The Cambridge Introduction to
British Poetry, 1945–2010

The Cambridge Introduction to British Poetry, 1945–2010 provides a broad overview of an important body of poetry from England, Scotland, Wales, and Northern Ireland from the postwar period through the present. It offers a comprehensive view of the historical context surrounding the poetry and provides in-depth readings of many of the period's central poets. British poetry after 1945 has been given much less attention than both earlier British and American poetry, as well as postwar American poetry. There are very few single-author studies that present the entirety of the period's poetry. This book is unique for the comprehensive richness with which it presents the historical and literary-historical scene, and for its close-up focus on a wide range of major poets and poems.

Eric Falci is Associate Professor of English at the University of California, Berkeley. He is the author of *Continuity and Change in Irish Poetry, 1966–2010* (Cambridge University Press, 2012). He has also published a number of essays on modern British and Irish poetry.

The Cambridge Introduction to
British Poetry, 1945–2010

ERIC FALCI

University of California, Berkeley

CAMBRIDGE
UNIVERSITY PRESS

CAMBRIDGE
UNIVERSITY PRESS

32 Avenue of the Americas, New York, NY 10013-2473, USA

Cambridge University Press is part of the University of Cambridge.

It furthers the University's mission by disseminating knowledge in the pursuit of
education, learning, and research at the highest international levels of excellence.

www.cambridge.org
Information on this title: www.cambridge.org/9781107542570

First published 2015

Printed in the United Kingdom by Clays, St Ives plc

A catalog record for this publication is available from the British Library.

Library of Congress Cataloging in Publication Data
Falci, Eric.
The Cambridge introduction to British poetry, 1945–2010 / Eric Falci,
University of California, Berkeley.
    pages   cm. – (Cambridge introductions to literature)
Includes bibliographical references and index.
ISBN 978-1-107-02963-7 (hardback) – ISBN 978-1-107-54257-0 (pbk)
1. English poetry – 20th century – History and criticism.   2. English
poetry – 21st century – History and criticism.   I. Title.
PR601.F35   2015
821'.91409–dc23   2015020635

ISBN 978-1-107-02963-7 Hardback
ISBN 978-1-107-54257-0 Paperback

Cambridge University Press has no responsibility for the persistence or accuracy of URLs
for external or third-party Internet Web sites referred to in this publication and does not
guarantee that any content on such Web sites is, or will remain, accurate or appropriate.

Contents

Acknowledgments

I would first like to thank all of my colleagues in the Berkeley English department. In particular, I'd like to thank Charles Altieri, C.D. Blanton, Mitch Breitwieser, Kathleen Donegan, Nadia Ellis, Catherine Flynn, Lyn Hejinian, Geoffrey G. O'Brien, Kent Puckett, Scott Saul, Sue Schweik, Namwali Serpell, and Emily Thornbury for their wonderful conversations about poetry, as well as for their friendship and support. My thanks are also due to those who have helped this project along as research assistants and interlocutors: Martha Avtandilian, Sanjana Bijlani, Monica Hay, Victoria Kim, Andrew David King, Sophia Mao, and Claire Rogerson. Ray Ryan has guided this project from the beginning, and I deeply appreciate his support and advice. I'd also like to thank Caitlin Gallagher at Cambridge University Press, Kim Husband at PETT Fox, Inc., and Ramesh Karunakaran at Newgen Imaging for their help seeing this book through the press. Serena Le and Wendy Xin read every page and provided invaluable suggestions and commentary, and I am tremendously grateful for their help. Finally, my love and thanks to Amanda Whitehead.

Thank you to the following for permission to reproduce copyrighted material from the poems listed:

- Bloodaxe Books for excerpts from Basil Bunting's *Briggflatts* (from *Collected Poems*, 2000);
- Carcanet Books for excerpts from Tom Raworth's *Ace* and *Writing* (from *Collected Poems*, 2003);
- Allardyce, Barnett, Publishers for excerpts from Veronica Forrest-Thomson's "Pastoral" from *Collected Poems*, ed. Anthony Barnett (Shearsman Books, in assoc. with Allardyce Book, 2008). Copyright © Jonathan Culler and The Estate of Veronica Forrest-Thomson, 2008;
- J.H. Prynne for permission to reprint "Chromatin" (originally published in *Wound Response* [1974] and reprinted unaltered in *Poems* [Bloodaxe Books, 2015], page 225). Copyright © J.H. Prynne;

- Tom Leonard for excerpts from "Six Glasgow Poems" (from *Outside the Narrative: Poems 1965–2009*, Etruscan Books and Word Power Books, 2009). Copyright © Tom Leonard;
- The Random House Group Ltd. for excerpts from Michael Longley's "Wounds," from *Collected Poems* by Michael Longley, published by Jonathan Cape;
- Wake Forest University Press for excerpts from Michael Longley's "Wounds," from *Collected Poems* by Michael Longley;
- Farrar, Straus and Giroux for excerpts from "Strange Fruit" from *Opened Ground: Selected Poems 1966–1996* by Seamus Heaney. Copyright © 1998 by Seamus Heaney. Reprinted by permission of Farrar, Straus and Giroux, LLC;
- Faber and Faber Ltd. for excerpts from Seamus Heaney's "Strange Fruit" from *Opened Ground: Selected Poems, 1966–1996*. Copyright © 1998 by Seamus Heaney;
- Denise Riley for excerpts from "A Note on Sex and 'The Reclaiming of Language'" (from *Selected Poems*, Reality Street, 2000). Copyright © Denise Riley;
- Oxford University Press for an eight-line excerpt from Geoffrey Hill's "Al Tempo de' Tremuoti" (from *Broken Hierarchies: Poems 1952–2012*, edited by Kenneth Haynes [2013], page 895).

Introduction

This book offers a broad account of British poetry after 1945 – its major trends, its central figures, its key texts, and the contexts out of which it has emerged. Chapters progress both thematically and chronologically, adumbrating particular movements, styles, and topics as they unfold over decade- or decade-and-a-half–long overlapping spans. The first five chapters cover different aspects of the period between 1945 and the mid-1980s, while the final three pick up the story in the 1980s and work their way toward the present. This is not an airtight chronology, however, and there are moments throughout when I jump ahead or retrace earlier steps in order to extend a story, reframe a connection, or preview an upcoming topic.

Such an organization is meant to present a coherent picture of the field. But it also spurs the argument that buzzes beneath the book's surface of exposition, description, and analysis. By reading across British poetry at various moments, juxtaposing disparate but proximate texts, I hope to show the variety and capaciousness of the work that constitutes the field rather than to present each chapter as a thematic silo. Of course, there are many times in the following pages when I place like next to like, but I have also sought opportunities to place like beside unlike. A number of the accounts of postwar British poetry that exist, and even the most powerful ones, tend to adhere to the silo model, either pitting factions or formations against each other or remaining within a narrow band of poetic practice. Al Alvarez both identified and perpetuated this tendency in the famous introduction to his 1962 anthology, *The New Poetry*, in which he describes the "machinery" of English poetry "since about 1930" as "a series of negative feed-backs."[1] The explanatory force of this analogy is quite real, but it also sets into motion two distinct but equally limiting methods of argument about that poetry.

First, it proffers a linear approach that obscures the complex and often incongruent unfurling of formal possibilities that has taken place over the past seventy years. And second, it models a species of antagonistic criticism that continues to flourish. The clearest form of this enmity is the ongoing impasse between so-called mainstream and experimental or innovative poetry, with well-known polemics appearing from both sides, whether Don Paterson's introduction to *New British Poetry* (2004), which repeatedly lambastes the hermetic difficulties of the "Postmoderns," or Andrew Duncan's series of volumes objecting to what he sees as the fundamental "conservatism" of British poetry in the twentieth century.[2] Postwar British poetry is certainly not unique in being a site of ardent and often scathing skirmishes among and between practitioners and critics. Furthermore, there have been many instances in which strong, polemical stands have been necessary and have revitalized the field. I will detail a number of these instances over the course of the following chapters. However, one unfortunate side effect of a persistent "negative feed-back" model has been a tendency to eschew discussions of texts' intricacies in favor of a too-heavy dependence on critical preconceptions. Keith Tuma has provided a valuable account of how twentieth-century British poetry has been underread, and so misunderstood, by American readers,[3] but it might also be said that postwar British poetry has been underread more generally, not only in the sense that it is read by fewer people than other forms of imaginative writing – the plight of poetry everywhere – but also that it hasn't been read closely or imaginatively enough.[4] My aim here is not only to introduce as fully as possible the range of British poetry written since the middle of the twentieth century, but also to look along the way at a selection of especially intriguing poems in depth and on their own terms.

By enmeshing texts, poets, and groups within a given historical span and set of contexts, this book implicitly argues that a poem, as a mode of cultural production, formally reshapes the various material pressures that nonetheless shape it. This is not, however, to say that poems merely reflect their historical circumstances or express preconceived contents or identity positions. To be sure, questions of position and identity – whether in terms of gender, race, ethnicity, class, or nationality – are vital when considering this body of work, and one of the major features of British poetry since the 1970s has been a significant increase in the number and prominence of women and minority writers. However, the poems that I highlight tend not to reduce to unequivocal statements of identity. Rather, by way of their formal investments and processes of unfolding, poems can register, critique, and remake identity positions. Poetic form is multifarious, and many factors come into play when considering any aspect of a text's substance. Does a poem rhyme or use traditional meters and stanza-shapes, or does it conform to a different sort of rhythmic organization, or to none at all? Does it take part in a conventional genre or mode, such as elegy, ekphrasis, or curse? Does it feature a coherent speaker, or does it seem less like a dramatic monologue and more like a crash of competing voices or textual shards? Does it focus on a natural scene or an urban site or a domestic interior, or does it seem to have no setting at all? Is there a narrative or argument within the text, or does it utilize some other sort of discursive strategy? Does it abide by a particular kind of structural limitation, either a well-established type like the fourteen lines and internal architecture of a sonnet or a *sui generis* rule that the poet invents? Is it heavily stylized and densely allusive, or does it aim to resemble something like everyday speech? And, if so, what sort of everyday speech does it resemble? All of these questions – and there are many more – contribute to our understanding of a poem's form, and they will underlie many of my readings to come.

However, the form that a poem takes is not simply a matter of choice for an aesthetic free agent who can survey the history of poetry and select from among its myriad options while remaining untethered to that history. Cultural circumstances and historical conditions favor certain options and make others seem less workable or propitious. History doesn't determine form, but a poem is nonetheless marbled by its context. Poetic forms encode their obligations, their debts, and their attempted freedoms. As such, they serve as complex and sometimes contradictory aesthetic enactments that are incessantly marked by their moment. The most significant and innovative poems to appear in the period within this book's scope are steeped in the history of poetry even as they respond to shifting conditions within Britain, and they appear across the spectrum of poetic practice and style, although the surrounding debate among critics, reviewers, and poets themselves has tended toward the construction and perpetuation of oppositional camps. My principal aim is to elucidate the formal genealogies of the wonderfully assorted body of poetry produced in Britain since 1945.

The phrase *in Britain* necessitates some further clarification. This book is primarily concerned with the poetry of England, Scotland, Wales, and Northern Ireland. I will not be focusing on poetry from places that had won independence from Britain before the middle of the twentieth century, nor will I focus on Anglophone poetry written in newly independent countries after decolonization.[5] On the one hand, it is vital to discuss poetry by colonial writers during the period of decolonization, especially in cases in which that work made an impact in the United Kingdom, and I take such matters up in Chapter 2. On the other hand, it is just as vital to differentiate between British poetry after 1945 and the much larger canon of Anglophone poetry or postcolonial poetry in English so as not to offer a totalizing narrative of global poetry in English that recolonizes distinct, emergent literary histories.[6]

As I begin to show in the next section of this introduction, the political ground of Britain has shifted massively in the postwar period, and the attenuation of the British Empire cannot help but be a significant factor in a consideration of the period's poetry. While the continued designation of that poetry as "British" invites investigation, *British poetry* remains a useful, if unstable, category, even though the larger geopolitical entity to which it refers has altered. Maintaining it as a designating term has the value of continually indicating the field's own historicity. With the empire's close and ongoing movements toward devolution and possible independence in Scotland, Wales, and Northern Ireland, the primary denotation of "British" is put into question. But as a literary-historical term, it retains vital connotative layers. In this book, *Britishness* will function mainly to suggest differentially shared sets of material, cultural, and geographical factors. With the exception of work from Northern Ireland – a region whose complex contemporary history and turbulent status within late-twentieth-century Britain it seems best to address in a separate chapter – I discuss poetry from different parts of Britain relationally, and so, for example, rather than a separate chapter on Scottish poetry, there are considerations of Scottish poets at different historical moments within several of the chapters that follow. This is manifestly not to say that all of the poets discussed in this book would identify themselves primarily as British. Rather, it is to say that an interlocking set of historical and sociopolitical conditions subtends, at least partially, their work. However, this claim is accompanied by the understanding that considering this work as *British* is much more useful as an initial way into it than as a final explanation of it.

At the end of the Second World War, Britain was – to adjust the title of Stevie Smith's most famous poem – both waving and drowning. It was a complex moment, and an array of crosscurrents shaped the United Kingdom in the decade or so after the Allied victory over the Axis powers. The defeat of Nazism and totalitarianism was a triumph for freedom and democracy, and Britain's key role in that victory brought hope and an upswing in national feeling. The Labour Party's surprising election in 1945 – over Winston Churchill's Conservatives – spurred the beginnings of the welfare state, and central to the story of the last seventy years has been an overall improvement in the material circumstances of a great many Britons, especially in the three decades after the end of the war, when changes wrought in the late 1940s were most keenly felt. Sir William Beveridge's 1942 *Report on Social Insurance and Allied Services* became the basis for crucial reforms in many spheres of life, and the postwar nationalization of key industries and resources aimed to ensure a more stable economy. For a number of reasons, the rigidities of the English class system loosened, and changes in government policy provided opportunities for many more people, most notably through the passing of an Education Act in 1944 (the Butler Act), which established a three-tier system of secondary education and ensured access for all students. Along with the National Health Service, the National Insurance Act, and other pillars of the early welfare state, the Butler Act aimed to produce a more equitable society.

This isn't to say that the English aristocracy lost its power or that the triangular hegemony of Oxford, Cambridge, and London failed to hold sway. Rather, it is simply to point out that Britain underwent immense changes in the second half of the twentieth century and that these changes had at their root not only national and global geopolitical shifts (more on which in what follows) but also internal shifts in how British society imagined itself and how people in Britain lived their lives. The playing field was certainly not leveled, but strict class-based stratifications began to be dislodged, however slowly and uneasily, while living standards and wages rose for much of the population. In addition, an overall liberalization of society meant increased rights, freedoms, and prospects for women, minorities, and marginalized groups, although racism and sexism continued to be systemic problems. While the major political parties disagreed about numerous aspects of the welfare state's makeup, the basic principle of it was at the heart of a political consensus that held until the 1970s, and there were periods of significant energy and optimism, especially from the late 1950s to the mid 1960s, when it was thought that many social problems had been largely solved.

Such progress is, however, part of a long-term narrative, and from another angle, Britain's postwar fortunes look much more like drowning than cheerily waving. If it was a period of social improvements, then it was also one of deep disillusionment. At war's end, Britain faced major challenges in almost every area, and a widespread sense of decline accompanied feelings of relief and renewed hope. The economy was massively damaged during the war, with Britain losing a quarter of its total wealth, and the postwar period featured a number of currency and balance-of-payments crises as the pound sterling's value in world markets was eroded. During the war, there had been huge military and civilian casualties, and German aerial bombings had caused major damage to cities throughout Britain. As Alan Sinfield notes, "by June 1941 more than two million houses in Britain had been damaged or destroyed; by the end of the war, two out of every seven houses were damaged, one-fifteenth of them beyond repair; in central London, only one house in ten escaped damage."[7] In addition, shortages and rationing continued for a time after 1945, and the pride of victory was tempered by continuing austerity in many areas of daily life. Such overwhelming human, economic, and material losses underwrote a definite sense of cultural decline, which became concretized in the rapid diminution of the British Empire from the late 1940s through the early 1960s.

In the aftermath of the war, it became quickly apparent that Britain had neither the clout nor the wealth to maintain its preeminent place on the global stage. Considering that the size of the British Empire actually grew slightly just after the war, when it took control of several areas once held by Germany, the economic peril facing Britain soon came to a head. The burden was unfeasible, and the reduced role of Britain as a global power, coupled with growing calls for independence in many colonized areas, made it clear that the British Empire, as it was currently constituted, was unsustainable. The Indian Independence Act was passed by Parliament in 1947, dividing British India into the independent dominions of India and Pakistan. Despite the attempt to portray the withdrawal from British India as smooth, sound, and efficient, it was a devastating process. According to Wendy Webster, "the communal violence produced by the partition of India led to an estimated 180,000 deaths in the Punjab, while ten and a half million Hindus, Muslims and Sikhs became refugees."[8] Other colonies worked for their own freedom via both armed resistance and political negotiation, and between 1957 and 1968 many colonies throughout the Middle East, Africa, and the Caribbean achieved independence. The speed of decolonization was dizzying, and as early as 1962, Anthony Sampson characterized the period as the "aftermath of empire."[9]

Along with imperial contraction, Britain's geopolitical role was dampened by the start of the Cold War and the rise of the United States and USSR as predominant global powers. Through the Marshall Plan, which began in 1948, the United States provided vital economic assistance to rebuild and bolster the British economy, but this also underscored Britain's reliance on the United States, especially in international matters. Additionally, American-style consumerism and popular culture entered more and more areas of individual and social life, and the increasing influence of mass media – especially television – assured the continuing presence of both in British society. According to Sinfield, only 4.3 percent of homes in Britain had television sets in 1950, a number that increased to "49.4 percent by 1956, and over 90 percent by 1964."[10] Such statistics point to the kinds of material gains that many people enjoyed, but they also demonstrate the growing power of mass media and the swift entrenchment of consumerism, which – it was feared – would lead to an erosion of the particularities of English cultural life.

These fears were not exclusively over the potential ramifications of American influence. As decolonization and the rise of the Cold War superpowers forced a drastic shift in its place on the global stage, Britain sought to maintain its stature as a world player. Through the creation of the Commonwealth, a loose confederation of former colonies and dominions with the UK at its center, Britain aimed to project a semblance of its former imperial power. However, the

Commonwealth never became the economic or geopolitical force that many hoped it would, since it had to compete with other bodies – the United Nations, the World Bank, NATO, the European Union – that more successfully took the lead in international affairs. As Britain positioned itself as both the indispensable ally to the United States and the center of a global Commonwealth, it also set itself more firmly – though always warily – within the community of Europe. After no small amount of hand-wringing and several failed applications (mainly due to French vetoes), Britain entered the European Economic Community in 1973 and has been part of the European Union since its formation in 1993. At the same time, it has found numerous ways to keep its distance from continental Europe, most famously by retaining its own currency rather than adopting the euro. As this last fact might indicate, the status of Britain in relation to other political and international bodies – as well as in relation to the discrete but conjoined entities that comprise the United Kingdom itself – has been in flux over the past seventy years.

Although it isn't the case that every sphere of post-1945 British cultural and political life reflects perfectly on every other, it may not be too much to suggest that Britain's conflicted position globally has analogues at other levels. If the figure for the immediate postwar years is a person who is both waving and drowning, then a relative of such a figure – one less perilously placed – might do for the period more broadly considered. Feelings of relief and renewed hope were striated by loss and unease. Revitalization was coupled with exhaustion. The war was won, but the cost was enormous, and the rapid unspooling of the Empire concretized the sense that something major and vital was gone. It was, many thought, to be a minor age, and, almost immediately, nostalgia for the glorious days of England and Empire became a recognizable and prevalent feeling throughout Britain. Such nostalgia was harnessed during significant moments, as in the coronation of Queen Elizabeth II in 1953, the pageantry and symbolism of which leaned heavily on Britain's imperial past and which was one of the first major events in Britain to rely on television's power to produce a sense of mediated simultaneity (Margaret Thatcher's exploitation of postimperial nostalgia in the run-up to the Falklands War in 1981 provides a different example of the manufacture of national feeling).

At the same time, and in many quarters, there was deep skepticism about the object of nostalgia. The history of the British Empire was, from this perspective, not one of enlightened glory but of callous colonialism and exploitation. The singular fact of the Holocaust exposed the barbarity at the heart of Western civilization. The circumstances of decolonization and the brutality of empire provided another form of civilizational exposure. Nearly simultaneously, then, there arose feelings of deep and irrevocable loss, of proud nostalgia for that loss, and of utter skepticism about what was lost. For T.S. Eliot, such a discomforting realization occurred at the start of the war. In *The Idea of a Christian Society* (1948), he writes about his reaction to the Munich Agreement, in which Britain, France, and Italy allowed the Nazis to annex the Sudetenland in a failed attempt to appease Hitler's Germany:

> I believe that there must be many persons who, like myself, were deeply shaken by the events of September 1938, in a way from which one does not recover; persons to whom that month brought a profounder realization of a general plight. It was not a disturbance of the understanding: the events themselves were not surprising. Nor, as became increasingly evident, was our distress due merely to disagreement with the policy and behavior of the moment. The feeling which was new and unexpected was a feeling of humiliation, which seemed to demand an act of personal contrition, of humility, repentance and amendment; what had happened was something in which one was deeply implicated and responsible. It was not, I repeat, a criticism of the government, but a doubt of the validity of a civilization. We could not match conviction with conviction, we had no ideas with which we could either meet or oppose the ideas opposed to us. Was our society, which has always been so assured of its superiority and rectitude, so confident of its unexamined premises, assembled round anything more permanent than a congeries of banks, insurance companies and industries, and had it any beliefs more essential than a belief in compound interest and the maintenance of dividends?[11]

Eliot's lament brings with it a deeply conservative ideology, and one might read the poetry he wrote during the war – the *Four Quartets* – as his attempt to revalidate a civilization that had been so shaken through a reassertion of Christian faith. But his commentary also exemplifies a much broader structure of feeling that continued after the war, though with a more muted theological component. Writers in Britain grappled with these incommensurable conditions in the immediate postwar period and beyond, and throughout this book, I show how these forms of ambivalence manifested poetically.

Certain forms of dissonance also characterized the world of British poetry at midcentury. As Stephen Spender points out in *Poetry Since 1939* (1946), poetry was very popular during the war: "despite paper rationing, the sales of poetry increased, and even less-known poets could reckon their sales as between 2,000 and 4,000 instead of in hundreds, as would have been their circulation before the war."[12] This wartime boom didn't last, and, indeed, poetry's overall fortunes within the mainstream publishing world have grown ever bleaker during the period that this book covers, despite several isolated periods of growth (especially during the later 1960s and early 1970s, and in the mid- to late 1990s). But other factors helped to bolster poetry's profile in the postwar years. The Arts Council in England was founded in 1945 – followed later by Arts Councils in Northern Ireland (1962), Wales, and Scotland (both in 1967) – and although literary activities made up a very small portion of the overall Arts Council budgets, such support was important. Additionally, the establishment of the BBC's Third Programme in 1946 provided a promising new media outlet for poetry, with George MacBeth's *The Poet's Voice* (later changed to *Poetry Now*) proving to be the BBC's most popular poetry broadcast program after its inception in 1957. As mentioned earlier, the 1944 Butler Act commenced a huge expansion of higher education in Britain, and the recommendations of the government's Robbins Report in 1963 led to the construction of new universities throughout the 1960s (often referred to as the "Plate Glass" universities to differentiate them from the ancient universities and the "Red Brick" universities founded in the early twentieth century). Over the longer term, this has made for more teaching opportunities for writers. Especially in the last twenty-five years, the position of *poet* has become institutionalized in Britain – supported by arts grants and formalized within university creative writing programs – even as the market for poetry has shrunk, and these forms of institutional support have their roots in the mid-1940s.

In *Poetry Since 1939*, Spender placed Eliot's *Four Quartets* at the top of the heap of poetry written during the war, and he continued to proclaim the centrality of W.H. Auden and the group of poets surrounding him in the 1930s – Louis MacNeice, Cecil Day Lewis, and Spender himself. Auden was still the most influential English poet of the time, although John Betjeman's cozy lyrics proved him to be the most popular, with his 1948 *Selected Poems* becoming a bestseller. Auden's place at the center of English poetry was, however, far from assured in the postwar years. At the same time that Spender praised Auden's technical brilliance, he sidelined him: "W.H. Auden went to America in the autumn of 1938 and stayed there."[13] Auden's departure for the United States at the start of the war marred his reputation in England, and while younger poets continued to learn from him, his absence allowed a strange disjoining to take place, as though there were two Audens, the important English poet of the 1930s and the one who left and was no longer worth considering. Philip Larkin, one such younger poet, typified this stance:

> I have been trying to imagine a discussion of Auden between one man who had read nothing of his after 1940 and another who had read nothing before. After an initial agreement by adjective – 'Versatile,' 'Fluent,' 'Too smart sometimes' – a mystifying gap would open between them, as one spoke of a tremendously exciting English social poet full

of energetic unliterary knock-about and unique lucidity of phrase, and the other of an engaging, bookish, American talent, too verbose to be memorable and too intellectual to be moving. And not only would they differ about his poetic character: there would be a sharp division of opinion about his poetic stature.[14]

The postwar fate of Auden's reputation exemplifies a larger phenomenon in English poetry just after the war and into the early 1950s, one produced by overlapping circumstances and best described as a complex hollow. While there were a number of major poets on the scene, there was also something of a vacuum. Yeats died in 1939, Auden left for the United States, and Eliot completed his career as a poet with the *Four Quartets*. Thus, the central poets of the 1920s and 1930s had, in different ways, left the field. Eliot remained a towering cultural figure, and as a director at Faber and Faber from 1925 until his death in 1965, he had a massive impact on the course of poetry in England. However, his own poetry could be positioned as part of a literary past, still to be reckoned with but also placed at a distance. Additionally, while soldier-poets such as Roy Fuller and Charles Causley survived the war and had long careers, several of the most promising young poets were killed in battle, notably Keith Douglas, Sidney Keyes, and Alun Lewis.

For emerging poets in the late 1940s and early 1950s, it was possible to distance figures like Auden and Eliot from the on-the-ground workings of the literary scene, which had the effect of clearing room for the younger figures to emerge. No such maneuvers were possible when dealing with Dylan Thomas. He was the most famous – and most notorious – poet in midcentury Britain and a figure with whom younger poets had to reckon directly. Thomas had been celebrated since his early poetry of the 1930s, and he became the most influential poet within a brief Neo-Romantic movement that flourished during the war. The active core of this movement were the self-proclaimed Apocalyptic writers, a group led by Henry Treece, J.F. Hendry, and G.S. Fraser. Other poets in this circle included Vernon Watkins, Norman MacCaig, Lawrence Durrell, George Barker, and Nicholas Moore. Three wartime anthologies edited by Hendry and Treece – *The New Apocalypse* (1939), *The White Horseman: Prose and Verse of the New Apocalypse* (1941), and *The Crown and the Sickle* (1944) – are the central documents of this movement, which while coming short of the full surrealism of David Gascoyne's 1930s poetry does follow up on certain surrealist tendencies. In addition to being influenced by the surrealists and Thomas's early work, the Apocalyptic writers drew heavily on D.H. Lawrence, William Blake, Franz Kafka, Sigmund Freud, and Herbert Read, as well as Christian eschatological writings, which gained new adherents during the war and with the start of the nuclear age.[15]

In his essay "How I See Apocalypse," Treece includes Fraser's explanation that Apocalypticism is "a life movement," one that "asks for freedom for man, as a complete living organism." Fraser distinguishes this from surrealism, which claims "freedom for man's automatic verbal mechanisms, but not for man himself" and so is a mere "*mechanical* sort of freedom, in which the subconscious fed out a constant stream of discreet images."[16] Compared to the densely intellectual poems typical of Auden's 1930s, Neo-Romantic poetry focused on the extremity of individual subjectivity, especially as it manifested in the unconscious's churn of images. The visceral mysticism and nearly animistic earthiness of Neo-Romantic poetry struck a nerve during the war, although it quickly faded, as is clear in Spender's comment in his 1946 pamphlet:

> At first the general impression produced by this poetry has been one
> of disintegration. If one compares anthologies such as *Poems from
> the Forces* and *The White Horseman* with the collection produced
> by the imagists or any other advanced movement since 1918, one
> notices at once the lack of rhythmic tension, the confused imagery, the
> over-literary fashions of thought, the uncritical writing which stakes all
> its ambition on a vague faith in inspiration or on some preconceived if
> chaotic attitude towards life.[17]

Treece had success after the war, continuing to publish with Faber and Faber and having an American edition of his *Collected Poems* published by Knopf in 1946 before turning to fiction in the 1950s, but the movement did not last, and the tenets that it espoused became subject to withering criticism as it was marginalized in the 1950s.

Although Thomas maintained some distance from the Apocalyptic poets, declining to sign their manifesto, he was the epitome of the Neo-Romantic movement and a formidable presence on the wider scene. While Thomas's reputation has ebbed, his position at mid-century was unquestioned, an opinion shared on both sides of the Atlantic. Here is Spender's verdict: "Thomas is a poet who commands the admiration of all contemporary English poets. He has influenced a number of younger writers who see in him an alternative to the intellectual writing of Auden. Of the poets under forty-five, he is perhaps the only one capable of exercising a literary influence as great as that of Auden."[18] The American poet Kenneth Rexroth's view, in the introduction to *The New British Poets: An Anthology* (1949), is even bolder: "If Auden dominated the recent past, Dylan Thomas dominates the present. There can be no question but that he is the most influential young poet writing in England today. The unanimity with which everyone except unreconstructed Stalinists and tame magazine versifiers points to him as the greatest phenomenon in contemporary poetry is simply astonishing." Rexroth hedges his bet by noting "that something like this was once the case with Auden," which "bodes ill for Thomas' reputation some ten years hence."[19] Ultimately, Rexroth was right, although it took longer than ten years for Thomas's posthumous reputation to decline, and his prediction couldn't have foreseen Thomas's premature death in 1953.

The dense and often inscrutable texts of Thomas's 1930s volumes – *18 Poems* (1934), *25 Poems* (1936), and *The Map of Love* (1939) – were, as mentioned, the model for much wartime Neo-Romantic and Apocalyptic poetry, but many of the poems collected in *Deaths and Entrances* (1946) were significantly more accessible than his previous work, a quality that certainly contributed to the volume's huge sales.[20] This small book contains a number of Thomas's most well known poems, and as John Goodby demonstrates in a pioneering reassessment of Thomas's work, these pastoral fantasias show him moving into more complex terrain at the end of his life. Goodby describes these later poems – such as "Poem in October," "A Winter's Tale," "Ballad of the Long-Legged Bait," "Over Sir John's Hill," "Poem on His Birthday," "In the White Giant's Thigh," and the incomparable "Fern Hill" – as "Cold War pastorals," a phrase that pinpoints the nuanced manner in which they intertwine multiple aesthetic, generic, and ideological investments while remaining within the mainline of British nature poetry.[21] Under Goodby's lens, the dark nostalgia for childhood that drives "Fern Hill" is at once an attenuated romanticism and the adumbration of an anxious postwar moment:

> And once below a time I lordly had the trees and leaves
> Trail with daisies and barley
> Down the rivers of the windfall light.[22]

The speaker's remembrance of his child self's "heedless ways," when he considered himself "lordly" even though he was under the thumb of time, is a variation on a Wordsworthian topos, but it also obliquely registers both the oppressive practices of wartime totalitarian regimes and Cold War fears of imminent annihilation.[23]

At the time of his death, Thomas was not only a famous poet, he was also something of a celebrity, with his public readings, radio appearances, and raucous American tours adding to his considerable legend. His play for voices, *Under Milk Wood* (1954), became a staple of the BBC's Third Programme throughout the 1950s, which kept his voice in the air well after his death. At the same time, the publication of his *Collected Poems* in 1952, coupled with his death at thirty-nine the following year, made it possible to consider his work as a completed entity. So, like Auden and Eliot – although for different reasons and with different effects – Thomas was both ubiqui-tous and removed from the poetry scene of the early 1950s. My descrip-tion of the period from 1946 to about 1953 as a complex hollow does not at all mean that intriguing and worthwhile poetry wasn't being produced. For example, and to remain in Wales: in addition to Thomas's poetry, two of the most significant Anglo-Welsh modernist texts appeared during that stretch: Lynette Roberts's *Gods with Stainless Ears: A Heroic Poem* (1951) and David Jones's *The Anathemata* (1952), in addition to the early volumes of R.S. Thomas. But for a number of reasons, many of them circumstan-tial, the moment was ripe for new writers and styles to come to the fore. Considering the issues that I have presented thus far, what did emerge is not surprising. "The Movement," which was the dominant formation in English poetry in the 1950s (and whose impact lingered well beyond), privileged a form of self-conscious moderation that often depended on nostalgia and a return to earlier traditions. This was partly out of frustration with what it saw as the extravagance of modernism but also reflective of the broader forms of disquiet that coursed through British culture in the middle of the century. If, for Thomas, poetry was "a burning and crested act," then the Movement writers who came after and reacted against his vivid and exces-sive example aimed for a more restrained, less flammable style of verse.[24]

Chapter 1

The Movement and Its Discontents

The first key signs of what came to be known as "the Movement" were two 1954 articles in *The Spectator*. In an August 27 piece titled "Poets of the Fifties," Anthony Hartley reviewed four volumes published by the Fantasy Press and, after describing their styles, influences, and shortcomings, concluded, "we are now in the presence of the only considerable movement in English poetry since the Thirties."[1] The emerging movement is typified by the early poetry of Thom Gunn, Donald Davie, George MacBeth, and Jonathan Price (the four poets under review), as well as John Wain, Kingsley Amis, Philip Larkin, and Philip Oakes (the other young poets mentioned by Hartley). The poets are influenced primarily by William Empson and, to a lesser degree, Auden, and what unites their poetry is its tone, which Hartley describes as " 'dissenting' and non-conformist, cool, scientific and analytical."[2] An article titled "In the Movement" and published in the October 1 issue continues Hartley's line of thinking, describing Auden and the 1930s poets as well as the nebulous output of the 1940s and early 1950s as part of a passing age and suggesting that "within the last year or so," there have been signs of a "new movement" in literature.[3] The unsigned essay, which was written by J.D. Scott, names Davie and Gunn as key poets in this new "movement" and adds several novels – by Wain, Amis, and Iris Murdoch – to the mix of representative texts. While admitting that the sample size is small, Scott nonetheless gives a fairly comprehensive summary of its attitudes and tendencies in what has become an oft-quoted encapsulation: "The Movement, as well as being anti-phoney, is anti-wet; sceptical, robust, ironic, prepared to be as comfortable as possible in a wicked, commercial, threatened world which doesn't look, anyway, as if it's going to be changed much by a couple of handfuls of young English writers."[4]

These and other articles, along with Wain's promotion of the new writers on his Third Programme series *First Reading* in 1953, helped raise their individual profiles as well as collate them. The success of Philip Larkin's *The Less Deceived* in 1955 brought more attention, and D.J. Enright first grouped the poets who we've come to identify with the Movement in his 1955 anthology, *Poets of the 1950s*. This volume was published in Japan, where Enright was teaching at the time, and didn't have much of an impact on literary discussions in England, but it did provide a template for Robert Conquest, who was assembling his own anthology, *New Lines*, which appeared in 1956. It included nine poets (all appeared in Enright's volume, all were educated at Oxford or Cambridge, and all but one, Elizabeth Jennings, were male) and was the pivotal anthology of midcentury poetry, as well as the text around which accounts of the Movement turn. Like the Movement more generally, *New Lines* had an outsized influence on the course of British poetry in the latter half of the twentieth century and helped shape a discourse and set of arguments around English poetry that linger today. Revisiting Conquest's text can help clarify these arguments and delineate the Movement's terms.

Alongside Donald Davie's early critical writings – especially *The Purity of Diction in English Verse* (1952) and *Articulate Energy* (1955) – Conquest's "Introduction" to *New Lines* is the Movement's defining document. Even though he suggests that what these poets "have in common is perhaps, at its lowest, little more than a negative determination to avoid bad principles," it is exceedingly clear just what those "bad principles" are and which are the writers who fail to avoid them.[5] In contrast to the "genuine and healthy poetry of the new period" (i.e., "the general tendency" best represented by the poets in this volume), poets in the 1940s made the "mistake" of "giving the Id, a sound player on the percussion side under a strict conductor, too much of a say in the doings of the orchestra as a whole."[6] Alongside the antimodernist feeling that runs through the Movement's discourse, the targets here are the Apocalyptic poets and Dylan Thomas in particular. By contrast, the "healthy" poets of the 1950s restored a "sound and fruitful attitude to poetry, of the principle that poetry is written by and for the whole man, intellect, emotions, senses and all."[7]

In the wake of the totalitarianism of the 1930s and the Second World War, the poets in *New Lines* are said to submit "to no great systems of theoretical constructs nor agglomerations of unconscious commands" and are positioned against the rise of Communism in Eastern Europe and Communist sympathies in postwar Britain.[8] Conquest, who would go on to expose the hypocrisies of the Soviet Union in more than twenty books, most famously in *The Great Terror: Stalin's Purges of the Thirties* (1968), suggests that the poets collected in *New Lines* revere "the real person or event" and that their poetry is free from "both mystical and logical compulsions."[9] They are united in their refusal of a common program, unlike unnamed groups of "doctrine-saddled writers forming a definite school complete with programme and rules."[10] The simple fact that *New Lines* poets have come upon these "healthy" principles of writing separately and "from various starting-points and by the discipline of practice" assures their "depth and soundness."[11] An overdependence on emotion, which results in a mistaken belief that a poet's task is simply to make "an arrangement of images of sex and violence tapped straight from the unconscious," requires the reestablishment of poetry's "intellectual component."[12] This nod toward Empson is followed by a warning about relying too heavily on intellectual "formulae" as the sole guarantor of poetry and, once again, Conquest stresses the importance of balance and moderation – of "health" – for the poets who will follow.

The opening poem in *New Lines*, Elizabeth Jennings's "Afternoon in Florence," begins with what one might take as a précis of the entire book:

> This afternoon disturbs within the mind
> No other afternoon, is out of time
> Yet lies within a definite sun to end
> In night that is in time.[13]

The particularity of the present is privileged over the weight of the past or the vagaries of the future. Seemingly Eliotic gestures toward timelessness or the infinite are curtailed, placed within the limits of the day and its "definite sun." The refusal to let myth, memory, or prophecy overwhelm attention to "the real person or event" drives the poem as Jennings shapes an "image of the city tangible."[14] Such paeans to balance and moderation pepper the volume, most notably in Larkin's wish for Kingsley Amis's newborn daughter in "Born Yesterday" ("May you be ordinary") and in Amis's own "Against Romanticism," which praises "a temperate zone" of "woods devoid of beasts" and "roads that please the foot."[15] In the worst cases, such an adherence to a mode of poetic "health" results in texts of lifeless scenery whose self-satisfied conclusions expose their paltry stakes. Many poems in the volume, however, exceed the limiting desire to avoid "negative principles," and a number have remained significant within the larger canon of postwar poetry. It is not a coincidence that two of the stronger poems in the anthology – Thom Gunn's "On the Move" and Donald Davie's "Remembering the Thirties" – partake the least of general Movement tenets as Conquest and others articulated them. Over the course of their careers, Gunn and Davie moved far away from their Movement-identified work, but they remain, apart from Larkin, the most significant poets connected to the Movement.

Davie's "Remembering the Thirties" both fulfills the volume's nonprogrammatic program and, ultimately, refutes the kind of moderation that Conquest endorses. Positioning the younger poets first as dutiful heirs and reenactors of the "sagas" of the 1930s poets (primarily the composite MacSpaunday group that orbited around Auden), "Remembering the Thirties" ironizes the fashioning of literary generations but also remains dependent on such fashioning.

After tracing the gap between one literary generation and the next, it wryly comments on the antique quality of the 1930s poets' commitments and styles and rebukes their adherence to "irony," to a "coy / Insistence on the quizzical."[16] In the penultimate quatrain, Davie comes round to what can stand as a Movement slogan: "a neutral tone is nowadays preferred." Were the poem to end with this Hardy-derived sentiment, it would fulfill the anthology's premises. Conquest's counsel to avoid "bad principles" is, after all, most likely to result in a scrupulously neutral poetry. And yet Davie quickly changes tack after coming to this point of rest:

> A neutral tone is nowadays preferred.
> And yet it may be better, if we must,
> To find the stance impressive and absurd
> Than not to see the hero for the dust.
>
> For courage is the vegetable king,
> The sprig of all ontologies, the weed
> That beards the slag-heap with its hectoring,
> Whose green adventure is to run to seed.[17]

Until the penultimate stanza, the speaker of "Remembering the Thirties" has relied on a knowing cleverness, appropriate for his stance as a younger poet antagonizing his elders. Within ABAB-rhymed quatrains locked into a just-flexible-enough iambic pentameter, the poem maintains a jaunty – if not quite neutral – tone as it seeks to open up space for itself by treating 1930s poetry as part of history (and of the history of poetry) rather than as living practice.

At this turn, however, the speaker reconsiders. Instead of seeing the previous generation's concerns and exploits as somehow ridiculous, the speaker now sees them as both "impressive and absurd." This newly positive perspective gives less weight to absurdities and ironies (now simply forms of "dust") than to the "hero" himself. The final stanza, apart from harnessing an excessively metaphorical style at odds with Movement tenets against excess, also relies on a kind of deliberate oddness. If a "neutral tone is nowadays preferred," then Davie's final quatrain cuts quite sharply against such a preference. Even if we read it as mock heroic rather than heroic, we are faced with the simple strangeness of the image pile. Rather than quietism or neutrality, the poem ends by promoting "courage." This "courage," however, is quickly transformed into a swamp monster on its last legs. As "vegetable king," it is both the source and waste of "all ontologies," the "beard" of "sprig" and "weed" that covers and "hectors" the "slag-heap." Davie ends the poem with a fierce postpastoral moment, admitting the continuing "green adventure" of such sprigs and weeds while simultaneously placing them within heavy industry's crushing machinations. The possessive pronoun "whose" can refer both to the "weed" bearding the slag-heap and to the "slag-heap" itself, and so both the literal and idiomatic meanings of the phrase "run to seed" are brought to bear upon the poem's conclusion. The weed will run to seed in that it will in some way propagate itself, while the slag-heap runs to seed in that it signals the degradation of the landscape. Whatever we make of these metaphorical shifts, they are clearly not "neutral": they refuse to bring the poem around to a conclusion that would fit the course of the previous eleven quatrains, and they significantly muddy the waters of the poem's rational structure.

The penultimate stanza concludes with the suggestion that the stance of the previous generation is indeed impressive (if also absurd), but instead of wrapping this new perspective into the poem's overall movement, the final quatrain undertakes a stylistic overturning. It leaves behind the argument that catalyzed it so far and submits instead to the (a)logic of metaphor. It refuses the strictures of Conquest's introduction. At the same time, the final stanza indexes a history of English poetry, from the Marvellian phrase "vegetable king" (reminiscent of the "vegetable love" described in "To His Coy Mistress") to the final line's wink-and-nod reference to Dylan Thomas, whose poems often trace "green adventures" via the gnarled thickets of metaphor. Instead of a "neutral tone," the poem concludes with a series of exuberant flourishes. Images flash and give way to others, and metaphors flicker and split. The object of the poem – the Auden generation – has been largely forgotten, and the poem's gimlet-eyed look at the 1930s has been dropped in favor of a glance toward Romanticism. Even though this glance is seemingly hip to its own absurdities and overstatements, it also comes to rest in a slightly cartoonish pastoral scene. Somewhat slyly, and then at its conclusion not slyly at all, "Remembering the Thirties" stands both as a prototypical Movement poem and as a refutation of the principles by which we tend to define the Movement.

That such an unsettled text is one of the most memorable poems in *New Lines* is deeply suggestive. "Remembering the Thirties" is a discontented poem. Rather than the "health" and "soundness" with which Conquest characterizes his anthology's poems, Davie's text is disconcerted. Later in this chapter, I will describe the more intensely discontented forms that were being produced in the 1950s. But it is worth noting that such formal discontentment wasn't at all limited to poetry that we now consider to be alternative to the "mainstream" as it is epitomized in the Movement. Indeed, several of the most discontented poems written in the two decades after the end of the war are by Philip Larkin, the still and central point of the Movement's turning world.

Larkin's poetry typifies all that the Movement, as well as a certain line of British poetry in its wake, could be said to stand for: moderation, formal soundness, a reliance on traditional lyric structures and modes, and a dependence on a centralizing and coherent (if disaffected) speaker. His poetry also displays the less attractive aspects of a little-England postwar mindset. It is not worthwhile to rebut charges of Larkin's xenophobia, racism, and sexism, especially after the publication of his letters and of Andrew Motion's biography, *Philip Larkin: A Writer's Life*. There are plenty of passages in Larkin's poems that crystallize one or another of his more offensive stances. Larkin's poetry is most often catalyzed by a kind of seething disappointment that registers as sour misanthropy or resigned fear. The two repeated lines that enclose each stanza of "Wants" encapsulate either pole: "Beyond all this, the wish to be alone"; "Beneath it all, desire of oblivion runs."[18] If there exists in Larkin an antidote to such a sense of despair, it would have to be located within Larkin's faith in poetic form itself. As Edna Longley puts it, "what he might be protecting, what might be at stake in his poetry, is the lyric's very survival. One of his gyres is the losing and finding of faith in form. And, for Larkin, form as pattern is inseparable from form as mystery."[19] Longley's reading of Larkin is a strong one, although it is difficult to reconcile her Yeatsian framework (gyres, mystery) with the actual substance of Larkin's work. More convincing would be to say that Larkin's dependence on – which may be another way to say his faith in – poetic form allows for his doubt of all else. Even this, however, draws the line too strictly between the form and the content of Larkin's poems and so lets too many poems off the hook. The primary reason the bitter meanness of Larkin's views could be shrugged off or downplayed by so many readers is that they are ceaselessly tuneful. "This Be the Verse," for all of its bile, is incorrigibly jaunty. The grace of Larkin's forms is quite real. That such formal grace often covers, and covers for, outbursts spewed against the world is just as real. If Larkin's poems, more than any others, speak for and to the condition of postwar Englishness, then their surface beauties are doubly damned.

I will not attempt to save the poetry from the less than praiseworthy (though hardly criminal) life of the poet, to sink the work into the morass of biography, or to claim the poems as indicative of an entire structure of feeling in postwar English writing. But I will suggest an alternate way to understand Larkin's slim and vital body of poetry within its historical moment. Larkin can surely be made to stand for postwar England: a nation grimly coming to terms with its quite different, and certainly diminished, geopolitical place (see "At Grass"); a glum society in thrall to capitalism (see "Going, Going") and locked into nostalgia (see "MCMXIV" and "Show Saturday"); a gone empire unable to hang on to its holdings (see "Homage to a Government"). And his poetry almost too readily glosses the status of individual life late in the millennium – alienated, hemmed in, at ease, and self-deceiving (see, among many others, "Reasons for Attendance," "Next, Please," "Wires," "Toads," "Poetry of Departures," "Skin," "Home Is So Sad," and "Money"). Larkin's poetry clearly reveals its historical moment, and his work is symptomatic of its circumstances.[20] What have remained further from critical view, however, are its moments of internal disconcertedness. Thematically and tonally, Larkin's poetry draws from the various modes of unease available in postwar England, and the poems' neat finish – their lively well-madeness – most often serves as a sardonic counterpoint. But some of the most fascinating passages in Larkin's *Collected Poems* feature moments of productive friction, wherein whatever we might call the poem's content is neither fully ratified nor fully masked by its form, but instead where the poem's internal tensions leave its content in a lurch.

These moments are scattered but crucial. They occur when content grates against form or when form unfolds its content strangely. Their objective correlative can be found in one of the most famous images from Larkin's poetry, in the odd and unassuming gesture of the speaker of "Church Going," who after entering an empty church removes his "cycle-clips in awkward reverence."[21] This poem, the central text in *New Lines*, stands like a quern-stone in 1950s British poetry, exhibiting many of its central concerns and modes. Its speaker is at once winning and pitiable, able to pinpoint the diminished circumstances of the church while understanding that his irreverence is a form of nostalgia. His visit is clunky and comical: he lets the "door thud shut" behind him, he speaks somewhat too loudly when he offers a mock reading from the lectern, and he fumbles with his bicycle clips. But after two stanzas, at the point when the speaker decides that the church "was not worth stopping for" and shows his dissatisfaction by tossing into the collection box a mere "Irish sixpence," he has second thoughts: "Yet stop I did: in fact I often do." This insight sets into motion several stanzas filled with speculations about what the impressive monument will be used for once "churches fall completely out of use." Once belief and disbelief have gone, all that will be left are the physical remains. The speaker imagines that even these bare remnants will become objects of attention and (however misguided) veneration by "some ruin-bibber" or "Christmas-addict." This moment of scorn turns into something else, however, when the speaker realizes that his speculation on the future use of the disused church has rebounded back onto him. He is in fact the only one there, and so he is placed in the position of the caricatures he was just lambasting: "Or will he be my representative // Bored, uninformed." The speaker undergoes something like a conversion; he apprehends the power of a place (an institution, a way of life, a culture) that he knows is obsolete and yet cannot quit visiting. Even the statement of his quasi-conversion is couched in the language of dismissal:

> For, though I've no idea
> What this accoutred frowsty barn is worth,
> It pleases me to stand in silence here.

Realizing that it, in the end, was indeed worth stopping for, our hatless speaker spends the final stanza praising the continued significance of a church that, for the previous six stanzas, was the object of gentle but unmistakable derision. It is now "a serious house on serious earth" that continues to draw people beyond its putative obsolescence, because

> someone will for ever be surprising
> A hunger in himself to be more serious,
> And gravitating with it to this ground,
> Which, he once heard, was proper to grow wise in,
> If only that so many dead lie round.

The final stanza displays the full grandeur of the poem's form. Larkin's nine-line stanzas borrow primarily from Keats and Yeats, although the richness of those poets' architectural forms are muted by Larkin's use of partial rhymes, some of which become increasingly remote, as in this final stanza's chiming of "earth it is" / "destinies" / "serious" as well as the rhyme on "surprising" and "grow wise in." As the meter becomes more insistently iambic, presumably to match the conclusion's tonal amplification, the rhymes fray. Even as the poem comes around to praising this "serious house on serious earth," it pulls back in the final lines by reasserting the sense of belated diminishment that dominated previous stanzas. Speaking now of the generic "someone" who will gravitate back to this place, the speaker sets such a move within the context of loss. This *was* a place "proper to grow wise in." And the source of the wisdom is unfathomable. It isn't the wisdom of scripture but the presumed wisdom of the inscrutable dead. And these dead – the tombs, the weathered headstones in country graveyards – are still "lying." They are unmoving and deceitful. The past offers no help, and the poem ends by undercutting its attempt to revalue what it had initially dismissed. The place is redeemed, but the human presence within it is denied.

Such a conflicted moment, when the two-faced coin of form and content is stretched and bent, is common enough in Larkin to be significant, manifesting sometimes as a rhetorical undoing (the "almost true" "almost-instinct" at the end of "An Arundel Tomb" or the "not untrue and not unkind" words in "Talking in Bed"),[22] and other times as a clash of registers (as in "High

Windows"). Larkin's poetry often tracks the insufficiencies and deceptions of the past (see "I Remember, I Remember") and occasionally attempts to redeem in the future a doomed present (see "The Explosion"). There are even moments of seeming transcendence, of an "unfenced existence" that is at once desirable and abyssal.[23] Quite often Larkin's poems fail to move past either of the stark impulses that frame "Wants": "Beyond all this, the wish to be alone"; "Beneath it all, desire of oblivion runs." Rather than fully enacting or suppressing either of these impulses, however, the poems that remain vital mingle the two together in moments of strange and shimmering discontentment.

One such moment occurs at the end of "The Whitsun Weddings," the title poem of his 1964 volume, which describes a speaker's train journey toward London. The Whitsun bank holiday brings tax advantages to those who marry on that day, and over the course of the poem, the speaker turns his observations of the many wedding parties at each station into scattershot social commentary. Composed in the long-stanza form that Larkin favored for many of his major pieces, "The Whitsun Weddings" catalogues his central motifs and typical stances. It begins with the speaker's escape from whatever obligation brought him north: "That Whitsun, I was late getting away: / Not till about / One-twenty on the sunlit Saturday / Did my three-quarters-empty train pull out."[24] The train journey allows for a wide-angled view of the changing English landscape that contains both pastoral remnants ("wide farms," "short-shadowed cattle") and the "floatings of industrial froth." Davie sees this amalgamation as the poem's primary achievement. While ultimately coming down against "Larkin's poetry of lowered sights and patiently diminished expectations," Davie praises "The Whitsun Weddings" as "heartening evidence of how the British poet might rise to [the] historically unprecedented challenge" of how poetry "should survive in a wholly urbanized and industrialized society."[25] Tom Paulin, who has written some of the most trenchant critiques of Larkin's work, especially about what Larkin's prominence in postwar poetry says about late-twentieth-century English culture, praises the poem, although backhandedly:

> "The Whitsun Weddings" lyrically documents a shabbily decent
> England before rising in its final stanza to a sacramental image of
> newly married love, fertility and disappointment ... the secular urban
> landscape is imbued with both religious and patriotic values (the
> arrow-shower carries a resurgent nationalist energy and emotion).
> Very deftly, Larkin combines a Yeatsian big-bang effect of magisterial
> visionary power with an undermining sadness whose dying fall and
> sense of diminished horizons is lyrical and deeply English.[26]

A good deal of the poem fulfills both Davie's and Paulin's sense of Larkin's strengths and limitations.

The noise of the wedding parties draws more and more of the speaker's attention, and the poem turns from describing the landscape to commenting on the people he sees: "girls / In parodies of fashion," "mothers loud and fat," "uncles shouting smut." While the poem's ten-line stanzas again show Larkin's reliance on Keatsian and Yeatsian architectures, this poem seems more like a riff on rather than a rescoring of Keats's "Ode on a Grecian Urn." People seen in passing are reduced to empty vessels for Larkin's casual scorn and bad faith. The weddings are all hollow monuments, "huge and wholly farcical." He watches everybody watching the new brides as they get on and off the train and compares the composite ritual to a "happy funeral" and a "religious wounding." "The Whitsun Weddings" repeats "Church Going" with a difference. Both poems critique the vitiation of cultural traditions within modernity, and both lament the diminished shabbiness of the present. In "Church Going," however, the speaker is able to reformulate a mode of value out of the empty monumentality of organized religion. "The Whitsun Weddings" struggles to assert such an alternative and is instead propelled by the inevitability of the train's arrival. Now surrounded by the various wedding parties, the speaker sees England momentarily through their eyes and wonders at their foreshortened horizons:

> none
> Thought of the others they would never meet
> Or how their lives would all contain this hour.
> I thought of London spread out in the sun,
> Its postal districts packed like squares of wheat.

Sitting in judgment, the speaker sees them as passive spectators of their own lives, unconcerned with possibilities that have already been foreclosed. The image of London as a wheatfield of postal districts is both lovely and set to unravel. The jigsaw-like shapes of bureaucratically constructed postal districts are nothing like the four-square regularity of wheatfields seen from above, and it seems incumbent upon the reader to recognize that the simile will not hold. The figure depends upon a reader to pry apart its tenor and vehicle in order to work against the conflation that it undertakes. And one can't simply point out the contrast between the "natural" phenomena of the wheat and the institutional phenomena of the postal districts, because the squares of wheat themselves are products of human management and industrial machinery. Additionally, seeing the wheatfields as "squares of wheat" requires a sustained bird's-eye view of the landscape, one that seems more likely to be a product of air travel than of train travel. A train traveler can of course find herself in a quasi-overhead position in relation to the surrounding landscape that she is passing, but it will be transient, subject to the whims of topography and the route of the tracks. Such local moments of course do not redeem the darker aspects of his poetry and worldview, but Larkin's best poems often offer such self-critical paths for readers to follow. In dismantling the logic of the simile, one is forced to read Larkin's poem against itself.

The conflation of postal districts and wheatfields prepares for the final image of the poem, one of Larkin's best known. As the train pulls into the station, the speaker feels "a sense of falling," a phrase that gathers up Larkin's essential themes: deprivation, decline, creeping limitations. Whatever change has been wrought during this "frail / Travelling coincidence" is at an end:

> And as the tightened brakes took hold, there swelled
> A sense of falling, like an arrow-shower
> Sent out of sight, somewhere becoming rain.

This image – which, according to Andrew Motion, calls up the scene at the Battle of Agincourt as depicted in Laurence Olivier's 1944 film version of *Henry V* – undergoes a series of fissures.[27] A "sense of falling" that coincides with the train's arrival at the station is figured instead as a departure, as the synchronized arrows are unleashed onto an enemy in the unseen distance. The violence of this image is submerged by the next link in the figural chain, when the arrows "become" rain. The arrow-shower ditches its metaphorical connotation and becomes simply a rain shower, but it seems crucial not to simply let these metaphorical transformations occur without pressing on them. Just as we are meant to mark the discrepancy between wheatfields and postal districts, so are we meant to pry apart the dead metaphor in "arrow-shower." The complex "big-bang effect" that Paulin describes is neither a contented grand finale nor an ironic instance of "diminished horizons." The instability of the final image disallows both options; it is a moment of figural unraveling that pries apart the poem's conclusion. A poet, as Larkin puts it in a 1979 interview in the *Observer*, "is really engaged in recreating the familiar, he's not committed to introducing the unfamiliar."[28] For the most part, "The Whitsun Weddings," as is the case for the bulk of Larkin's slim body of poetry, is committed to such recognizable forms of recreation. The final stanza of this poem, however, introduces a species of significant unfamiliarity: the final figure is alienated from itself, strewn across the split metaphor embedded in "arrow-shower." The social contradictions that the speaker can neither ignore nor move beyond are refracted in the several fissile images, but such metaphorical torsions might also outstrip the negativity or sullenness of the thematic substance by providing a concluding image of compacted, if not unified, lyric intensity.

My unpacking of several of the knottier moments in Larkin's poems is not meant to suggest that he is, against all appearances, an experimental poet. Newness was not part of Larkin's or the Movement's project. They were mainly interested in conserving traditional forms of English poetry and cultural life. Movement poetry dominated the literary landscape in the 1950s, and it remained influential for the rest of the century, largely due to the continued prominence of Larkin. But as an actual movement, it was extremely short lived. Blake Morrison locates the heart of the Movement in the years between 1954 and 1956: "By the beginning of 1955, sufficient Movement work had appeared for some reviewers to be sure that it represented the 'literature of the 1950s.'"[29] A quite brief period of emergence set up a mid-decade apex with the appearance of Larkin's *The Less Deceived* in late 1955 and *New Lines* in 1956. Morrison writes, "it would be as difficult to give a precise date for the dispersal of the Movement as it is to give a precise date for its inception. The group had never been officially formed; nor was it ever officially dissolved. It is arguable, however, that 1956 was a crucial turning-point, and that after this date many of the factors which had brought about the development of the group ceased to operate."[30] If the group ceased to cohere internally around 1956, then it also faced pressure from external factors. The remarkable success of Ted Hughes's very un-Movement-like debut volume, *The Hawk in the Rain* (1957), signaled that Movement values did not hold the field, and in several quarters, reaction against the Movement was resolute.

The most considerable contemporary rebuttal to Conquest's *New Lines* and the Movement came from Al Alvarez. In the introduction to his own anthology, *The New Poetry* (1962), he offers a description of the course of poetry in England, a passage I mentioned briefly in the introduction: "since about 1930 the machinery of modern English poetry seems to have been controlled by a series of negative feed-backs."[31] These feed-backs are designed to steer English poetry away from modernist experimentation and back toward traditional styles and forms as espoused by a figure like Thomas Hardy. In Alvarez's reading, the Movement is the third negative feed-back: the work of the 1930s, especially Auden's "light verse" and his imitators, is the first, and the Neo-Romantic poetry of the 1940s, with Dylan Thomas as the "new master," is the second.[32] Alvarez directly targets Conquest and the *New Lines* poets, calling their work "academic-administrative verse" that is bland and conformist. He goes so far as to create a synthetic poem that contains lines from eight of the nine poets in Conquest's anthology in order to demonstrate the Movement's "unity of flatness."[33] Using the speaker of Larkin's "Church Going" as his model, Alvarez describes the standard-issue Movement poet:

the image of the post-war Welfare State Englishman: shabby and not concerned with his appearance; poor...; gauche but full of agnostic piety; underfed, underpaid, overtaxed, hopeless, bored, wry...the poet is not a strange creature inspired; on the contrary, he is just like the man next door – in fact, he probably *is* the man next door.[34]

His reading of the Movement is not entirely inaccurate. Certainly, writers like Amis, Larkin, and Davie espoused varieties of moderation and conservatism that epitomized certain aspects of British society and English cultural life. Instead, Alvarez favors the "strange creature inspired" model of the poet, a mash-up of D.H. Lawrence's "psychological insight and integrity" and T.S. Eliot's "technical skill and formal intelligence" that he calls "the new depth poetry."[35] This explains why Ted Hughes and Thom Gunn, along with John Berryman and Robert Lowell, are the primary figures in Alvarez's canon. But it also explains the ultimate limitations of Alvarez's critique as well as of his anthology: his *New Poetry* isn't all that new.[36] It includes some of the key younger poets who emerged in the late 1950s (Hughes primarily), but it also includes six of the nine poets in *New Lines*, along with several other writers whose work doesn't offer much in the way of newness or contrast strongly with Movement poetry. And many of the most interesting and important writers of the 1950s and early 1960s are left out entirely. Like Edward Lucie-Smith's *A Group Anthology* (1963) – which assembles poems written by members of "the Group," a regular workshop started by Philip Hobsbaum at Cambridge in the early 1950s – Alvarez's anthology positions itself as an alternative to the Movement, a maneuver that obscures the resemblances between Movement poetry and that which was set against it, as well as the broader historical shifts around which these anthologies converge.

If Conquest's *New Lines* catches a moment of cultural retrenchment that spans the decade after the war as well as a sense of "declinism" that lingered beyond the 1950s, then the two editions of Alvarez's popular anthology coincide with a moment of broader expansion and liberalization in the 1960s. Especially after the election of Harold Wilson's Labour Government in 1964, a number of policy shifts made for a more liberal society. Strictures against divorce and abortion were loosened, antidiscrimination legislation was passed, and homosexuality was decriminalized with the passage of a Sexual Offenses Act in 1967. Within such a context, progressive political groups prospered, with the Campaign for Nuclear Disarmament continuing its protests and the antiwar movement burgeoning in response to the expanding conflict in Vietnam. The end of the ban on Lawrence's *Lady Chatterley's Lover* presaged a relaxation in censorship and, along with a rising youth culture throughout the decade, contributed to the possibility of new kinds of thinking about sexuality

and social relations, although conservative views – especially regarding sex
and race – continued to predominate in many spheres. As Dick Hebidge points
out in *Subculture: The Meaning of Style* (1979), links were formed between
white youth cultures and urban black cultures – mainly via American music –
but significant racial tensions continued to exist, with groups of "Teddy boys"
responsible for violence against West Indian communities within the context
of a larger backlash against liberal postwar immigration policies (issues that
I cover in more detail in the following chapter).[37] Throughout the 1960s – and
the postwar period as a whole – modes of retrogression and expansion exist
in dialectical tension with each other, and both are visible within the period's
poetry. It isn't simply that *New Lines* encapsulates 1950s English conservatism
while Alvarez's *The New Poetry* symbolizes 1960s liberalism, but rather that
both anthologies evince the range of ideological positions that characterized
Britain at the time.

The 1960s proved to be a vibrant time for the arts, although the economic
optimism that lay beneath this vibrancy did not last long. The Beatles, who
formed in 1960 and released their first album in 1963, quickly became international figures and paved the way for a flourishing rock-n-roll scene throughout Britain. Their hometown of Liverpool became a lively cultural and literary
scene, and the so-called Liverpool poets – Roger McGough, Adrian Henri, and
Brian Patten – combined rock-n-roll and poetry into popular mixed-media
happenings. Their 1967 anthology, *The Mersey Sound*, published in the Penguin
Modern Poets series, was a bestseller and remains in print, having sold a half
million copies over the course of its life.[38] Although popular culture – and popular music especially – continued to chip away at poetry's audience, Randall
Stevenson suggests that

> support for poetry was … strong during the 1960s, a relatively buoyant
> time for the genre in general. Several mainstream publishers expanded
> their poetry lists at the time – Cape in 1963, Macmillan in 1968, and
> Secker and Warburg in the 1970s – while Chatto and Oxford University
> Press continued longer-established commitments, and Faber and Faber
> remained a key outlet throughout the period. As in other areas, Penguin
> was particularly successful in the 1960s, its Modern Poets series selling
> half a million volumes during the decade and in the early 1970s.[39]

Many regional cities had flourishing arts and literary scenes in the 1960s
and 1970s, but London – or, in the terms of the 1960s, "Swinging London" –
remained the cultural center whose values held sway. English theatre and fine
art scenes successfully adapted styles of pop art and abstract expressionism
imported from the United States, and additional financial support – both

public and private – led to an increase in gallery shows, exhibitions, and the-atre companies. In the poetry world, the influence of beat and hippie culture was apparent in the growing popularity of poetry readings. Events such as the International Poetry Incarnation – a June 1965 happening at the Royal Albert Hall that drew more than 6,000 people and a host of internationally famous writers – harnessed the energies of bohemia to bring poetry into the vortex of 1960s counterculture, a vortex concretized in Michael Horovitz's *Children of Albion: Poetry of the "Underground" in Britain* (1969). Immortalized in Peter Whitehead's film and book, *Wholly Communion*, the Poetry Incarnation drew on the frisson of Allen Ginsberg's legendary reading at Better Books the pre-vious month, just after he had been declared *Kral Majales* ("King of May") in Prague and then swiftly kicked out of Czechoslovakia. The middle part of the decade saw the materialization of a many-tentacled cultural underground, complete with hundreds of cheaply printed and often short-lived magazines, experimental theatre and performance art, and multipurpose venues that aimed to be arts centers and community hubs.

Old and new cultural forms pressed against each other, and we can find a proleptic image of such overlapping ideologies at the start of Gunn's "On the Move," a seemingly prototypical Movement poem that moves well beyond its terms. "On the Move" begins as a variation on a familiar pastoral scene, with the speaker watching a "blue jay scuffling in the bushes" and a "gust of birds / That spurts across the field."[40] These quiet observations are interrupted by the "dull thunder" of a biker gang:

> On motorcycles, up the road, they come:
> Small, black, as flies hanging in heat, the Boys,
> Until the distance throws them forth, their hum
> Bulges to thunder held by calf and thigh.[41]

One form of social life disturbs another as the sexualized masculinity of urban and suburban youth culture – Teddy boys, Mods, Beats – overwhelms the roadside observer and his bucolic spot of time. "On the Move" encapsulates both the aesthetic ideology of the Movement and, albeit anachronistically, the later resistance to that ideology within the different cultural energies in the 1960s. Gunn's early work straddles these formations, a straddling that is dra-matized in numerous ways in "On the Move." What remains to be considered are the kinds of poetry being written at the time that can be explained neither by the Movement model nor by models set up in reaction to it.

Alvarez's "negative feed-back" paradigm offers one critical narrative to explain the course of poetry in Britain between the 1940s and the early 1960s. But this model misses important work of the period that neither correlated with

Movement tendencies nor took an active stance against them. The two poets I'll turn to now, Stevie Smith and W.S. Graham, produced some of the most significant poetry in the midcentury, but they have tended to be overlooked by critics, partly because they don't fit into the kinds of literary narratives constructed by figures like Conquest and Alvarez. This sense of "unfittingness" is not merely a literary-historical circumstance: for these poets, it is inherent to the textures of their work. If Movement poetry could produce, perhaps despite itself, instances of formal innovation or generative uncertainty, then Smith and Graham each exemplify a much more serious engagement with the possibilities provided by modernist poetry while simultaneously adapting the main traditions of English verse for their own ends. Their work remains productively caught between these two currents and offers a different set of formal possibilities, many of which would be taken up by later writers.

Smith is one of the most significant English poets of the postwar era, although she doesn't appear in many of the period's anthologies. Most anthologies of the time failed to adequately represent women writers, despite the popular and critical success of such poets as Anne Ridler, E. J. Scovell, and Kathleen Raine. The only woman poet in *New Lines* is Elizabeth Jennings, while Alvarez includes no British women in *The New Poetry*, although he does find room for Sylvia Plath and Anne Sexton in the second edition. *New Lines – II* includes two women out of twenty-four poets. That midcentury anthologists overlooked Smith was misguided but unsurprising. Smith gained prominence in the 1930s, primarily as a novelist but also as a poet. She was featured in *The Faber Book of Twentieth Century Verse* (1953), but her career hit a rough patch in the late 1940s and 1950s, with several poorly selling volumes in the decade after the war. Her 1957 volume, *Not Waving But Drowning*, however, signaled a reemergence that would last until her death in 1971. She became a popular performer of her poetry, and her penchant for wearing children's clothes and keeping her hair very short made her a memorable, even iconic persona within the English literary scene of the 1960s. Praised by Larkin and Lowell and one of Plath's self-declared "obsessions," Smith produced one of the most significant bodies of work among modern English poets.

Nonetheless, her work has never quite fit within the predominant accounts of twentieth-century poetry. Martin Pumphrey crystallizes the difficulties of "placing" Smith's work:

> Any discussion of Smith's poetry that is to do more than confirm it
> as an amusingly idiosyncratic, critical anomaly must confront the
> implications of the uncompromising use of play and fantasy that is its

most distinctive characteristic. To single out as important simply those poems that can be read most easily as "serious literature" is to evade the critical challenge of Smith's full poetic performance.[42]

Smith's endemic playfulness is of a sardonic and often disturbing sort. Based in a number of traditional genres, such as children's stories, fairy tales, nursery rhymes, and ballads, her lyrics use the jauntiness of form to cover a darkness of substance. Like Larkin, Smith's abiding concerns are death and myriad forms of despair and disappointment (social and romantic, existential and quotidian), and she counterpoints the severity of these concerns with a lively and ceaselessly mischievous surface. Smith is a writer of darkening and alienated cheer, an attenuated Romantic who rewires certain forms of Victorian light verse by forcing them to take in modern ennui and postwar anomie, as in the short poem "In the Night," a single-quatrain poem in trimeter that begins by looking for companionship but ends by thinking "only of the people I should like to bite."[43] Smith's typical stance is playfully fiendish, doubly pulsed with deathliness ("Come Death. Do not be slow") and mordant humor ("Our Bog is dood, our Bog is dood").[44] She is, with Larkin, England's preeminent poet of disappointment.

However, Smith's forms tend to be more thoroughly discontented than Larkin's. Rather than his tidy quatrains or grander stanzas that hold within them a mass of bleakness, Smith's poems continually spill out from and unsettle themselves. Her meters rarely stay on their tracks, as in the final line of "In the Night," which sets the quatrain's rollicking trimeter wobbling. As Christopher Ricks has pointed out, the key to her tone is in its refusal to answer the question of "whether her innocence *is* mock-innocence or not."[45] She is much more likely than any other British poet in the midcentury to write in a straightforwardly parodic or satirical vein about English culture or the literary establishment (see "This Englishwoman," "The Choosers," "The Bishops of the Church of England," "Souvenir de Monsieur Poop," "To School!," or "To an American Publisher"). She is also much more likely to write poems that willfully court sentimentality (see the wonderful "A House of Mercy"). Additionally, the drawings that accompany a great many of Smith's poems contribute to an overall sense of ambiguity, because a reader is never quite sure how to read the pairing of text and sketch.

Although Smith claimed that her drawings weren't made to suit particular poems, she was insistent that they be included in her volumes, and part of her trouble finding suitable publishers in the 1950s had to do with this insistence. At times, a drawing provides an emblem for a poem, as in Smith's well-known retelling of "The Frog Prince," wherein a drawing of an uncomfortably lounging and perhaps sybaritic frog sits beneath the poem's last line, a visual signature of the frog speaker who realizes his unhappiness and asks for his disenchantment: "Come then, royal girl and royal times, / Come quickly."[46] In other instances, the drawing problematizes the text. "The River Humber" is a dawn poem in praise of the river, told from the perspective of a speaker who can oversee the entire vista: "The river Humber" lying "in a silken slumber," the sun rising over the river and the mists, the places still in dark "upon the waters' farther reaches."[47] Between the poem's title and the unfurling of this peaceful scene, however, there is a drawing of a woman floating face-up in the water. If we equate the speaker of the poem with the figure in the drawing, then the poem narrates not a visualized moment but a wholly imagined one. If the woman in the drawing is a personification of the river, then the combined poem and drawing end up conducting a more complicated examination about the gendering of the natural world, and the river's "deeper slumber" plays a subtle variation on Smith's primary theme: an inevitable and sometimes wished-for death.

There are also a number of poems whose accompanying drawing actively undoes the text, the most famous example of which is "Not Waving but Drowning." The poem begins with a third-person speaker who gives a series of contradictory descriptions of a man who is both dead and moaning, and who, in any case, nobody can hear. From the beginning, claims about the dead man are deeply problematic: if he is dead, then the fact that he couldn't be heard would be utterly self-evident. It isn't that nobody heard him and therefore he died, but rather that nobody heard him because he was already dead. The second line unspools further the first line's untenable logic: if he is moaning then he isn't dead, and if he can be said to be moaning, then the initial claim, that he couldn't be heard, can't be true, since the speaker heard him. The poem makes it impossible to ascertain the status of the man. He is dead but moaning. He is both "still" (a kind of death) and still moaning (surely a kind of life, even if it's a soon-to-be finished one).

The next pair of lines further undercuts the simple misunderstanding described in the title by giving over the poem to the dead yet moaning man who describes his plight, talking back to the third-person speaker of the first two lines and presenting the truth of his condition. It now seems as though the initial speaker has misread the scenario. Either the second speaker is not dead – since he is able to respond – or is speaking from beyond death in order to correct the mistaken impression of the earlier speaker. The dead man states that he "was much further out than you thought" ("you" now refers to the first speaker and, more generally, to the people watching him from shore), and that he is neither "still" nor "lying."[48] It isn't only that the initial speaker and the crowd mistake waving for the flailing of a drowning man but that the first speaker didn't seem to register movement in the first place.

The second stanza moves back to a third-person perspective as it mourns the death and tries to explain it, only to have the dead man reply in the third and final quatrain with a forceful repetition of his earlier rebuttal:

> I was much too far out all my life
> And not waving but drowning.[49]

The speaking dead man provides an entirely new timeline for his death: it is not a single fatal moment in the too-cold water but a systemic and life-long drowning. A political allegory is surely possible. This is the title poem of a volume that Smith published in 1957, just after the Suez Canal Crisis signaled the severe attenuation of Britain's global power and just before a series of successful independence movements in British colonies in the Caribbean and Africa (more on both in the next chapter). It suggests that what seems like a fairly quick shift of fortune for the British Empire (recently waving, but now drowning) is not simply a precipitous downfall caused by the massive loss of wealth in World War II and altered geopolitical circumstances but rather a much longer-term event: an empire that had long been precariously overextended.

Whatever we do with the political reading – a reading that becomes infinitely more complex when we take into account all of the contradictions in the poem's logic and voicing – we also have to take into consideration the picture that comes at the end of this poem about a dead man who is, nonetheless, still moaning and talking. Taking up the bottom half of the page on which the poem appears is a drawing of a figure waist deep in water whose long hair comes down to obscure parts of the face and chest. This illustration looks like a woman, or is at least less definitively gendered than the dead man in the poem. The wrists of the person depicted are submerged (so the figure is certainly not waving), and unless the drawing happens to capture the moment when the figure has propelled herself out of the water (though, oddly, with her hands still submerged), then the woman is not drowning but standing in water that happens to come to her waist. The woman's mouth is closed and she is even smiling a bit, both of which seem unlikely to indicate speaking or moaning (although, of course, moaning doesn't necessarily require an open mouth or neutral expression). Smith's picture perhaps switches the sex of the figure in the poem, but it also goes to great lengths to reverse everything the central figure is said to be doing: not waving, not drowning, not moaning, not larking, not laying, and not dead. This poem is wrenched out of alignment in nearly every possible way.

As mentioned earlier, part of Smith's late career success had to do with her public performances, both live and on the radio, and Norman Bryson has given a wonderful description of seeing Smith read her poems at King's College, Cambridge, in the late 1960s: "the dominant tone was of cheerfulness exaggerated, as if the rise and fall of a cheery, vernacular voice were pushed higher and lower and became a stylized sing-song that wasn't cheerfulness but had an alienated relation to cheerfulness…the performance was unnerving because it was so excessive."[50] Bryson's description of Smith's alienated cheerfulness reveals something important about English culture in the mid-century, specifically about the intertwining of postwar relief and late-empire anxiety. It also catches something quite significant about midcentury poetry in Britain. Even poets who returned to so-called "traditional" forms and stances found that those forms could no longer work in traditional ways. Robert Conquest's call to abjure the path of modernist experimentation and return to "the central principle of English poetry, and use neither howl nor cypher, but the language of men," reprises William Wordsworth's 1802 "Preface" to *Lyrical Ballads*, but it could in no way lead to poems that comfortably remodeled nineteenth-century and early-twentieth-century lyric forms, whether Wordsworth's, Tennyson's, or Hardy's.[51] As we've seen, such an attempt by Movement poets often brought about varieties of textual friction or alienation. For poets outside of the Movement orbit and who were more interested in following up on certain strands within poetic modernism, such local instances of discomfort expanded into more systemically discontented texts.

This is certainly the case for W. S. Graham's "The Nightfishing" (1955). Graham was born in Greenock on the Firth of Clyde, west of Glasgow, and spent much of his adult life in Cornwall. His early work, published in four volumes in the 1940s and influenced by Dylan Thomas and the Apocalyptic poets, is densely figurative and syntactically wrenched, remaining obscure even to many of its sympathetic readers. "The Nightfishing" is the title poem of his 1955 volume, the first of his to be published by Faber and Faber, and an object of Eliot's praise. In a 1950 letter to Moncrieff Williamson, Graham writes, "a nice letter from Tommy E., saying thinks the N.F. is a whizz for sticking together and being a long poem."[52] It is one of the key poems of the 1950s, and yet it tended not to figure into contemporary debates, whether those debates centered on the Movement or alternatives to it. Like Smith, Graham didn't feature in some of the important anthologies of the period, and his distance from the English and Scottish literary circuits furthered a sense of his isolation. Graham, who early on chose to pursue poetry as a full-time endeavor and faced economic difficulties throughout his life, disappeared from view after *The Nightfishing*, reemerging in 1970 with *Malcolm*

Mooney's Land, which was followed by *Implements in Their Places* (1977) and *Collected Poems 1942–1977* (1979). His career developed in relative obscurity, and much of the attention paid to him has been posthumous. Since his death in 1986, there has been a steady resurgence of interest in his work, the apex of which occurred around the time of Faber's publication of Graham's *New Collected Poems* in 2004.[53]

It isn't hard to understand why Graham's poetry had been undervalued for so long. His early work often borders on impenetrability. Even in its more lucid moments, as in the final lines from "The Narrator," the first section of his 1944 volume, *Seven Journeys,* it remains primarily concerned with its own coming into being:

> What summer eyes perched deep within a dream
> Could bring the god the child and the rose to speak.
> What tongue like a stamen stemmed on a kiss or a grave
> Is yet enchanted into form.[54]

Such self-entwined moments are common in Graham's work, and his frequent abandonment of normative syntax and penchant for excessive figuration – what Edwin Morgan has described as "linguistic intoxication" – would all but assure his marginalization in a literary moment guided in part by Movement principles of clarity and accessibility.[55] Additionally, Graham remained uninterested in uniting poetic projects with political ones, and so, in a Scottish literary climate dominated by Hugh MacDiarmid and his amalgamation of Scottish nationalism and Scottish literature, Graham's densely meditative poems could be read, and were read by MacDiarmid and others, as irresponsibly quietist. His later work, while significantly clearer than his poetry of the 1940s and early 1950s, remains primarily concerned with the poem as an act of radical communication. Many of these poems are absorbed into their own processes of utterance, and Graham's primary aim throughout his writing career was to examine the basis of the poem as a dialogic act, one that takes the writer and the reader to "the other side / Of language."[56] Often, his poems stage this dialogue as one that occurs within the writing subject, a split between "I" and "me" (which, of course, also functions as a kind of "you"), while at other times Graham more directly addresses the people in his life, especially his wife Nessie Dunsmuir, and the painters of the St. Ives school – Peter Lanyon, Bryan Wynter, and Roger Hilton in particular – who were his close friends in Cornwall.

For Graham, then, a poem is a made event, a "lyrical contrivance" that continually accounts for its own unfolding.[57] One of the clearest statements of his poetics occurs in "The Constructed Space," from *Malcolm Mooney's Land:*

> I say this silence or, better, construct this space
> So that somehow something may move across
> The caught habits of language to you and me.[58]

The poem is an utterance and a construction that becomes a conduit of both silence and speech. It is an act of communication, but the message communicated is the utterance that is the poem itself rather than any detachable content that it might contain. His most significant work, situated at the pivot between his earlier opacities and his later ease into clarity, is an extended meditation on the way in which poetry rerenders experience into the "constructed space" of the text, thereby becoming not a representation or account of that experience but a new experience in its own right.

"The Nightfishing" tells the story of a small-hours fishing expedition. Graham includes several Scottish or Scottish-sounding place names throughout, but the land- and seascape is a composite one, likely amalgamated from his childhood in Greenock and his time in Cornwall. The poem is divided into seven sections totaling 479 lines, and it includes a variety of stanza shapes and line lengths. Orbiting around the third section – 38 octaves that describe in detail the fishing journey – are six shorter poems that provide alternate perspectives on the expedition. The first invokes the soundscape of the harbor and works to simultaneously establish and estrange the writing self. The second section comprises a brief sea shanty. The fourth is a song to a lover on shore. The fifth includes a brief poetics: "All words change in acknowledgement of the last. / Here is their mingling element."[59] The sixth stages a dialogue between two versions of the writing self as it recollects the voyage. The final section reprises the first, repeating the sounds of the "sea bell" as one journey (one self, one poem) is finished and another is in the offing. As one might imagine, "The Nightfishing['s]" search for herring is not simply a fishing trip. The sense in which this voyage is something closer to a metaphysical quest is apparent from the justly admired opening lines:

> Very gently struck
> The quay night bell.
>
> Now within the dead
> Of night and the dead
> Of my life I hear
> My name called from far out.[60]

Like many poets before him, Graham uses the conceit of the sea voyage to delve into a series of issues at the heart of the poetic enterprise: the inevitability of death, the odd relationship between the mortal self and the cyclical world, the sense in which the self is not simply a self but an uneasy amalgam of self-like emanations that overlap and overwrite each other. Throughout the poem, motifs and images interweave and repeat, and so the out-and-back telos of the nightfishing expedition is juxtaposed with the tidal repetitions of the poem's rhythms. Carefully orchestrating phrase boundaries and line boundaries in order to effect the text's wave-like pacing and steeping the poem in dense patterns of assonance and consonance, Graham rarely presents the scene from above or from afar, insisting instead on situating the reader within the boat along with the speaker and the crew. Much of the poem takes place precisely at sea level:

> The tethers generous with floats to ride high,
> And the big white bladder floats at hand to heave.
> The bow wakes hardly a spark at the black hull.
> The night and day both change their flesh about
> In merging levels.[61]

Many of lyric poetry's most common topoi make an appearance in "The Nightfishing," coming to the surface between talk of the water and the waves and the haul of silvery herring. This quest poem is also a self-elegy, a work song, an extended nocturne, an almost-aubade at its close, a meditation on language, and a love poem (to the sea, to the lover on shore, to the text's own internal processes). At times, the fishing trip starts to resemble a metaphysical or spiritual trek, while at others, it threatens to become purely a conceit for the making of a poem.

But what is crucial about "The Nightfishing" is that it never fully turns over into any of the other generic types toward which it occasionally points. The fishing trip remains a fishing trip. The material facts of the poem – a boat, a crew, shore birds and diving birds circling, the dark seam of water that may indicate herring, the moon, the water, rough waves – are never entirely subsumed into a symbolic narrative. Graham's method here is not mythic. It draws on the modernist projects of Eliot and Pound but swerves away from fully investing its fishing trip with mythic or historic power. Or one could say that Graham is unable or unwilling to leverage his narrative of herring fishing into a totalizing poetic vision. In either case, this unresolved tug at the poem's core is the source of its value. The speaker never gains dominance over "this sea which utters me," either visually or otherwise, and so the poem remains doggedly tethered to its environment.[62] The speaker also never fully consolidates into a self-identical subject but rather remains haunted by its own doubles, the unbiddable power of sea and weather, and language itself ("I uttered that place / And left each word I was").[63] "The Nightfishing" is fully realized, and its relatively consistent tone and register provide large-scale cohesion. At the same time, however, it is productively wobbly, remaining dissatisfied with the generic or formal solutions available to it. Its refusal to leave behind the particularities of the fishing trip – the "harbour oil," the "sheared water," "the slowly diving nets," "our hacked hands" – in order to pursue a more abstractly spiritual or metapoetic voyage keeps it moored in the actual.[64] At the same time, it will not relinquish metaphysical gestures, even if they remain latent within the poem's dark waters.

"The Nightfishing['s]" intergeneric tension and estranging syntax characterize the phenomenological investigation at the heart of Graham's work. At the same time, "The Nightfishing" is a materialist text in that it remains connected to the realities of the fishing trip. But Graham's poems tend to focus less explicitly on politics and history or on the prerogatives of poetry as a social practice. One of the open questions for postwar writers concerned how poetry might respond not only to the destruction and brutality of the very recent past, but also to the longer history of exploitation that defines European imperialism. For Jon Silkin, whose journal *Stand* staged debates of these issues during the 1950s and 1960s, "the real question" was how to write socially committed poetry that consolidated some of the gains of modernism, especially imagism, without slipping into didacticism. In the introduction to *Poetry of the Committed Individual* (1973), he asks, "how might a hermetic or imagistic art be engaged with an art that wanted without compromising its essentiality to be socially oriented, involving, as this does, some movement towards the discursive [?]"[65] One of the featured poets in Silkin's anthology was Geoffrey Hill, whose long writing career has been animated by the question of poetry's role in relation to politics and history. In the introduction, I described a complex structure of postwar English feeling in which optimism at the war's end was tempered by disappointment at Britain's imperial decline, both of which were marbled with a deep skepticism concerning just what was being celebrated or lamented. This structure of feeling is one of discontentment, and I've tracked various modes of formal discontentment in the poetry of the 1950s. Hill's early poetry embodies a different kind of discontentment, one unsure of the role of poetry itself in the face of widespread skepticism about the future (and past) of English culture.

Like that of several of the Movement poets, Geoffrey Hill's earliest collection appeared as part of a series of pamphlets from Oscar Mellor's Fantasy Press, which began in 1951 and was a key outlet for young Oxford poets, as well as for several American poets resident in Oxford in the early 1950s, most notably Adrienne Rich and Donald Hall. After his 1952 Fantasy Press Poets pamphlet, Hill continued to publish in journals, and his first full volume, *For the Unfallen: Poems 1952–1958*, was published by André Deutsch in 1959. In this volume, Hill shows himself to be a strong formalist, and his adherence to traditional forms of English poetry – rhymed quatrains, the sonnet, an iambic pentameter base – would seem to link him to the Movement poets. And yet the relaxed formality of poets like Amis or Larkin is worlds away from what G. S. Fraser, in a review of *For the Unfallen*, calls Hill's "chillingly distinguished formality."[66] Hill's early work is characterized by its increasingly vexed syntax, its austere authority, and its continual unease with the role of poetry in a European civilization so lately ravaged by war and atrocity. At once a visionary poet and a writer of unyielding skepticism, Hill takes up traditional forms in order to put systemic pressure on the ideals, beliefs, and ideologies of English and European culture. Though formally masterful, Hill's poems turn this mastery against itself by using it to articulate intractable dilemmas surrounding art's ethics and to stage the insoluble paradoxes of individual and social life.

In *Articulate Energy: An Inquiry into the Syntax of English Poetry*, Donald Davie writes,

> Systems of syntax are part of the heritable property of past civilization, and to hold firm to them is to be traditional in the best and most important sense. This seems ungracious to both Pound and Eliot, who have both insisted upon the value of the European civilized tradition, and have tried to embody it in their poems. Nevertheless, it is hard not to agree with Yeats that the abandonment of syntax testifies to a failure of the poet's nerve, a loss of confidence in the intelligible structure of the conscious mind, and the validity of its activity.[67]

Davie's credo, which might be taken as a Movement mantra, suggests that a return to syntax is a return to traditional, civilized values. Hill's early poetry does conform to "systems of syntax" but works to deconstruct the link between "systems of syntax" and what we might call "systems of civility." There is indeed a strong strand of Blakean sublimity in Hill's work, in which the poet assumes far-reaching powers of declaration and prophecy. This is most apparent in the earlier texts in *For the Unfallen*, which is arranged chronologically and attaches dates of composition to each poem. But as the volume proceeds, the vatic powers of poetry are more insistently questioned and troubled. The ability of a poem to perfect aesthetically a subjective moment, a philosophical or ethical dilemma, or an historical instant or process comes under incisive investigation. This is most apparent in the book's elegies: Hill's impulse to elegize and memorialize the dead – especially victims of historical violence – is increasingly frustrated by the impossibility of doing justice to the dead within a poem's rarefied shape. Vincent Sherry summarizes this point: "Hill's language seeks to be both the medium of aesthetic perfection and a force field of historical violence. If the individual work, as an aesthetic whole, achieves a formal perfection, as such lifting us away from history, its parts are still heavy with history, immersing us in the matter of bloody fact."[68]

A handful of thematic clusters predominate in *For the Unfallen*: the creative power and responsibility of the poet, the presence of the past within the present, the ethics of elegy and remembrance, the sheer weight of the dead upon the concerns of the living, the importance of traditional structures and institutions, the failures and iniquities of those same institutions, the need for just speech and action and the difficulty of the same, the potential for eloquence and passion to deaden into hollow custom, the intertwining of religious belief and deep doubt, the dangers of modern commerce, and the difficulty of ascertaining true value. In later volumes, Hill relates these issues more specifically to the matter of England and Europe, but in *For the Unfallen*, they tend to be approached via mythic and Biblical analogues. Several texts reference historical events and personages, and one of the key poems in the volume, "Two Formal Elegies," specifically positions itself as a post-Holocaust text, dedicated as it is to "the Jews in Europe."[69] But the poems generally abstract their scenes and narratives from particular events, while it remains clear that Hill means to test poetry's capacity for historical examination. In this he follows Eliot's call in "Tradition and the Individual Talent" for poets to be historically minded and to write with a feeling for "the mind of Europe."[70] But as *For the Unfallen* proceeds, Hill approaches this civilizational mind with increasing skepticism.

"Genesis," the volume's first poem, displays a poet of nearly unbridled power:

> Against the burly air I strode
> Crying the miracles of God.[71]

Even as the speaker comes to understand the innate violence of creation and civilization ("By blood we live... / There is no bloodless myth will hold"), the syntax of the poem remains firmly under the speaker's control.[72] An oracular stance, which owes much to Blake and Yeats, appears occasionally throughout the volume but is usually subdued by elusive ambiguities and syntactical snares. Epiphanies and moments of creative dominion become harder to come by, and poems frequently end with questions, doubts, or disappointments. The inability to harness poetic speech for epiphanic realization becomes a theme of its own:

> For though the head frames words the tongue has none.
> And who will prove the surgeon to this stone?[73]

The volume cycles through a series of deaths, many of them "deaths by water," as it attempts to find a suitable mode of elegy. The paradoxical weight of the drowned comes to overtake the speaker's desire to atone for their unwilling sacrifice. Hill's elegies are rigged to fail, and attempts to memorialize "those varied dead" are shown to be merely aesthetic gestures that "deceive[s] with sweetness harshness."[74] In "Metamorphoses," "Elegiac Stanzas," and "After Cumae," poetry's pretensions to vatic knowledge are exposed and undermined. In "Of Commerce and Society" and "To the (Supposed) Patron," such deceptive gestures are linked to modern Europe's obsession with trade, commerce, and profit. In "A Pastoral," the redemptive power of art, its claim to provide recompense via its elegiac motions, is satirically redescribed as a mere display of decency that masks justice. Throughout *For the Unfallen*, eloquence, civility, and custom are rethought as the tools of barbarism and subjugation. As the volume proceeds, every word and well-turned phrase becomes a potential site of guilt and falsity, and art merely a place where "history can be scraped clean of its old price."[75] Each poem is an instance of trammeled speech, and Hill's rigorous forms are self-delighting and self-despising.

For the Unfallen is both guilty beacon and earnest warning. It reviles the "bad perjurable stuff" from which many modern poems are made but also recognizes itself in that same stuff.[76] It is mistrustful of its own well-wrought shapes and yet continues to aim for aesthetic repletion. It satirizes the baseness of modern English and European culture but returns again and again to the icons and myths of that culture, if only to describe their deceptive inadequacies. As does Larkin, Hill keeps faith with traditional forms but pressurizes those forms so that they can bear the weight of their recalcitrant, ambivalent materials. In these ways, *For the Unfallen* may be the key volume of poetry produced in Britain in the 1950s. It registers, with relentless force, the varied stresses that shaped poetry in the wake of the war and in the face of a new and seemingly more perilous geopolitical dispensation. Hill's early work draws together a number of influences – from Blake, Hopkins, and Yeats to Eliot, Empson, and Allen Tate – without fully assimilating any of them. Rather than the Movement's studied avoidance of modernist experiment, Hill registers modernist poetry's key concerns while remaining supremely distrustful of modernity itself. If Larkin voices a certain strand of postwar English feeling – insular, wishing for comfort and ease, both satisfied and anxious – then Hill's first volume might be said to articulate a different sort of feeling, though one not entirely divorced from the first. The eminently legible disappointments of Larkin's poetry become baroque connivances in Hill's. The damage of history weighs upon nearly every line in *For the Unfallen*, but nowhere is found a moment of full respite. If in Larkin's work the occasional unsettled passage, as at the end of "The Whitsun Weddings," is, precisely, occasional, then for Hill, such moments are constitutive: "No manner of address will do."[77] At a moment of cultural and political refashioning, Hill's poetry stages the inability to disentangle the past from the present and vexes itself by considering its implication within the course of history's, and England's, modern progress: "To put up stones ensures some sacrifice."[78]

Chapter 2

Decolonizing Poetry

The conditions that brought about the rapid dissolution of the British Empire after World War II had been developing since the late nineteenth century, but they were quickened by the war's devastation and aftermath. Postwar realignments of geopolitical power, as well as the systemic damage that the war inflicted, ensured that Britain had neither the political nor the financial resources to maintain its empire. The 1956 Suez Canal Crisis crystallized these shifting dynamics, and that year – which, as we've seen, is also and fittingly the apex of Movement poetry – continues to be understood as a crucial marker of Britain's altered position. After the United States halted Britain's attempt (in league with France and Israel) to invade Egypt in order to maintain its access to the Suez Canal, which had been nationalized by President Nassar in July 1956, it was clear that Britain's imperial reach had diminished. Colonies that had been aiming for political independence for decades found and seized their moment. Other colonies that had less well-developed independence movements became caught up in the wave of decolonization that swept through the Caribbean and Africa, the famous "winds of change" that Prime Minister Harold Macmillan described in a 1960 speech in South Africa. Between the 1947 Indian Independence Act and the late 1960s, much of Britain's empire in Africa, the Middle East, Asia, and the Caribbean was dismantled. Without attempting a full survey of postcolonial poetry in English, and without aiming to incorporate all narratives of emerging national canons into a monolithic story of "global English literature," this chapter will consider some of the ways in which poets responded to the complex process of British decolonization from the 1950s through the 1970s.

The effects and implications of decolonization were many and multifarious. Burgeoning independence movements were fed by the desire for freedom and political autonomy, by feelings of ethnic and cultural pride, and by anger at the violent, coercive history of British imperialism, especially the legacy of the transatlantic slave trade. Such wide and deep animosity among colonial subjects was, however, often tempered by genuine feelings of affinity for and a sense of belonging to Britain. As Anne Spry Rush points out in reference to the

Caribbean, "from the late nineteenth-century through the twentieth-century colonial period, education was, for West Indian children, an immersion in Britishness."[1] Wartime propaganda and political rhetoric engrained the idea of a democratic, egalitarian British Empire fighting a global war against tyranny, and many colonial subjects joined the British military on those terms. This problematic discourse remained active after the end of the war, projected into a vision of a liberal, progressive Britain that would ensure the welfare of all of its subjects, and many people throughout the colonies continued to affiliate themselves with British culture even as they simultaneously supported political independence. The two Colonial Development and Welfare Acts passed by Parliament in 1940 and 1944 demonstrated a commitment to increasing resources for expanding education and other projects, even during a time of financial constraint. Although they were less successful than hoped, the attention paid to social and economic issues helped shore up support for British policy in the colonies and sought to cast an image of imperial unity. Additionally, the 1951 Festival of Britain and Elizabeth II's coronation in 1953 each bolstered a sense of national and imperial recovery after the turmoil and austerity of the war years. The spread of film and television helped ensure that such major events were seen throughout the empire, enhancing the image of a global British community as the political stakes of that community were being pulled away.[2]

One of the strategies to foment continued imperial unity in the immediate postwar period was the formation of the British Commonwealth, the umbrella term designating the new structural relationship between Great Britain and its dominions and former colonies. The actual unifying force of the Commonwealth was short lived, cresting, perhaps, with Elizabeth's coronation and troughing in the later 1960s and early 1970s, when Britain turned more fully to Europe as a primary economic partner. Much of the Commonwealth's significance was and continues to be symbolic rather than material, with the arts and culture playing a central role in maintaining the links between Britain and its former colonies. However, one feature of the Commonwealth's early history has shaped the course of postwar Britain: emigration from current and former colonies into the United Kingdom, what the Jamaican poet Louise Bennett famously described as "colonization in reverse."[3] While there had always been a small stream of migrants from the colonies into England, immigration policies established after the end of the war encouraged large numbers of people to migrate to the British mainland. The postwar labor shortage in England made immigrant labor necessary, and the 1948 Nationality Act's broad definition of citizenship – all Commonwealth subjects were recognized as British citizens who had the right to live and work in the United Kingdom with their families – made settlement in England an appealing and viable option.

Large-scale colonial migration first began in the West Indies in the late 1940s. The docking of the SS *Empire Windrush* at Tilsbury on June 21, 1948, carrying 492 passengers from various parts of the Caribbean (mostly men) is an iconic moment within the formation of contemporary Britain, and, according to Anne Spry Rush, 115,000 West Indians migrated to Britain between 1952 and 1962.[4] Despite their legal status as British citizens and the need for their labor, colonial immigrants experienced widespread racism and discrimination, especially during periods of economic weakness. Black immigrants faced both institutionalized racism and informal discrimination in matters of employment, social relations, and, as Wole Soyinka powerfully dramatizes in his well-known poem "Telephone Conversation," housing. Racially motivated attacks, such as the 1958 Notting Hill riots, occurred frequently, and right-wing politicians presented arguments against immigration in racist and often apocalyptic terms, with Enoch Powell's infamous 1968 "Rivers of Blood" speech in Birmingham the nadir of such discourse.

After the progressive 1948 Nationality Act, immigration policy in Britain became increasingly restrictive. The 1962 Commonwealth Citizens Act introduced quotas based on skills and employability, while the 1968 Commonwealth Immigrants Act and the 1971 Immigration Act placed further limits on inward migration from former colonies into Britain, especially from the West Indies, Africa, and Asia. The 1981 British Nationality Act reversed its 1948 predecessor, limiting full citizenship to those people born with at least one parent who held British citizenship. This astonishing turnaround in citizenship policy shows the centrality of postwar immigration within broader – and usually anxious – debates about Britishness and the vexed joint of ethnicity and nationality. As Ashley Dawson suggests, "the migration of colonial subjects to the British metropolis forced this mongrel nation to reckon with its long history of imperialism and racism."[5]

Ever-tightening immigration policies are part of this postwar reckoning with British "imperialism and racism." One aspect of this story, which I take up in Chapter 6, takes place in the 1980s and continues into the present. It features poets, often the children of immigrants who arrived in the first waves of postwar migration, who consider questions of ethnic identity and cultural affinity as inhabitants of a thoroughly postcolonial Britain. The other, which is the central topic of this chapter, involves poets born and raised in the colonies who came of age during or just after the war and who had to negotiate the conditions of decolonization as they were developing. This earlier part of the story is difficult to pin down geographically. It is key to an account of British poetry in the twentieth century, but it isn't centered in the British Isles. Rather, it occurs throughout the Atlantic world and comprises a complex narrative of transit, migrancy, displacement, and transatlantic interaction.

One of the central tasks of colonial poets in the period was to negotiate a sense of double, conflicted belonging – of, as Derek Walcott puts it in an early poem, being "divided to the vein."[6] The speaker of Walcott's "A Far Cry from Africa" catalogues and critiques the brutalities of "colonial policy" as he considers the 1953 slaughter of a Kikuyu tribe by Mau Mau rebels in Kenya, but he ends the poem caught between an intractable set of identities, obligations, and desires:

> Where shall I turn, divided to the vein?
> I who have cursed
> The drunken officer of British rule, how choose
> Between this Africa and the English tongue I love?
> Betray them both, or give back what they give?
> How can I face such slaughter and be cool?
> How can I turn from Africa and live?[7]

The geographical triangulation that Walcott offers here – a Caribbean poet writing in the voice of one caught between Africa and England – maps onto a subject position bifurcated between racial solidarity and a strong sense of cultural Englishness. This passage indexes many of the difficult choices faced by individual colonial subjects and colonial societies more generally, as well as some of the strategies used to navigate such tortuous conditions. For the speaker, it seems impossible to face fully the actuality of Britain's imperial violence – "such slaughter" – and still carry on. But it also won't do to turn away from the knowledge of such a history and simply "live." One solution might be to turn away from both England and Africa so as not to have to choose between them, but this would indicate a form of betrayal. Another would be to "give back" to both what they give, but the precise connotation of the phrase remains ambiguous. Does "give back" have the sense of "return," or perhaps "retaliate against"? What kinds of politics are forwarded here? Active resistance to colonial rule? A negotiated settlement between one's multiple forms of identification? A continual state of unsettled anxiety brought about by attempting simultaneously to "curse" imperial Britain and "love" English language and culture – to be at once Caliban and Prospero?

The poem presents rather than decides among these choices, and its explicit indecision is signaled implicitly in its metrical patterning. The questions in the final lines are rendered in smooth, perfectly formed iambic pentameter verses – a knack for which is surely part of what has been "given" Walcott during his complicated immersion in English literature and culture. The poem's general metrical pattern is strategically curtailed at a significant moment – "I who have cursed" – but the reinstallment of iambic pentameter immediately following lessens the effect of the speaker's cursing of "British rule." One of Walcott's indispensable early poems, "A Far Cry From Africa" troublingly and productively charts the complexities of postcolonial subjectivity during the moment when independence movements and colonial wars reshaped the political substance of Britain's colonial world.

The questions that animate Walcott's speaker are not only individual or rhetorical. While many colonies gained their independence through a negotiated settlement or some form of Parliamentary consent, and while Britain's postwar colonial wars tended not to be protracted military affairs as in the case in Ireland during and after the Great War, there was still a great deal of violence and turmoil during the decades of decolonization. Some independence movements featured revolts and armed resistance, as in Kenya, Cyprus, and Malaya, while others became caught up in the ideological torsions of the Cold War. Often the leftist politics of anticolonial groups came into conflict with the American-led struggle against communism, which played into local political dynamics and shaped Britain's response to specific independence movements. Poets and writers were often actively involved in such events.

In British Guiana, the victory of the socialist politician Cheddi Jagan and his People's Progressive Party (PPP) in the 1953 election (the first to feature universal suffrage in the colony) led to a suspension of the constitution, with British troops and security agents intervening to overturn the results. The British government, unhappy at the prospect of a communist regime in Guiana and feeling pressure from the United States, declared a state of emergency and ruled the colony directly for three years, claiming that it was preventing a communist takeover of the country. Jagan was removed as prime minister, and he and his wife, along with other members of his political party, were arrested. One of the founding members of the PPP, and a close colleague of Jagan's, was the poet Martin Carter. He was arrested in October 1953, just after Britain declared a state of emergency, and detained without charge at an American military airbase in Guiana until January 1954.

That same month, a small London publisher with leftist leanings published Carter's volume, *Poems of Resistance from British Guiana*. Carter spent part of his detention on hunger strike, and many of the poems directly address the past and present of British imperialism, as in his call for resistance and revolution at the end of "I Clench My Fist":

> Although you point your gun straight at my heart
> I clench my fist above my head; I sing my song of FREEDOM![8]

This passage, although closer to propaganda than much of his other work, displays the inextricability of Carter's poetry of the 1950s and 1960s from the anticolonial movement in British Guiana. His well-known poem "University of Hunger" provides a rich example of the interplay between political vision and poetic form:

> is the university of hunger the wide waste
> is the pilgrimage of man the long march
> The print of hunger wanders in the land.[9]

Clearly referring to Carter's own time on hunger strike during his incarceration, the poem transforms "hunger" into a broader metaphor for systemic deprivation and want. Carter's dependence on iambic pentameter (typical of his work throughout the 1950s and 1960s) produces a cadence of despair as various images of misery are fused together and captured within the meter. Just as the iambics in "I Clench My Fist" mimic the actions of British troops, so in "The University of Hunger" is the fundamental English poetic meter mobilized to dramatize the effects of British oppression and incursion.

At the same time, Carter incorporates occasional Creole words and syntax in order to introduce a form of linguistic resistance within poems about political resistance. The opening lines of the quoted passage are statements, not unpunctuated questions, and they use a common Creole English syntactical pattern in which the subject is elided (in this case, the subject pronoun *it* and the relative pronoun and verb *that is*). By fronting the copula, the poem disjoints standard English. It splices in a form of Creole English in order to provide a species of grammatical resistance alongside of its catalogue of stasis and lack:

> is air dust and the long distance of memory
> is the hour of rain when sleepless toads are silent
> is broken chimneys smokeless in the wind
> is brown trash huts and jagged mounds of iron.[10]

Carter's poetry is by turns prophetic and realist, aggregating isolated images into a litany of anticolonial feeling. The turn to elemental features with mythic undertones ("air dust," "hour of rain," "sleepless toads") is a common one within postcolonial poetry in English, sometimes serving to counterpoint images of urban or industrial modernity with a presumably precolonial plenitude and other times providing an alternate system of cultural value outside the orbit of the imperial West (with its "jagged mounds of iron"). Carter's lines set the stage for such an alternative space, one in which images of impending hope and regeneration ("the hour of rain") are placed within the continuing desolation of "the university of hunger."

British Guiana was granted its independence in 1966 and renamed Guyana, and Carter remained politically active throughout the 1950s and 1960s, taking a position as Minister of Information and Culture in the People's National Congress in 1967. His time in government was disillusioning, however, and he resigned three years later. Alongside an article in the *Sunday Graphic* announcing his resignation, Carter published a short poem, titled "A Mouth Is Always Muzzled," that expresses his disappointment with the Guyanese government and his realization of the wide gulf between the promise of national independence and the Machiavellian actualities of postcolonial politics:

> In the premises of the tongue
> dwells the anarchy of the ear.[11]

The poem draws dichotomies – between clear speech and chaotic chatter, between resolved purpose and anarchic spectacle – that encapsulate the difficulties of adhering to political and social ideals while steeped in the everyday machinations of institutions, where clarity of vision and speech becomes an inevitable casualty of bureaucracy's obfuscating rhetoric. It also recognizes the simple fact of material need ("the food it eats to live"), as well as the obligation of abstract political ideals to take into account concrete necessities, and such an amplification of the subjective concerns of the lyric speaker into a consideration of large-scale social conditions underlies Carter's work.

One of the major issues for British colonial poets writing in the middle decades of the twentieth century was finding an audience and a mode of publication. West Indian fiction was quite successful in the 1950s, with Andrew Salkey, Jean Rhys, George Lamming, Samuel Selvon, Wilson Harris, and V.S. Naipaul pursued by major London publishers. West Indian poets, however, appeared much less frequently on the lists of key poetry houses.[12] Carter's *Poems of Resistance from British Guiana* is one of the very few West Indian poetry volumes published in England in the 1950s, and Walcott's *In a Green Night: Poems 1948–1960*, published by Jonathan Cape in 1962, was the first volume of postwar West Indian poetry brought out by a major London press. Walcott and Edward Kamau Brathwaite, whose first book, *Rights of Passage*, was published in 1967 by Oxford University Press, are the only black Caribbean poets who had volumes published regularly by English publishers before the 1980s. Bruce King states it even more plainly: "with few exceptions, such as Walcott and Brathwaite, black poets were ignored by mainstream British publishers until the mid-1980s."[13]

One prominent example of an important Caribbean poet ignored by London publishers is Louise Bennett. Bennett, known as Miss Lou on her many radio and television shows, was a ubiquitous presence in Jamaica and a globally famous figure, and her dialect poetry and monologues reached a wide audience. She produced a number of albums and volumes, most notably *Dialect Verses* (1942) and *Jamaica Labrish* (1966), but it took a while for her to be taken as a serious poet within the West Indies, and she was not considered within the British poetry scene. Within such a climate, poets sought alternative outlets, and journals such as *Bim*, *Focus*, the *Caribbean Quarterly*, and *Kyk-Over-Al* became key fora for new Caribbean writing and criticism. Another significant forum was *Caribbean Voices*, a weekly BBC radio program that debuted in March 1943 and ran through the 1950s, first under the leadership of Una Marson, a Jamaican journalist and writer who had produced several programs for the BBC's Colonial Service, and then of the Irish-born Henry Swanzy after Marson's departure in 1945. Marson and Swanzy had strong connections with key figures in the Caribbean, such as Frank Collymore and John Figueroa, who served as informal talent scouts for *Caribbean Voices*. Even when Swanzy and the program were criticized as being yet another form of colonial imposition or for taking the best new writing out of the Caribbean, the program continued to be a catalytic force. It simultaneously strengthened the link between Anglophone Caribbean writers and the metropolitan center and encouraged the development of a distinct West Indian literary tradition. These were not necessarily compatible projects, and the kinds of tensions brought to the surface within the context of *Caribbean Voices* resemble those found within postcolonial poetry more broadly.[14]

Swanzy was a strong supporter of the young Derek Walcott, whose first appearance on *Caribbean Voices* came in 1949, the same year that his work first appeared in *Bim* and a year before he entered the newly established University College of the West Indies.[15] Walcott's poetry, with its vivid descriptions and its focus on Saint Lucian landscapes and Caribbean content, was bound to draw the attention of Swanzy, who favored writing that attended to local culture. Walcott's deep strengths as a phrasemaker, an image spinner, and a deft worker of the iambic line, along with his ability to assimilate features of modernist poetry into his own emerging style (primarily Auden, Yeats, Thomas, and Eliot), gave his early work a compelling authority, and his reputation in London grew throughout the 1960s.[16] His second volume with Cape, *The Castaway*, sold more than 1,000 copies in its first year.[17] Apart from a few poems that emerge out of trips to England and the United States, his work focuses on the particularities of the West Indies and his own experiences there. Nevertheless, a good deal of Walcott's early poetry wrestles with questions that also faced émigré writers in London, such as those he asks at the end of "A Far Cry From Africa." Even within Saint Lucia, Walcott was an insider's outsider. His middle-class family, Methodist upbringing, Catholic secondary education, and mixed heritage (both of his grandfathers were white, while both of his grandmothers were African) meant that he was a somewhat unplaceable figure, as in the self-portrait drawn in the early chapters of his autobiographical poem, *Another Life* (1973). His intellectual and cultural formation was "wrenched by two styles," and such a wrenching has shaped his poetry's continuing investigation into the tensions between the history of colonialism in the West Indies and the possibilities of articulating a strong form of postcolonial subjectivity.[18]

His early poetry extensively maps these multiple forms of ambivalence: by directly treating the end of empire (as in "Ruins of a Great House," "Two Poems on the Passing of an Empire," and "Verandah"); by considering the fortunes of a small island such as Saint Lucia within the larger orbit of Western modernity and global capitalism ("Prelude"); by shaping his own development as a mélange of influences, myths, and forms of knowledge ("Origins" and *Another Life*); by taking up archetypal figures such as Crusoe or Odysseus within a Caribbean perspective ("Crusoe's Island," "Crusoe's Journal," "Sea Grapes," and, of course, his epic *Omeros*); by depicting the West Indies as both a site of celebration ("A Sea-Chantey") and of continuing historical trauma ("Lavantille"); and by devising a voice and lyric texture that can shuttle between standard English and a Creole vernacular dialect (see "Tales of the Islands," "Parang," and especially "The Schooner *Flight*"). Walcott's poetry is strongest at the moments when it manages to leverage subjective narratives and descriptive scenes into larger commentaries on the history of the West Indies and, more precisely, on the erasure of that history by the multiple devastations of European imperialism. In such moments, ambivalence remains a generative force, and George Lamming describes Walcott as "a model of the ripened ambivalence that makes impossible demands of the heart, tears it to pieces by a contradiction of origins, and finally offers it to the dubious consolation of a livable despair."[19]

Walcott's method of turning impossible contradiction into a form of consolation often revolves around acts of naming and renaming. In "The Muse of History: An Essay" (1974), Walcott grants the poet, and especially a poet of the New World whose native history has been obliterated by imperialism and the slave trade, an "Adamic vision," the prerogative to re-name the places and things of the world.[20] In "A Sea-Chantey," this yields a celebratory list of place names – a "litany of islands" and "rosary of archipelagoes."[21] Later poems complicate this Edenic impulse by recognizing and attempting to account for the massive and traumatic absence at its heart. Because European imperialism has abolished the native history of the islands – "there is too much nothing here" – and because, nevertheless, the material, political, and social implications of that imperial history shape the islands' present – "the middle passage never guessed its end" – an act of postcolonial naming can never quite be originary.[22] Walcott's favored image for this doubly binding colonial condition is the wound, as in the conclusion of "Lavantille":

> Something inside is laid wide like a wound,
>
> some open passage that has cleft the brain,
> some deep, amnesiac blow. We left
> somewhere a life we never found,
>
> customs and gods that are not born again.[23]

The "something inside" is both the historical fact of the middle passage and the knowledge of that fact for those who have come after. Walcott's collective "we" cannot simply be born anew to a world that the Adamic poet can make by naming. Nor, however, can there be a return to past traditions and cultural forms that have been lost. Birth and death are closely juxtaposed, and each is imprisoned in the other. This tension between creation and destruction, between forms of life and life's erasure, is encoded within Walcott's other primary leitmotif: the sea itself, which comes to stand for absolute loss and devastation – of people, of cultures, of history – and for the possibility of newness.

"The Sea Is History" allegorizes this toggle, ironically describing a slave ship's transatlantic passage and the slave trade itself in biblical terms. Responding to, presumably, a European's question about the absence of Caribbean history, the speaker of "The Sea Is History" harnesses the teleology of the biblical books in order to name that which the European imperial project – often using the same biblical progression to justify its actions – decimated:

> Where are your monuments, your battles, martyrs?
> Where is your tribal memory? Sirs,
> in that grey vault. The sea. The sea
> has locked them up. The sea is History.[24]

The speaker decolonizes the bible by forcing it to account for the history of black people in Africa and the Caribbean and subsequently rescales the poem to construct a new allegory in which the minor motions and petty maneuverings of colonial and neocolonial officials are figured in a litany of blatantly unheroic animals. The poem concludes with a hopeful moment in a tide pool:

> and then in the dark ears of ferns
>
> and in the salt chuckle of rocks

> with their sea pools, there was the sound
> like a rumour without any echo,
>
> of History, really beginning.[25]

Moving from imperial "monuments" and the hugeness of the sea to the micro-environment of a shoreside sea pool, the poem presents a politics of locality while unraveling the largest and most systemic of Western ideologies. And yet even this redemptive moment of postcolonial reinscription (the volume in which this poem appears was published in the same year that Saint Lucia gained its independence) is figured as deeply ambivalent. History "really" begins as a nonhistorical sonic event – a nonechoing sound that resembles a rumour (which is, it might be said, all echo) – within the anthropomorphized auditory systems of plants and rocks. The implications of such a metaphorical schema are multiple, and they are deliberately curtailed: the grand statement "of History, really beginning" is, almost too ironically, positioned as the poem's final line. "The Sea Is History," one of Walcott's most important poems, finds its start only as it ends. Such a moment reveals his larger project. The great struggle of Walcott's poetry – from his 1948 self-published volume, *25 Poems*, through the lyrics and long narrative poems of the 1970s and 1980s, to his reimagining of Homer's *Odyssey* within a Saint Lucian context in his 1991 epic, *Omeros*, and into his late poetry – has been to find a way to begin.

Shabine, the speaker and protagonist of Walcott's long poem "The Schooner *Flight*," includes an instance of complex self-definition within his opening monologue:

> I'm just a red nigger who love the sea,
> I had a sound colonial education,
> I have Dutch, nigger, and English in me,
> and either I'm nobody, or I'm a nation.[26]

The key coordinates of postcolonial subjectivity (and of Walcott's poetry) are represented in this passage: a sense of geographical specificity and attachment, a hybrid ethnic and racial identity, an intertwining of standard and creolized forms of the colonial language, an ideological formation that is both empowering and alienating ("a sound colonial education"), and an ambivalent relationship to the larger social and political structures that surround and produce the self. On the one hand, Shabine is overlooked, a "nobody" within the normative, white model of the British subject. On the other hand, Walcott's entire oeuvre is premised on the possibility of leveraging such an absence, and here the alliterative link between "nobody" and "nation," especially when triangulated with the rhyme on "education," produces a strange sense of plentitude that outflanks the putative either/or structure. By upending the part/whole relationship that usually sponsors a notion of a national belonging, Walcott reopens a famous question, one famously asked by MacMorris in Shakespeare's *Henry V*, "What ish my nation?" The same question is put to Leopold Bloom by an adamant Irish nationalist in the "Cyclops" chapter of *Ulysses*. The Jewish Bloom answers, "Ireland...I was born here. Ireland," and when asked to define a nation, replies that a nation is "the same people living in the same place."[27] These two quotations condense many of the issues central to this chapter, and the questions posed by MacMorris and to Bloom are ones that had particular resonance in postwar Britain. With the dismantling of the British Empire and the creation of newly independent countries that nonetheless maintained a connection to Britain, new answers to the question – "what is a nation?" – had to be found.

Of course, one of the simplest answers is that "a nation" is exactly what a newly independent colony became, and nationalism remained an important ideological force within the British Isles and the colonies during decolonization. As I've described in the previous chapter and will outline in a different context in the next chapter, the end of the empire produced a necessary rethinking of the nation of England and of the nature of Englishness. There were also questions about how to reimagine or redesignate relations that were important and ongoing but that couldn't be solved within the discourse of nationhood or of empire. In the 1950s and 1960s, the Commonwealth was imagined to be one sort of solution, and, as mentioned earlier, the arts were often asked to construct and bolster links between Britain and its newly independent former colonies. Walcott curated a selection of new Commonwealth writing for an issue of *London Magazine* that was meant to promote the 1965 Commonwealth Arts Festival, one of the major such linkages. Among several weeks' worth of events in Cardiff, Glasgow, Liverpool and London, there were a number of poetry happenings.[28] The festival's anthology, *Young Commonwealth Poets '65*, grouped poets by "nation" and arranged them alphabetically, giving equal status to widely disparate political entities. Within the anthology, England exists on equal footing with Scotland, Northern Ireland, Canada, Zambia, and dozens of other political entities. Several established poets are represented (Lamming, Carter, Walcott, Edwin Morgan, Roy Fisher, Roger McGough, Ian Hamilton Finlay), and many younger poets who would go on to become major figures make appearances (Brathwaite, Les Murray, Fleur Adcock, Seamus Heaney, Michael Longley). The poets are separated by nationality but equalized within the table of contents' abecedary. Such an arrangement offers a veneer of equality (which was central to the discourse around the Commonwealth) while masking or ignoring the quite real inequalities that continued to exist among them.

The only exception to the organizational logic of *Young Commonwealth Poets '65* is its arrangement of Caribbean poets, who are grouped under the general heading "West Indies" and then broken down into subsection by individual country or island. Ironically, the West Indian poets are united in a volume published three years after the dissolution of the West Indies Federation, a ten-island group lasting from 1958 to 1962 that was envisioned as a cohesive political unit. The Federation was marred by internal conflicts from the beginning, as the desires and priorities of the different islands prevented a coherent regional unit from succeeding in the long term. And, for the most part, the logic of the nation-state rather than the federated or regional unit dominated political developments during British decolonization.

Groupings and informal federations of artists, writers, and intellectuals, however, have been a central and lasting feature of the period's cultural life. Indeed, the story of postwar British poetry is often told as a continuing battle between one faction of poets and another or presented as a kind of tribal map. One of the most significant groups of artists and writers in postwar Britain was the Caribbean Artists Movement (CAM). Founded by Edward Kamau Brathwaite, Andrew Salkey, and John La Rose in London in 1966, CAM was a driving force in the development of West Indian literature in Britain and the Caribbean. Between 1967 and 1972 (with the first three years being the most lively), CAM organized meetings, lectures, readings, art exhibitions, performances, and three large conferences (in 1967, 1968, and 1969). A dozen CAM newsletters were produced in London between 1967 and 1970, and *Savacou: A Journal of the Caribbean Artists Movement* appeared regularly throughout the 1970s. Most of the key figures in Anglophone Caribbean literature participated in CAM, and its loose organizational structure and panoply of events encouraged wide involvement. CAM was committed to promoting Caribbean art and culture, but there wasn't a single group manifesto or uniform political ideology. The topics that most interested the group can be seen in the titles of some of its major talks. At the first CAM meeting, in January 1967, Orlando Patterson gave a talk titled "Is there a West Indian Aesthetic?" In July of that year, C.L.R. James spoke on "The Contribution of the West Indies to European Civilization." At the third CAM conference in August 1969, Edward Brathwaite lectured on "Africa in the Caribbean." The movement's activities waned as central figures (Brathwaite especially) moved away from London at the end of the 1960s. Additionally, the spread of radical student organizations and the rise of Black Power movements led to an increasingly politicized atmosphere around the group and among West Indians in Britain generally. This was especially the case after Stokely Carmichael, author of *Black Power*, visited London and gave several speeches in 1967, most notably a talk at the Congress on the Dialectics of Liberation in July of that year, which led to his banishment from Britain. CAM was composed primarily of middle-class intellectuals and artists, and the inevitable gap between CAM and working-class black immigrants was magnified during this period, which featured class-based struggles and calls for direct political resistance rather than discussion and analysis of the social and cultural situation.[29]

Brathwaite was the CAM secretary from its inception until his move to Jamaica in 1970, and he and his wife Doris were the key organizational forces during CAM's most successful period. One of the signal events in CAM's history was Brathwaite's public reading of *Rights of Passage* at the Jeannetta Cochrane Theatre in Holborn in March 1967. It had just been published by Oxford University Press, and the reading, as Anne Walmsley has it, "effectively launched its publication and its poet."[30] The event was not only a major triumph for Caribbean literature in Britain, it also underlined the importance of oral traditions for West Indian poetry. Part of CAM's project, and of Brathwaite's in particular, was to emphasize the importance of native Caribbean and African musical and spoken-word practices and to find a way to bring serious attention to these aspects of folk culture in the West Indies.

Brathwaite's concept of "nation language" emerged from his experiences in CAM and from his doctoral research at Cambridge, which appeared as *The Development of Creole Society, 1770–1820* (1971) and which laid the groundwork for his later historical studies, *Contradictory Omens: Cultural Diversity and Integration in the Caribbean* (1974) and *Folk Culture of the Slaves in Jamaica* (revised edition, 1981). In a 1979 talk at Harvard University, Brathwaite differentiated among four strata of language in the Caribbean: the "imposed" and "imperial" languages of English, Dutch, Spanish, and French; creole English, "which is a mixture of English and an adaptation that English took in the new environment of the Caribbean when it became mixed with other imported languages"; "*nation language*," "which is the kind of English spoken by the people who were brought to the Caribbean, not the official English now, but the language of slaves and labourers, the servants who were brought in by the conquistadors"; and "the remnants of ancestral languages still persisting in the Caribbean," which includes the languages of the Amerindians, "a destroyed people," Hindi, Chinese, and "survivals of African languages."[31] Creole English and "nation language," as well as the various "ancestral languages," had to "submerge themselves" beneath the imperial languages.[32] This "underground language," an ongoing dialectical exchange rather than a standardized structure, "was itself constantly transforming itself into new forms."[33] "Nation language" is "the *submerged* area of that dialect which is much more closely allied to the African aspect of experience in the Caribbean," but it is deliberately contrasted with the term *dialect*, which, for Brathwaite, "carries very pejorative overtones."[34]

The task of the Caribbean poet is to harness the resources of one's "nation language" in order to bring to the surface the African and Afro-Caribbean features embedded within English lexical and syntactical forms, what Brathwaite calls "its contours, its rhythm and timbre, its sound explosions."[35] This involves, first, a Poundian redux: an active breaking or ignoring of the pentameter as the dominant meter and an attunement to the oral tradition of Caribbean spoken word and song. Brathwaite celebrates figures like Louise Bennett, Mighty Sparrow, and Big Yout, who had been ignored by the literary mainstream and whose mastery of Caribbean folk rhythms and of calypso and reggae makes them emblematic nation-language poets. Poets who embrace nation language will move Anglophone Caribbean writing out of its "first phase," the central feature of which is exile to the metropolis, and will be part of a larger process of cultural healing.[36] As he puts it in a talk given at the 1971 Conference of the Association for Commonwealth Literature and Language Studies at the University of the West Indies in Mona: "the writer should [get to] know his society, and history, and do what he could to heal the dichotomies, especially between folk and elite…the healing process had to begin with a recognition of the resources of the folk, we ourselves turning our eyes from overseas back to the ground of ourselves."[37] Despite the danger of essentialism implicit in Brathwaite's formative concept, his theories about nation language and creolization have been deeply influential. Just as influential has been Brathwaite's early poetry, in which he offered a model of nation-language literature alongside his theorization of it.[38]

Rights of Passage is a linked series of poems that focuses widely on black cultural and historical experience. It traces the effects of the transatlantic slave trade on Caribbean and African societies by incorporating a vast array of images, myths, figures, settings, and practices from native and folk traditions in the black Atlantic world. Along with *Masks* (1968) and *Islands* (1969), the other two books that make up *The Arrivants*, *Rights of Passage* inscribes a cycle of departure and return. Recounting the violence of capture, the horror of the middle passage, and the trauma of slavery while occasionally stitching in moments of hope and potential regeneration, the trilogy comprises an epic miscellany of transatlantic history. Rather than proceed with a single developmental narrative of an individual or group, Brathwaite juxtaposes a number of micronarratives in different forms: blues, work songs, laments, prayers, calypsos, chants, and all sorts of lyric subgenres. The poems' rhythmic intensities are catalyzed by Brathwaite's adaptation of jazz and Afro-Caribbean music. And much of their structural scaffolding is derived from his knowledge of folk practices and rituals such as *voudon*, *kumina*, and limbo.

"Wings of a Dove," one of the trilogy's great individual poems, draws on such a multitude of rhythms, tones, and genres. It begins with a description of "Brother man the Rasta / man" before transcribing a people's collective cry: "Down down / white / man, con / man, brown / man.[39] It then offers an ironic retraction or explanation of the people's shout in a heavier dialect before concluding with a chant-like prayer whose heavy enjambments and syncopations complicate the rhythms that have come before:

> So beat dem drums
> dem, spread
>
> dem wings dem,
> watch dem fly
>
> dem, soar dem
> high dem,
>
> clear in the glory of the Lord.[40]

The "dem" that punctuates every couplet is the sort of excessive sonic material – textual noise – that Brathwaite considers key to nation language: "Noise is that decorative energy that invests the nation performance. Unnecessary but without which not enough."[41]

The Arrivants, in addition to being a nation-language performance, is a text deeply marked by Anglo-American modernism. Eliot's influence can be traced through the trilogy, as can Yeats's and Pound's, each (and there are of course others) remixed within the poem's mélange of perspectives and styles. "Calypso," the poem following "Wings of a Dove," contains multiple registers and rhythms in its four short parts. It moves from a lyric catalogue describing the Caribbean's formation ("The stone had skidded arc'd and bloomed into islands") to a sardonic evocation of the sugar trade that finishes with an Eliotic flourish: "and young Mrs. P's quick irrelevant crime / at four o'clock in the morning."[42] It then weaves Eliot's grim jauntiness into blues-inflected portraits of "black Sam" and "John with the European name."[43] The poem concludes in a calypso chorus with a heavy beat and a defiant collective voicing:

> Steel drum steel drum
> hit the hot calypso dancing
> hot rum hot rum
> who goin' stop this bacchanalling?[44]

Like *The Waste Land*, *The Arrivants* doesn't feature a single speaker but rather a shifting series of voices who reappear throughout. One such voice is "Tom," a composite character derived from the title character of Harriet Beecher Stowe's *Uncle Tom's Cabin*, who appears initially as a locus of shame and weakness but is also a transformative figure factored out over the course of the volume: as "timid Tom / father / founder / flounderer"; as "Selassie God," the Ethiopian king and Rastafarian messiah; as "this poor / land- / less, harbour- / less spade"; as "Brother Man the Rasta / man"; and as "the boy now nigratin' overseas."[45] Such personas often diffuse into a voice more like the poet's own, which itself is frequently flipped into a seemingly impersonal "I" or "we" that ventriloquizes a social or racial collectivity. In the same way, location is rarely constant; instead, *Rights of Passage* shuttles across and up and down the Atlantic seaboard and throughout the Caribbean, Africa, England, and the United States, constantly metamorphosing character, scene, rhythm, and speaker in order to anchor the book's primary motifs: forced migration, geographical displacement, and exile.

What amazes about the trilogy is Brathwaite's facility with scale and scope, his ability to make cohere a Poundian historically minded epic. Poems move from commentary on political events and social issues to ritual-like passages of great auditory power (see "South" and "O Dreams O Destinations"). Portraits of individual, often anonymous black figures are juxtaposed with wide-angled scenes of Caribbean and African landscape and seascape, which are themselves interlaced with glimpses of black life in northern cities. Precisely observed images of death, destruction, and waste are followed by exhortations to build anew that which the slave trade has destroyed ("Prelude"). Elegy can turn quickly to satire and then to solitary prayer and then to collective chant ("New World A-Comin'" and "All God's Chillun"). Poems that catalogue stark questions about African, Afro-Caribbean, and African-American historical experience ("Mammon" and "Postlude/Home") are answered by poems that return to the lived grain of that experience in order to imagine a future ("Epilogue"). Brathwaite's intertwining of nation language and standard English revolutionized the possibilities for Anglophone poetry, and Lawrence Breiner has gone so far as to describe the trilogy as "for its time and place a functional equivalent to the work of Dante or Chaucer."[46]

In *Masks* and *Islands*, motifs ramify and build upon each other as the exilic wanderings of *Rights of Passage* settle into a more consistently plotted journey from West Africa (*Masks*) through London and back to Jamaica (*Islands*), following Brathwaite's own itinerary from the mid 1950s to the early 1970s. Unlike the other parts of the trilogy, *Masks* stays in one place, remaining in Africa throughout and focusing exclusively on African cultural, religious, and artistic practices. After the invocatory "Libation" – which consists of a prayer to the Akan earth goddess ("Prelude"), a detailing of the ritual instruments

("The Making of the Drum"), and a chant-like text that renders the drums' music ("Atumpan") – the arc of *Masks*' symbolic narrative runs from the movements of precolonial African kingdoms through the colonial incursions and the start of the transatlantic slave trade, ranging over the continent while focusing its gaze most frequently on West Africa and the Ashanti Kingdom (present-day Ghana). There is, once again, no consistent "I" that carries over from text to text, and many poems adopt the voices of early kings or of various imagined figures in precolonial and early colonial Africa. But as the volume progresses, the speaker who appears most frequently seems a stand-in for the poet, an exile returning to Africa generations later. The "home- / less departer" considers, again and again, the consequences of European colonization, both its immediate human devastations and its effects centuries later (see, especially, "The New Ships").[47] These moments of despair occasionally give way to regenerative celebrations and moments of partial hope (see "Adowa" and "The Forest"). The final section of *Masks* articulates a double return. At the symbolic level, the return is to Africa. At the structural level of *The Arrivants* as a whole, the return is to the Caribbean. Enfolded within this pair of quite different arrivals are the contradictions built into the diasporic imagination. Brathwaite considers this double return to opposite sides of the Atlantic key to the "healing process" that is the responsibility of the Caribbean writer. The concept and practice of nation language impels this process, impossibly poised between colonial languages, native languages, and the insurgent creolizations that ceaselessly transform both. Simon Gikandi has illuminated this notion. Expanding on the importance of Edouard Glissant's theorization of Creole (which he calls a "language of Relatedness" rather than a "language of Being") for Brathwaite's own account of "nation language," Gikandi writes, "if, on the one hand, Creole literatures function as acts of refusal, it is a refusal which, on the other hand, is constructed at the point of interface, at the junction where the European language meets the African voice. What happens when these two faces meet is the key to understanding Caribbean poetics."[48]

Islands, the final part of the trilogy, stages this complex return and locates the "point of interface" in the postwar Caribbean, complicating further the dialectical move that occurs at the end of *Masks*. The "point of interface" that is the West Indies is not only a geographical palimpsest (a variety of local African cultures underlie and have been altered by a variety of local Caribbean cultures) but also a temporal one. The precolonial, pre–middle passage African past cannot be regained but also cannot be laid aside. It is, as Walcott's vision often has it, an absence or a kind of wound. Brathwaite's aim in *The Arrivants* is to offer a mode of suturing. He revivifies African and Afro-Caribbean songs, dances, myths, and forms of knowledge while keeping in mind that these

practices are governed by unaccountable loss and by continuing oppression
and injustice. The poems in the trilogy coalesce rather than conclude: they
return to the ancestral, the mythic, and the elemental not so as to indicate that
an individual or a culture in the middle and late twentieth century can gainsay
history and remake its origins, but so as to suggest that such a coalescing is
both impossible and necessary. Such forms of newness are, from the start, acts
of repair. The project of the individual texts in the trilogy is to be

> now waking
> making
>
> making
> with their
>
> rhythms some-
> thing torn
>
> and new[49]

This "waking" and double making operates as a kind of hopeless hope, one that
may not restore the past, remake the present, or assure a different future but
that can, nonetheless, continue to suggest such possibilities. The trilogy tracks
the hopeful moments of decolonization and independence as they give way to
the less hopeful actualities of postcolonial governance, as well as to the continuing neocolonialism of global capitalism and to the cultural colonialism of the
tourist economy. Brathwaite's early trilogy maps these transnational vectors
within the Caribbean context and plots the linguistic, aesthetic, and political
arcs in which such vectors travel.

What we might call Brathwaite's "elemental modernism" is a strategy that
several key postcolonial writers took up in the late modernist period. Jahan
Ramazani describes such "hybridizing literary strategies" as indicative of
postcolonial poetry's redeployment of "modernist bricolage" tactics, among
which he names "translocalism, mythical syncretism, heteroglossia, and apocalypticism."[50] These are certainly tactics that Brathwaite employs, as do many
significant postcolonial figures within Ramazani's canon of contemporary
transnational poetry in English, which includes writers such as Christopher
Okigbo, Okot p'Bitek, A.K. Ramanujan, Lorna Goodison, and Agha Shahid Ali
(in addition to Walcott, Brathwaite, and Bennett). In a number of decolonizing
poems, these formal strategies underwrite a double return that is both spatial
and temporal. Such poems seek to regain the precolonial past or to find those
aspects of earlier cultures that have survived the devastations of imperialism
or that can be productively remade. However, any such returns are bound to
be partial and precarious. Brathwaite's notion of nation language is predicated

on a revaluation of African and native languages that have been submerged under imperial languages. But the insurgent, subversive creolizations that constitute nation language do not successfully restore native authenticity. Rather, they are acts of bricolage that constellate Afro-Caribbean cultural and aesthetic forms with those of European modernism. These texts suture together within their mottled forms the temporal and spatial discontinuities that are founding conditions of postcolonial writing.

There are a number of factors that make Anglophone West Indian poetry an especially important part of the story of post-1945 British poetry, which is why I have given it such attention in this chapter.[51] However, this isn't to say that there weren't poets of note writing in English in East and West Africa, India, or other places during the period of decolonization. In Africa, metropolitan publishers were eager to take advantage of new book markets in newly independent countries in the 1950s and 1960s. A number of African writers found large audiences in Britain and throughout the English-speaking world, touched off by Amos Tutuola's *The Palm-Wine Drunkard* (1952) and the massive success of Chinua Achebe's *Things Fall Apart*, published by William Heineman in 1958, which helped to fund Heinemann's entire African Writers Series for a long while afterward. Due in part to Achebe's success and influence, the novel became the privileged form of English-language African literature, as Gareth Griffiths points out: "of the first twenty-six titles published by Heinemann in their African Writers Series, twenty-one were classified as a fiction (that is novels and short story collections), three as non-fiction (all autobiographical accounts), and only one as poetry, and one as drama."[52] The first generation of major writers in Anglophone Africa – Achebe, Wole Soyinka, and Ngũgĩ wa Thiong'o – worked primarily in genres other than poetry. More importantly, many writers in Africa have linked decolonization and independence to the avoidance of English as a literary language, what Ngũgĩ has famously called "decolonizing the mind." This has made the distinction between developing African literary canons and postwar British literature somewhat sharper. Okot p'Bitek's long narrative poem, *Song of Lawino* (1966), along with his follow-up volume, *The Song of Ocol* (1970), did find success with an English-language audience, but both poems are translations by p'Bitek himself of his original poems in Acoli, which places them in a somewhat different category.

That being said, several major figures did write poetry. Although it isn't the work for which Wole Soyinka – the first African Nobel Prize winner – is famous, his early poetry is significant. In poems such as "Death in the Dawn" or "Around Us, Dawning," "modern" events – an airplane flight, a car crash – are rendered in densely metaphorical language that utilizes the basic elements of land, sky, season, and animal, while many other poems in *Idanre and Other*

Poems (1967) unfold as tortuous psychological or psychosexual meditations that also weigh the violence in 1960s Nigeria (see "Massacre, October '66," one of Soyinka's most powerful poems). The poems in *Idanre* and *A Shuttle in the Crypt* (1972) feature all manner of syntactical compactions – inversions, elisions, reversals, archaisms, unexpected juxtapositions – as Soyinka draws upon the dense figurations of the metaphysical poets as well as on the tight stanzas of mid-twentieth-century Anglo-American figures like William Empson, Allen Tate, and the early Robert Lowell. Soyinka frequently incorporates figures and images out of Yoruban myth and culture, especially in the long poem, "Idanre." The turmoil felt by the speakers of his poems is rendered in highly pressurized phrases, starkly defamiliarizing images, and combustible rhythms. His is a difficult, sometimes rebarbative style, but such difficulty is fitting and compels attention, especially in *A Shuttle in the Crypt*, which consists mainly of poems written when Soyinka was imprisoned and placed in solitary confinement for nearly two years by the Nigerian government.

Soyinka was imprisoned because of his support for Biafran secessionists who were in the middle of a civil war with the Nigerian government. After Nigeria won its independence in 1960, tensions among the country's three major ethnic groups – the Hausa and Fulani in the north, the Yoruba in the southwest, and the Ibo in the southeast – and among various government factions increased until three eastern states declared an independent republic of Biafra. Government forces attempted to put down the coup, and the Biafran War lasted from July 1967 until January 1970, when the Biafran army surrendered. One of the many, many victims of the war was the poet Christopher Okigbo, who was born in 1930 and died as a member of the Biafran forces in August 1967. He was part of a group of Nigerian poets, along with Soyinka and John Pepper Clark, who attended the University College, Ibadan in the early 1950s and who were associated with the important student journal there, *The Horn*, and the Mbari Artists' and Writers' Club. The poetry he produced during his brief career is at the very center of the canon of modern African poetry, and the densely allusive and elusive sequences that constitute *Labyrinths* – *Heavensgate* (1962), *Limits* (1964), *Silences* (1965), and *Distances* (1964) – provide the most concentrated example of elemental modernism in the period.[53]

Okigbo's poems are differently difficult than Soyinka's, and the challenge of reading *Labyrinths* has less to do with barbed syntax and more to do with the difficulties of following the metaphorical and allusive logic of Okigbo's vision. The poems together comprise a spiritual and historical quest, and in a preface to *Labyrinths*, Okigbo describes the sequence as "a fable of man's perennial quest for fulfilment."[54] Okigbo was raised a Catholic but was also deeply knitted into the Igbo tradition, and his syncretic vision combined with a deeply modernist sense of form to produce a voice that both takes very seriously its own aesthetic vocation and can cultivate a stance of sardonic despair in the style of early Eliot. However, it is important to note that Okigbo's sense of his calling as a poet goes well beyond the aesthetic:

> I am believed to be a reincarnation of my maternal grandfather, who used to be the priest of the shrine called Ajani, where Idoto, the river goddess, is worshipped. This goddess is the earth mother, and also the mother of the whole family. My grandfather was the priest of this shrine, and when I was born I was believed to be his reincarnation, that is, I should carry on his duties. And although someone else had to perform his functions, this other person was only, as it were, a regent. And in 1958, when I started taking poetry very seriously, it was as though I had felt a sudden call to begin performing my full functions as the priest of Idoto."[55]

His curtailed but powerful body of poetry is founded on such orphic functions, and around his work has grown an aura of almost prophetic significance, no doubt spurred by his untimely death in battle.

Heavensgate is a series of prayers, invocations, praise poems, satires, visions, and curses. There are poems in which the speaker ("prodigal," "initiate," "newcomer") addresses a composite beloved (a river, a goddess, a mother, a lover, a lioness, "my white queen," "mother Idoto," "Anna"); poems in the voices of local characters, such as Jadum (whom a note describes as "a half-demented village minstrel") and Upandru ("a village explainer"); poems of rites and community festivals; poems that make oblique reference to contemporary events in Nigeria ("and the hand fell with Haragin," who was the chairman of the Nigerian Salary and Wage Commission in 1965); poems that entwine spiritual vision and sexual awakening (see "Watermaid"); and poems that move quickly from transcendence to anomie.[56] While *Heavensgate* is the most dependent of the four sequences on its modernist precursors, it also shows Okigbo's ability to range widely among his preferred materials and styles, moving from the opening poem's simple, hopeful invocation ("Before you, mother Idoto, / naked I stand"), to a tone of Eliotic alienation ("The stars have departed, / the sky in monocle / surveys the worldunder"), to the prophetic voice that dominates *Limits*, *Silences*, and *Distances*:

> Dark waters of the beginning.
>
> Rays, violet and short, piercing the gloom,
> foreshadow the fire that is dreamed of.[57]

As in the quoted passage, the poems throughout *Labyrinths* simultaneously unfold several time frames: the daily and diurnal (this passage is the opening of an *aubade*, a dawn poem), the ritual, the mythic, and the apocalyptic or messianic. The poet's journey takes place in an abstracted and heavily symbolic African environment, but as with the multiple time frames within the sequence, it is usually difficult to pin down a precise geography or to get comfortable in a single, consistent setting. After the preparatory gestures of *Heavensgate*, the poems' textures become more concentrated. Rather than shuttling among styles and registers – as he tends to do in *Heavensgate* – Okigbo works to compact them in a single amalgam, as in this description of the beginning of a drum song:

> And the drums once more
> From our soot chamber,
> From the cinerary tower
> To the crowded clearing.[58]

The drums emerge from their tomb – "soot chamber," "cinerary tower" (a *cinerarium* is a place to keep ashes) – to take part in the ritual playing, and in doing so they remake both the Yeatsian tower and the Keatsian urn. Instead of Keats's urn's "unheard melod[y]" Okigbo's drums awake like the "unheard sullen shriek" of a sacrificed ram, and then, even more strangely, like the synaesthetic "shriek" of incense, the intense smell of which is made audible.[59] The anticipated syncopations of the drums are presaged by the quatrains' uneven rhyme patterns. Heavy half rhymes in the first stanza ("more" / "chamber" / "tower") thin out in the following two stanzas, which feature half rhymes only on the first and third lines ("awake" / "shriek"; "blood" / "deployed"). At this point, the drums, having already changed from ash to incense to animal, morph into two different – and seemingly disparate – delivery systems:

> Liquid messengers of blood,
> Like urgent telegrams,
> We have never been deployed
> For feast of antelopes...[60]

The drums are first metamorphosed into "liquid messengers of blood" (which, in an overwritten fashion, might just mean "blood" – its own substance and carrier) and then into "urgent telegrams." The beating of drums becomes the beating of blood becomes the (much lighter) "beating" of the telegraph machine. Perhaps made of antelope hide themselves, the drums necessarily haven't been "deployed" – a military figuration clearly designed for the reader to notice – for the "feast of antelopes," an event that may result in the skin of the sacrificed animals from which the drums themselves might later be made.

Okigbo foregrounds elements of Igbo ritual and knits those elements into a developing spiritual and psychological voyage, but his figural transformations reveal quite different economies and scales, just as the whole of *Labyrinths* works at multiple levels at once – constructed from African themes and materials, inscribed by disparate forms of European and American poetic modernism, and mottled by their tense and unfinished interplay. In the parabolic lyrics of *Limits*, the dialogic and elegiac ceremonies of *Silences* (alternating first between *Crier* and *Chorus* in "Lament of the Silent Sisters" and then between the long-drums and the elephant horn and among the various ancestral drums in "Lament of the Drums"), and the dream-like poems, in *Distances*, of a near mystical psychic homecoming, Okigbo undertakes a multipart spiritual journey. The journey also mortars his vast surround – Igbo totem and myth, West African flora and fauna, European and American literature, Nigerian history, classical Greek and Roman culture, and European modernity's array of action and damage. Even as he turns to a clearer style to confront more directly the violence of Nigeria's civil war, he maintains his preference for elemental terms and figures – "iron birds," "a night of deep waters," "a path of stone," "a dance of death," "this iron dance of mortars" – as he assumes a definite prophetic stance at the very end of his war-shortened life: "I, Okigbo, town-crier, together with my iron bell."[61]

My construal of "elemental modernism" and its centrality to the poetry of British decolonization is not simply a respinning of modernist primitivism. It is a widespread mid-century tactic, one in which poets chart the complex difficulties and horrors of modernity by way of a broken return to elemental forces – to the environment and the animal world, to the natural history of earth, and to early civilizations, myths, and religions. This mode is central to modernist poetry more generally and is one that critics and readers have long recognized. In the postwar period, such a mode has intriguing historical implications. As I've shown, for poets from decolonizing places, this mode becomes a means to articulate aesthetic independence from imposed imperial norms and to revalue native experience while drawing on and experimenting with models of European modernism and the English literary tradition. For poets in Britain and in England in particular, such an elemental poetics has quite different ramifications, as can be seen most powerfully in the early poetry of Ted Hughes.

In his extremely successful first volume, *The Hawk in the Rain* (1957), and then in the several volumes that followed – *Lupercal* (1960), *Wodwo* (1967), and *Crow: From the Life and Songs of the Crow* (1970/1972) – Hughes established himself as a virtuoso of animal poems. Not necessarily as a nature poet in the tradition of the Romantics or Georgians, but as a writer for whom animals become the primary means to track psychic complexities ("The Hawk in the Rain"), to meditate on violence and history ("The Jaguar" and "Thistles"), and to describe and catalyze the poet's act of writing ("The Thought-Fox"). Hughes's imagination tends heavily toward the primal and the instinctual, and animals become "something more near / Though deeper within darkness" that provides the immanent material from which to fashion accounts of the self and its strange depths.[62] The roughened texture of his poems alternates between precisely observed details and mythic abstraction, as in "The Horses," in which the speaker first comes across a group of horses during a predawn walk and quickly turns them into emblems of an ancient world void of people. He sees the horses

> Huge in the dense grey – ten together –
> Megalith-still. They breathed, making no move,
>
> With draped manes and tilted hind-hooves,
> Making no sound.
>
> I passed: not one snorted or jerked its head.
> Grey silent fragments
>
> Of a grey silent world.[63]

The speaker circles back around to take another look, although this time he is "stumbling in the fever of a dream" after the sun has "erupted silently." Now, however, the horses have "draped stone manes," and their "tilted hind-hooves" are "stirring under a thaw."[64] The sun animates while the poem immobilizes them, symbolic statues within the speaker's psychic gallery.

Heavy on assonance, consonance, alliteration, and half rhyme but wayward in their metrical patterns, Hughes's early poems fashion an aesthetics out of animals and envision individual subjects and larger social relations via the prism of nature. The picture that most often results is of a violent, atavistic world in which all the substance of civilization and culture is stripped away to reveal the primal, base forces that drive human actions. This is, to be sure, poetry keen to plumb the individual and collective unconscious, and Freud and Jung are key avatars. But as the scope of Hughes's vision grows, at once more impressive and more monstrous, it becomes clear that he is also considering the force of history itself. *Crow* is the dark heart of this project, and the gathered poems about Crow's violent, death-filled birth, his berserk childhood, his bouts with god, his wanderings and battles, and his sundry acts of destruction constitute a myth of negation. Crow is civilizational anti-matter. He is both the barbarism at its core and the inassimilable excess that it extrudes:

> Crow straggled, limply bedraggled his remnant.
> He was his own leftover, the spat-out scrag.[65]

The episodes are consistently violent and exude a general sense of misan-thropy and misogyny, one that is only somewhat leavened by Crow's darkly comic nature. *Crow*'s cartoonish nihilism emerges out of Hughes's thorough-going cultivation of primitive violence as an operating principle, but it is also historically attuned. *Crow*'s parables of "horror without redemption" regis-ter abstractly the world-historical destruction of recent events – the Second World War, the Holocaust, the war in Vietnam, colonial wars in Africa and India – and the sense of impending cataclysm produced by the tensions of the Cold War.[66] Crow becomes, for Hughes, a principle of elemental nega-tion, a metaphorical figure to carry and to devour the multifarious evils of the modern world.

Not all of Hughes's poetry is as parabolic as *Crow*. Much of it is attentive to the particulars of Britain, and the environment of England often serves as a psychic sink. "Pike," for most of its eleven quatrains, concerns the violent and brief lives of pike, "killers from the egg," three of whom the speaker keeps in a fish tank, "behind glass, / Jungled in weed."[67] One pike eats another, and then one of the remaining two dies attempting to eat the last: "One jammed past its gills down the other's gullet."[68] Remembering a pond he once fished and imagining within its depths "pike too immense too stir," the speaker hatches an image that spurs the rising psychic unease that ends the poem. The pond, filled with tench that "had outlasted every visible stone / Of the monastery that planted them," as well as with actual and imagined pike, is compared to the country itself:

> Stilled legendary depth:
> It was as deep as England.[69]

The pond becomes a mythical metonym for the nation, a reservoir of legend and history as well as a locus of psychological trauma. Considering Britain's shrinking scope in the postwar period, this "deepening" of England can be read as a compensatory gesture, as a return to elemental features that might elide, mitigate, or redirect historical realities. As decolonization proceeded, then, a related – perhaps causal – move was a "deepening" of England itself. And poets tapped the depths of such locales.

Chapter 3

Local Modernism

The twin pressures of decolonization and devolution have shaped Britain in the latter half of the twentieth century and into the early decades of the twenty-first. These pressures joined with others to force a large-scale rethinking of the "place" of Britain – as an archipelago, a set of differentially interlocking internal geographies, and an island nation balancing its relationships with the United States, the Commonwealth, and, somewhat more warily, Europe. As Britain's empire diminished, and as the status of the Celtic areas of the British Isles shifted within emerging devolutionary and nationalist movements, the unspoken stability of the English center could not hold. The far peripheries of the British Empire disintegrated, while the near peripheries reconsidered their relationship to the metropole.

Poets like Hugh MacDiarmid and Edwin Muir in Scotland, R.S. Thomas in Wales, and John Hewitt in Northern Ireland sought to articulate distinct cultural and political spheres outside England and Englishness while still necessarily operating within a larger British ambit. Thomas's Welsh nationalism was tied to a bracing conservatism, whereas MacDiarmid, a lynchpin of the Scottish nationalist movement that gained momentum throughout the century, routed his nationalism through his commitment to communism. This pairing proved thorny, and MacDiarmid, famously, was kicked out of the Scottish Nationalist Party for his communist beliefs and out of the Communist Party for his nationalism. John Hewitt's formulation of regionalism and his articulation of a distinctive Ulster geographical, social, and cultural space was meant in part as a bulwark against both Irish nationalism and an exclusively Anglo-Protestant version of Northern Ireland. Such imaginative and cultural readjustments were occurring within the space of a changing England as well. Postwar deindustrialization and suburbanization reshaped many cities and their hinterlands and altered the relationships among the country's regions, especially between the southeast (the home counties and an ever-spreading London) and the midlands and the north. The homogenizing effects of a rising consumer culture and an infiltrating mass media (heavily influenced by American culture) threatened the vitality of local practices and, in certain ways, reinforced the hegemony of the metropolitan center. At the same time, the potential loss of regional specificity sparked an interest in local histories and traditions. The vein of "place poetry" that I examine in this chapter – which orbits around an extended reading of Basil Bunting's *Briggflatts* – is catalyzed by its complexly stratified local concerns.

A series of partial paradoxes inflects this important strand of postwar poetry. As the British Empire contracted, the metropolitan center could no longer implicitly define itself by way of its imperial periphery. It could not be the unstated term against which difference was to be measured. In his study of late modernist English writing, Jed Esty describes a shift from "the fading significance of English universalism to the emergent significance of English particularism," which is indicative of a "resurgent concept of national culture" that occurs alongside the end of empire.[1] What Esty calls an "anthropological turn" in English culture is apparent not only at the level of the nation but also at that of the region and the locale.[2] The reconceptualization of England as particular rather than universal helped make alternate concepts of England possible. That is to say, the dismantling of the concept of "English universalism," which occurred as the imperial systems undergirding that concept were dismantled, allowed for a secondary – a rebound – dismantling of "English particularism," since the particularism that was often produced worked actively against a concept of Englishness.

At the same time, these secondary particularisms – whether MacDiarmid's Scottish nationalism or the regional particularism of Bunting's Northumbria – have been undercut by the totalizing forces of modernization, the mass media, and global capitalism. The rise of tourism and the heritage industry in Britain from the 1960s forward is a signal example of this process.[3] Various forms and instances of local culture and community are brought to the surface and revalued at the moment when material and economic circumstances make them untenable as living communities. They become viable again only within the frame of "heritage" and as sites within a tourist economy, both of which forces necessarily empty them of their lived density and social repletion. Leftist thinkers such as Richard Hoggart and Raymond Williams linked the rise of heritage and tourist industries to the evaporation of community-based forms of art in the standardized haze of "pop" culture. Many writers in this period became interested in the poetic potential of place and locality, and their aesthetic engagements were inevitably shot through with the kinds of contradictions that characterized their materials.

These engagements have taken many shapes. As we have seen, Hughes's early turn to the elemental and the primitive is a seemingly ahistorical project mottled with historical problems. In David Jones's long poem *The Anathemata*

(1952), early Wales and Roman Britain provide the linguistic, mythological, and iconographic pieces from which the Catholic Jones assembled a mosaic of gathered fragments that concern the geologic, topographic, and civilizational history of the British Isles and are placed within the ritual space of the Catholic liturgy. In a very different register, Charles Tomlinson spun together features of American objectivism and English landscape poetry in volumes such as *A Peopled Landscape* (1963), *American Scenes and Other Poems* (1966), and *The Way of a World* (1969), which document and reflect upon his wide-ranging travels through England, Europe, and North America. And there were of course many instances of nostalgic lyricism seeking to keep alive the pastoral images of a rural past or to lament the vague blandness of the present, a version of ideological retrenchment most familiar as the "little Englandism" associated with Larkin, Amis, and the Movement. The final, nearly hopeful plea of Larkin's "Show Saturday" – "Let it always be there" – can be juxtaposed with the darker realization of his "Going, Going" so as to give a sense of at least one range of poetic engagement with the changing circumstances of England. After derisively lamenting that in the too-near future England will be "bricked in / Except for the tourist parts" and linking its future ignominy to its increasing ties to Europe (he calls a future England the "first slum of Europe"), the speaker of "Going, Going" describes the fullness of the loss:

> And that will be England gone,
> The shadows, the meadows, the lanes
> The guildhalls, the carved choirs.[4]

Larkin captures both a long-embalmed desire within postwar English thought and society ("let it always be there") and the understanding that this desire is for an England that is, simply, gone.

For other poets, especially those more amenable to the legacy of modernist experimentation, the matter became one of finding forms that would suffice to render such changed circumstances. An important feature of this search was a renewed interest in the possibilities of the long poem, although in ways that veered away from the totalizing impulse and epical length of Pound's *Cantos*. Rather, the texts at the center of this chapter can be considered within the rubric of what C.D. Blanton and Nigel Alderman have dubbed the "pocket epic," which they describe as a diverse "genre of minor or local epics" that are widespread in British poetry in the middle and late twentieth century.[5] Many of these "pocket epics" are interested primarily in delineating a particular space or region, and along with the central texts of this chapter – Roy Fisher's *City* (1961), Bunting's *Briggflatts* (1965), and Hill's *Mercian Hymns* (1971) – poems such as Patrick Kavanagh's *The Great Hunger* (1942), Jones's *The Anathemata*, and John Montague's *The Rough Field* (1972) typify this strand of poetic production. One might also consider poems examined in earlier chapters, such as Graham's "The Nightfishing," Walcott's "The Schooner *Flight*," or Brathwaite's *The Arrivants*, as quite different reflexes of the "pocket epic." The more capacious and heterogeneous formal possibilities inherent in the long poem or multipart poem make it an exceptional mode in which to explore a range of issues – cultural, historical, political, geographical, and biographical – that attach to the notion of "place."

These poems can mobilize the resources available in both narrative and lyric modes, as well as integrate historical and documentary materials, to present the complexities of a place and its history. Longer, prismatic sequences or extended series allow for a more intensive investigation of the relationship among the individual, the community, the locality, and the larger world than might the brief lyric. Such investigations gained a good deal of traction in the postwar period when the "place" of Britain was being rethought, and so, according to John Kerrigan, these "long poems, or broken sequences, respond to devolutionary and internationalizing pressures by crossing localized memoir with historical excavation."[6] Although there are of course plenty of long poems in postwar Britain that don't deal directly, or even implicitly, with issues of place and location, the intensity with which poets in the 1960s and 1970s harnessed and renovated modernist forms and techniques in order to delve into the history and culture of a specific region is central to the story of the modern long poem in English, and this intensity has inflected British poetry up to the present.

One of the earliest postwar poets to merge modernist forms and local materials was Roy Fisher. Fisher, who grew up and lived in Birmingham until the 1970s and has spent the past several decades living in rural Derbyshire, has written that "Birmingham's what I think with," and he is best known for his loco-specific poetry about Birmingham and environs, especially his two long poems, *City* (1961) and *A Furnace* (1986).[7] Fisher has been described as a neo-modernist and a retro-modernist poet, and he is simultaneously one of the major British poets of the postwar period and a writer who seems perpetually described as "underappreciated." He is one of the few poets whose influence crosses over the mainstream/innovative divide, and unlike many other writers, he has remained remarkably free of the factional entanglements that inscribe contemporary British poetry. Fisher triangulates a tradition of English nature poetry, American poetic modernism (especially the work of William Carlos Williams and several of the Black Mountain poets), and European forms of modernist abstraction and surrealism, and then channels it all through his own specific experience of living in the declining English industrial belt. In doing so, he fashions a body of work that extends lyric poetry's ability to delineate the intricacies of subjective experience while simultaneously charting the collapsing logic of industrial modernity in England.

Unlike other poets who, as we'll see later in the chapter, devise their own varieties of place poetry by taking recourse in the mythic, the archaeological, and the historical, Fisher's Birmingham remains primarily a place to "think with" in the present. He is interested in tracking the continuities and disjunctions between Birmingham past and present, but his poems tend to be based on the experience of living in a place rather than of digging under it. The "I" of his poetry resembles a surveyor more than an excavator. His attention to the particularities of place is related to his larger concerns about the nature of perception, the phenomenology of bodily experience, and the interaction between humans and their environments. The formal stakes of his poetry – its general refusal to settle itself in a single discursive center or linear pattern, its highly visual nature that manages to transcend mere scene painting, its maintenance of a point of view that is both encircled within its environment and necessarily distanced from it – all make for texts of tremendous capaciousness, driven by what John Kerrigan calls a "receptiveness fed by detachment."[8]

Peter Barry writes that *City* "is the most powerful literary account we have in poetry of the widespread experience in mid-century Britain of urban loss and destruction, a three-stage process comprising, first, the Blitz during the Second World War, then the wholesale 'redevelopment' and 'slum clearance' of the 1950s and 1960s, and finally the de-industrialization of the 1970s and 1980s."[9] Originally assembled by Michael Shayer out of Fisher's poems, prose passages from unpublished "diary observations," and parts of what Fisher has called a "preposterously apocalyptic *bildungsroman*," *City* initially appeared from Migrant Press in 1961.[10] Fisher revised the text for its next appearance in 1963 (in the journal *Living Arts*), and this version is the one that appears in his 1968 *Collected Poems* from Fulcrum Press and his subsequent *Collected* volumes.[11]

City is composed of untitled prose paragraphs and titled poems. There is no standard pattern to the shifts between prose and poetry, just as there is no linear narrative or symbolic arc that allows the poem to be read teleologically. It is best understood as a spatial form that has no single center but rather what one poem calls "an irregular radial plantation of these props."[12] The prose paragraphs (thirty-eight in total, separated by the poems into seven sections) describe the damage and vacancy of post-Blitz Birmingham, offer instances of situated viewing, provide historical contexts for and second-order reflections on the city's development, present general profiles of the city's citizens as well as more detailed portraits of several city dwellers, and generally feature a roving urban eye/"I" who is often walking the city at night and meditating on the alternate cycles of destruction and progress that shape it. The ten poems include brief lyrics that outline and reflect on a particular scene or view of the postwar, late-industrial city ("North Area," "By the Pond," "The Sun Hacks," "The Poplars," and "The Wind at Night"); a poem in tercets that describes the deaths and funerals of several of the speaker's relatives during bomb attacks on the city ("The Entertainment of War"); a long poem that is by turns ode and elegy for an unnamed "hero," possibly referring to the city itself in the style of Williams's *Paterson* (the second part of "Lullaby and Exhortation for the Unwilling Hero"); several song-like lyrics that feature refrains and densely metaphoric imagery (the first part of "Lullaby and Exhortation for the Unwilling Hero," "The Hill Behind the Town," and "The Park"); and a prose poem that describes the fashioning of a "tree" out of "steel stakes" and a variety of refuse and abandoned materials and that serves as an *ars poetica* for the entire text ("Starting to Make a Tree").[13]

Much of the prose in *City* is evocatively realist, detailing urban particulars or providing commentary on the city's inhabitants, politics, history, or architecture. These passages sometimes extend into self-reflexive musings that trouble or dislocate the speaking self. Fisher's prose occasionally moves into a more poetic, even surrealist register, as when the envisioned cityscape metamorphoses into "a composite monster, its unfeeling surfaces matted with dust: a mass of necks, limbs without extremities, trunks without heads; unformed stirrings and shovings spilling across the streets it had managed to get itself provided with."[14] Just as the prose moves among several styles of description and evocation, so do the poems alternate among several lyric registers. There is a heavily visual discourse that figures the details of the city with a tone of Eliotic grimness:

> by the butchers' cars, packed tail-to-kerb,
> Masks under white caps wake into human faces;

a highly rhythmic and sonically rich style in the song-like poems:

> Sullen hot noon, a loop of wire,
> With zinc light standing everywhere,
> A glint on the chapels,
> Glint on the chapels;

and a more self-reflexive mode that attempts to account for the ways in which the individual subject renders what is perceived:

> All I have done, or can do
> Is prisoned in its act:

I think I am afraid of becoming
A cemetery of performance.[15]

The tension between the prose sections and the poems, as well as the stylistic shifts within the prose pieces and the poetry, catalyzes the larger conceptual stress that inheres throughout *City*. This tension, given its most concrete expression in the passage just quoted, draws together several problems: how to negotiate the Romantic inheritance of a centralizing lyric subject after such a subject has been fractured and dispersed within modernist poetics; how to find a poetic form adequate to the multiple transformations that characterize postwar Birmingham; how to incorporate the actualities of industrialized, suburbanized England without taking recourse in pastoral nostalgia; and how to construct a poetic texture that includes a perceiving, writing subject without that subject assuming the false authority of an older model of lyric poetry.

The modular form of *City* helps keep these various tensions alive. *City* is both a single text and a series of discrete texts whose divisions are marked (as when a poem's title appears after a stretch of prose, thereby indicating the "end" of the untitled prose section) as well as muted (as when the interjection of a new untitled prose section retroactively indicates the end of a poem). Fisher's paradoxical phrase, "a cemetery of performance," is operative at every point. Because the discrete sections of *City* don't have a clear narrative or symbolic trajectory, it is easy to think of them as potentially rearrangeable. A reader could "perform" the text differently by reordering sections. At the same time, there is a clear sense of solidity to each of *City*'s textual structures. A reader might thread her way through them in different ways or with different inflections, but as separate modules, they are coherent and concrete forms – a movable cemetery of texts. *City* renders place as an always-problematic juxtaposition of discrete but interacting parts and environments, which Fisher describes in one of the prose sections in terms of the encounter between nature and the built world: "the society of singing birds and the society of mechanical hammers inhabit the world together, slightly ruffled and confined by each other's presence."[16]

The uneasy articulation of human making (industrial and otherwise) and the natural world in Fisher's *City* is one of the central areas of concern in the "place poetry" of the 1960s and 1970s. This topic is fundamental to what remains the key such text in the period: Basil Bunting's *Briggflatts*. The appearance of *Briggflatts* in the mid-1960s was galvanizing, not least because it marked the surprising reemergence of a writer who had fallen out of the story of modern British literature. Bunting was an important, though largely overlooked writer in Pound's circle in the 1920s and 1930s, and much of the poetry

that makes up his slender *Collected Poems* (first published in 1968) was composed during those decades. Besides *Redimiculum Matellarum* ("A Necklace
of Chamberpots"), a small volume privately published in Milan in 1930 that
received a single review (from his friend Louis Zukofsky), and *Poems 1950*
(mostly containing work written in the 1930s and published with Pound's
urging by a small press in Galveston, Texas), Bunting published no volumes
of poetry until his resurgence during the final decades of his life. Born in
1900 in Newcastle and educated at several Quaker schools in Yorkshire and
Northumberland, Bunting was imprisoned as a conscientious objector during the latter part of the Great War. He spent the 1920s and 1930s moving
among England, Paris, Germany, the United States, the Canary Islands, and
Rapallo, Italy. He joined the Royal Air Force in World War II, deciding that
the danger posed by Hitler outweighed his innate pacifism, and he eventually
became an intelligence officer and interpreter in Persia. He stayed in Iran after
the war, working as a diplomat, a foreign correspondent for the *Times*, and, so
the story goes, a British spy. Expelled from Iran in 1952, Bunting returned to
Northumberland, where he spent much of the rest of his life.[17]

Bunting had written very little poetry since the 1930s, although his 1951
long poem, *The Spoils* – which draws from his war experience and is steeped
in Arabic and Persian literature and culture – is one of the most intriguing
World War II poems in the British canon. He was, in part at least, spurred back
into writing by Tom Pickard, a young poet who, along with Connie Pickard,
organized an important reading series at Morden Tower, which was the nerve
center of a poetry renaissance in Newcastle. Bunting composed *Briggflatts* in
1964 and 1965 and first read it at Morden Tower in December 1965. Published
in *Poetry* (Chicago) the following month and soon after in a small volume by
Fulcrum Press, *Briggflatts* was immediately recognized as a major work. His
public performances became touchstone events, and Bunting quickly became
an iconic figure for many of the young poets who spearheaded the British
Poetry Revival in the 1960s and 1970s.[18]

Briggflatts is several things at once. It is a version of a Poundian modernist
epic, although, at around 700 lines, it is much closer in length to Eliot's *The
Waste Land* than to Pound's *Cantos*, Olson's *The Maximus Poems*, or Zukofsky's
A. It is precisely and baroquely shaped, and its five parts cohere into a unity
that, apart from Eliot's two long poems and David Jones's *The Anathemata*,
is unmatched in modernist long poems in English. It is heavy with allusions,
parataxis, sharp transitions, and recondite knowledge, incorporating several
touchstones – the seventh-century manuscript of the *Lindisfarne Gospels*,
several sonatas by Giuseppi Domenico Scarlatti, moments from Dante's
Commedia – as compositional and structural catalysts. It is a fully realized

instance of Bunting's version of objectivist poetry and fulfills the principles of "imagism" as Pound, along with H.D. and Richard Aldington, had laid them down more than 50 years before:

1. Direct treatment of the 'thing' whether subjective or objective.
2. To use absolutely no word that does not contribute to the presentation.
3. As regarding rhythm: to compose in the sequence of the musical phrase, not in sequence of a metronome.[19]

It is – in the complexity of its technique, the density of its form, and the scope of its materials – a fully modernist poem.

At the same time, it is a deeply British poem, steeped in English literary history and the history of the British Isles, and as invested in reinventing the modernist lyric as it is in following up Poundian innovations in modernist epic.[20] As Eric Mottram has written, "it is not the least moving experience of *Briggflatts* that it also embodies a commitment to the great British tradition of lyrical poetry from Wyatt and Spenser to Swinburne and Yeats, concretely audible in the sound and movement of the work."[21] One of its key presiders is Wordsworth, Bunting's model of a Northern poet, whose distinctive sonic characteristics had been wrecked or ignored by the southern English literary establishment ("southrons" in Bunting's Northern parlance). It is also, and perhaps at only one level, a deeply nostalgic poem. Its subtitle is "an autobiography," and much of the poem tracks the biographical context of Bunting's life as it follows a seasonal cycle from spring to winter. The first, fourth, and fifth parts take place entirely in the North of England. The second section moves from London south through Europe to Italy and the Mediterranean, mapping Bunting's own travels in the 1920s and 1930s. According to a sketch of the poem that Bunting made during an interview and that has since circulated widely, the third is the only one not to be explicitly linked to a season, consisting as it does of a woodman's dream-vision.[22] Based on a Persian legend of Alexander the Great's interview with an angel on a mountaintop, the vision draws on Bunting's knowledge of Firdosi's massive eleventh-century epic poem, *Shahnameh*, in which the story of Alexander appears. When the woodman wakes up halfway through the section, we are back in Bunting's Northumbria, where we remain for the remainder of the poem.

The cyclical motion of the poem – through the four seasons, from Northumbria out into the wider world and back again – underwrites much of its thematic material. *Briggflatts*'s fundamental theme is the passing of time and the transience of experience. It is at the crux of the childhood love affair that Bunting outlines in the first section and that is the emotional core of the poem (*Briggflatts* is dedicated "For Peggy": as a teenage boy, Bunting spent many summers staying with the family of a school friend, John Greenbank, in the village of Briggflatts; Peggy Greenbank was John's sister and Bunting's childhood sweetheart). It focalizes the poem's repeated considerations of the nature and value of art. It underlies Bunting's historical vision and his construal of a distinct Northumbrian culture as a counterweight to the hegemony of southern England. And it frames the dialectic of regeneration and decay that saturates the text.

Part of the pleasure of the poem, meanwhile, is its rich panoply of people, animals, and landscapes. The famous opening introduces *Briggflatts*'s primal scene, as the poet addresses a bull (the first member of the poem's extensive bestiary) cavorting on the banks of the Rawthey River near Briggflatts:

> Brag, sweet tenor bull,
> descant on Rawthey's madrigal,
> each pebble its part
> for the fells' late spring.
> Dance tiptoe, bull,
> black against may.
> Ridiculous and lovely
> chase hurdling shadows
> morning into noon.[23]

The river sings, above which the bull descants (a descant is an ornate melody played or sung over a tune), above which the poet addresses in forceful tones bull and river and scene. The bull dances as it sings, chasing shadows that are themselves "hurdling" through the day, as burgeoning spring fills the landscape (fells, dale, furrow) and tints the bull's hide:

> May on the bull's hide
> and through the dale
> furrows fill with may,
> paving the slowworm's way.[24]

Like the bull, which appears in several forms over the course of the poem, the "slowworm" that moves through the opening scene becomes a composite symbol at the heart of *Briggflatts*. It signals sex and death, time and its passing, love and its absence, and it reappears at nearly all of the poem's pivotal moments.

Part of Fisher's burden in *City* is to consider the impress of industrial modernity on the natural world, and in *Briggflatts*, Bunting takes on an analogous burden, although one considerably rescaled:

> A mason times his mallet
> to a lark's twitter,
> listening while the marble rests.[25]

The introduction of the stonemason offers a second avatar for the poet (also, Peggy Greenbank's father was a stonemason), and the mason's inscriptive art is set against the musical art of bull and river to give the poem a double method of composition. The chiseled permanence of the stone counterpoints the transient tunings and movements of music and dance, although neither is able to represent the actual fullness of the lived world or of the experienced moment. The gravestone that the mason carves is the emblem of this dilemma: its inscribed name names no one, necessarily spelling out a "man abolished."[26]

At this point, the first section, which consists of twelve thirteen-line stanzas, turns to the story of the adolescent lovers. The world in which they move, kiss, and touch is a preindustrial pastoral space, although hints of death are never far from the surface. They watch the mason work, walk in the fields and through rain, and listen to sheep and peewit. Their actual lovemaking is prefaced by a brief mention of the death of Eric Bloodaxe, a tenth-century Viking king who is one of the poem's key figures, and this darker story signals the turn that will take place at the end of the section. Writing – both the forms of inscription described within the poem and the writing of the poem itself – is projected as a means of transmuting the loss of love, but at this point, such transmutations cannot be made to suffice. Time cannot be regained, and the generative symbols from the poem's first several stanzas are wasted or debased:

> Dung will not soil the slowworm's
> mosaic. Breathless lark
> drops to nest in sodden trash;
> Rawthey truculent, dingy.[27]

Song, dance, and writing have all been damaged or cancelled, and the pastoral beauty of the opening stanzas has been ruined. Just as love has proved transient, so have spring, the bull's life, the lark's vitality, and the stonemason's inscription. However, the slowworm still makes its mosaic among dung, and such a transformation of loss or waste into value will become part of the poem's overall aim.

None of the other sections of *Briggflatts* has the chiseled symmetry of the first. The variousness of the stanza forms in sections two through five can, along with demonstrating Bunting's technical facility, suggest a larger structural and thematic point. If the first section depicts a moment of plentitude – a pastoral world in which human making and the songs of the natural world are "timed" together and in which love, sex, and pleasure comprise a unity rather than instances of shame, guilt, or proleptic loss – then the rest of the poem, having lost this pocket of innocence, works through a series of heterogeneous formal shapes in order to find a means of recompense.

As many commentators have pointed out, *Briggflatts* is, in part, a quest poem. The formal and experiential perfection of the opening section cannot be replicated, and the middle sections of the poem map a quest for a time that has been lost, as well as for a poetic form to register – and perhaps repair – this loss. Part two begins as a gentle parody of Eliot's *The Waste Land*, with the "poet appointed" in London and sunk in a morass of urban decadence and decrepitude, only able to mate "beauty with squalor to beget lines still-born."[28] An oblique prayer to one who may know his fate prefaces an ocean voyage that commences northward under the thumb of a domineering sea captain and then turns southward to the Mediterranean. Although the poet's view of the "flying fish [that] follow the boat" gives him a way forward poetically, the overall tone remains one of disappointment and self-castigation:

> It looks well on the page, but never
> well enough. Something is lost
> when wind, sun, sea upbraid
> justly an unconvinced deserter.[29]

Even though the poet remains downtrodden and unsure of his project, the second section features some of the poem's most notable passages. Bunting uses the deft and complex patterning of the Lindisfarne Gospels' "plaited lines" to construct an equally complex poetic texture.[30] Utterly unlike the consistent stanzas and style of the first section, the second is a gallery of forms and modes. Long verse paragraphs alternate with a variety of lyrical texts: a sea shanty, quatrains on the sensory pleasures of Italy, a hermetic work poem, a poem on the death of Eric Bloodaxe that repeats a single vowel sound to end every line, a shoreside lyric that develops the poem's bestiary while analogizing certain animals with the musical forms of certain composers. The end of the second section, meanwhile, travels farther along the Mediterranean, ending up in Crete and retelling the moment from Virgil's sixth Eclogue in which Pasiphae, husband of King Minos, mates with a bull after being cursed by Poseidon, a coupling that produces the Minotaur. Bunting presents this coupling as both unnatural and, in problematic, even misogynistic ways, pleasurable, at least for the bull, which "gloried in unlike creation."[31] Such a sexual union, driven by lust and the result of a god's anger, reverses the adolescent pair's sexual experience in the first section. The "unlike creation" designates the monstrous result of this coupling and becomes another way to "upbraid" the poet, a warning for the "unconvinced deserter."

The third section, in which a band of companions attempts to find a usable path through a dusty, charred shoreside, pushes such implications even further. The long verse paragraph that opens the section (and that takes up its majority) offers all manner of grotesquerie as it, as mentioned earlier, depicts "Alexander's trip to the limits of the world" and his interview with the angel.[32] This trip to the mountaintop, past cliffside gulls and shit-eating scavengers, is at the same time an underworld journey, and the third section, untethered from the seasonal pattern that unites the others, becomes *Briggflatts*'s excremental hell-canto. Along the way, Bunting mocks "southrons" and the market-based values of the capital, and the band of companions has to make its way past "turd-bakers," "hags," "long rotted corpses," beggars advertising "rash, chancre, fistula," and all manner of madman and beast.[33] His soldiers turn back, desiring their home in Macedonia, but Alexander continues, scaling the peak until he sees Israfel, the angel who in the Qu'ran stands poised to blow his trumpet to mark the final judgment at God's command. An image of the angel brings this long stanza to a close, as it is clear that God's call will not be given: "Yet delay! / When will the signal come / to summon man to his clay?"[34] The stanza break coincides with a change of scene, as Bunting introduces a just-waking woodman who had been knocked out by an "adder's sting."[35] The adder is revealed to be the slowworm, which sings its song into the woodman's drowsy ear and which presumably is the source of the woodman's dream-vision of Alexander's journey. The slowworm celebrates his own place at the center of the natural cycle, and his call for the coming of autumn echoes as the woodman is "led home silently through clean woodland": "Swaggering, shimmering fall, / drench and towel us all!"[36]

The rains requested by the slowworm have come and gone by the time the fourth section begins: "Grass caught in willow tells the flood's height that has subsided."[37] The long-lined verse paragraph that follows contains some of the most obscure writing in the poem as it fills out the Celtic-based Northumbrian cultural tradition that it means to construct. The gallery presented includes Aneurin and Taliesin, medieval Welsh poets; Columba and Columbanus, early Irish missionaries; Aidan and Cuthbert, key early figures in the Christian church in Northumbria; along with anonymous "Clear Cymric voices" and "Girls in Teesdale and Wensleydale."[38] Within this autumnal elegy, in which the poet hears "Aneurin number the dead," there is a dense weave of figures and animals, many of them reappearing from earlier sections along with familiar thematic concerns: "Today's posts are piles to drive into the quaggy past / on which impermanent palaces balance."[39] This entire section – stuffed with images and motifs that don't fully coordinate – textually incarnates a "quaggy past" that can't be repaired. Part of the trouble is the art of poetry itself, which, compared to the nobility of the medieval Welsh poets composing songs on the battlefield to honor the dead, has become a "pedant's game." Close reading is disbarred as a mode of understanding – "Follow the clue patiently and you will understand nothing."[40] And the passage ends with an exceedingly strange set of images that resists comprehension: lice crawling from the seams of a "jacket shrunk to the world's core" in order to reach a "wall of flame" in which "they'd crackle like popcorn in a skillet."[41]

This apocalypse in miniature triangulates the end of the third section's dream-vision (the lice are versions of the slowworm) and the catalogue of animal life and death that comes just before. But it is hard not to feel as though the poem is at an impasse. The poet certainly seems to sense this and turns from the crackling lice to a second-order meditation on one of *Briggflatts*'s key presiders:

> It is time to consider how Domenico Scarlatti
> condensed so much music into so few bars
> with never a crabbed turn or congested cadence,
> never a boast or a see-here.[42]

This regathering of compositional strength coincides with the sun rising, as the poem takes a cue from the natural cycle and tries to begin itself again. The final stanzas of the fourth section condense and recapitulate the first two. First, there is a counterfactual aubade in which the poet's young love is pictured making scones and bacon after the night's lovemaking. Some of the purity of the first section's adolescent sexuality returns even as the future loss of love is ensured and better understood: "Goodbye, dear love // …We have eaten and loved and the sun is up."[43] After this farewell, we are returned to the second section's image of the poet in the city, and this section ends with the poet singing his rat-song, a deliberate overturning of the slowworm's song of cyclic fecundity and regeneration: "Where rats go go I, / accustomed to penury, / filth, disgust and fury."[44]

A three-line tag at the end of the rat's song pivots the poem into its final movement and serves as another recapitulation for a text that can't help but turn back and replay the past. Another dawn is offered as the reader's eye is drawn quickly from the rat scuffling in the corners to the dawn sky: "Stars disperse."[45] The heavenward turn previews the final section's astronomical interests, and its reiteration of the poem's central theme allows a reader to see clearly just how the final section goes about suggesting a solution to the problem of pastness and loss that has plagued but also generated its entirety. This winter section contains few of the obscurities or difficulties of previous sections, and it is here that Bunting's hope to emulate the limpid condensations of Scarlatti is most stunningly achieved. As in the opening, but with a difference, the texture is sonically compressed and visually rich as the poet traces several scenes: first, seabirds, "lace of frost" on shore-rocks, a fishing line with a "nosegay" of worms for bait, and "silver blades of surf"; and then shepherds and "sweet turf," dogs being led from "Tweed and Till and Teviotdale" and "Redesdale and Coquetdale," and ewes "heavy with lamb."[46] We are again in the pastoral plenitude of Northumbria and nearing a moment of peace: "silence by silence sits / and Then is diffused in Now."[47] The poet's gaze turns skyward, and he envisions the procession of winter stars accompanied by the music of flutes, harps, drums, horns, and strings. The diffusion of then into now touches off the near diffusion of the celestial into the terrestrial: "starlight is almost flesh."[48] Stars – their sheer, unaccountable distance from each other and from us – become an answer of sorts to the quandary of time's passage. They don't solve the transience of human life, but they reframe it: "Then is now. The star that you steer by is gone."[49] This truism, that the starlight we see is ancient light, hastens the poet's return to the poem's primal scene: "light from the zenith / spun when the slowworm lay in her lap / fifty years ago."[50] Bringing its two incommensurable time frames together at least momentarily, the poet can begin to conclude, setting aside the book he has made ("the sheets are gathered and bound, / the volume indexed and shelved"), realizing the pastness of the past despite its dispersion into the present, and actively finishing his autobiographical epic with a transfusion of ancient lyric:

> Starlight quivers. I had day enough.
> For love uninterrupted night.[51]

The section's final line is an adaptation from Catullus (*"nox est perpetua una dormienda"*), and this last diffusion of "then" into "now" is both a fulfillment of love and love's scattering.

The fifth section's final lines offer a species of unfinished conclusion in another way: they aren't quite the final lines of the poem. A three-stanza coda immediately follows, and the explicit sense of dislocation within these stanzas unmoors the unity just achieved. Quickly recapitulating several of the poem's central settings and scenes, the coda concludes with a final glance at Eric Bloodaxe. The accouterments of his reign are strewn about, and the final stanza poses a pair of vexing questions that problematizes the fifth section's strategy of repairing time:

> Where we are who knows
> of kings who sup
> while day fails? Who,
> swinging his axe
> to fell kings, guesses
> where we go?[52]

The coda is a not insignificant interruption of the finale's "uninterrupted night." Its two concluding questions reframe the poem, moving from autobiography to history and from the particularities of the poet's life to the communal – though entirely unspecified – "we." But they also enact the fifth section's hard-won knowledge. Each of the questions is situated on either side of the equation, "Then is now." The first asks about the location of a "we" positioned in a time something like "now" who might know something about the past. It seems to take place in the past: kings dine at nightfall. But it takes place in the past from the position of the present: a "we" who don't know from where (or from when) to know this past. The second question inverts this temporal and spatial structure: someone in the past ("who") swings his axe to kill a king and wonders ("guesses") "where we go." The "we" of the first question is the "we" of the second, but the temporal perspective has been switched. The final stanza itself is a modified chiasmus, and this strangely doubled moment spins together present and past. The "we" of the coda has opened out beyond the smaller circle of the poet but still remains in a Northumbrian context, thinking not just about any king's but about Bloodaxe and his killer.

Just as the poet of *Briggflatts* seeks to implant "then" into "now" in order to regain something of his childhood love, and of his past more generally, so does the poem interfuse forms. Bunting merges an epic impulse with a lyric engine in order to construct a long poem that is both expansive and powerfully condensed. He exfoliates an autobiographical narrative so that its larger cultural and historical patterns ramify. He fashions a unique species of modernist long poem while drawing heavily from the habits of English lyric. And he is able to fashion a text of wide international scope that is at the same time bedded in the specific, though in part imagined, locale of Northumbria.

Bunting's unique position – straddling high modernism and late modernism and returning to poetry when he was, in many minds, already part of a poetic past – certainly underlies *Briggflatts*'s peculiar power, but it also helps ensure its singularity. At the same time, it can also be argued that it indexes late-twentieth-century British poetry. Its commitment to a particular place and cultural tradition links it to the work of regionalist writers such as Hewitt or George Mackay Brown. Its attempt to frame its location as a counterweight to the metropolitan center of London and southern England connects it with the more overt nationalist and decolonizing projects of R.S. Thomas and Hugh MacDiarmid. Bunting shares an interest in incorporating patterns and effects from the minority and historical languages of the British Isles – Welsh, Irish, Old English – with poets like Dylan Thomas, Austin Clarke, David Jones, Bill Griffiths, and Seamus Heaney. And much of *Briggflatts* is resolutely lyric and rural, which is evidence not only of its deep links to Wordsworth but also of Bunting's affinities to a wide range of mid-twentieth-century poets who remained committed to a lyric tradition in the line of Thomas Hardy and Edward Thomas.

That *Briggflatts* both indexes postwar British poetry and is an exceptional text is only a partial paradox. One of the features of this body of work – and a throughline in this volume – is its constitutive variety. Many of its representative texts look remarkably unlike each other, even when those texts emerge from similar formations or are written by the same person. Many of the figures who have been at different moments positioned as central – Larkin, Hughes, Heaney, Duffy – have distinct, signature styles that seem not to change much over the course of their careers, although a closer inspection would reveal shifts and ruptures within their oeuvres. But some of the most notable works written by a number of the most important figures (including one or two of those listed) are unrepresentative of their work as a whole. One such text is Geoffrey Hill's *Mercian Hymns*, which is both his most well known and his least characteristic work. It is also Hill's contribution to the motley gallery of British "pocket epics."

Hill's *Mercian Hymns* brings us back to the Midlands, although to a quite different version of the Midlands from what we are given in Fisher's *City*. A departure from his earlier volumes, which were featured at the end of the first chapter, *Mercian Hymns* consists of thirty sections made up of brief strophes in prose, or "versets." The metrically dense lines and compacted stanzas of his first several volumes, as well as of much of his subsequent work, give way to a freer prose form that, nonetheless, remains syntactically complex and heavily rhythmic. Just as Bunting uses figures from the Northumbrian past to catalyze *Briggflatts*, so does Hill use King Offa, the eighth-century king of Mercia, as an organizing principle for his own sequence. Many of the sections describe some aspect of Offa's reign, although the *Mercian Hymns* are not entirely or exclusively "about" Offa. Running underneath, alongside, and above the Offa stories are autobiographical vignettes, and many of the sections recreate moments from a childhood in the Midlands that resembles Hill's own (Hill was born in Worcestershire in the West Midlands in 1932). Again like Bunting in *Briggflatts*, Hill intertwines the past and present, and there is a continual thrill in his staging of anachronism.

This is clearly seen in the poem's opening address to Offa, in which he is called both "king of the perennial holly-groves" and "overlord of the M5."[53] This first hymn establishes some of the historical facts of Offa's reign over Mercia: he is installed in its capital (Tamworth) and credited with creating the "historic rampart and ditch" that is his namesake, expanding the kingdom, instituting the first workable form of English currency ("moneychanger"), collecting taxes ("saltmaster"), and being a "friend of Charlemagne."[54] But he is also an anachronistic figure in the twentieth century, the "overlord of the M5" who is later said to be driving through the Vosges in his "maroon GT."[55] After the speaker completes his litany of titles and names, the king responds with insouciant and modern-sounding authority: " 'I liked that,' said Offa, 'sing it again.' "[56]

Throughout *Mercian Hymns,* Hill juxtaposes idioms and registers in such ways, moving among strata of diction and lexis as he crosses the eighth century with the twentieth. Interspersed within vignettes about Offa's reign – his naming, his construction of a dike to separate his kingdom from that of Powys in Wales, his crowning, his laws, his desk, his coins, his sword, his (apocryphal) trip to Rome, his battles, his tyranny, and his funeral – are moments from mid-twentieth-century Britain. Some are historical events: World War II (hymn XXII), the coronation of George VI in 1936 (hymn III), and Enoch Powell's "Rivers of Blood" speech in 1968 (hymn XVIII).[57] Others refer more intimately to a childhood that might be (or might as well be) Hill's own. Some of the most remarkable passages occur when descriptions of a child exploring nature come to bear the weight of English history:

> Gasholders, russet among fields. Milldams, marlpools that lay
> unstirring. Eel-swarms. Coagulations of frogs; once, with
> branches and half-bricks, he battered a ditchful; then sidled
> away from the stillness and silence.[58]

The thickly intertwining consonants and modulating vowel sounds replicate the "coagulated" scene. The shifting rhythms often ironically counterpoint their contents, as in the jaunty dactylic rhythm in the second half of the strophe that describes the child's violence. This hymn proceeds to relate a brief narrative about how the young protagonist beats his friend, Ceolred (an earlier Mercian king), after Ceolred loses the boy's toy airplane. Just as the use of the word "flayed" in this passage inflates massively the violence of the schoolboy fight, so does the boy's retreat to his "sandlorry named *Albion*" knowingly infantilize the tyranny of Offa's reign.[59] In 774, Offa declared himself king of the English ("*Rex Totius Anglorum Patriae*"), here satirically rendered by Hill as a boy playing with a toy truck named *Albion* (the oldest known name for Britain).[60] The two figures – Offa and a mid-twentieth-century figure who is alternately "I" or "he" – are often woven together in such ways, but the strange anachronism involved in this weaving never dissipates. By being in both eighth-century Mercia and the twentieth-century Midlands, the poem remains fully in neither. The seeming autobiographical "I" never fully settles, and the depiction of Offa is arch and knowing enough so as not to let readers forget that they are involved in an improbable bait and switch: "Not strangeness, but strange likeness."[61] By way of this productive anachronism, the hymns examine the pressure of the past upon the present, the use (and misuse) of the past, the iniquities of history as well as of contemporary structures of governance and power, and the critical obligations of poetic utterances to anatomize the power structures that constitute them.

The deeply serious, constitutionally wary, and incisively ironic voice of Hill's early poetry has not disappeared in *Mercian Hymns*, but it has been made wryer. Moving among idioms and tones, Hill presses every word and phrase, testing denotation against connotation and connotations against each other so as to reveal their multiple meanings and their unspoken implications. Offa is presented both as a tyrant and as a rapacious industrialist, and Hill's caricatures indict authoritarians both ancient and modern:

> Dismissing reports and men, he put pressure on the wax, blistered it
> to a crest. He threatened malefactors with ash from his noon cigar.[62]

Moments of intense lyric and descriptive power are rendered suspect by hints of violence and indications of damage: "Coiled, entrenched England: brickwork and paintwork stalwart above hacked marl."[63] The England of *Mercian Hymns* is an "ancient land, full of strategy" where "tracks of ancient occupation" (here, Offa's Dyke itself) still run through England's late industrial phase, where "frail ironworks" rust and hearthstones are likened to "charred lullabies."[64] The sequence ends with the poet/child's "last dream of Offa the King," in which the king vanishes, leaving behind "coins, for his lodging, and traces of red mud."[65] These three totems – signaling the world of politics and economy, the built environment, and the land itself – coalesce to offer a reprisal of the central features of Hill's investigation into the structures of power and violence that have shaped England.

Each of the poems I have looked at so far sets itself on a specific patch of ground, but each estranges its ground by incorporating that patch's thick and gnarled history, as well as the poet's own experience of it, into the text's broader formal and discursive motions. If Hughes's comparison, in "Pike," of a particular pond in England to England itself naturalizes the relationship between place and history, then, in varying ways, the texts examined here produce formally the disjunctions between the two. Each seeks to locate a mode of poetic value by excavating the past of Britain and using, as C.D. Blanton notes, "local terrains as alternative sites of historical inscription."[66] By setting their long poems within a particular place, these poets aim to construct artifacts that also reveal their own processes. Inscriptive figures litter both *Briggflatts* and *Mercian Hymns*, and the style of writing in both poems might lead a reader to think that the poets aim to construct static artifacts – inscriptions that can outflank historical change. But, and in this Hill and Bunting further resemble Fisher, the processual nature of the poetic artifact outflanks its permanence or solidity. Even though Bunting states, "Pens are too light. / Take a chisel to write," the multifarious and changeable form of the long poem forces a reading that is mobile, revisionary, and in process.[67] In the same way, Hill's refusal to allow *Mercian Hymns* to settle comfortably into one historical moment makes for a text that, despite its deeply earthy and visceral language, is always up in the air, switching between centuries without ever resolving one in the other. And Fisher's aggregated gazes at postwar Birmingham do not combine to offer a single subject position that can capture and master its surroundings but rather a set of modular perspectives that remain productively un-aligned. In quite different ways, each poem forestalls easy consumption.

Hill's use of Offa, like Bunting's use of the *Lindisfarne Gospels* and Eric Bloodaxe, seeks to revivify or re-enchant the present by turning to the British past. But the extended form of each poem, which makes for moments of significant uncertainty and forces a reader to juxtapose different sections and register the discrepancies between them, affords a textual and interpretive openness that productively complicates the conservative nature of their backward glances. This tendency toward "open forms" is a crucial aspect of the next chapter's topic: a period of renewed modernist innovation in the 1960s and 1970s known as the British Poetry Revival. The open forms favored by writers associated with the Revival offered a way to escape or bypass what were seen to be the narrow limits of the English lyric tradition as it had been construed by poets in the postwar years. Many of the innovative works of the British Poetry Revival were, we might say, site specific. Writers conducted their investigations of specific places while registering continually the ways in which any such locale is produced by and shot through with global currents and flows – economic, political, and environmental. And so as a conclusion to this chapter and a vault into the next one, I will end with a brief consideration of Peter Riley, a key figure within the British Poetry Revival and a poet who offers a version of "local modernism" that both follows up on and redirects the models conceived by Fisher, Bunting, and Hill.

Much of Riley's poetry in the 1970s and early 1980s, especially in *Lines on the Liver* (1981) and *Tracks and Mineshafts* (1983), concerns, as he puts it, "lead mining in the carboniferous limestone zone of Derbyshire and North Staffordshire."[68] Composed in the wake of successful strikes by British coal miners in 1972 and 1974 but before the much less successful strike in 1984 and 1985 – when Margaret Thatcher's Conservative government held out against Arthur Scargill's National Union of Mineworkers until they ended their strike

without winning their demands and thus lost much of their political power –
Riley's work in the period is attuned both to the abstract and conceptual potential of mines as models of inner life and poetic making and to the particular
economic and social conditions that obtained within the mining industry. In
"A Note on Vein Forms," which contains detailed descriptions of the primary
features of rock veins and mining practices, Riley mobilizes the metaphorical
power of what he calls "the mining environment":

> A mass of ore is a "lode" and mining is a matter of "following the
> lode." Veins are "quick" (with ore) or "dead" (without ore), and a vein
> exhausted by mining is also called "dead," so that in this metaphor
> the process of mining is a combat aimed at killing the vein. Much of
> the traditional vocabulary of the trade, and mine-name etymology,
> represents the ore as a living substance or animal in this way.[69]

For Riley, a mine's complex system of caves does not merely offer a set of figural
transpositions. Mining's history is central both to the long history of human
labor and systems of value and to industrial capitalism. The mine is, in a quite
literal way, "a world lost for the sake of the world."[70]

Like *City*, both *Lines on the Liver* and *Tracks and Mineshafts* combine poetry
and prose sections as they consider the geological, cultural, and economic
aspects of mining in the Peak District. In doing so, they frequently adapt the
"vein form" of the mines themselves, describing the history of mining in the
area, explaining the makeup of mines, and assembling a flexible set of analogues and metaphors for the networks of caves and the embedded ore. The
whole environment of a mine and its surround becomes "a figuration of the
self at work in perception and creation."[71] The nature of limestone sediments
is "best understood in the images of sleep and suspension, whereas the intru-
sive minerals may be understood in images of dream and death."[72] Riley uses
the estranging quality of such places made underground in order to conceive of larger social and economic relations as they transform the natural
environment.

In "King's Mine," from *Tracks and Mineshafts*, the prose strophes recall the
versets of *Mercian Hymns* as they register images of the manhandled earth lit-
tered with the remains of industry ("clinker," in this context, can refer to concrete, bricks, or general industrial waste):

> Teeth marks on the shoulder and flank of the hill, scatter of clinker
>   in the grass, compacted rain-washed mounds glittering with small
>   surfaces of calcite and quartz.[73]

The nonlinear texts move from prose to free-verse passages, replicating the
overground and underground expeditions that they describe, and sometimes

offering warnings about our too-excessive interference into the ground we live on: "We mould the materials of earth to our own rhythms / ignoring the backlash – we sink into the ground."[74] Riley has suggested that the industrialization of mining in fact helped spur its demise, partly because the "factorisation of the mine," ostensibly a form of "technological efficiency" leading to increased revenues, misunderstood the nature of the materials it was meant to find.[75] Instead of ascertaining and understanding the spatial rhythms of minerals as they are distributed under the earth, large-scale mining operations sought to "mould" those rhythms to their own need for "efficiency" and profit. Thus, "the backlash": "the metal and us had had enough of each other, and the socio-industrial structures were not versatile to move on."[76] A particular sort of place – both at its surface and into its depths – here refuses to countenance the operations performed upon it.

Riley's mine-poetry filters distinct realms of experience through the centripetal metaphor of the mine, while at the same time refusing to allow the metaphor to fully explain or falsely equate disparate realms:

> Flesh scores lines
> in the calcium slag of earth and the spirit
> wakes, the needle enters the groove,
> polar tension shakes the circuit, which
> responds, gapes, tremors, issues
> forth into the acts of day, for good.[77]

The mine does not become a too-simple metaphor for the spirit, the psyche, or the city. Rather, it floats among figural levels, sometimes adhering at the level of the individual body ("flesh scores lines") and sometimes at the level of the planet ("polar tension shakes the circuit"). These lines might be said to follow a shifting "vein" of figures. The body ("flesh") becomes a machine (something that could "score lines" in the earth), while the earth's solidity is undermined by the comparison to "calcium slag." Out of this clinker of figures comes the awakening spirit, which is immediately materialized as something like a record player. The "lines" that "flesh" had earlier scored in the earth are transposed into the groove of a record that the needle – the spirit – enters. One pseudo-penetration ("flesh" scoring lines into an earth that is actually the nonsolid "calcium slag") produces another (the immaterial spirit/needle "enters" the groove). The circular rotation of the record player sparks the next figural substitution, wherein the needle is now seemingly connected to a compass. There is also a kind of figural expansion at work, as the bodily/terrestrial frame gives way to one that is atmospheric or even planetary: "polar tension shakes the circuit." This becomes a second-order metaphor for the shaken metaphors that comprise the section, as the "circuit['s]" relays are continually broken. The litany of verbs describes an eruptive motion that intersperses this "circuit" into the "acts of day." The turn to larger ethical and political matters later in the poem (both individual acts done "for good" and peace as a project of the "inhabited city") cannot be fully clarified by these images, but the composite matter of these lines from "Material Soul" – the opening poem in *Tracks and Mineshafts* – remains powerfully attuned to the intertwining of personal, social, and civilizational experience, while the passage itself is figuratively disjoined.[78]

If part of the large-scale dilemma of postwar Britain was to come to terms with the loss of empire and its altered place in the world, then a natural move was to look inward. These inward turns often contained backward glances, and many locally modernist texts undertook a double movement – into specific matters of British history and into the changing status of the literal ground. I have focused on what seem to me to be the central texts in this vein, but there are of course many others. They are part of a period of extraordinary poetic energy and innovation in the 1960s and 1970s, one that continued to flourish even as the somewhat illusory nature of the 1960s economic expansion became clear and as the 1973 oil crisis presaged a period of global economic contraction. During this interval, widespread arguments over the practice and status of poetry itself occurred with a force that continues to ramify. The locus of this activity is what has become known as the British Poetry Revival.

Chapter 4

Late Modernism

The British Poetry Revival – a many-centered configuration of poets, poems, little magazines, small presses, reading series, and conferences – has had a decisive effect on the course of poetry in the past half century.[1] While it comprised nothing like a unified program, many of its key figures were friends and colleagues, and the groups that formed had deep affinities, sharing influences and antagonists. Seeking to resist the leanings of the Movement, as well as the institutions and aesthetics of mainstream English poetry, writers such as Eric Mottram, Bob Cobbing, J.H. Prynne, and Tom Raworth incorporated Objectivist and Projectivist practices from the United States; positioned writers like Ezra Pound, William Carlos Williams, Charles Olson, Basil Bunting, and Hugh MacDiarmid as presiding figures; and made allies with Black Mountain, Beat, and New York School poets. By the early 1970s, poets associated with the Movement were easy targets. They were writing less and less actual poetry while occupying positions of significant and easily assailable influence, such as Larkin's editorship of *The Oxford Book of Twentieth Century English Verse* or John Wain's stint as the Oxford Professor of Poetry (1973–1978). However, their aesthetic preferences held sway, with the short, first-person lyric of moderate scope remaining the form of choice. Much of the energy of the Revival went toward critiquing the dominance of this form and the ideologies underlying it.

The Revival encompasses the performance and concrete poetry that swirled around Cobbing in London; the lyric experiments of Wendy Mulford and Denise Riley; the varieties of innovative work emerging from Scottish poets such as Edwin Morgan, Ian Hamilton Finlay, and Tom Leonard; the dense late modernist texts of Prynne and his circle in Cambridge; and varieties of demotic regionalism, most notably the poets who clustered around Bunting in Newcastle, especially Tom Pickard and Barry MacSweeney. In this sense, the title of Andrew Crozier and Tim Longville's *A Various Art* (1987), the first major anthology to feature poets associated with the Revival (albeit one heavily weighted toward poets in the Cambridge wing), rings quite true. Revival poets draw heavily on American and European modernist poetics, but a number of their signal projects are – to continue the previous chapter's theme – resolutely local. Many of the Revival's key texts deal with British, English, or Scottish matters – or with global matters in their British inflections – but they tend not to be "about" Britain in a straightforward way. It isn't possible, or desirable, to derive a standard "Revival" style from what is a huge and assorted body of poetry, and so when I refer to the British Poetry Revival or to "Revival poets," I mean to indicate an extended period of practice and production, beginning in the early 1960s and lasting into the early 1980s, in which a quite large number of writers – much larger than I have space to survey here – aimed to extend poetry's scope through a multitude of approaches and formal means.

Robert Sheppard sketches the term's history:

> The British Poetry Revival was first proposed by Tina Morris and Dave Cunliffe in the eighth issue of their underground magazine *Poetmeat* around 1965 … It was subsequently used as the title of a 1974 Polytechnic of Central London conference: "The British Poetry Revival (1960–1974)", and of its conference essay, by Eric Mottram. Ken Edwards and Barry MacSweeney have both adopted this term. Mottram also used the term in his revised essay "The British Poetry Revival, 1960–1975", an important survey, published in 1993.[2]

Sheppard's overview condenses several of the Revival's key aspects, especially its dependence on a thriving little magazine and small press scene that operated outside of mainstream literary channels. *Poetmeat* was one of the many little magazines that highlighted alternative poetry and countercultural art and one of the 539 that, according to Richard Price, were founded in Britain between 1960 and 1975.[3] Often short lived and usually cash strapped, these little magazines acted as the Revival's circulatory system. A representative though extremely selective list includes Peter Finch's *Second Aeon*, Ian Hamilton Finlay's *Poor. Old. Tired. Horse.*, Cobbing's *And* and *Writers Forum*, Peter Hodgkiss's *Poetry Information*, Andrew Crozier and Peter Riley's *The English Intelligencer*, and Crozier and Tim Longville's *The Grosseteste Review*.[4] Generally ignored by establishment publishers, many of these exploratory poets started presses to publish their work and that of fellow travelers. Asa Benveniste's Trigram Press, Stuart Montgomery's Fulcrum Press, the Cape Golliard Press directed by Raworth and Barry Hall, Crozier's Ferry Press, and Hodgkiss's Galloping Dog Press were among the many homemade operations that featured inventive work with very little outside funding apart from the occasional use of university photocopiers or supplies.[5] The Association of Little Presses, founded by Cobbing and Montgomery in 1966, became an important center of advice and exchange for publishers and poets, or, as was usually the case, poet-publishers.

These small-press volumes and little magazines, while unavailable at what Eric Mottram called "the controlling High Street booksellers," were stocked at the network of independent bookshops that served as meeting places and reading venues, such as the Trent Book Shop, Allen Halsey's Poetry Bookshop in Hay-on-Wye, Unicorn in Brighton, the Paperback Book Shop in Edinburgh, and several shops in London – Indica, Turret, Compendium, and, especially, Better Books.[6] Just as small presses and magazines tended to exist in a symbiotic relationship, so did reading series and bookshops tend to emerge together. Usually, the existence of a bookshop inspired the commencement of a reading series, but the inverse also occurred, as in the case of Tom and Connie Pickard's Morden Tower reading series, which generated the Ultima Thule shop nearby. Reading series could also spark larger happenings, and the mid-1970s featured the Cambridge Poetry Festival in 1975 (and repeated in 1977 and 1979), the annual International Sound Poetry Festival organized by Cobbing between 1974 and 1977, and several conferences on Modern British Poetry organized by Mottram at the Polytechnic of Central London's Centre for Extra Mural Studies, in June 1974, October 1974, and June 1977. These occurred during the brief "takeover" of the staid Poetry Society by poets associated with the Revival and coincided with Mottram's tumultuous period as editor of the *Poetry Review*, the Poetry Society's house publication and, previous to his editorship between 1971 and 1977, a redoubt of traditional verse. Mottram's unceremonious deposal by the Society's conservative factions and the subsequent resignations of most of the poets associated with Mottram marked the end of one phase of the Revival. These events and their aftermath remain alive in discussions about experimental poetry in Britain, and they underlie the continuing schism between so-called mainstream poetry and Revival poets and their heirs.[7]

Perhaps the single unifying feature of the poetry associated with the Revival has been its abiding though not uncritical interest in American poetry. Pound and Williams were the favored high modernists, and Donald Allen's path-making anthology, *The New American Poetry* (1960), provided a set of blueprints that British poets absorbed and redrew. Ginsberg, Gregory Corso, and Lawrence Ferlinghetti were already well known by the time of their appearance at the 1965 International Poetry Incarnation. New York School poets were influential for Lee Harwood and Tom Raworth, both of whom spent significant time in the United States. Charles Olson and the Black Mountain poets were key interlocutors for the Cambridge poets, and Prynne's friendship and correspondence with Olson was decisive in his poetry of the 1960s. Olson's "Projective Verse" essay, part of which consisted of a reply to a letter from the British poet, then Cambridge student, Elaine Feinstein, was read quite closely by nearly all the Revival poets. One way to understand the trajectory of early Revival poetry – especially Prynne's – is to consider how poets adapted and moved beyond or around Olson's Projectivism.

Little magazines and small presses were keen to feature recent American poetry, but American poets tended not to appear on the lists of the major English publishing houses, and so a small cache of volumes – such as Allen's anthology and *Penguin Modern Poets 19* (1971), featuring Raworth, John Ashbery, and Harwood – became polestars for poets looking for strategies outside those favored by the Movement. In a similar way, several poets helped catalyze a transatlantic conversation, with Raworth, Donald Davie, Gael Turnbull, and Ed Dorn acting as turbines of poetry across the North Atlantic (to steal and alter a phrase of Dorn's). Dorn, who taught for a time at Essex University, was an especially crucial figure, and his importance is concretized in Prynne's dedication of his 2005 *Poems*, which reads, "For Edward Dorn / his brilliant luminous shade."[8]

While American poets were central to the British Poetry Revival, British poets tended to be overlooked in America, a state of affairs that began much earlier in the twentieth century, and a condition of transatlantic poetic history accounted for most fully by Keith Tuma.[9] Somewhat ironically, then, the first substantial gathering of Revival poets was a 1971 issue of the American journal *Triquarterly* (volume 21), edited by John Matthias. It was later published by the Swallow Press in Chicago as *Twenty-Three Modern British Poets*, but – unsurprisingly – did not find a publisher in Britain. A half century after the beginning of the British Poetry Revival, alternative British poetry continues to depend on a thriving though sometimes precarious set of small presses, along with several larger publishers – Salt, Shearsman, Carcanet, and Bloodaxe – that have shown a commitment to publishing experimental work, while establishment publishers such as Faber and Faber or Jonathan Cape have remained uninterested.

Tom Raworth is one of the Revival's central poets. For much of his career, his reputation has been greater in the United States than in Britain, and a good deal of his poetry has been published initially by small American presses. While he has ties to all of the Revival's myriad formations, his work has always tended to stand somewhat apart.[10] Like several of the Revival poets – Cobbing and Allen Fisher especially – Raworth is hugely prolific, with several dozen volumes and chapbooks appearing over the past fifty years. Ginsberg and the San Francisco poets were important early influences, and the poetry in his first full volume, *The Relation Ship* (1966), tends toward brief and playful texts that keep themselves occupied by ephemera. They resemble torn-off lengths of the insouciant mind's tickertape or small textual games whose lightness reproduces the evanescent mental flittings that they document; "Stag Skull Mounted" from *Moving* (1971) is exemplary in this regard. His work of the 1970s and 1980s is marked by a shift toward longer poems made up of very short lines, often only a word or two long. Texts such as *Ace* (1974), *Writing* (1982), and *Catacoustics* (1991) comprise gusts of language running down the page. His poems splice together collage and montage, mobilizing the heterogeneous spatial possibilities inherent to the former and the temporal velocity intrinsic to the latter.

It is a truism of Raworth criticism – perhaps the only truism – that his work is propulsive, both weightless and unremitting, a feature that is intensified by his remarkably, often alarmingly fast public performances. The thin strips of text quicken the reading eye, and near-constant shifts of person, perspective, and context make it impossible to aggregate anything like discursive or narrative continuity. Streams of language coalesce in isolated moments but rarely build into larger units. This passage from *Ace* both describes and enacts Raworth's practice:

> nothing
> behind poetry
> look
> a
> like
> or is it
> an an
> but
> why.[11]

Not every page of *Ace* atomizes with such playful ferocity, but this litany of grammatical particles, moving from a brief *ars poetica* through a scatter of small words, gives a good sense of the typical energy of his work, as well as of the difficulty of isolating or excerpting passages away from the full run of the text. Brian Reed describes a typical Raworth page as "a hasty agglutination of unfinished thoughts." This, in Reed's reading, is not a slight or a critique. He goes on in the same passage to laud the thoroughly decentered quality of Raworth's poetry:

> It must be pointed out ... that even when classed among the writings of outliers and experimentalists, the poem's speedy shuffling-through of topics, settings, and frames of reference remains unique to Raworth. There seems to be a roving, spotlight-like center of attention with drastically curtailed knowledge of what has come before and what is to follow.[12]

Raworth's readers, then, are most often in positions of significant precarity, and this is key to the poetry's vertiginous pleasure, as in this passage from *Writing* (1982):

> your country gives you
> metal pieces
> coloured
> by fragility of life
> a belt buckle
> of imitation antique brass
> flickers in as
> though the cuts
> were frame to frame
> while memory nags
> at persistence of vision
> from screen to drawing
> no matter
> what
> is a sudden change
> for in this area
> that cannot be
> called a landscape
> as anything may happen
> i turn to write
> instead of read
> waking this morning
> with a sore head[13]

As good a primer of his compositional process as there is in his large body of work, this passage quickly turns from observation and description to second-order reflection. The belt buckle is first the object seen and then the prism through which the poem models itself ("as / though the cuts / were frame to frame"). The representational surface ceaselessly shifts, from "metal pieces" to "belt buckle" to "screen to drawing" to landscape to text ("i turn to write / instead of read"), as we are given both figures through which to "screen" the poem and a set of disjunctions that we can't visually navigate, a condition of mental "slowness" that we are made to share with the hungover speaker and his "sore head." As the passage above suggests, with its wary mention of military honors (the "metal pieces" that "your country gives you"), Raworth's poetry often includes a substantive critique of politics specifically and of the ideologies of poetry more generally. "West Wind," which marks Raworth's reentry into British culture and politics in the 1980s after extended periods living abroad, is the most forceful of Raworth's political poems, with multiple references to Margaret Thatcher and the neoliberalism of 1980s England. Even when he does not attend so directly to politics or culture, however, his work is radical for the ways in which it so thoroughly defamiliarizes the practice of reading.

Ace (1974) is in many ways his most complexly composed short-lined long poem of the period. Its four sections, not including the slightly later coda, "Bolivia: Another End of Ace," might correspond to the four suits in a deck of cards, and there are a number of references to cards and card games through-out, including several interspersed images of cards that delineate the sections. Each part is made up of thin strips of left-justified text, twenty-five lines to a page, primarily consisting of just one or two words per line, with a handful of three-word lines scattered throughout and just seven four-word lines in the entire book. The first section, subtitled *in think*, is by far the longest, at 26 pages. Section two, *in mind*, contains nearly 19 pages, while sections three and four (*in motion* and *in place*) contain just over eight and just over three pages, respectively. The poem reduces itself as it moves along. "Bolivia: Another End of Ace" consists of twelve pages divided into five brief subsections (*in transit, in part, in consideration, in love,* and *in conclusion*).

On one level, then, the poem is highly partitioned, and the repeated syn-tactical structure of the subtitles encourages a reading that seeks to unite the sections into some sort of coherence. On another level, however, the sepa-rate sections do not build upon each other, and any such attempt is stymied in several directions, not least by the fact that the volume (both in its two 1970s editions and in its 2001 reissue by Edge Books) doesn't contain page numbers, a feature it shares with a number of the Revival's pamphlets and chapbooks. The act of referring to earlier passages and rereading later passages in light of earlier ones is hindered, not to say entirely forestalled. One can, of course, just add page numbers by hand, and this signals one of the central conditions of Raworth's poetry: readers are consistently made into cocreators. Removing a basic technology of the book – page numbers – makes it, on one level, much less reader friendly. At the same time, it also encourages a tremendously tactile experience: flipping back and forth between pages, holding one's thumb in a page while embarking ahead, adding Post-it notes or folding over page cor-ners. The collage-like images that divide the sections add to this sense of DIY reading, of being "in" the book, as the section headings suggest. The impro-visational tactics that readers employ to handle the book are replicated in the rapid shifts and disruptions that constitute *Ace*'s basic operational mechanism. It is "about" the experience of reading it rather than some extractable meaning or theme.[14]

This fulfills one long-lasting premise of modern poetry, emerging out of the nineteenth-century French symbolists and Walter Pater, that form and content are inextricable. Part of Olson's argument in "Projective Verse" modulates this basic notion, and he quotes approvingly Robert Creeley's comment, "form is never more than an extension of content."[15] Fulfilling an Olsonian tenet, *Ace* moves rapidly from perception to perception, and it meets Olson's further demand that a poem be a "high-energy construct and, at all points, an energy discharge":[16]

> i glow
> and flicker
> change
> but first
> a present
> that fits me
> to a t
> no mist
> but sky
> and we
> beneath it
> in our minds
> never
> prevented
> life growing
> by caring
> we changed
> selfishness flashes
> SHOCK
> SHOCK
> in the mountains
> we
> used.[17]

The present of the poem – both its gift and its time frame – "fits me / to a t," a fit that is replicated by the enclosed lyric moment that occurs next: "no mist / but sky / and we / beneath it." This enclosure of selves sits strangely around the "glow / and flicker" that charges the poem, and the potential hypostasizing of a self that begins to build – "selfishness flashes" – has to be "shocked" out of the text. This first happens literally, by way of a capitalization motif that is repeated sporadically throughout *Ace*, and then allusively, as Raworth riffs on a passage at the opening of *The Waste Land* in which Eliot ventriloquizes the Countess Marie Larisch's 1913 memoir, *My Past*: "In the mountains, there you feel free."[18] Raworth here links to the ur-poem of high modernism, the grafted passage serving as something like a shock absorber in this utterly different poetic texture. The speed of Raworth's poetry doesn't lend itself to certain strategies of "close reading," but this isn't because there aren't complexities to be found. Indeed, Raworth's quickly turning mobiles encourage a reading that isn't so much distracted as it is unstably attentive. We pay constant mind to the page but are prohibited from aggregating that attention into a reified interpretive product that we might call a "reading" of the poem. Raworth grabs our attention and most often manages to keep it, but his poems perpetually force us to reroute our attentiveness.

Ace is both disjunctive and formally consistent: its lines repel each other in nearly every way except for their uniform unspooling down the page. It tacks between the full collaging that characterizes Roy Fisher's *The Cut Pages* (1970) and the much more gentle and sporadic proceduralism of a text such as Gael Turnbull's *Twenty Words, Twenty Days* (1966). Although many Revival poets have adapted procedural and conceptual practices from American and European postmodern poetry, they tend not to adopt such procedures entirely. Of course, writers such as Cobbing or Ian Hamilton Finlay can be readily identified with movements in concrete and sound poetry, but in large part Revival poets tend not to be programmatic. This returns us to the theme of variousness that underlies this chapter.[19] Raworth, for instance, is often thought to be a singularly distinctive poet, as John Wilkinson has suggested: "what seems indisputable is that Raworth's poems are different from any others."[20] This is of course true and not true, and one might think about Anthony Barnett, a writer featured in *A Various Art* and associated with the Cambridge circle, as a poet whose short lines offer analogous but quite distinct experiences of forward momentum. In any case, Raworth's singularity is, counterintuitively, somewhat typical of poets associated with the Revival, whose work often looks and reads nothing like each other's.

This is the case even for the strongest and most consistent formation of the Revival: the multigenerational cluster of poets surrounding J.H. Prynne in Cambridge. Prynne has been hugely influential as a teacher and as an example, but his remarkable, difficult work remains an inimitable force rather than the kernel of a coterie style (even as the circle around him has or has had nearly all of the features of a coterie). I will now turn to several poets associated with the Cambridge portion of the Revival, but I don't mean to suggest a potted literary history of an easily encapsulated movement. Some writers within the Cambridge formation, such as Peter Riley and Denise Riley, have made or will make more substantive appearances in connection with other issues, while others are part of later chapters' stories.[21]

As John Wilkinson notes, " 'Cambridge poetry' begins with *The English Intelligencer*, a near-legendary worksheet edited by Andrew Crozier and Peter

Riley between 1966 and 1968."[22] Initially circulated to twenty-eight people, with the list of participants ultimately growing to sixty-six, *The English Intelligencer* was not, Wilkinson points out, exclusively a product of Cambridge,[23] but it was the first venue for a number of important early poems by Cambridge poets, including Riley, Crozier, Prynne, John James, and Wendy Mulford. Initially edited by Crozier, with Prynne acting in an important advisory role, *The English Intelligencer* was distributed in regular installments – every several weeks – and was numbered continuously throughout the thirty-six issues that appeared.[24] Crozier edited the first 274 pages, which were distributed between January 1966 and March 1967, with Peter Riley taking over editorial duties from April 1967 until December 1967. All told, there are 533 numbered pages, with additional batches of unnumbered pages distributed after Crozier reassumed the editor's post. The project continued until April 1968, by which point nearly 1,000 pages of poetry, letters, and commentary had been produced. From the beginning, the central forces behind *The English Intelligencer* seem disappointed by its lack of critical rigor. Lots of poets sent poems, but many fewer sent critical responses to other's poems or more general critical prose. There were occasional letters contributed, but they tended to be from the same several participants, and the kind of ongoing exchange that was desired rarely materialized.[25] Nonetheless, the epistle remained the preferred mode of commentary for Cambridge poets. Not until the 1990s, with writers like Wilkinson and Milne, did this formation begin producing a more publically minded critical prose.

After the end of *The English Intelligencer*'s run, Crozier remained a key figure, because of both his own work and his crucial duties as editor, publisher, critic, and anthologist. In addition to *The English Intelligencer*, he edited *The Wivenhoe Park Review* and *The Grosseteste Review*, founded Ferry Press in 1964, and, as previously mentioned, coedited *A Various Art*. These efforts, which also included the recovery of neglected modernist poets like Carl Rakosi and John Rodker, have sometimes threatened to overshadow his own poetry, which draws simultaneously on English Romanticism and American modernism, primarily the work of Pound and Williams.[26] The influence of Olson is clear throughout much of his work, especially in what Edward Larrissy calls Crozier's "mistrust of egotistical language."[27] The spine of Crozier's poetry is constituted by a clutch of long poems – usually sequences or series – that articulate a mode of being in the world that does not depend upon the continual capture of exterior objects within the subject's orbit. Significant poems in this vein include *The Veil Poem* (1974), *Pleats* (1975), *Duets* (1976), *High Zero* (1978), and "Free Running Bitch" (first published in Iain Sinclair's anthology, *Conductors of Chaos*, in 1996).

This passage from *High Zero*, a long poem containing 24 stanzas of 24 lines each, typifies the way his poems encounter the world:

> Light is in the curtains
> like a bright veil of numbers
> that rises in folds over and over
> and the calculus of persistence
> undogmatic and fluent in its changes.[28]

"Undogmatic and fluent in its changes" is a motto of Crozier's aesthetic ethos, and the displacement of activity and affect from the subject to the space around the subject is cognate with his primary formal strategies: prosodic and grammatical flow that is achieved by way of extremely light punctuation, constant but not attention-grabbing enjambment, and a subtle reliance on the mere ghost of an iambic pentameter substructure.

Such strategies can be seen with vibrant clarity in *The Veil Poem*, Crozier's most well known text. A fusion of Wordsworthian Romanticism and Olsonian open field composition, its ten sections (numbered 0 through 9) offer a series of observations and meditations founded in an ekphrastic impulse – in the form of postcards sent to Crozier by Jeffrey Morsman, who is the poem's dedicatee.[29] The postcards source a number of the poem's basic images – most conspicuously the arches that appear throughout – but Crozier is interested in scene painting only as a kind of prefatory stationing that enables his phenomenologically minded speculations. A nocturne that occurs on domestic thresholds (window, porch, yard, garden), *The Veil Poem* unfolds the processual, experiential nature of subjective life. Its desire to remain incomplete and provisional is signaled (perhaps too preciously) by the first section's subtitle: "(left unfinished)."[30] The deliberately unclosed parenthesis establishes a sense of inherent contingency that contrasts with the opening poem's objectivist pastoral register as it presents a spot of late modern time.

Crozier's interest gradually moves from the visual scene to the perceptual, affective, and epistemological processes that underlie and construct it. He tracks the play of dark and light, the perceptual activities that produce the outer world, the outer world's incessant overwhelming of the senses, and the ceaseless, interactive mutability between an environment and a subject entrenched within it. Discrete paths of seeing are traced and recorded as the speaker seeks reciprocity between the seer and the seen, a poetics that wants to become an ecology:

> There is no radiant source within
> these walls, they hold the sunlight to
> define their intricate arcing.[31]

As here, Crozier's lines often break in gently unexpected places, a formal feature that coincides with the speaker's meditation on his place and ontological nature: "Which side of these doors am I?"[32] *The Veil Poem* occasionally touches on moments of English domesticity ("the people / off the train come out their back doors / to potter about"), and moves ultimately toward an image of non-instrumentality couched in marital harmony:

> The dust beneath my
> fingernails is all the wisdom I have
> to take with me upstairs to my wife.[33]

The complexities of this moment display the tension at the poem's center. Crozier wants to uncenter the lyric self but also to retain something of the space or atmosphere in which that self speaks. The accomplished poem and whatever wisdom it affords is not the achieved artifact, but some uncountable remainder ("dust beneath my / fingernails") that both attaches to the poet – literally "under" his body – and persists outside of his possession. Knowledge and wisdom are not, finally, within the domain of the lyric subject, but attaining such a nongrasping form of subjectivity requires a paradoxical double-step. The experience of "non-domination," to adjust a phrase that Crozier uses in section 1, cannot but occur within the torsions of lyric, a genre long derided for its ideologically complicit self-regard. Crozier's partial solution to this dilemma is to retain a central lyric "I" but also to place that "I" within an environmental and conceptual manifold in which it undergoes constant displacement:

> Here at the centre of every intersecting circle
> each infinite yet wholly itself
> whichever way you turn a way is offered
> for you to carry yourself.[34]

The lyric subject is destabilized in *The Veil Poem* but remains at least partly intact. Crozier's poetry settles itself on the limen between reality and language, seeking to delineate the intricacies of phenomenological experience in linguistic forms that will inevitably repel or misshape that experience.

A much more forceful articulation of the necessity of linguistic artifice and autonomy as the fundamental prerogatives of modern poetry can be found in the work of Veronica Forrest-Thomson, another central figure in Cambridge poetry. In her posthumous volume, *Poetic Artifice: A Theory of Twentieth-Century Poetry* (1978), Forrest-Thomson triangulates later Wittgenstein and Eliot as part of an argument about the singularity of poetry that manages to balance an adherence to Empsonian ambiguity and an impulse toward deconstruction. She states her position quite clearly at the start of her monograph: "Poetry is not, of course, independent of ordinary linguistic categories; if it were it would be unintelligible. What happens is that ordinary linguistic categories are subsumed and altered by rules specific to poetry. Phonological and grammatical structures have different functions in the medium of poetry."[35] This assertion underwrites her theory of "Artifice" (a word capitalized throughout the volume), which she positions as a necessary bulwark against the weak naturalizations that typify a great deal of contemporary work. Against the thinly thematic poems of Larkin or Hughes, she argues for an approach that dwells "at length on the play of formal features and structure of relations internal to a poem."[36] Key to Forrest-Thomson's approach is what she calls the "image-complex," which might be considered a later reflex of the Eliotic objective correlative: "An image-complex consists of a blending of two or more areas of extended meaning; like traditional metaphors, it brings various non-verbal properties together in a new verbal structure."[37] These "image-complexes" are internal to the poem and connect the different levels of its structure. The "disconnected image-complex" is, for Forrest-Thomson, "a particular twentieth-century phenomenon," which "suspends our reading between empirical and discursive imagery and forces us to make connections which neither discourse itself nor the world already contains."[38] We are always thrown back upon the internal relations of the poem's form, and, in the modernist poetry that Forrest-Thomson favors, upon its place between the "old languages which we inhabit and the new world which emerges from an assimilation and transformation of these languages."[39]

Forrest-Thomson's theory of poetic artifice both describes and goes beyond her own poetry. At the time of her death in 1975 at the age of twenty-seven, Forrest-Thomson had published two volumes of poetry and a number of critical articles. Her poetry moves quickly from the overly arch modernist lyrics that make up *Identi-kit* (1967) to the Wittgensteinian variations on concrete and sound poetry in *Language-Games* (1971). Her poems are heavily allusive, underwritten by footnotes, and bolstered with quotations from critics and philosophers: ironically pedantic poems ensconced in the frisson of the university. They raid canonical texts, stitching together homages to Eliot, Pound, Baudelaire, and others out of grafted fragments. Forrest-Thomson constantly experimented with forms, tones, and attitudes, and every poem seems like a kind of trial piece. *On the Periphery* (1976) appeared posthumously, and it shows Forrest-Thomson finding new ways of articulating her poetry and her theoretical program. "Pastoral" translates this program into an "image-complex" more viable and compelling than in many of her earlier parodic texts. Drawing a sharp distinction between nature and language, the poem begins with a scene that is at once quite vivid and entirely unreal, a different version of the late-modern pastoral offered in *The Veil Poem*:

> They are our creatures, clover, and they love us
> Through the long summer meadows' diesel fumes.[40]

The play of vowel and consonant in these opening lines refracts their oddity of address; a speaker addresses not "lover" but "clover" and refers to another group – "they" – who "love us." The fissured deictic pairing rebounds upon the poem's programmatic interest in the fissure between language and reality, and the poem's "us," driving along the meadow's edge, is doubly estranged from the world at the start of the second quatrain: "Jagged are names and not our creatures." Considering the multiple forms of estrangement implicit in the first two quatrains, the sudden collision in the final stanza might be said, using Forrest-Thomson's own terms, to transform the poem from an "image-complex" based on disconnection to a "disconnected image-complex." The poem describes the moment just before the car hits something and then the moment after, when language has already intervened:

> The gentle foal linguistically wounded
> Squeals like a car's brakes
> Like our twisted words.

The poem takes cognizance of its own machinations as the cleft between language and the world carried thus far as a theme is restaged performatively as a series of broken similes: the foal's squeal is said to be like the sound of the car swiftly braking, which is said to be like the sound of "our twisted words." The double implication of the initial image of the foal – it is both wounded *in* and wounded *by* language – is brought to the surface in the self-reflexive final phrase, and in this brief text, Forrest-Thomson both thematizes the core of her theory of poetic artifice and enacts it via the intricacies of sound, deixis, and figuration.

Forrest-Thomson added a dedication to one copy of "Pastoral" that remains among her papers: "for J.H. Prynne / il miglior fabbro."[41] Playing Eliot to Prynne's Pound, Forrest-Thomson's annotation suggests not only the importance of Prynne as a colleague and interlocutor during her time in Cambridge but also as a model for the kind of poetry that she most valued: "Since language has appropriated the non-verbal world and distorted it to suit the requirements of society, Prynne is engaged in restoring language to the condition of reality in its pre-mediated state."[42] Prynne hovers over Forrest-Thomson's poems, as he does over Cambridge poetry (and English poetry more generally) of the last five decades, and it is to him that I now turn.

Prynne's formidable body of poetry has assumed a position like the one Bunting attributed to Pound's *Cantos* – the Alps that must be faced and will be long and perilous in traversing – and I can attempt nothing like a full climb here. The recondite difficulty of his poetry makes any kind of summary gesture impossible, and most critics and commentators have had the most success focusing almost exclusively on a single poem or small volume at a time.[43] In addition to the challenges presented by the work itself, which in any case limits the size of his readership, Prynne's remoteness from the major circuits of the literary world has been largely self-enforced: after his early and eventually disowned volume, *Force of Circumstance* (1962), published by Routledge and Kegan Paul, he has chosen to publish with small presses in limited print runs or to privately produce his work. His collected volume, *Poems* – first published in 1999 and reissued and expanded in 2005 and 2015 – has made the entire scope of his work widely available, but for much of his career, he has deliberately cultivated a smaller audience. So, if Prynne's poems do seem like a later version of the Poundian Alps, then they are also a huge and imposing mountain range for which, for a good stretch of time, few had the coordinates.

J.H. Prynne was born in 1936 and has spent the entirety of his career at Cambridge University as a librarian, teacher, and Fellow of Gonville and Caius College. Prynne's work of the late 1960s, in *Kitchen Poems* (1968) and *The White Stones* (1969) especially, is indebted to Olson's open field poetics as well as to his anthropological speculations in essays such as "Human Universe." As Forrest-Thomson notes in the earlier quotation, Prynne's early work is interested in a restoration of origins, as in the opening lines of "Die a Millionaire":

> The first essential is to take knowledge
> back to the springs.[44]

As he lays out in clearer terms in "A Note on Metal" (1968), this project of return or restoration entails a critique of the abstraction of value that has characterized human society since "the early Bronze Age," and so Prynne's poetry, throughout and at its heart, is concentrated on economics.[45] The impossibility of any such return to origins is recognized later in "Die a Millionaire":

> The fact is that right
> from the *springs* this water is no longer fit
> for the stones it washes: the water of life
> is all in bottles & ready for invoice.[46]

Driving much of Prynne's work is the realization of the already-imbricated nature of our knowledge and experience and their determination by ideological forces outside of our ken, what he calls in several early poems "the twist-point." The depredations and iniquities of consumer capitalism, as well as the instrumentalization of modern life, become constant targets of his scorn and ire:

> All this by
> purchase on the twist-point, the system gone
> social to disguise
>   the greed of ambition
> swimming in great seismic shocks through
> the beds of our condition.[47]

Prynne's poetry is materialist in quite a number of ways, as John Wilkinson has pointed out, and in addition to the extended critique of global capital and political economy, it is concerned with the actual substances underlying "the beds of our condition," whether geological, biological, or digital.[48] His work draws heavily on technical and scientific discourses, but instead of raiding these fields for glittering vocabulary or vibrant analogies, Prynne works through their conceptual and ethical implications. And the materiality of language itself is, to quote Wilkinson, "asserted at every turn through its historical and social thickness; efforts to warp the expression of humanity must reckon with the deep resources as well as the resistances of this stuff."[49]

What Prynne calls "the acrid wavering of language, so full / of convenient turns of extinction" makes for poems of fumy thickness.[50] Nearly every word is deflated and repressurized so as to reveal both its history – its etymological, idiomatic, and figurative traces – and the ideological material that clings to it. This, to be sure, makes for a reading of exceeding slowness and deliberation, an antithesis to Raworthian speed. Many poems activate recognizable generic conventions – whether the quest poem, as in "Aristeas, in Seven Years"; the love poem, as in "The Stranger, Instantly"; the Wordsworthian walking poem, as in "Thoughts on the Esterházy Court Uniform"; the nocturne, as in "The Moon Poem"; the shore poem, as in "Living in History"; the scenic vista poem, as in "The Western Gate"; or the travel poem, such as "Chemins de Fer." There are even a few poems that have relatively clear plots and stable diegetic spaces (see "Foot and Mouth" and "One Way At Any Time" for two instances). However, even preliminary generic tags are barely adequate for the dense texture of observation, meditation, and intellection that comprises any given poem.

These difficulties are compounded by Prynne's eschewal of a coherent lyric speaker. The language joined together and presented as a single "poem" is rarely guaranteed by a unified voice or perspective. The poems before *Brass* (1971) methodically problematize the subject, no longer a site of plentitude or knowledge, nor a locus of modernist fracture, nor a postmodern hollow, but rather a wavering and unstable effect of the structures of late capitalism. Prynne's post-*Brass* poems more fully negate a coherent speaking/writing subject, but they also often decline a human-based perspective. In order to fully interrogate the "beds of our condition," his poems operate at a scale that is either much larger than the human or much smaller – the geologic or the cellular.

One key early example of the former tendency is "The Glacial Question, Unsolved." It begins with and in "the matter of ice" and tracks the complexities of glaciation and deglaciation on the landmass of Britain.[51] The poem is about the overall southward movement of glaciers during the Pleistocene epoch, the basic geological condition in which "we" live, and its own unfolding works through this "condition of fact."[52] Dense with references and often resembling an academic lecture, the poem nevertheless doesn't utilize scientific knowledge in order to "humanize" the enormity of glacial action, nor does it simply deconstruct the supposed objectivity of scientific discourse in order to expose its entrenched ideologies and repurpose it as a form of lyric power. Instead, "The Glacial Question, Unsolved" seriously considers its governing question. Its decentering of subjective experience is key to its aim of envisioning a large-scale geological process and of understanding patterns of human society as distant, marginal effects of that process, as can be seen in the poem's final lines:

> We know this, we are what it leaves:
> the Pleistocene is our current sense, and
> what in sentiment we are, we
> are, the coast, a line or sequence, the
> cut back down, to the shore.[53]

The "we" that is hailed in these lines comprises no actual human community but is rather a kind of deictic scatter – deposits left by glaciers – that is continually subject to false or broken equations ("we are, we / are"). The "matter of ice," both the topic of glaciation and the actual matter *in* ice that will be eventually left behind by glaciers, is, eventually, "us," but an "us" that can't be occupied by writer or reader.

The difficulty of occupying the pronouns that Prynne's poems offer is systemic. His poems' scalar and perspectival shifts are made more difficult to navigate by the interweaving of multiple technical registers, a point made by N.H. Reeve and Richard Kerridge in their pioneering monograph, *Nearly Too Much: The Poetry of J.H. Prynne*: "the space set out by a Prynne poem often seems to be space in which different 'knowledges' or discourses pass, meet and collide with each other, in such variety that no reader is likely to process and internalize them all."[54] When these various knowledges are riveted together and shot through by Prynne's materialist critique, words and phrases become both opaque and newly magnetized by their strange new contexts, as in this passage from "A New Tax on the Counter-Earth":

> It is cash so distraught
> that the limbic mid-brain system has absorbed
> its reflex massage. We move into sleep portioned
> off in the restored liner, and the drowsy body
> is closer to "nature", the counter-earth.[55]

Syntactical linearity is made to take on something like an extra dimension as the lexical freight of each phrase is repacked. Disparate discourses are repositioned by the series of grammatical relays and verbal switches ("it is," "that the," "sleep portioned / off in") that simultaneously stage sentence-forms and disallow usual notions of sense and reference. Sentences become tracks of thought and response, just as the larger structures of stanza or verse-paragraph come to resemble cognitive trail maps.

Indeed, what my extraction of quotations from several poems misses is the arduous intensity of thought and linguistic effort that each poem undertakes. One reason why criticism on Prynne has tended toward varieties of line-by-line commentary is that this often seems like the only way to approach poetry that is so entirely resistant to summary and paraphrase.[56] In "Mental Ears and Poetic Work," first given as a talk at the University of Chicago in 2009, Prynne describes the "active poetic text" as "characteristically in dispute with its own ways and means, contrary implication running inwards to its roots and outwards to its surface proliferations: not as acrobatic display but as working the work that, when fit for purpose, poetry needs to do. These are the proper arguments of poetry as a non-trivial pursuit, the templates for ethical seriousness."[57] In order to actively "work the work," I will look closely at one poem in order to display the vigilant granularity of Prynne's "poetic thought."[58]

"Chromatin" was first published in *Wound Response* (1974), and the volume's title cues the poem's investigation of the chemical and biological aspects of physiological and psychological life. Its close-packed stanza of sixteen lines visually replicates the compactions of thought and figuration that occur within:

> The prism crystal sets towards the axis
> of episodic desire: lethargy and depression
> cross the real-time analogue: currents level
> and historic matching blurs into locked-on
> receptor site blockade. Stable mosaic at

adrenal print "you" are in white "I" see a
moving shade by the door it is *my wish* to
be there running on ("mental confusion,
tremors, anxiety") and breaking the induced
blockade I truly am by the door shaking or
the frame goes to gel. Visual sonar
arrhythmia blocks fading brocade made
pressure crisis you and the flowers in
pliant flicker real time! I surmount
the uptake gradient, cognition by
recount, the homeric icefields unfold.[59]

The great majority of the lines have between nine and eleven syllables, with three lines that stretch to twelve syllables, and one (the second) that goes for fifteen. There is not a regular metrical pattern, but the poem's unfolding is shaped by near ceaseless enjambment and a tendency towards medial caesurae. The systemic effect of the enjambment is intensified by the large number of lines split midphrase, often leaving an article, preposition, or conjunction hanging at the end of a line. We might say that these angular effects analogize the "prism crystal" mentioned at the beginning – the lines are heavily faceted, there are edges everywhere. A number of sound patterns run through the poem, and one central sonic motif (an "axis / of episodic desire") is the alternation between voiceless velar plosives (*crystal, axis, episodic, cross, currents*) and bilabial nasals (*moving, my, mental, tremor, am*), a pattern that first appears in the title word. This tacking between /k/ and /m/ produces a further "axis" as the vocal apparatus moves back and forth from the front of the mouth to the back – from upper throat to lips – when rendering the poem's sound structure. As is often the case in Prynne's work, "Chromatin" is sonically dense, but it eludes a typical or traditional pattern of density: its patterns emerge like the chromatin itself when hit with dye.

At first glance, "Chromatin" doesn't look particularly rebarbative. It conforms in many ways to what we expect a poem to look like, and it doesn't contain a massive amount of what we might call "external information" – allusions, technical or specialized language, historical references, or data. If we imagined this poem within the context of the *Norton Anthology of Poetry*, there might only be five footnotes: four definitions (the title word, *receptor site, adrenal,* and *arrhythmia*) and a citation for the quoted phrase in the middle of the poem ("mental confusion, / tremors, anxiety"). This, however, isn't an allusion in the sense that it serves as a textual spark that alerts a reader to another text but rather seems to be a nondescript and untraceable fragment of a list of possible side effects or symptoms. The title indicates that this poem is in contact with scientific discourses, but what exactly is the role of biological knowledge within the poem? Chromatin is the combination of DNA and proteins that makes up the nucleus of a cell and that is crucial within the production of chromosomes. It shapes the genetic material so that it can fit into the cell and strengthens and protects DNA so that it can undergo mitosis. So, chromatin might provide a mental analogue for the poem itself. It allows for a dense packing of nuclear material within the cell, a feature that is echoed by the densely packed poem, which, like chromatin during certain stages of the cell cycle, is not linear but highly compacted and interwoven. The asyntactical quality of the poem's four sentences are reminiscent of the multilayer, hyperlinear packaging of chromatin within a cell, but this resemblance provides a pointer about how the poem works rather than a primer that helps to ascertain its potential meaning.

The other technical terms are all related to biology, but they don't necessarily have much to do with chromatin (apart from "receptor site"), and the poem veers off into a number of other discourses or fields over the course of its sixteen lines: gemology ("prism crystal"), sexuality ("episodic desire"), and psychology ("lethargy and depression"). Between the presence of these discourses about desire and feeling and the extremely attenuated narrative that sketches a romantic relationship gone wrong, we might even feel safe wrapping this poem back into a familiar world of love lyrics. If we isolate certain sections and ignore what surrounds them, we get a fairly clear poem about some kind of heightened moment of domestic energy and perhaps violence: "'you' are in white 'I' see a / moving shade by the door it is *my wish* to / be there running on … and breaking the induced / blockade I truly am by the door shaking or / the frame goes to gel." Reading the poem as an oblique record of romantic or sexual crisis allows us to make performative sense of the agrammatical quality of certain lines:

> arrhythmia blocks fading brocade made
> pressure crisis you and the flowers in
> pliant flicker real time!

In such a reading, these lines "succumb" to the emotional pressure on the figure voicing them, although it is difficult, if not impossible, to locate a coherent lyric speaker that could obtain for the entirety of the poem.

The refusal to offer a consistent "I" around whom a lyric utterance can be organized is a near-constant strategy for Prynne, but even though we don't have a lyric speaker or a guiding mind, we do have all sorts of lyric bodies operating at multiple levels of appearance: the intracellular ("chromatin"), the cellular ("receptor site"), the glandular ("adrenal print"), the physiological and anatomical ("lethargy," "tremors," "arrhythmia"), the psychological ("depression," "anxiety"), and even the neurological ("currents level," "visual sonar"). The poem attempts to articulate something like a fractal logic of the body and its processes: just as a nonlinear, heavily compacted organization defines the workings inside the nucleus, so does such a logic exist at higher levels of mental and physical existence, what the poem glosses as "cognition by / recount." Rather than a narrative structure, there appears an intricate pattern that takes on various shapes throughout the poem: "prism crystal," "stable mosaic," "fading brocade." We must work among isolated phrases because the poem's organizing logic isn't that of the sentence as a temporal unfolding but rather as a spatial container.

Indeed, the one thing that remains prohibitively difficult about reading "Chromatin" is making sense of the entirety of each of its four sentences. This, perhaps, is the point. Each sentence thwarts most attempts to align its basic components. In the first sentence, the relationship among subjects, verbs, and objects remains elusive both across and within the three independent clauses. It is almost as though Prynne assembles nonarticulating parts so as to signal the poem's reliance on mosaic or brocade patterns rather than linear ones. The second sentence is an elaborate run-on that models the "mental confusion" at its parenthetical center. The third sentence does away almost entirely with verbs as it simply lays words next to each other without a clear sequencing: there are several verb-like parts in the sentence ("blocks," "made," "flicker"), but they don't work in a verb-like way. The final sentence offers a clear subject-and-verb structure ("I surmount"), but this act of subjective overcoming is attached to the rate of absorption in various biological and chemical processes. The "uptake gradient" is not something that an individual could "surmount" – it isn't a function of will or determination or even of volition. Disparate existential levels are rammed together, and we might read the final sentence's second clause as a second-order reflection on or abstraction of this process. The final clause of the poem, however, introduces an entirely new analogical plane. We've moved from the inside of a cell to a huge geographical and temporal expanse. Not only are we asked to imagine icefields, but we are also asked to consider "homeric icefields," so, perhaps, icefields as they would have existed during the time of Homer. We're then asked to imagine them "unfolding," a geological process that would occur over thousands of years. Both the unfolding of icefields and the unfolding of DNA are processes outside our ability to cognize them: we have to depend on a kind of "recounting" – a story or metaphor or technology of sensory extension.

If the final phrase extends the poem's fractal logic and its use of figuration to conduct a large-scale argument – a kind of homeric simile – then it is also the most stunning performance of that logic. It folds a rhyme into its last two words (a pararhyme on -*fields* and -*fold*) as though to gesture playfully at the typical concluding couplet of the sonnet form that it superficially resembles. The word "icefields" folds in on itself, a field encircled by /s/ sounds. Each of the letters of the line's opening word – "recount" – are recounted in the words that follow it, with the fullest recounting taking place when the end of "homeric" replays, with a slight vocalic modulation, the beginning of "recount." This morphological stub is partially resounded at the start of "icefields." What I mean to say here is that while the poem's final line doesn't "solve" the poem or clarify its many complexities, it is surely a powerful resolution – sonically intricate and imagistically sublime. It is a very lyric ending to a strangely lyric poem, offering an instance of rich closure to a text that in so many other ways remains open and enigmatic.

Such a strong concluding move is typical of Prynne's poetry, and "Chromatin" is an important transitional piece that furthers aspects of his earlier concerns, prepares for certain features of his middle-period work of the 1980s and early 1990s (with *The Oval Window* [1983] as an important apex), and predicts the more profound resistance to syntactical order and coordination that characterizes his later work, an arc that might be said to begin with *Her Weasels Wild Returning* (1994). Prynne's nearly impenetrable late texts have staggered even some of his most faithful adherents, but they can be seen as intensifications and extensions of his approach since *White Stones*. In his 2009 talk at Chicago, he addresses the matter with remarkable candor:

> I am rather frequently accused of having more or less altogether taken leave of discernible sense. In fact I believe this accusation to be more or less true, and not to me alarmingly so, because what for so long has seemed the arduous road into the domain of poetry ("what does it mean?") seems less and less an unavoidably necessary precondition for successful reading. The task, however, is not to subside into distracted ingenious playfulness with the lexicon and cross-inflectional ideomatics, but to write and read with maximum focused intelligence and passion, each of these two aspects bearing so strongly into the other as to fuse them into the enhanced state once in an old-fashioned way termed the province of the imagination.[60]

Distancing himself from "distracted ingenious playfulness," Prynne's vision of poetry remains, in its broadest terms, a modernist one, and even – in its knowing reference to "the province of the imagination" – a very late reflex of English Romanticism, albeit a vision that dialectically pushes both to their furthest implications. Prynne's poetry is designed to be read with one's full attention on its complex turns of syntax, line, and argument. Every word choice and line break seems the product of maximum compositional deliberation, no matter how inscrutable the effects may be. His are radically well-made poems. Other strands of activity associated with the Revival took quite different paths.

John James was a central contributor to *The English Intelligencer* and he is usually placed within the Cambridge orbit, but his work is much more indebted to Frank O'Hara and the New York School poets and to William Carlos Williams behind them. Much of his work of the period is committed to a species of precise casualness and intimate immediacy:

> I know you will enter the room in 25 seconds
> a freesia or two in your green lapel
> the storm in the chimney shaking.[61]

James's poems are both restless and relaxed. As the beginning of his sequence *Narrative Graffiti* has it, they aim to record "our acknowledgement / of the world, the variousness of that response,"[62] but they are also "always / on the prowl // for the materials / of your existence."[63] Committed to preserving the fundamental lyric duo of "I" and "you," James's poetry aims to document something of the transience of human experience. And so many of his poems, appearing as slight records of mundane happenings and exchanges, are marbled with a sense of loss: "nowhere else is quite the same today / franking these letters of dispersal."[64]

James has also worked in a more disjunctive style, as in "Talking in Bed" and other poems in *Striking the Pavilion of Zero* (1975), although his work never approaches the aggressively disconnected surface that characterizes the work of another key contributor to *The English Intelligencer*, Barry MacSweeney. MacSweeney also had deep connections to the scene in Cambridge and published his precocious first volume, *The Boy from the Green Cabaret Tells of His Mother*, in 1968. A prodigy in the mold of Rimbaud or Dylan Thomas, MacSweeney – who was born in 1948 – was a Northern poet who drew heavily on Bunting's poetics as well as the work of Tom Pickard. He also had links to the London avant-garde scene, but his favored posture was that of an outsider or vagrant. The wolf is his poetry's spirit animal, as in his sequence *Brother Wolf* (1972). His early poetry is dedicated primarily to love and eros – "women I chased on the lawns of Albion" – as he works through a series of influences, especially nineteenth- and twentieth-century French poetry, as well as Chatterton, Shelley, Bunting, and Prynne.[65]

MacSweeney's style remained highly mobile, with different models taken up, inhabited, and discarded very quickly.[66] His 1970s poems aggregate disjointed phrases into baroque chains that aggressively shift tone and register as they revisit several key areas of interest: politics, sex, love, popular culture, and the often tragic and self-damaging bearings of poets and artists. Throughout his career, he adopted various hazardous artists as stand-ins and interlocutors, composing knowingly seedy variations on Romantic (and romanticized) stereotypes, what "Black Torch Sunrise" calls "elegiacs & glittering heroes / sour with mediocre filmwork."[67] *Odes: 1971–1978* begins with "Just 22 and I Don't Mind Dying: Official Poetical Biography of Jim Morrison," a shuffling of quasi-surrealist imagery intercut with obliquely rendered moments that evade narrative development. The several dozen odes that follow comprise brief phrasal bursts grooved down the middle of the page whose self-dramatizing litanies continually rename their own conditions of extremity and remain attuned to the erotic junk of contemporary consumerism. A number of long poems from the same period, such as "Colonel B," "Liz Hard," and "Jury Vet," careen between sardonically fawning anatomizations of popular culture, especially the fashion industry, and what he calls at one point "gamey bedroom porn."[68]

Within these rough textures, MacSweeney's own position is on the gritty margin, among "the gutter realm / of citizens."[69] Simultaneously lamenting the economic messes of the 1970s and lambasting Britain's turn toward conservative politics later in the decade, MacSweeney frequently aims to stitch a mode of political critique into his lyric self-lacerations. His thematics of self-destruction and self-loathing reaches an apex (or nadir) in *Hellhound Memos* (1993), which consists of dispatches from an underworld of addiction and ecstatic mayhem. The hellhound motif is taken from Robert Johnson, who is one of the sequence's presiders and who takes his place in MacSweeney's gallery of tragic avatars. Less disjunctive than his earlier odes but also less manifestly about MacSweeney's own alcoholism and recovery than his later work in *The Book of Demons* (1997), *Hellhound Memos* intertwines MacSweeney's retrofitted Romanticism with his distinctive version of nasty pastoral, as in this passage from "Hellhound Rapefield Memo":

> Filth it is a monument.
> O lanceolate leaves the truth is yours!
> A monument. Pink-suited hellhound over it.
> I fear for my cusloppe, my betany, my bane, my cranesbill, my cuckoo
> pinting gob of wayside spit.[70]

The flowers catalogued are both venerated as part of the elegiac motion and trashed – roadside plants "watered" by spit.

Although MacSweeney's bristly lyricism is often dependent on a retrograde image of wounded masculinity that shades too easily into sexism, his aggressive fissuring of normative denotation – his jerking of signifiers away from their signifieds – can be more positively read as an intensification of a sound-based poetics that MacSweeney learned from Bunting. Indeed, MacSweeney's poetry often reads as a kind of punk *Briggflatts*:

> No pink clues
> as
> fuck seeds
> dance
> &
> rage.[71]

The sheer physicality of language in this passage from "Jury Vet" is, to be sure, uncomfortably forceful as it collapses sex and violence. But its sonic exuberance and attention to the shape and play of words are indicative of key strands within the Revival and link MacSweeney to figures like Maggie O'Sullivan (who will be discussed in more detail in Chapter 7) and Bill Griffiths.

MacSweeney's combination of experimental syntax and layout with a thematic focus on psychic and social extremity recalls Griffiths's pamphlets of the 1970s. In texts like *Cycles* (published in 1976 but written between 1970–1974) and *War w/ Windsor* (1976), Griffiths critiques political and social injustice in contemporary Britain, focusing particular ire on the state's control of violence and its dependence on incarceration. Much of his material was drawn from his own experiences, which included a period as a Hell's Angel and a stint in Her Majesty's Prison Brixton, but also from that of other prisoners who Griffiths knew and supported. His poems are shot through with dialect, slang, and a range of vernacular terms, and they advance in short, skewed bursts, as in the opening of one of the *Cycles* texts:

> Morning s'blue
> early, edgy, special
> lay like a gun
> in await
> some sort sun's exploding
>
> castellated
> a shitting hole, shat in
> (solitary)
> holy spirit![72]

Moving vertiginously among lexical registers and riveting displaced phrases together, Griffiths aims to route a Foucaultian analysis of the structure of power and the iniquity of its institutions through the heavily accented short lines that he favors. His anarchic lyricism draws from Ginsberg, William Burroughs, and Michael McClure, as well as from a tradition of English lyric that runs from Bunting and Hopkins through Keats back to Old English poetry (a subject in which Griffiths earned a doctorate from King's College, London in 1987 and that is a central focus of his work from the mid-1970s).

Most of Griffiths's work was self-published by his own Pirate Press and produced with Bob Cobbing's help at the Poetry Society's printing shop at Earl's Court, an unexpected bastion of innovative writing and publishing for a brief period in the middle of the 1970s.[73] Griffiths was also deeply involved with Cobbing's Writers Forum and his many sound and concrete poetry projects. The sheer extent of Cobbing's aesthetic activities is remarkable and, like Crozier, the legacy of his prolific duties as editor, organizer, publisher, and one-person infrastructure for experimental poetry in London has tended to outshine his own massive body of work.[74] The Writers Forum workshops began in 1952 and met regularly (every two to three weeks) for much of the rest of Cobbing's life. Cobbing was at the center of a configuration of writers who stressed the performative nature of poetry. They built on the growing popularity of poetry readings and harnessed the energy of the 1960s counterculture – especially as described by Jeff Nuttall in *Bomb Culture* – to integrate performance and making as part of a broader ethos of poetic community. This community featured many collaborative projects among Cobbing, Griffiths, O'Sullivan, cris cheek, Peter Finch, Paula Claire, Lawrence Upton and others, as well as standing groups of performance poets, the most significant of which were *jgjgjgjgj*, a trio consisting of cheek, Clive Fencott, and Upton, and *The Koncrete Kanticle*, made up of Cobbing, Griffiths, and Claire. This scene peaked in the mid- to late 1970s, buoyed by a lively arts and cultural climate that carried over from the 1960s. Its waning was connected to the economic difficulties of the 1970s and the political redirection later in the decade. cris cheek links the "deterioration" of the alternative British poetry scene to the rise of Thatcher and the political shifts of the 1980s:

> For the best part of a decade from 1980 there was only really occasional Kings' readings, the Subvoicive series curated by Gilbert Adair, and Bob Cobbing's Writers' Forum workshops. Allen Fisher ran workshops at Goldsmith's College which generated a focus and produced the Robert Sheppard, Adrian Clarke axis, and there were occasional programmes such as the RASP session in South London put together by Reality Studios and Spanner [two small presses]. But really the scene, which had been a steaming scene, went flat.[75]

Nonetheless, cheek's description suggests that a good deal of poetic activity persisted even after the scene contracted in the 1980s, and Cobbing remained at the center of a number of circles until his death in 2002.

In works like *An ABC in Sound* (1965), *Six Sound Poems* (1968), *The Five Vowels* (1974), and *Jade-Sound Poems* (1976), Cobbing brought poetry back to its fundament. His early sound texts and visual poems incorporated many of the elements underlying lyric: chants, inscriptions, riddles, catalogues, and game forms such as anagrams and abecedaries. Many of his works abandon words or recognizable letter combinations. Each page of *Jade-Sound Poems*, for instance, consists of a string of letters, symbols, numbers, diacritical marks, and/or punctuation marks arrayed in a single curving tower down its middle. The font and position of the symbol string changes with every page, and it is almost as though one is looking at the DNA strand of a new language emerging from the grainy, off-white paper. By composing below the level of verbal coherence or semantic meaning, Cobbing sought to get to the root of language's double system of sound patterns and visual marks. If words are no longer imagined to be part of a signifying system, then they begin to revert to more freely malleable sonic and inscriptive materials: "the shape, the mark on the page, is the significant thing and any mark or shape on the page, any texture can be read, can be interpreted as sound."[76] Working across the visual, literary, and sonic arts and allowing their borders to be almost entirely porous, Cobbing drew on a long tradition of modernist sound and visual poems – including Guillaume Apollinaire's *Calligrammes*, Russian *Zaum* poetry, Hugo Ball's *Lautgedicht*, and Tristan Tzara's Dada texts – as well as on the international concrete poetry movement that flourished from the mid-1950s through the 1960s.

Cobbing drew from a huge range of conceptual practices and production techniques in order to render the pages that would become the visual scores for his sound texts. Although vocal performance was a necessary aspect of the realization of his aesthetic vision, Cobbing's compositions began as visual forms: "one simply composes the textures and the lines and the shapes and sees what sounds come out."[77] He used cut-ups, found texts, and permutations of both found and newly composed texts to generate materials for his poems, and he often made further alterations by manipulating printing and copying technologies. Many of his poems are made up of language that has been blurred, overprinted, distorted, or rescaled, and so encountering his work is often more of an act of looking than it is of reading, even as one realizes that the seemingly nonsensical shapes and figures serve as sonic cues for Cobbing's performances.

Sensations of the Retina (1978) diagrams this process, beginning with a prefatory page that lays out several basic motifs: "Concretion from within creates the specific place / Taut, radiant, articulate but strange to language."[78] After several visually descriptive phrases, the poem attempts to transmute the visual into the aural:

EYE   STANDING   AT   EXTREME   PERIMETER
LISTENS
BECOMES THE MEDIUM OF THE HEARD

After this readable page appears a typewriter poem that uses the letters of the previous page's final lines – "A voluble cascade of rippling water / Emancipates the l i g h t" – to construct a pattern that resembles a "voluble cascade" of letters, a metamorphic inkblot. The next eight pages are fully concrete: abstract designs featuring a preponderance of black ink in a heavily overtyped and overprinted texture. Occasionally, the edges of what were once letters become visible, and some of the images might loosely recall the verbal descriptions on the first page, but *Sensations of the Retina* remains, as does the best of Cobbing's work, "strange to language." Routed through a genealogy of modernism quite distinct from that of the Cambridge poets, although of course sharing several key points of contact, the London node of the British Poetry Revival was not exclusively devoted to sound or concrete poetry, as this chapter's final turn will show. But attention to process, performance, and collaboration was a hallmark of this moment and has presaged some of the more intriguing projects in British poetry in the last several decades.

While Cobbing was the epicenter of concrete and sound poetry in England, there was a counterbalancing force to the north. Beginning in the very early 1960s, several Scottish writers began to steer away from the domineering Scottish nationalism that attached to Hugh McDiarmid, as well as from the more traditional forms of poets like Norman MacCaig and, slightly later, Douglas Dunn. In early books such as *The Dancers Inherit the Party* (1960) and *Glasgow Beasts, an a Burd, Haw, an Inseks, an, aw, a Fush* (1961), Ian Hamilton Finlay combined folk materials and experiments in Scots into a sparely pastoral objectivist style. His "Orkney Lyrics" resemble some of Lorine Niedecker's miniatures, while the title poem of *Glasgow Beasts, an a Burd, Haw, an Inseks, an, aw, a Fush* composes a bestiary in Scots whose demotic playfulness influenced slightly later figures like Edwin Morgan and Tom Leonard. First gaining recognition as a translator of European poetry, Morgan was a stylistic shape shifter, and his major early books, *The Second Life* (1968) and *From Glasgow to Saturn* (1973), contain a plethora of surreal, concrete, and sound texts in addition to more traditional poems. In "The Loch Ness Monster's Song," Morgan imagines a transcription of that fictive beast's peculiar music:

> Sssnnnwhufffll?
> Hnwhuffl hhnnwfl hnfl hfl?
> Gdroblboblhobngbl gbl gl g g g g glbgl.[79]

Meanwhile, "Canedolia: An Off-Concrete Scotch Fantasia" begins with a rash of exclamations – "oa! hoy! awe! ba! mey!" – and then unspools a series of questions and nonsensical, Jabberwockian answers about a place or event:

> *what is it like there?*
> och it's freuchie, it's faifley, it's wamphray, it's frandy, it's sliddery.[80]

Unlike the more abstract sound texts of Cobbing and others in London, Morgan's work remains undergirded by a basic adherence to mimesis or representation, either using sound or concrete techniques to produce an extended form of communication, as in his rendering of Nessie's song, or – as in the lexical adventures in "Canedolia" – maintaining basic syntactical and grammatical structures even while generating a litany of nonsense words and neologisms.

Like Morgan, Tom Leonard has worked in a variety of concrete, permutative, and pattern forms throughout his career, but a very different kind of sound poetry appears in his earliest and still most well known work, the *Six Glasgow Poems* (1969). In each of these brief poems, Leonard renders the concrete particulars of working-class speech patterns of Glasgow, his home city, into a singular orthography whose vernacular energy repels the dominance of Received Pronunciation. A dynamic speaking voice drives Leonard's dialect poems, and the *Six Glasgow Poems* are miniature dramatic monologues or conversation pieces. "Good Style," the last of the *Six Glasgow Poems*, provides a forceful defense of his project:

> helluva hard tay read theez init
> stull
> if yi canny unnirston thim jiss clear aff then
> gawn
> get tay fuck ootma road[81]

Anticipating the kind of linguistic defiance that characterizes Linton Kwesi Johnson's dub poetry, Leonard's speaker acknowledges the "difficulty" of his poems' appearance – "helluva hard tay read theez init" – but also rebuts any sort of accommodation. The poem's refusal to offer itself in more accessible terms is not only an act of political resistance but also indicative of an aesthetic obduracy that is characteristic of a good deal of concrete and sound-based poetry.

Nowhere is this better seen than in Finlay's concrete work, which took up an increasing amount of his time and energy after the comparatively conventional books of the very early 1960s. Like a number of figures central to the Revival, Finlay promoted new poetry through his editorial and publishing activities. He produced twenty-five issues of *Poor. Old. Tired. Horse.* (*POTH*) between 1961 and 1967 (taking the title phrase from a poem by Robert Creeley), publishing an eclectic and broadly international selection of sound and concrete poetry, as well as a good deal of Scottish, American, and English poetry and texts in translation. Finlay avoided uniformity, and, as Morgan recalls, each issue was something of a surprise: "some issues were thematic, some general; some illustrated, some not; some hand-drawn, some printed; some with fine artwork and layout, some with – not so fine. Few magazines encouraged such a marked sense of anticipation from number to number."[82] Along with the Wild Hawthorn Press, which he founded with Jessie McGuffie in 1961, *POTH* became the primary outlet for Finlay's own poetry. Concrete poems first appeared in the sixth issue of *POTH* (March 1963), with a page devoted to Augustos de Campos and Noigandres poetry from Brazil. Within a few years, Finlay had turned fully to concrete work. After a move to a shepherd's cottage ringed with moorland named Stony Path in Dunsyre (about twenty-five miles from Edinburgh) in 1967, he and Sue Finlay, his wife and collaborator, turned most of their energies toward creating the gardens and landscapes that have made the grounds and structures surrounding Stony Path – renamed Little Sparta in 1979 to indicate Finlay's increasingly complex classicism – one of the most important artistic endeavors in late-twentieth-century Britain.

The totality of Finlay's project traverses a huge span of artistic practice, and, like Cobbing, Finlay identified himself primarily as a poet even though he worked across a number of forms – gardening, sculpture, land-art, architecture, and visual art.[83] What united his endeavors was a commitment to revealing the intensely spiritual and ultimately ethical relation between humans and the natural world. His works are devoted to recomposing this relation, and his early dissatisfaction with traditional poetic forms and with conventional language itself is connected to his desire to enunciate a different mode of being. In a 1963 letter to Pierre Garnier, Finlay explains his turn:

> "Concrete" began for me with the extraordinary (since wholly unexpected) sense that the syntax I had been using, the movement of language in me, at a physical level was no longer there – so it had to be replaced with something else, with a syntax and movement that would be true to the new feeling ... "concrete" by its very limitations offers a tangible image of goodness and sanity; it is very far from the now-fashionable poetry of anguish and self ... It is a model, of order, even if set in a space which is full of doubt ... I would like, if I could, to bring into this, somewhere the unfashionable notion of "Beauty."[84]

His "unfashionable notion of Beauty" led him in several directions. He created variations on Renaissance *emblemata* with the fishing boat and the battle ship serving as dialectical symbols of his neoclassicism; complex pattern poems such as "Acrobats" in which the page takes on the properties of a painter's canvas; and poem-objects or garden poems – many of which would take their place on the grounds of Little Sparta – in which his texts were cut into stone, marble, glass, and wood, as in the early sandblasted poem, "Wave Rock."[85] His one-word poems began appearing in the final issue of *POTH*, with the bind between a poem's title (which could be more than one word) and its content (one word only) modeling Finlay's own reaching toward symbiotic order. One of his most well known one-word poems, entitled "The Boat's Blueprint," displays this with crystalline beauty. In *Poems to Hear and See*, a 1971 selection of his concrete work, the poem is printed with an aqua-blue, nearly sage background behind the title phrase, which appears in white block letters bordered in a darker blue-green tint. The poem's single word – "water" – appears below, in a lowercase italic font whose hue matches the blue border of the title phrase.[86] As Finlay's classicism expanded its range of reference beyond the Greeks, taking in the mythology and ideologies surrounding the French Revolution as well as attempting (quite controversially) to rescue a variety of neoclassicism that was coopted and ruined by the Third Reich, he remained committed to concretizing a complex pastoral philosophy at Little Sparta as well as in the huge body of printed work that he produced until his death in 2006.

Finlay's work recenters a matter I examined in the previous chapter and that has occasionally surfaced in this one: that of place. Again and again, we find poets keen to survey the place of Britain and the historical conditions that have shaped its modern environments, both natural and built. The importance of place in contemporary British poetry is a well-worn critical path, but for good reason. Poets have been obsessed with it – an obsession that has a number of causes, manifests in a number of ways, and is apparent at nearly every point on the spectrum, from the most achingly experimental texts to the coziest poems of the mainstream. The most significant work to emerge out of the London tributaries of the Revival – Allen Fisher's *Place* – is, as its title suggests, one such project, and I will conclude this chapter with a brief and necessarily cursory trek along a few of the many paths that it offers.

Like Cobbing's, Fisher's corpus of poetry is massive and spread among many dozens of pamphlets and small-press publications. Like Iain Sinclair's *Lud Heat* (1975), *Place* is fixed on a particular patch of London and constitutes a data-rich, open field poem indebted to Olson and, more urgently, to Mottram's presentation of Olsonian poetics and emphasis on the importance of research in open field composition. But unlike Cobbing's immense but discontinuous series of publications or Sinclair's singular volume, Fisher's *Place* is a multipart project whose parts often shifted places and metamorphosed. It wasn't published as a whole until 2005, several decades after its writing, and even that edition of *Place* does not constitute a "complete" edition, with Fisher's near decade-long process of composition, revision, and recombination forestalling anything like a definitive, static text. As a poet and visual artist, Fisher has consistently sought to display the process and remnants of a work's construction within the work itself. He has worked in conceptual forms at certain points in his career, but *Place* is processual rather than procedural; it does not unfold according to a predetermined rule or design but rather shapes itself according to the demands of the experiences and materials that underlie the project's evolving scope.

Place was composed between 1971 and 1978 and grew out of Fisher's art and writing activities in London, especially his involvement in the *Fluxus*-inspired *Fluxshoe* performance collective in 1972 and 1973. It was published in four major parts – *Place* (1974), *Stane* (1977), *Becoming* (1978), and *Unpolished Mirrors* (1985) – plus the shorter pamphlet *Eros: Father: Pattern* (1980), but additional sections appeared along the way, and several pieces were eventually subsumed into other sections or refitted for different purposes. Robert Hampson tells us that "the sets that constitute each book were shuffled, re-shuffled, cut into each other to lay bare the constant re-presentation and re-vision of the work, the work as praxis not object, the notion of 'open-field composition' (deriving from Olson) combining with the desire to de-mystify the process of composition."[87] In a prose note published well after the writing of *Place*, Fisher clarifies the importance of praxis, introducing a concept he calls "the complexity manifold" as a gathering of "the aesthetics at all levels and all functions of a poet's production, both consciousness and product." This manifold is "responsible for what is gathered and held, ordered, disrupted, retained, and lost. Poetics, in this sense, spins across the epistemological boundaries of scale and energy."[88] *Place* is an extended textual gathering of materials concerning the Borough of Lambeth, south of the Thames. Fisher, who lived in this area throughout the period of composition, explores its history, geology, and infrastructure, and the long poem constitutes a manifold of research and response. The first book of *Place* begins by describing Fisher's processual practice:

> this set takes the form of an essay
> in fragments   that brought together
>   bring about their own symmetry
> their own chaos
>
> any poetry within this essay is for me inseparable
> from the flow   so that
> it seemed best not to tear away from the commonplace.[89]

As Fisher assays to get beneath and behind present-day Lambeth, he follows its marked streets and unmarked paths, examines its landmarks and the events that they mark, and traces its long history of occupation – from pre-Roman tribes through his own moment.

Many of the pages of *Place* present his research notes, historical annotations shot through with stark lyricism:

> 457 ad. Britons defeated at Crayford, 4000 dead.
> London deserted, the tides eat the Causeway.
> London gone like Tadmor, Tyre & Carthage.[90]

The object of such presentations is partly to record an effort of discovery – one that is concretized in the lists of "resources" accompanying each volume – and partly to contextualize the extended critique of modern capitalism and industry that occupies Fisher throughout. Instead of understanding and coexisting within the environment, Fisher's urbanites are alienated from the places where they live, and he wants to bring to the surface a city hidden beneath modernity's wastes: "London   junction of roads   energies / pathways & leys."[91] Rather than a city-space produced and regulated by bureaucracy and the needs of capital, Fisher conceives of an urban locale that comprises an "imaginary map of energies" and that is responsive to deeper patterns and cycles of human civilization that are "essentially directed by earth."[92]

A good deal of *Place* is given over to describing the paths and places that Fisher comes upon, mapping the routes of underground rivers or sewer systems, listing his itinerary while he tracks the routes taken by others, and speculating on the connections between different strata of London's history. Along the way, there are assorted found texts, diagrams, inserted pieces of the archive, instructions about stone cutting, a prose letter to two friends about the "rising damp" problem in their house,[93] a poem in the voice of Samuel Matthews (a historical recluse who was murdered in Dulwich Wood in 1802), and a copy of a 1975 letter Fisher wrote to the "London Borough of Lambeth" including a commentary on the importance of ley lines, a report of "a large unidentified flying object" "seen today over Coldharbour Lane," and a call to cease demolishing houses on that road.[94] Additionally, *Place* displays Fisher's own network of literary influences and interlocutors. There are letters to Mottram, Sinclair, Robert Duncan, and Chris Torrance; a poem for Pound and then another one on the occasion of his death; a translation of Lorca dedicated to Jack Spicer; several poems after Louis Zukofsky and one after Georges Bataille; and homages to MacDiarmid, Baudelaire, and Olson. Indeed, part of the charge for Fisher is to differentiate his own long place poem from those of his American exemplars:

> to list is not enough
>
> listings have been made

fishers' ships out of Gloucester
sediments in Paterson.[95]

Such a desire to differentiate *Place* from Olson's *The Maximus Poems* and Williams's *Paterson* partly explains the shifts that occur as the project evolves.

This "change in priorities," announced in *Becoming*, is fully realized in *Unpolished Mirrors*.[96] Here, Fisher continues the locodescriptive and annotative style of the earlier books, but also introduces a more prophetic and visionary voice derived from William Blake – an increasingly central figure for Fisher – and most often placed in the mouths of several avatars whose monologues dominate *Place*'s final volume. Moving back and forth across London's history, touching down repeatedly at moments of great destruction – the Great Fire of 1666 and the Blitz in 1940 and 1941 – *Unpolished Mirrors* features several archetypal or historical characters – the artist, the gardener, the doll, Christopher Wren, Watling – who model different positions in relation to art, life, and society. The role of the antagonist is played by Watling, the bourgeois noble Londoner and self-proclaimed "perpetrator of city life as oppression."[97] Even as *Place* becomes increasingly allegorical, any didacticism is leavened by its nonteleological construction and by the lightness achieved by the loose juxtapositions spread over a huge textual space. *Place* succeeds as the ardent record of a massive exploratory project, with individual poems and passages gaining resonance because of their proximity and because of the sheer constructive force that holds them together: "this poem clings together on its preparation."[98] When such constructive force wanes, the project must be left behind, as in "Wren's monologue," which contains the poem's apotheosis:

> I have been the historian too long
>   immersed in wreckage hurled at my feet
> stay   try to awaken
>   strength in the fragments.[99]

Here, Fisher's renunciation of his own immersive strategy in *Place* is immediately countermanded. He expresses a wish to be done with the poem that he has been writing, but then a voice tells him to "stay." "Awaken[ing] / strength in the fragments" encapsulates Fisher's method, but it is also a late rescoring of modernist epic fragmentariness, as seen in Eliot's *The Waste Land* and Pound's *Cantos*.

As we have seen throughout this chapter, writers associated with the Revival were keen to revisit American and European modernism so as to reimagine its contours within their own contexts. They also strove to reroute a tradition of English poetry that had, to their minds, too easily sidestepped the implications of modernist innovations. The Revival had, to be sure, major drawbacks, the central one being the paucity of women and black poets within its circles. It is, nevertheless, a significant part of the story of poetry in Britain since 1945, although its full history remains to be written. The sheer volume of work produced by the writers touched upon in this chapter – not to mention the work of myriad poets I have not had space to discuss – is formidable, and some of it remains in far-flung editions. The intense demands that it places upon readers means that it will always have a somewhat limited audience, and so it is no surprise that we have a much shakier account of the British Poetry Revival than we do of, say, the very different poetic revival happening simultaneously in Northern Ireland. A good deal of sorting out remains to be done: basic acts of exegesis are needed for many texts, and the full arcs of many poets' oeuvres remain largely unaddressed. Even compiling a bibliography of a poet's work and then actually laying hands on the work can be a hefty task, especially for audiences outside the Revival's origin-places, readers without access to a large research library, or those not in possession of, as John Wilkinson quips, "patience, money and the right contacts."[100] This has, in the past, made the study of this work something of an insider's game, insinuating an elitism of access that cuts strongly against the generally leftist politics of many Revival poets. This problem has lessened in a digital age. But a different problem remains: the polemics of the past several decades have much too bluntly cleaved the entirety of poetic production into two camps: the establishment versus the experimental. One of the effects of this polarization is that too little energy has been devoted to a patient consideration of the precise stakes of the projects that have been undertaken. Throughout this book, I mainly discuss poetry across spectra of aesthetics and geography relationally in hopes of presenting as capacious a picture as possible. In the next chapter, however, I zero in on a body of Northern Irish poetry that is coeval with an extended political and military struggle that concerned, among other matters, the geographical definition of Britain itself, and which it seems best to approach from within its own unique context.

Chapter 5

The North

By devoting a separate chapter to the body of poetry connected with the outbreak of violence in Derry in October 1968 and the ensuing thirty-year period of strife known as "the Troubles," I do not mean to imply that Northern Irish poetry is entirely self-contained. The poets at the core of this formation – Seamus Heaney, Michael Longley, Derek Mahon, John Montague, Paul Muldoon, Tom Paulin, Medbh McGuckian, and Ciaran Carson – certainly constitute a closely linked community akin to those that featured in previous chapters, but they also have deep ties with British, American, and European poets. I also do not intend this chapter to offer a comprehensive account of Northern Irish poetry, nor, of course, of post-Yeatsian poetry from the Irish Republic. My aim, rather, is to register and comprehend the significance of poetry from Northern Ireland in relation to developing canons of contemporary poetry in the British Isles.[1] Northern Irish poets have become increasingly well known in Britain and the United States since the 1970s, and the massive size of Heaney's British readership alone speaks to the centrality of Northern Irish poets to the concerns of this book. Heaney was, along with Ted Hughes, by far the best-selling poet in the U.K. for the last decades of the twentieth century; and for periods in the 1990s and 2000s, Heaney's books accounted for two thirds of all contemporary poetry volumes sold in Britain.[2]

The importance of the Troubles within the postwar history of Britain makes it imperative to understand Northern Irish poetry within a larger historical context, and the complexity of that history shapes my decision to consider it in a discrete chapter. As part of the treaty that ended the Anglo-Irish War (1919–1921), the island of Ireland was partitioned into two entities. The Irish Free State (Éire) made up the bulk of the island and became politically independent from Great Britain (it remained for a time a dominion of the British Empire but left the Commonwealth in 1937 and became the Republic of Ireland). Northern Ireland, consisting of six counties in the northeast part of the island (Fermanagh, Armagh, Antrim, Down, Tyrone, and Londonderry), remained part of Britain. The historical province of Ulster included an additional three counties (Monaghan, Donegal, and Cavan) that were incorporated into the Irish Free State. Because of historical patterns of English settlement in the North, especially during the plantation of Ulster throughout the seventeenth century, Ulster is the heart of unionism and Protestantism in Ireland. Unionists in the early twentieth century were prepared go to any length to demonstrate their loyalty to the British crown, which included taking up arms not only against Irish nationalist and Republican factions but also against Britain itself in order to prevent their absorption into an Irish Free State that they considered to be antipathetic to their interests and in thrall to the Roman Catholic Church. Keeping Northern Ireland within Great Britain became a necessary condition not only of peace between Ireland and Britain but also of the political independence of the Irish Free State.

Protestants were a minority population island-wide but a slight majority in the North, and much of the history of Northern Ireland since its founding has been one of constructed inequality as Protestant majorities sought to maintain political and economic hegemony. However, as more and more Northern Catholics benefitted from increased opportunities available within the postwar welfare state, there was a push for reforms, and groups in Belfast and Derry took cues from civil rights movements in Europe and the United States. The Northern Irish Civil Rights Association (NICRA) was formed in 1967, campaigning for a reform of voting policies, an end to electoral gerrymandering, changes in public housing and public employment processes, the repeal of the Special Powers Act, and the disbanding of the Ulster Special Constabulary (the B-Specials), a police reserve force that was entirely Protestant and considered by many Catholics to be discriminatory.

Mapped onto this sectarian conflict is a colonial one. Since partition in 1921, Irish Nationalists and Republicans in the North and South have tended to see the British presence in Northern Ireland as a form of colonialism, and during the Troubles, the Irish Republican Army expended at least as much energy trying to get the "Brits Out" as they did wreaking havoc on Protestant life in the North. For Nationalists, the geographical unit is equivalent to the political one, and it was only with the 1998 Good Friday Agreement, the culmination of the Northern Irish peace process that brought an end to the Troubles, that the Irish government removed the provisions from its Constitution that claimed the entire island as its territory. The political struggle for Irish independence has always been couched in larger questions of ethnic and cultural identity, the status of the English and Irish languages within Ireland, and the longer history of British imposition. In this way, poets like Heaney and Montague can be thought of alongside late colonial and postcolonial writers like Brathwaite and Walcott, and the issues that dominate Northern Irish poetry in the period resemble those examined in Chapter 2. Recentering a discrete Irish cultural heritage has long been a project of modern Irish literature, and poets writing during the Troubles continued this task, adapting their projects to the distinct conditions of Ulster.

It is also important to consider the economic issues underlying the political and sectarian strife. The Northern Irish economy depends greatly on the British economy, and so when the British economy faltered, as it did many times after WWII, Northern Ireland was affected greatly (as was the Republic of Ireland, but in different ways). Linen production and shipbuilding propelled Ulster and especially Belfast into a position of economic strength in the nineteenth and early twentieth centuries (the *Titanic* was built in a Belfast shipyard). But as these industries declined, the economic deterioration was precipitous. There weren't enough jobs to go around, and because Unionists dominated governments, tended to be better educated, were able to acquire more skills, and had more connections, most of the decent jobs (by design and by manufactured "coincidence") went to Protestants. There were, then, significant class issues involved, although socioeconomic inequalities were often overshadowed by political and historical explanations for the violence. It isn't a coincidence that many of the most extreme views – Republican and Loyalist – tend to be found among the lowest economic classes, who have borne the brunt of the violence and turmoil.

The Troubles began, according to many, in October 1968 after police clashed with marchers in Derry who were protesting discriminatory public housing policies. In January of the following year, the People's Democracy (a civil rights group made up mainly of students, and somewhat more radical than the NICRA) led a protest march from Belfast to Derry, which was attacked by Loyalists at Burntollet Bridge. Major clashes ensued several months later between residents of a Catholic area in Derry and the Royal Ulster Constabulary during what has come to be known as the Battle of the Bogside. British Army troops entered Derry in August 1969 to put down the fighting. They initially had the support of many Catholics, who hoped that the army would be a source of protection against what was seen as a biased police force. However, the official formation of the Provisional Irish Republican Army (PIRA) added another paramilitary force to the streets, and continuing clashes increased tensions over the next several years. The institution of internment without trial in August 1971 and, more intensely and horrifically, the deaths of fourteen unarmed civilians at the hands of an elite British parachute regiment during a civil rights march on January 30th, 1972 (an event known as Bloody Sunday), made it utterly clear that civil order had broken down. In March 1972, the government at Westminster prorogued the Northern Irish government and ruled the province directly, a situation that continued (apart from a brief stretch in 1974) until power was devolved to a cross-party Northern Irish Assembly as part of the historic Good Friday Agreement.[3]

The period between 1971 and 1976 was the deadliest of the Troubles, with more than 1,700 deaths in that period (compared to more than 3,600 for the entire stretch from 1968 to 2001). By this point, the literary renaissance that had started before the outbreak of violence was well established, and Heaney, Mahon, and Longley had each published several volumes and gained significant reputations. After attending Trinity College, Dublin in the late 1950s and early 1960s, Longley and Mahon returned to Belfast, where they were part of an energetic group of young writers that included Heaney, James Simmons, Stewart Parker, and Edna Longley. Philip Hobsbaum became a crucial organizing figure upon his arrival in Belfast, establishing a writing and reading group based on his earlier efforts in London. The legacy of the Belfast Group has been a point of debate among participants, but it clearly was an important space for a number of those involved and especially productive for Heaney. *The Honest Ulsterman,* founded by Simmons in 1968, served as a key outlet for nearly all the poets associated with the Northern Irish renaissance, and Simmons's forceful and provocative editorship assured its centrality within cultural and literary debates. Heaney's first volume, *Death of a Naturalist* (1966), gained wide acclaim, and debut volumes by Mahon (*The Night Crossing*, 1968) and Longley (*No Continuing City*, 1969) were clear signals that a formidable group of poets was emerging. This emergence predated the Troubles but would become inextricably linked to them. It is impossible to say whether the social and political crisis spurred great poetry or if great poetry would have happened anyway. But, however we choose to understand the unlikelihood of so many important poets appearing in such a small place in such a short time, it is certainly the case that the Troubles became a structuring principle for the work and its reception.

As Terence Brown has written, "the Northern Renaissance was a renaissance for a particular kind of poem," and a predilection for the brief, well-made lyric continues to hold, even as Muldoon and Carson have pursued ever more audacious and zany species of well madeness.[4] The open, experimental forms that characterize the British Poetry Revival aren't apparent in this renaissance, but this isn't to suggest that Northern Irish poets simply repeated old forms or spurned innovation. We might say that they have been most interested in experimenting inside the lyric rather than outside its basic structures. Continuing to draw on a Yeatsian inheritance, they have been able to maneuver around within that inheritance more freely than did midcentury Irish poets, mainly because these immediate predecessors – primarily Louis MacNeice, Patrick Kavanagh, and John Hewitt – helped to absorb the pressures of Yeats's legacy and to make its key aspects newly and differently available for later poets. Traditional English lyric genres and strategies were at the heart of the renaissance in the North, but this did not yield standard Movement-style poems. Rather, sound patterns were thickened, rhyme schemes made to absorb the lexis and dialect of English as it is spoken in Northern Ireland, and lyric subgenres skewed so as to accommodate a different range of affective investments, speakerly needs, and cultural scenarios. Torqued by the turmoil in Ulster and shot through with ambivalence, these poems both draw from and rework the traditional storehouse of English poetry.

Such undertakings are keyed to the place and history of Northern Ireland. As we have seen, a great deal of postwar British poetry is resolutely local, exfoliating regional histories, cultures, and geographies. Considering the intense pressures of and on particular places in Northern Ireland, one might similarly expect a great deal of intimately proximal poems, texts that live the Troubles, as Derek Mahon puts it, "bomb by bomb."[5] But while several later poets, primarily Ciaran Carson, formulated a style that managed to render the actualities of life in Troubles-era Belfast, earlier poems about the Troubles tended to offset themselves from the specifics of the conflict. From its start, poets were called upon and, perhaps more importantly, felt themselves to be called upon to respond to the outbreak of violence. This call to act as spokespersons, or to provide artistically minded social commentary, was one that many of them resisted from the start. And so one strategy for writing of the Troubles without writing about them became to dislocate them geographically, historically, or both.

Such dislocations took many shapes. In *North*, the 1975 volume that is the Troubles' central poetic document, Heaney approaches contemporary Northern Ireland via Iron Age "bog bodies" found preserved in Scandinavian bogs. In one of the most famous poems of the period, "A Disused Shed in Co. Wexford," Mahon thinks through issues of violence and historical conflict by meditating on a mushroom shed on the grounds of a hotel abandoned during an earlier period of strife, the Anglo-Irish War and Irish Civil War (1919–1923). Longley's most poignant poems take up the Troubles by refracting them through a consideration of World War I and especially of his father's war experience. In *The Rough Field* (1972), a lyric archive of discrete poems, historical quotation, literary sampling, woodcuts, sectarian emblems, familial remembrances, and social critique, Montague presents himself as a spokesperson for his townland (Garvaghey, a transliteration of the Irish *garbh achaidh*, means "rough field") and his nation, but he also positions himself as a returning exile whose cosmopolitan experience – in Paris, New Haven, Berkeley – allows him to gaze like an outsider with an insider's eyes. A number of Muldoon's poems are set, in some fashion, in Troubles-era Belfast, but his most significant and extensive investigations of colonial violence, ethnic strife, and historical enmity take place far from Northern Ireland, and most often in North America, exploring the decimation of Native American populations by English and European settlers. Medbh McGuckian, who wrote her most politically and historically engaged poetry in the years between the 1994 IRA ceasefire and the 1998 Good Friday Agreement (and just after), filters her investigation of the Troubles through the intricately elusive metaphorical and symbolic scrim that is her work's most characteristic feature. For the key poets of the Northern Irish renaissance, then, the Troubles tended to be approached obliquely. Such maneuvers were common both to writers who have spent much of their careers outside Northern Ireland and to those who lived the Troubles bomb by bomb.

Although overshadowed by Heaney, Michael Longley is in many ways the fulcrum of contemporary Northern Irish poetry. Remaining in Northern Ireland for his entire career and a key figure at the Arts Council from the early 1970s through the early 1990s, Longley has been a central presence in Belfast for the last half century. The cumulative dedications in his *Collected Poems* index the Northern Irish literary and cultural world.[6] Longley is the great miniaturist of twentieth-century Irish poetry, and his tightly caulked stanzas tend in four directions. Long married to Edna Longley, Northern Ireland's most formidable literary and cultural critic, Michael Longley has produced many frank and moving poems about love, sex, and marriage. Second, beginning with *No Continuing City* and continuing through his most recent books, Longley's work comprises a lyric field guide of his home places and especially of Carrigskeewaun, a townland in County Mayo where he has long had a cottage. His miniatures offer a different kind of ecological lyric than does Heaney's famous poetry of digging and agriculture, and if, as we will see, Heaney's typical speaker in his 1960s and 1970s poetry resembles an archaeologist or anthropologist, then Longley's is a birdwatcher and naturalist (among many others, see "Carrigskeewaun," "Autumn Lady's Tresses," "The Comber," and "The Beech Tree"). Third, he returns repeatedly to the classics, reconstructing moments and stories from the Greek and Latin canons – primarily Homer and Ovid – in the form of crystalline lyrics that serve as *romans-a-clé* of his literary circles (see "Remembering the Poets" and "The Group") or oblique commentaries on the Troubles (see "The Butchers" and, especially, "Ceasefire").

Along with his love poems, nature sketches, and classical distillations, Longley's poetry is concentrated in elegies, and it is in this genre that he has produced his most significant work about the Troubles. Most frequently and notably, Longley juxtaposes a consideration of his father's service in World

War I with poems memorializing individuals killed in the North. "Wounds," collected in *An Exploded View* (1973), begins with his father's wartime memories:

> Here are two pictures from my father's head –
> I have kept them like secrets until now.

The first picture captures the patriotism and sectarianism that led many Northern Irish Protestants to enlist:

> First, the Ulster Division at the Somme
> Going over the top with 'Fuck the Pope!'
> 'No Surrender!': a boy about to die,
> Screaming 'Give 'em one for the Shankill!'

The second frames the "London-Scottish padre / Resettling kilts" of the dead after the battle.[7] The poem then turns to his father's own death, a half century later, and memorializes him alongside the more recent dead: "Three teenage soldiers, bellies full of / Bullets and Irish beer, their flies undone"; a child killed accidently by a stray bullet while sleeping ("heavy guns put out / The night-light in a nursery forever"); and a bus conductor shot randomly by a "shivering boy" who "wandered in" to his house, leaving the children and "bewildered wife" of the innocent man he just killed with an atrociously casual apology: "I think 'Sorry Missus' was what he said."

Without additional commentary or reflection, "Wounds" narrates several discrete deaths, forcing them to shed light on each other. They are made equally futile, notwithstanding their quite different circumstances. The supposed glory of the deaths at the Somme is problematized by the soldiers' fierce sectarianism. This sectarianism, fifty years later, is behind the deaths of another set of young British soldiers, who are, this time, unarmed ("their flies undone"), just as the bus conductor is unarmed when he is "shot through the head" and collapses "beside his carpet-slippers." Each death is placed like a totem or keepsake within his father's coffin, who didn't die in battle but whose life has been shaped by his war experience. A variation on Yeats' group elegies, Longley's "Wounds" draws its power from its refusal to frame the deaths its describes. It moves between past-tense narrations of the deaths and present-tense speech acts ("Here are two pictures"; "I bury beside him / Three teenage soldiers") and lets the connections and discordances between the deaths remain unstated. Unlike the Heaneyesque elegist, who continually reflects on and worries over his own position, the typical voice of Longley's elegies relies on epitaphic understatement, as in the portraits that comprise "Wreaths" or the flavor/ flower catalogue that constitutes "The Ice-Cream Man." While in no uncertain terms engaging in sincere acts of poetic remembrance, Longley's elegies underline their own inadequacies as memorials. He is skeptical of the power of religious doctrine or belief to make sense of the killings (see especially the second two "Wreaths": "The Greengrocer" and "The Linen Workers"), and his work of the 1970s is marked by a powerfully subtle anguish, one that implicitly distrusts poetry's need to make sense of the violence and death that it must nonetheless continue to register.

In the first part of his early poem "Letters," titled "To Three Irish Poets" and addressed to Simmons, Mahon, and Heaney, Longley includes a subtly wry comment on the proliferation of Troubles poetry:

> Now every lost bedraggled field
> Like a mythopoeic bog unfolds
> Its gelignite and dumdums.[8]

Ironically collapsing three quite different versions of the same patch of ground (the natural, the mythic, and the militarized), Longley also collapses several modes of writing about place. At the same time, he offers a sidewise glance at the many "mythopoeic" methods at work in postwar poetry. The tendency of writers across the British Isles to reenchant space can be read as a symptom of the historical condition of decolonization, or as a type of critical nostalgia that aims to rearticulate an idealized version of a pastoral Britain that it both knows never quite existed and understands as forever gone. But spinning together the actual ground and the place-made-myth within the context of violence in Ulster – *gelignite* is a material used for bombs and *dumdums* are types of bullets – faces a different dilemma: one that has to consider current crisis within its intertwining of place, history, and myth. This dilemma, though powerfully captured by Longley in this passage, is not one that has preoccupied him throughout his career. It is, however, at the heart of Heaney's work of the period.

Heaney's early poetry – from *Death of a Naturalist* (1966) through *Field Work* (1979) and *Station Island* (1984) – comprises an increasingly complex series of metaphorical overlays. From "Digging," the first poem of his first volume and one of his signature pieces, through the place-name, or *dinnseanchas*, poems in *Wintering Out* ("Anahorish," "Toome," and "Broagh"), Heaney repeatedly attempts to orchestrate discrete realms of knowledge and experience so that they speak in each other's terms. History – personal, familial, cultural – is made cognate with the natural and animal world, which is made cognate with the complex linguistic makeup of Ulster English and the tradition of Irish literature in English, which is made cognate with the agricultural labor that defined Heaney's early life at Mossbawn, the family farm in County Derry.

From the beginning, the thick sonorities and compounded rhythms of his texts aimed at a near-onomatopoeic alignment of sound and sense (see "Death of a Naturalist" and "Churning Day" for early examples). Heaney's poems are constitutively inweaving or inwoven (to borrow and adapt Christopher Ricks's famous and ceaselessly useful formulation).[9] They seek to resolve one form of life into another: the personal into the cultural, the religious into the aesthetic, the environmental into the psychological, the political into the mythical. The poem is the mechanism of alignment between the various attempted resolutions: "I rhyme / To see myself, to set the darkness echoing."[10] Beginning with *Wintering Out*, this project homed in on the relation of language to place, what he calls "bedding the locale / in the utterance."[11] Heaney charges his excavational imagination to sound out the multiple strands of his linguistic inheritance – English, Anglo-Irish, Ulster Scots-Irish, Irish Gaelic, Anglo-Saxon, Norse – in order to draw them into his own thickening "word-hoard." Such a project is extended in *North* as linguistics, anthropology, archaeology, and poetics are joined in a single quest for "antediluvian lore" that pushes "back / through dictions," from "Elizabethan canopies" through "Norman devices" and "ivied latins / of churchmen" to the "scop's / twang."[12] Throughout his work of the 1970s, this mode doubles as a way to resist the hegemony of a narrow view of what constitutes proper English and its literary tradition, as he writes in "Singing School": "Ulster was British, but with no rights on / The English lyric."[13] The short-lined quatrains that litter *Wintering Out* and *North* revel starkly in the language's philological many-mindedness.

Heaney's complexly centripetal stance is, in many ways, at the center of both the very large body of praise and the smaller – though vociferous – body of criticism that has attended his work. More than anything else, he wants to provide a form of unity, not only connecting varieties of experience but also articulating them within each other's terms. Such a tendency toward chiasmic enfolding manifests at every level of his poetry, and examples of the self-swallowing phrase, figure, or pattern run like an ore-seam through his books: "the flowerbeds / Bends low"; "Islands riding themselves out into the fog."[14] At its worst, Heaney's inweaving imagination produces well-wrought species of oversimplification – poems that too easily accept and exploit the conflation of the binary of England and Ireland with the conflation of male and female or that are too quick to read culture and language in the terms of nature and landscape. At its best, it makes for poems that draw together, via dense sound and lush metaphor, disparate areas of life into a momentary but – to go Heaney-ish for a moment – gravid relation.

The start of the Troubles shifted the conditions and prerogatives for writers in the North. Because of his early and swiftly growing fame, as well as his tendency to position poetry, as he puts it in one of his most famous essays, "Feeling Into Words" (1974), as a "revelation of the self to the self," the "restoration of the culture to itself," Heaney felt especially compelled to consider the role of poetry amid social turmoil and political violence.[15] In the same essay, he concretizes this shift: "from that moment ["summer of 1969"] the problems of poetry moved from being simply a matter of achieving the satisfactory verbal icon to being a search for images and symbols adequate to our predicament."[16] At about the same time, Heaney happened upon P.V. Glob's *The Bog People: Iron-Age Man Preserved* (1965), which describes the discovery of various bodies found preserved in peat bogs in Northern Europe, mainly in Scandinavia, but also in Ireland and the United Kingdom. The book contains evocative and detailed accounts of the bodies and the conditions of their discovery, speculative overviews of Iron Age culture, and hauntingly vivid images of the bodies that Glob, an archaeologist, had studied. In the images of these bodies, mostly victims of murder and, perhaps, ritual sacrifice, Heaney hit upon a potential set of adequate "images and symbols" through which to consider the situation in contemporary Northern Ireland. He first wrote "The Tollund Man," which was included in *Wintering Out* (1972), and then produced a series of "bog body poems" – "Bog Queen," "The Grauballe Man," "Punishment," and "Strange Fruit" – that are at the center of *North*.

The story of *North* is well known, and I will rehearse the history of its reception only very briefly here.[17] *North* remains Heaney's most polarizing volume, but it has generally been polarized upon Heaney's own terms: the "adequacy" of its chosen "images and symbols" to render the trauma of the Troubles. For many readers, it is his most significant volume, providing what Yeats calls, in a phrase Heaney adapts, "befitting emblems of adversity."[18] For others, Heaney's use of the preserved Iron Age bodies – or, to be more precise, images of those bodies – to symbolize sectarianism and colonialism in Northern Ireland is exploitative or oversimplified. Heaney was seen to fetishize, and even glamorize, violence and death. For such critics, history is flattened out, made into an endless cycle of brutality and murder in order to suit the poet's allegorizing imagination. In addition, the poems depend on a conceptual conflation of land and women that is the most troubling aspect of Heaney's early poetry. Considering the problematic ways in which the bodies in "Bog Queen," "Punishment," and "Strange Fruit" are turned into sexual objects, feminist critiques of Heaney's poetry have tended to gravitate toward *North* as containing some of the most notorious examples of Heaney's regressive gender politics (also see "Ocean's Love to Ireland" and "Act of Union").[19]

Critics who aim to rescue the poems point to Heaney's clear awareness of the licenses that he's taking and to his understanding of his complicit appropriations. Either way, what has been less frequently noticed is the over-arching trajectory of the "bog body" poems as they are arranged in the volume. It is crucial that the four primary poems of the embedded suite – "Bog Queen," "The Grauballe Man," "Punishment," and "Strange Fruit" – are arranged in pre-cisely that order: this sequence enacts the process by which Heaney attempts to find a mode of representation that can hold ethics and aesthetics together.[20] Considering that these are essentially ekphrastic poems – based as they are on the images in Glob's book – we might say that the bog poems sketch a poetics of ethical seeing. Heaney's most powerful tactic is his penchant for transfor-mational figurations: his ability to "describe" via metaphor or sonic play. In the bog poems, the descriptions of the bodies are in many instances figurative from the start. This approach quite easily leads to a kind of aesthetic objectification, and in the first poem in the sequence, "Bog Queen," Heaney allows himself to speak in the voice of one of the earliest discovered bog bodies, a female corpse found in County Down in 1781. He grants himself access to the entirety of her history and interiority, claims knowledge of the long period between her Iron Age death and her eighteenth-century "resurrection," and is able to both see the body and see into it – the poet is voyeur and anatomist. The "bog queen" is repeatedly positioned as a passive sexual object or as a figurative womb of the earth. The turfcutter who discovers her corpse repeats her original death and burial. She is then violated another time when a "peer's wife" bribes the turfcutter to dig her up, and the poem ends with her rising again from the bog. Her hair mutates into a "slimy birth-cord / of bog" and she is "reborn" piece by piece: "hacked bone, skull-ware, / frayed stitches."[21] This corpse blazon reen-acts the bog queen's original death in multiple ways and, combined with the overt sexualization of the bog queen and the fact that her imagined voice mir-rors exactly Heaney's usual lyric register, makes for a deeply problematic poem that never quite moves beyond aesthetic objectification.

As though realizing "Bog Queen['s]" failings, Heaney takes a different tack in "The Grauballe Man." Instead of speaking as the bog body (albeit in a voice that sounds like Heaney's), "The Grauballe Man" features a speaker who looks at but can't see into the corpse. As though to repent for the sins of the previous poem, the speaker remains on the surface of the body (and of the picture of the body), figuratively describing its vivid features but refraining from speak-ing as the body or allowing himself knowledge of its history. This is certainly another kind of objectification, but the speaker's refusal to *see into* the body (or its psyche) does seem to be an advance from the previous poem. The speaker is much more self-aware about his own tactics of representation and appropri-ation. He makes explicit that he is working from a memory of a photograph of the body, which now "lies / perfected in my memory."[22] The double valence of *lies*, dangling off the edge of the line to emphasize its shiftiness (a maneuver that Heaney repeats from the poem's first stanza), suggests the mediated and fabricated nature of the poem's representation, a self-reflexivity that is amplified in its final, complex stanzas.

The image of the bog body, lying "perfected" in memory, is then made to hang "in the scales / with beauty and atrocity."[23] The Grauballe man's violent death is figuratively repeated (he is "hung"), but the poem then moves beyond simply recapitulating the death (one of the faults of "Bog Queen"). Heaney triangulates three different and, frankly, incompatible images as he tries to balance "beauty and atrocity": the image of the Grauballe man (and, by extension, the poem "The Grauballe Man" that recreates this image); the famous Roman marble, "The Dying Gaul"; and "the actual weight / of each hooded victim, / slashed and dumped."[24] The poem's conclusion is a double move: it aims to grapple with the ethical implications of its own acts of radical seeing and also to register the continuing inadequacy of its search for "images and symbols" by which to understand violence in Northern Ireland. That is to say that while its self-awareness is an improvement over "Bog Queen," this precise self-awareness leads to the final unbalancing that occurs at the poem's end. In trying to balance "beauty and atrocity," the poem compares the bog body first to the Dying Gaul, and then to "actual" but anonymous victims of, presumably, the violence of the Troubles. So instead of two images balancing each other, we have three images that remain significantly unbalanced in the poem's scale pans. If "The Grauballe Man" realizes the problem implicit in "Bog Queen" and begins to account for it by changing its own strategy of representation, then its conclusion – a scuttling of the poem's figural scale – acknowledges the poet's need to renovate his vision once again.

The body described in the next poem, "Punishment," was, like the Grauballe man, discovered in 1952. Unlike the Grauballe man, who was found in Denmark, the so-called Windeby girl was discovered in Northern Germany (it was later determined that the Windeby girl was actually a young boy, information that wasn't available when Heaney wrote the poem). In certain ways, this is the most problematic poem of the bunch, and it has been subject to the most heated criticism, mainly concerning the poem's gender politics. The deeply objectifying gaze of "Bog Queen" appears in a different guise here. Instead of speaking for the bog body, Heaney assumes a third-person stance, but unlike "The Grauballe Man['s]" objective third-person narration, the speaker in "Punishment" has a good deal of omniscience. The figuration of the bog girl is deeply, uncomfortably sexualized, and the accouterments of her death, which remain on her corpse, are grotesquely reimagined as marriage totems.

As the speaker intensifies his troublesome speculations about the girl's sexual history and the possible reason for her murder, he moves from talking about her to talking to her, from metaphorical description to direct address. The poet's gaze careens between objectification of the girl and self-accusation: he calls her his "poor scapegoat" and himself an "artful voyeur" of her corpse.[25] That these descriptions appear as part of an address to her makes them seem like apologies or confessions, a transposition of the kind of self-questioning that drives the final stanzas of "The Grauballe Man." And indeed, the final two stanzas of "Punishment" repeat the earlier poem's direct comparison between the bog bodies and contemporary victims of violence. Without any warning, the self-lacerating speaker – who has earlier admitted that he would have partaken of the bog girl's punishment by casting "the stones of silence" – transforms the Iron Age victim into a contemporary Northern Irish Catholic girl who is punished in a different way. The speaker confesses that he has "stood dumb" when the girl was "cauled in tar" and left weeping "by the railings," going on to admit that he would

> connive
> in civilized outrage
> yet understand the exact
> and tribal, intimate revenge.

During the Troubles, young Catholic girls were publically shamed and violated in such ways as a punishment for dating British soldiers, an act understood to be a betrayal of the community. The speaker again admits his own failures to act against such violence, and, if nothing else, his difficult honesty keeps the poem from collapsing into an ethical quagmire. But redressing these failings is not within this poem's reach, and so Heaney must again revamp his mode of seeing and, thus, his basic strategies of representation.

"Strange Fruit" both fulfills and wrecks the four-poem sequence, and its importance must be considered on these dual grounds. Reseeing the Windeby girl and focusing on an image of the body's head that appears in Glob's book, "Strange Fruit" undertakes to construct a more ethically viable representation of the girl. If the inadequacy of "Punishment" is that it collapses the distance between the bog body and the contemporary Northern Irish girl who appears in its final stanzas, then "Strange Fruit" is careful to see the image of the head for itself: "Here is the girl's head like an exhumed gourd."[26] Again describing the body by comparing it to a part of nature, we might say that "Strange Fruit" begins by simply repeating Heaney's usual tactic. However, the key to this line doesn't seem to be the nature of the tenor or vehicle of the figure but rather the clear indication that figuration is occurring: "Here is the girl's head *like* an exhumed gourd." The basic figural engine of the bog poems is metaphor, not simile, and while there are several similes scattered throughout, Heaney's choice to begin "Strange Fruit" with a sentence that simply lays out a simile is significant. It allows for the head of the girl to appear on its own terms before it is placed in different ones. This pattern is repeated in descriptions of the girl's nose and eyeholes. Heaney is attempting a new kind of seeing here, one that recognizes that he is looking at an image of a long-dead corpse that is now a museum object (it is described as "an exhibition").

The shift is most profound in the poem's final lines, but before I turn to them, I want to suggest several ways in which "Strange Fruit" is also a deeply disruptive text that undermines those that come before it. Most noticeably, the poem adopts a different form from the narrow quatrain that is the preferred stanza-shape for the bog poems. An unrhymed sonnet in loose pentameter, "Strange Fruit" forces a significant readerly adjustment: instead of burrowing down the page using the spade-like quatrain stanzas, our pace slows, an effect that is amplified by the preponderance of end-stopped lines in the octave. At the turn of the sonnet, the poet drastically changes his view. Looking away from the girl's head (or the picture of it), Heaney introduces another figure from ancient history at the start of the sestet:

> Diodorus Siculus confessed
> His gradual ease among the likes of this:
> Murdered, forgotten, nameless, terrible
> Beheaded girl, outstaring axe
> And beatification, outstaring
> What had begun to feel like reverence.

Diodorus Siculus was a Greek historian who travelled widely throughout the Mediterranean and wrote a forty-volume world history, fifteen of which survive. This sudden turn to a seemingly arbitrary figure is quite unlike the earlier classical reference in "The Grauballe Man," whose mention of the Dying Gaul is relevant because one of the images in Glob's volume eerily resembles the pose and contour of the Roman marble. In any case, the reference to the Greek historian seems primarily to be a well-placed deflection or to provide a moment of pause before the speaker turns back to the girl and constructs the most astonishing speculative moment of the entire volume.

Offering a collage of verb tenses, the poem imagines the moment of the girl's death in such a way as to undo (or multiply) its temporality. The girl is placed firmly in the far past ("murdered, forgotten, nameless") but also in the present moment of two entirely different times: she is "outstaring" both the present instant of her death by axe blow (which is in the far past of the poem) and the present instant of the poem's attempt to beatify her. Recalling the speaker's wish in "The Tollund Man" to "risk blasphemy" and consecrate the bog where the body was found as a holy place, the ending of "Strange Fruit" begins to follow the same path, but then stops.[27] Moving from the progressive to the pluperfect, the poem ends by placing itself in the sort of grammatical unreality that has conditioned the entirety of the bog poems' imaginative charge. The girl is let go: she outstares both her own death and the poem's designs upon her. Of course, her bid for freedom is constructed by the poet, but it is significant that Heaney ends with a moment of nonmastery, especially in an arc of poems in which figural mastery is often assumed.

So, in quite a number of ways, "Strange Fruit" fulfills Heaney's aim to articulate a poetics of ethical seeing: at poem's end, the object – "the girl's head" – outsees its subject. The corpse's profound difference "outstares" the poet's designs upon it, and the speaker is left in a temporal and spiritual lurch. The poem is left undone: it had only "begun to feel like reverence," and both the object of the emotion and its structure founder. This foundering is, as I've suggested, also apparent in other ways, the most crucial of which is Heaney's choice of title. Within the internal logic of the poem, "Strange Fruit" is an apt title – the girl's head is initially compared to a gourd, and then her skin and teeth are compared to prunes. However, Heaney takes his title from a song made famous by Billie Holiday. "Strange Fruit," written and composed by Abel Meeropol (Lewis Allan) and first published in 1937 in a Marxist periodical, is about the lynching of black men in the American South. Like Heaney's bog body poems, Meeropol's poem was sparked by a photograph, and this in part can explain Heaney's appropriation of the title. In another way, however, Heaney's allusive introduction of an entirely different historical context of murder and violence is adamantly not justified. If the project toward which the bog body poems move is the ability to hold different moments of violence next to each other without collapsing them or using one moment to fully explain the other, then Heaney's title upends the progress of the sequence, while the unfolding of the poem itself completes it. The bog body poems are simultaneously compelling and disconcerting, a point that is demonstrated by the large body of criticism that is alternately attracted to and repulsed by them. These poems not only invite attraction and repulsion but also perform a process by which both might intertwine to become the basis of a more ethically attuned stance toward suffering and violence within the depths of history as well as in the mire of our own world.

In retrospect, the keenest critique of Heaney's *North* appeared, anachronistically, in the same year. Derek Mahon's *The Snow Party* was also published in 1975, and it contains a number of his most well-known poems, many of which express deep skepticism about a poet's public role. "The Last of the Fire Kings" is most forthright in this regard: the speaker claims to be "through with history," finished with the "barbarous cycle" in which he is subject to the "fire-loving / People" who expect him to agree to his own sacrificial death in order to "release them / From the ancient curse."[28] At once an allegory about the Troubles and a poem set in the Belfast of the Troubles, it partially embodies the "place out of time" that the speaker wants to find, and, along with texts such as "The Snow Party," signals Mahon's attempt to locate a place for poetry apart from the urgencies of history.[29]

Mahon, who was raised in a Protestant working-class neighborhood in northern Belfast, has lived the great majority of his life outside Northern Ireland, and his sense of a poet's responsibility to a particular place and culture runs counter to Heaney's and, indeed, to Longley's. Although Heaney positions himself as a kind of exile in his work of the later 1970s, Mahon's entire oeuvre is premised upon a sense of displacement and partial estrangement. The well-known final lines of "Afterlives" give a clear sense of his constitutive bearing within the particular context of the Troubles:

> Perhaps if I'd stayed behind
> And lived it bomb by bomb
> I might have grown up at last
> And learnt what is meant by home.[30]

The slant rhyme on *bomb* and *home* shows the uncanny quality of Mahon's notion of home, while the elegant trimeters demonstrate Mahon's career-long commitment to the metrical richness of the English line. A productive alienation is at the heart of Mahon's poetry and is powerfully evident in "A Disused Shed in Co. Wexford," a meditation on pastness, forgetting and the forgotten, history and its wastegrounds, and obsolescence and decay. After seeking a place "where a thought might grow" and moving through several geographically disparate abandoned sites, the poem settles upon "a disused shed in Co. Wexford, // Deep in the grounds of a burnt-out hotel."[31] It then turns its attention to the "thousand mushrooms [who] crowd to a keyhole" of the shed and who have been "waiting for us in a foetor / Of vegetable sweat since civil war days." Many of the atmospherics from the poem are drawn from J.G. Farrell's novel, *Troubles*, which concentrates on a once-majestic hotel in Wexford destroyed during the Anglo-Irish War, and so Mahon has found a place that is "out of time" in several ways. Like a number of poets writing "about" the Troubles, Mahon displaces his lyric scene.

Over the course of six ten-line, irregularly rhymed stanzas that move between tetrameters and pentameters, Mahon considers the plight of the abandoned mushrooms, but the exact nature of his consideration remains indeterminate. Instead of the insistent metaphorization that characterizes Heaney's bog body poems, Mahon's representation of the mushrooms is both more matter of fact and more audacious. From the moment of their introduction, the mushrooms are animated and humanized, and by the fourth stanza they are a community complete with modes of social stratification (based on which mushrooms are closer to the door and, so, the light). However, the exact nature of the developing allegory remains ambiguous. Mahon continually stitches in details that remind the reader of the fact that he is still talking about mushrooms, but he also so flagrantly humanizes the mushrooms that it seems naïve to mention his dependence on the pathetic fallacy: the poem so fully and blatantly invests in the pathetic fallacy that it seems to come out the other side.

The penultimate stanza begins by describing the shock of exposure, as the mushrooms are discovered after "a half century, without visitors, in the dark." They are awoken by a "flash-bulb firing-squad" who, on the surface, are tourists but who, allegorically, can have multiple references. The presence of numerous cameras may also refer to Northern Ireland during the period of the poem's composition (it was first published in *The Listener* in 1973), when the violence was spiraling out of control and the media descended upon Ulster. At the same time, the descriptions of the mushrooms upon their discovery are somewhat too extreme to apply comfortably to Northern Ireland. The extremity of the mushrooms' abjection suggests that another allegorical scenario may be developing: they are being compared to the victims of a much more murderous regime than any that has ever existed in Northern Ireland. The final stanza clinches this second allegorical turn when it compares the mushrooms to the "lost people of Treblinka and Pompeii." At the moment when the comparison to the Holocaust is stationed with the mention of the Nazi concentration camp, the allegory splits again, comparing the mushrooms also to the Romans who were buried at Pompeii by the eruption of Mount Vesuvius in 79 A.D. Incomparable scenarios are made to substitute for one another. Just as Mahon's dependence on the pathetic fallacy is so blatant as to be at least somewhat self-mocking, so too is his comparison of the mushrooms to survivors of the Nazi death camps so unsuitable as to be offensive and, at the same time, strangely shrewd.

It is as though Mahon sets his allegory to fail. What might have been a well-turned symbolic narrative about Northern Ireland or the iniquities of history generally is rendered untenable when the Holocaust is introduced as a possible target of the allegorical design. In this case, then, the poem has to revert to being primarily about mushrooms: knowing that a reader simply won't accept the suggested comparison between abandoned mushrooms

and Holocaust survivors, Mahon subverts any potential allegorical energy. We
are forced to see the mushrooms on their own terms, unable to responsibly
compare them to anything else. This makes the final six lines of the poem, in
which the mushrooms "seem to" speak directly and ask to be saved, particularly affecting. The collective mushrooms ask the "you" who has found them
not to abandon them again:

> 'Let not the god abandon us
> Who have come so far in darkness and in pain.
> We too had our lives to live.
> You with your light meter and relaxed itinerary,
> Let not our naive labours have been in vain!'

What status does such an appeal have? How might it affect a reader who is no
longer able to read allegorically? Do we simply suspend our belief a bit further
and accept that these mushrooms are nothing but mushrooms and yet still
compel our ethical attention? Or has the entire venture become ridiculous?
What do we make of mushrooms that are able to pun on the name of the tourists' photographic equipment (the "light meter"), turning it into a self-reflexive
description of the metrical patterns of the poem that we're reading? Mahon
presses so hard on a set of lyric conventions – pastoral, allegory, apostrophe –
that they become unreadable as such. And yet the mushrooms' plight and plea
become, if anything, more poignant, even though we are able to read them as
nothing other than themselves.

The internal pressure that Mahon puts on lyric conventions is intensified
by Paul Muldoon, Medbh McGuckian, and Ciaran Carson, poets at the core
of a second generation of the Northern Irish renaissance. If Longley, Heaney,
and Mahon approach the Troubles obliquely, tilting some notional prototype
of well-madeness in order to accommodate the volatile, insoluble knots that
characterize social and political life in the North, then the following generation knocks any such lyric prototypes wholly out of alignment. This is a secondary displacement that rebounds upon the first: the thematic obliquity of
the first generation is adapted as a set of formal tactics and absorbed back into
the interiors of the lyric. Instead of, say, moving on from the well-made poems
of Heaney, Mahon, or Longley and into the open forms that characterize some
British and American innovative poetry, Muldoon, McGuckian, Carson, and
Tom Paulin, among several others, continue to rely on the generic conventions of lyric both as internal shaping forces (the continued prominence of
lyric speaker or subject) and as a set of exoskeletons and architectures.[32] In
the remainder of this chapter, I will move briskly through several poems that
exemplify this shift and then conclude with a turn through Paul Muldoon's

long poem, "The More a Man Has the More a Man Wants." This is a signal Troubles poem of the 1980s as well as a key text in the body of "new narrative" poetry in Britain, a topic to which I will turn in the next chapter.

As the violence of the 1970s continued, and as inmates at Long Kesh Prison (The Maze) took up blanket protests, "dirty" protests, and hunger strikes to resist the conditions of their imprisonment, political solutions in Northern Ireland seemed remote. This sense of an impasse was intensified with the victory of Margaret Thatcher's conservative government in 1979. The death of Bobby Sands and nine other hunger strikers in 1981 can be seen as a retroactive turning point, a moment when the possibility of a political settlement instead of an armed solution began to be, however distantly, glimpsed by key figures in the IRA who saw the value of a huge propaganda victory as well as the potential importance of electoral representation in the British Parliament. On the whole, however, the situation in Northern Ireland remained precarious throughout much of the 1980s and early 1990s, and the poetry of that period is scored with anxieties, uncertainties, and frustrations.

In volumes like *A State of Justice* (1977) and *The Liberty Tree* (1983), Tom Paulin has sought to highlight the progressive, cross-sectarian republicanism that flourished in late-eighteenth-century Ireland, contrasting it with the intractable orthodoxies of contemporary Northern Protestantism that have led to a stilted and insular culture. In "Desertmartin," a small village in Country Londonderry, Paulin leaves no doubt about his sense of cultural diminution:

> Here the Word has withered to a few
> Parched certainties, and the charred stubble
> Tightens like a black belt, a crop of Bibles.[33]

Northern Protestantism in the late twentieth century is, for Paulin, "a culture of twigs and bird-shit" that can do nothing but repeat outworn pieties, "waving a gaudy flag that it loves and curses."[34] Skeptical like Mahon but even more willing to castigate actually existing Protestant society – both the "Big Man" (Ian Paisley) and the "wee people" who follow him – Paulin's lacerating gaze turns upon itself in the final lines of "Off the Back of a Lorry," a poem that catalogues the junk and paraphernalia that constitute a gaudily vacant culture.[35] Inverting the ending of Mahon's "Afterlives," which laments a lost opportunity to learn "what is meant by home," the speaker at the end of "Off the Back of a Lorry" admits his abject dependence on his own empty culture:

> they build a gritty
> sort of prod baroque
> I must return to
> like my own boke.[36]

Paulin's satirical writing takes in the grim particulars of the Troubles and uses those particulars to project allegories about state-sponsored violence and the injustice of politics. His pessimism is clearly seen in "A Just State," a darkly ironic title for a poem that begins with a statement of near disgust – "The children of scaffolds obey the Law" – and ends with a line that puts the scaffold to use: "A hemp noose over a greased trap."[37]

Like Paulin, Ciaran Carson aimed to locate a form "adequate," to return to Heaney's resonant phrase, to the on-the-ground conditions of life in a conflict-torn city. After a long silence following his apprentice volume, *The New Estate* (1976), Carson published two volumes in quick succession that established a new kind of Troubles poetry. In *The Irish for No* (1987) and *Belfast Confetti* (1989), he works exclusively in a long line that is at once tensed and meandering, drawing energy from the oral traditions of Irish storytelling and *craic* (Irish shorthand for pub talk, jokes, songs, and banter) and the reel forms of Irish traditional music. At the same time, Carson takes his home city of Belfast as his primary subject, producing texts dense with the anxious vibrancies of a heavily divided and militarized urban space.

The typical Carson narrator is a kind of Benjaminian *flâneur*, although one for whom explosive violence is always potentially imminent:

> Suddenly as the riot squad moved in, it was raining exclamation marks,
> Nuts, bolts, nails, car-keys. A fount of broken type.[38]

These opening lines of "Belfast Confetti" describe and enact the moment a bomb detonates during a confrontation between paramilitary forces and the police. "Belfast confetti" is a local phrase that refers to the projectiles hurled during such clashes. Here, the "confetti" – nuts, bolts, car-keys – is the shrapnel of the bomb as well. The poem's subject is hemmed in and can't get any purchase on his rearranged surroundings. The explosion that is narrated within the poem becomes enacted in the staged breakdown of language itself. Punctuation collides with cartography, and both systems are confounded: the explosion is "an asterisk on the map."[39] Inverting Heaney's centripetal tendencies, Carson's figural overlays collide and ricochet off each other. It isn't so much that Carson tries and fails to locate adequate symbols for the Troubles but that he unrigs the process of representation from within, showing how the violence exceeds attempts to symbolize and, so, organize it. Instead of the hermeneutic depths of Heaney's bog, we are given the fluctuating surfaces of Carson's city.

"Belfast Confetti" is written in the nine-line, two-stanza form that Carson favors for the short poems in his 1980s volumes. Often, the break between the five-line stanza and the four-line one marks a perspectival shift, moving from a decentered, unmoored subject in the first stanza who is entirely enmeshed in his environment to a more coherent subject in the second who has gotten visual traction on the scene, even if the scene itself remains as chaotic as it was before. These poems generally limn a single moment, compacting all its complex materials into the nine-line mold. Carson alternates his nine-line forms with long, intricate narrative poems – still in very long lines – that move among shifting strata of observation, memory, conversation, and reflection. The typical Carsonian narrator of these longer poems is both intimate and unreliable, and the poems combine *craic* with lyric reflection, as in the opening of "Hamlet":

> As usual, the clock in The Clock Bar was a good few minutes fast:
> A fiction no one really bothered to maintain, unlike the story
> The comrade on my left was telling, which no one knew for
> 　　certain truth:
> *Back in 1922, a sergeant, I forget his name, was shot outside*
> 　　*the National Bank....*[40]

"Hamlet" is a study in precarious time and wayward memory, and it shuttles among the snug confines of pub talk, occasional etymological digressions, and sidelong comments about the "exploded fragments" of Troubles-era Belfast.[41] The story about the soldier killed in 1922 links the late-century Troubles in the North with the troubles that accompanied the creation of the Irish Free State. Meanwhile, the "ghostly" tin can that was heard the night of the soldier's murder, and whose rattling signaled trouble for years afterward, links the poem's interest in the haunting of the present by the past with literature's most famous textual ghost. Bits from Shakespeare's play appear in order to solidify the poem's thematic focus on father-and-son relations, a frequent topic for Carson, as well as to refract the Northern Irish Troubles through Shakespeare's England.

In "Hamlet," as in a number of Carson's long narrative poems, stubs of stories, parables, folk tales, and memories of historical events continually overwrite each other in a palimpsestic unfolding that is replicated by the poem's props and its figural tendencies:

> As someone buys another round, an Allied Irish Banks £10 note
> 　　drowns in
> The slops of the counter; a Guinness stain blooms on the artist's
> 　　impression
> Of the sinking of *The Girona*; a tiny foam hisses round the salamander
> 　　brooch
> Dredged up to show how love and money endure, beyond death and the
> 　　Armada,
> Like the bomb-disposal expert in his suit of salamander-cloth.[42]

Here, representation and figuration slide into and away from each other: a mention of the money soaked in beer draws focus to the image on the money (of a ship sunk during the Spanish Armada in 1588 and whose wreckage has belonged to the Ulster Museum since 1972). This, in turn, leads to an associative slip spurred by the mention of the salamander brooch found in the *Girona's* wreckage: the salamander's legendary affinity for fire becomes the basis for a comparison with the fireproof suit of a "bomb-disposal expert." Such slippages drive Carson's poetry. He uses a compound lyric-narrative style in order to incorporate the particulars of Belfast's history and to show how these particulars are constantly reshaped within individual and communal memory: "We try to piece together the exploded fragments."[43] This patchwork poetics incorporates an incessant sociality in which the encounter between text and reader is made analogous to the continuous dialogue at the pub. Reversing Eliot's image in *The Waste Land* of the pub keeper as the enforcer of time, the ending of "Hamlet" offers one of the most optimistic images in Carson's 1980s volumes:

> The barman's shouts of *time* will be ignored in any case, since time
> Is conversation; it is the hedge that flits incessantly into the present,
> As words blossom from the speakers' mouths, and the flotilla
>   returns to harbour,
> Long after hours.[44]

Conversation itself – its digressions, tangents, confusions, and open-endedness – becomes not an adequate symbol of the Troubles but a necessary practice that counteracts the ideologies and violence dominating this period in Northern Ireland.

Carson's usual speaker in *The Irish For No* and *Belfast Confetti* is either walking the streets of Belfast or sitting in one of its pubs, ceaselessly attentive to exteriors and details from his surroundings. By contrast, Medbh McGuckian's poetry is primarily interested in delineating the complexities of inner life, and her speakers are often positioned at a domestic threshold. This certainly has gender implications, and McGuckian, along with writers such as Eavan Boland, Paula Meehan, Nuala Ní Dhomhnaill, and Eiléan Ní Chuilleanáin, have been creating a distinct form of Irish feminist poetry since the 1970s. McGuckian's work, especially her first four volumes – *The Flower Master* (1982), *Venus and the Rain* (1984), *On Ballycastle Beach* (1988), and *Marconi's Cottage* (1992) – provides an extensive account of the psychological intricacies that attend pregnancy and motherhood, and her attention to the interior life of sex and gender is singular in recent Irish poetry.[45] Her work is well known for its obliquity and hermeticism, and for many early readers, its seeming avoidance of sense and normative syntax was either a deep flaw or a sign of its status as a species of *écriture feminine*, a model of women's writing theorized by several continental philosophers, primarily Luce Irigaray, Julia Kristeva, and Hélène Cixous. The deep resistance of McGuckian's poetry is, in this view, due to its attempt to fashion a writing that inscribes female experience on its own terms rather than within literary and, indeed, linguistic structures that are fundamentally patriarchal. And so the startling figurations and logical leaps that are her work's most characteristic features seek to articulate bodily, affective, and psychological experiences that do not conform to normative, and highly gendered, poetic discourse.

This makes for a poetry that continually turns inward, reflecting on its own conditions as it retells "the story / Of its own provocative fractures."[46] A different kind of inweaving is at work than is the case in Heaney's poetry, and McGuckian's most powerful figures are able to do several things at once. They seem to tell us exactly how to read them while remaining inscrutable at the level of denotative reference. They provide "images and symbols" that are both intensely vivid and extremely difficult to comprehend. They retain the trappings of syntax and grammar while forcing such structures to carry semantic content that is inappropriate to their logic. One can never quite get to ground in McGuckian's poetry, and the kaleidoscopic character of her work is both its most distinctive feature and its most substantial hurdle, a readerly condition that McGuckian depicts again and again, "a waterfall / Unstitching itself down the front stairs."[47] That McGuckian is forthright about her poetry's potentially hazardous obscurity – "My words are traps / Through which you pick your way" – only amplifies its obscurity, cloaking it in an openness that her poetry both offers and denies.[48]

Such seeming privacy or secrecy does not signal a lack of interest in the outer world but rather forces a reconsideration of the public role of poetry by way of its very recalcitrance to shared meanings.[49] It isn't that McGuckian's poetry is opposed to a more recognizably public poetry like Heaney's but that it is dialectically entwined with it. Maintaining a number of familiar lyric conventions and materials but suspending them in an unfamiliar context or estranging them from their usual function, McGuckian is able to project a lyric texture that is deeply uncanny. Her poems are filled with highly symbolic structures, images based on a common lyric stock, and a continual interplay between the always fissile positions of a speakerly "I" and a readerly "you" – that strange and open deictic bind at the heart of lyric writing. But a poem's act of saying rarely yields a coherent said, and the frustration that is an inevitable aspect of her poetry's reception can be read as a substantive if cryptic form of engagement with the actualities of the Troubles. What looks to be deeply apolitical poetry exclusively concerned with the inner fluctuations of the self is, in addition to that, an extensive response to historical conditions and perhaps an argument concerning those conditions, one that operates by way of negation and at a far remove from the particulars of history and politics.

As Carson and McGuckian were publishing their early volumes, Paul Muldoon had already gained a significant reputation on both sides of the Irish Sea and had, by the end of the 1980s, become a more influential figure than Heaney for young poets in Britain and Ireland, even as Heaney's overall cultural and literary clout intensified.[50] Muldoon's virtuosity has been lauded from the beginning, and his early volumes are filled with increasingly dexterous feats of rhyme and wordplay, ever-more-intriguing variations on traditional forms (primarily the sonnet), and an expanding corpus of oddly angled parables, wryly ironic character and animal sketches, and quirky narrative poems. Like McGuckian, Muldoon is generally thought to be a difficult poet, but while the challenge of McGuckian's poetry is utterly immanent, a Muldoon poem is difficult because of some unstated knowledge that lies outside the text. This sometimes becomes a matter of tracking down missing information, references, or obscure allusions whose discovery clears up a poem's opacities. As time went on, this sort of difficulty increased exponentially, and volumes like *Madoc: A Mystery* (1990) and *The Annals of Chile* (1994) can be said to be encyclopedic because this is precisely the tool one needs in order to work through them. However, considering that many of Muldoon's references are specific to his particular life, one quickly realizes that an encyclopedia isn't quite sufficient.

The other sort of difficulty inherent to Muldoon's poetry, and the sort that I'll focus on here, has to do with its incessant narrativity and simultaneous refusal of certain kinds of context or information that would normally be expected in a narrative text. This makes for poems that resemble nothing so much as short lyric stories, but that also contain some hollow or absence that disallows a full sense of narrative completion to emerge. At times, as in "Why Brownlee Left," the title poem of his 1980 volume, the hollow is the central figure of the poem, in this case the farmer Brownlee, who simply vanishes one day while ploughing his fields, leaving his two horses

> Shifting their weight from foot to
> Foot, and gazing into the future.[51]

The unclosed rhyme on "foot to" and "future" enacts Brownlee's unknown fate and foreclosed future. At other times, the narrative is self-contained but premised upon an incredible act of narrativity. In the title poem of *Meeting the British* (1987), two sorts of aporia deflect off of each other. The poem tells of a meeting between Native American chiefs and leaders of the British forces during the French and Indian War (1754–1763) from the perspective of the Native Americans. The speaker describes meeting "General Jeffrey Amherst" and "Colonel Henry Bouquet," who present the Native Americans with gifts. Here is the last of the poem's nine rhymed couplets:

> They gave us six fishhooks
> and two blankets embroidered with smallpox.[52]

The poem presents an act of impossible speaking: a Native American chief voicing a poem in English and at one point "calling out in French," a calling out that is rendered in English. It isn't just that Muldoon composes a dramatic monologue in the voice of an imagined figure from the past. He also writes it in a language that the imagined speaker wouldn't speak (English) and that is really a silent stand-in for another language (French) that the speaker expresses surprise at his ability to speak.

Evincing quite a different sort of self-reflexivity than typifies McGuckian's work, Muldoon here points out the impossible nature of the poem he is delivering. The poem as linguistic artifact is decoupled from the poem as act of lyric speech, and this decoupling is exaggerated by the anachronism stitched into the final line. The one thing that the speaker would not be able to say at the end of the poem, no matter the language, is that the blanket is "embroidered with smallpox." Extant letters between Amherst and Bouquet discuss the possibility of deliberately infecting Native American tribes with smallpox by lacing blankets with it, and massive numbers of Native Americans, having no immunity to the disease, were killed by smallpox in the period. The knowledge of this act of germ warfare is, of course, unknown to the speaker, whereas it seems to be known by Bouquet and Amherst within the poem's diegesis (both of whom cover their noses with lavender-scented handkerchiefs in order to protect themselves). Of course, the information can also be known by Muldoon and his readers. So, it is an impossible speaking on several counts, a seemingly straightforward text about colonial violence and genocide in early America that contains its own undoing. Muldoon's poems most often exist in a space of constitutive between-ness, what one poem calls an "eternal interim."[53] They toggle between the straightforward and the utterly cryptic, and when they approach the Troubles, they tend to collapse the banal and the momentous. Such asymmetrical writing is another response to Heaney's theory of adequation, a rejoinder to the mire of political intransigence and continuing violence. Any kind of writing that might counter the emptiness of political rhetoric and the cynicism of journalism may have to be inappropriate.

In *Improprieties: Politics and Sexuality in Northern Irish Poetry*, Clair Wills argues that such a sense of inappropriateness or impropriety is central to this body of work. Muldoon's most impressively inappropriate text about the Troubles is the long poem that concludes *Quoof* (1983). "The More a Man Has the More a Man Wants," its title referring to a well-known pub song, is a lengthy caper poem – of which Muldoon has written several (see also "Immram," "Madoc: A Mystery," and "The Bangle [Slight Return]") – composed of forty-nine variably rhymed and sporadically metered sonnets. Muldoon has said that its forty-nine stanzas are linked to the forty-nine–part Trickster Cycle of the Winnebago Indians, as depicted in Paul Radin's *The Trickster: A Study in American Indian Mythology* (1956), and the metamorphic, fantastical quality of the Native American trickster authorizes the main character's rambunctious shape shifting. Muldoon's poem revolves around the adventures of a mercenary on the run known as Gallogly, his name a corruption of the Irish word for *young foreign warrior*, who is being pursued both by British security forces and a Native American named Mangas Jones, variously identified as Apache, Mescalero, and Oglala Sioux. The poem begins with Gallogly waking the morning after a romantic encounter and just before the security forces are about to ambush him as he gets out of bed:

> At four in the morning he wakes
> to the yawn of brakes,
> the snore of a diesel engine.
> Gone. All she left
> is a froth of bra and panties.
> The scum of the Seine
> and the Farset.
> Gallogly squats in his own pelt.[54]

After his first escape, Gallogly cuts a convoluted path through Northern Ireland, trying to elude the security forces who will eventually catch up with him. As can be seen in the running together of Belfast and Paris ("the Seine / and the Farset"), the metamorphic logic that governs Gallogly's own shape also underlies the poem's morphing spatiality. Mapping a madcap geography of the Troubles, the poem jumps from place to place in Ulster as it traces the movements of its roving protagonist. A long *aisling* (a dream vision) in the middle of the poem takes Gallogly to America (stanzas 21–36), where he, among other exploits, climbs into the horse in Picasso's *Guernica* at the Metropolitan Museum of Art (stanza 23) and enters a cartoonish underworld bar filled with Irish revolutionary leaders (stanza 31).

Muldoon's ironic use of the *aisling* mode, key to Gaelic literary tradition and a genre that often served to forward a vision of Irish nationalism, is one of the many intertextual frames piled atop his deeply cryptic narrative. In addition to the Winnebago trickster cycle and the *aisling*, the poem mashes in allusions to Robert Louis Stevenson's *Kidnapped: The Adventures of David Balfour* and *Treasure Island*, Heaney's "Personal Helicon," "Broagh," "Blackberry-Picking," and "Punishment," Dante's *Commedia*, Ovid's *Metamorphosis*, Frost's "After Apple-Picking," Stein's "Sacred Emily," Yeats's *Green Helmet and Other Poems*, Elizabeth Bishop's "The Filling Station," and John Montague's *The Rough Field*, as well as to earlier poems in *Quoof* (and there are surely more than have been mentioned here). It also stitches in passages from Thoreau's *Walden*, Shakespeare's *Sonnets*, Huxley's *The Doors of Perception*, Knut Hamsun's *Hunger*, a speech of Winston Churchill's, Carroll's *Alice's Adventures in Wonderland*, Frost's "For Once, Then Something," and Stevenson's *Strange Case of Dr. Jekyll and Mr. Hyde*. Operating simultaneously as an allusion generator and an occasional cento, the poem cuts between parodic modernism and postmodern pastiche in a kind of textual jitter that mirrors Gallogly's haps and mishaps.

There isn't space to detail all of the protagonist's adventures – nor is there general agreement about exactly how those adventures unfold – but over the course of the poem, Gallogly undergoes a number of ordeals and trials. He has a few brief affairs (stanzas 1 and 7), manages several escapes from his pursuers (stanzas 12 and 15), is shot through the chest (stanzas 13 and 14), takes revenge (stanza 19), experiments with hallucinogenic drugs (stanzas 11 and 29), steals several getaway vehicles and plants a bomb in at least one of them (stanzas 5, 7, 9, 40, and 48), turns into the bird-man Sweeney from the medieval Irish text *Buile Suibhne* (stanzas 18 and 20), has his long dream vision, and is captured and imprisoned in the Armagh Jail (stanzas 37–39), from which he may or may not escape at the end (stanzas 42 and 45–46). The poem concludes, seemingly, with Gallogly's death, when he is blown up by a bomb planted at a gas station that explodes in the penultimate sonnet (stanzas 47–49).

Along the way, we hear about the movements of the security forces who are in pursuit of Gallogly as well as various crimes that have, seemingly, little to do with our main character. Throughout, there are also several inconclusive vignettes about Mangas Jones's search for Gallogly (stanzas 2, 10, and 17), and the poem finishes with a more thoroughgoing refusal to conclude, in the form of a one-word ghost fiftieth sonnet that appears after the forty-ninth cryptically addresses the aftermath of the poem's final act of terrorism. The "self-same pump attendant" who appeared earlier pulls clear the mangled body of the terrorist, presumably our protagonist, and listens to his mock last confession, a nearly nonsensical reprisal of several of the poem's more cryptic moments:

> those already-famous last words
> *Moose ... Indian.*
> 'Next of all was the han'.' 'Be Japers.'
> 'The sodgers cordonned-off the area
> wi' what-ye-may-call-it tape.'
> 'Lunimous.' 'They foun' this hairy
> han' wi' a drowneded man's grip
> on a lunimous stone no bigger than a...'
>
> 'Huh.'[55]

As the last of the many grotesquely mangled bodies that appear in the poem, the dying Gallogly may use his final breath to name one of his pursuers, but his words remain inscrutable. The poem's last lines are given over to a conversation between observers of the explosion's aftermath – a kind of chorus or peanut gallery that has appeared once before (stanza 10) – who speak in a scrambled dialect that at various moments can appear as English, American, Scottish, and Northern Irish (*sodgers* in particular has several different dialectal valences). *Japers* is an obsolete word meaning trickster or deceiver, and even when he seems to be in pieces – a point darkly underlined by the reference to Stevenson's *Jekyll and Hyde* – Gallogly's shape shifting continues to seep into every aspect of the text's dynamics. The final conversational shrug is also the poem's ultimate refusal to be a proper or coherent narrative poem or to justify any of its outrageousness. Muldoon's poem is a many-leveled parody to be sure, with Heaney's mode of poetic exemplarity and high seriousness coming in for particular critique. If it occasionally seems to revel in its own forms of negation and grotesquerie, then its exuberant misanthropy also has the value of demonstrating the inadequacy of much of the discourse that had come to characterize poetry's response to worsening conditions in Northern Ireland.

"The More a Man Has the More a Man Wants" also catches and catalogues a number of trends that characterize British poetry in the 1970s and 1980s, ones that I've been tracing in the past three chapters and will continue to examine in the next. Focusing on the particular place of Northern Ireland but scrambling the sense of that place's coherence, Muldoon unplaces or misplaces the kind of place poetry developed by Heaney, Bunting, or Hill. Along with Carson and, in quite a different way, McGuckian, Muldoon reroutes the depth-model of place poetry, with its diggers and endless strata, into a play of disparate surfaces. His commitment to traditional forms is both deep and deeply profane, a kind of wonderfully bad faith best seen in his career-long dependence on and upending of the sonnet. But this same tendency toward extreme formal play – apparent in the massively complex word and rhyme lists that predetermine the unfolding of his long poems of the 1990s ("Incantata," "Yarrow," "Third Epistle to Timothy," and "The Bangle [Slight Return]"), and the kinds of repeating syntactical and sonic motors that generate much of his work in the 2000s – yields a style of quasi-conceptual writing that links him to more explicitly innovative poets in both Britain and North America. Finally, Muldoon's insistent narrativity, his propensity to write poems that resemble small (albeit zany and oblique) stories much more than they do efforts to express or construct a subjectivity, signals the movement toward poetic narrative that characterizes a good deal of British poetry in the last two decades of the twentieth century.

Chapter 6

New Narratives

Considering the cumulative energies of the British Poetry Revival and the Northern Irish Renaissance, poetry in the United Kingdom from the mid-1960s through the 1970s was at a zenith. All the more surprising, then, that Blake Morrison and Andrew Motion describe the two decades prior to the publication of their 1982 anthology, *The Penguin Book of Contemporary British Poetry*, as a "spell of lethargy."[1] To be fair, when Morrison and Motion state that "very little – in England at any rate – seemed to be happening" for "much of the 1960s and 70s," their geographical disclaimer recognizes the intense poetic activity in Northern Ireland.[2] Indeed, one thing that Morrison and Motion get right in their presentation of contemporary British poetry is the centrality of the Northern Irish poets within the late-twentieth-century Anglophone canon. Heaney is quite consciously placed as the anthology's presiding figure, and Longley, Mahon, Paulin, Muldoon, and McGuckian are given substantial room. Of the three narratives that the anthology espouses, its focus on Northern Irish poetry has proved to be the most durable.

The other two central suggestions that they make about the poetry they collect – and, implicitly, about the mainstream of British poetry at the time – have had various degrees of traction. They are right to say that their poets turn away from a focus on the personal or empirical (as in, respectively, Alvarez's and Conquest's versions of postwar poetry) and embrace "ludic and literary self-consciousness" and "metaphor and poetic bizzarrerie," but this claim is at once somewhat too broad and much too thin, even if one puts aside for the moment the large body of important work from the 1970s and 1980s that is quite directly autobiographical.[3] Isolating the poets included in their anthology as unique exemplars of a self-conscious, metaphorically rich poetry misconstrues the previous generations of poets against whom Motion and Morrison set their selection. The most notable purveyors of "poetic bizzarrerie" in the volume are the Martian poets – Craig Raine and Christopher Reid primarily – and Motion and Morrison's emphasis on the period's notable inventiveness is weakened by having to rest upon this limited vein of work. The third trend they spot is a new attention to the "provincial and the working-class" brought

155

by poets such as Douglas Dunn and Tony Harrison, whose "background and upbringing" have set "them at an angle to the cultural establishment."[4] Such an assertion, however, misreads as "new" a feature prominent in British poetry since the midcentury, as earlier chapters have suggested. What does seem new, as Motion and Morrison point out, is that the focus on economic status and social class is conducted in poems that quite deliberately set themselves within "establishment culture" and "adapt and vary its poetic forms for their own ends." Perhaps only in retrospect, the mainstream success of poets like Harrison and Dunn sits strangely against the anthologists' description of them as lynchpins in a new British poetry of "alternative traditions" that resists the values of the mainstream.[5]

Motion and Morrison's anthology has been a lightning rod ever since its appearance, and it has been criticized on nearly every front. Positioning the volume as the successor to Alvarez's 1962 anthology, their choice not to include any poet who was featured there makes for some significant gaps (any book appearing in 1982 and describing itself as an anthology of *contemporary* British poetry that doesn't include Hughes or Hill seems odd indeed). For many reviewers, critics, and readers, its canon is too narrow, too homogenous, and too committed to preserving an enervated mainstream. It includes no black British poets, a limited sampling of poetry by women, and none of the experimental poetry produced within the British Poetry Revival. Motion and Morrison's decision to feature Northern Irish poets was their strongest canonical intervention, but even this had its detractors, not least among the poets themselves. Heaney is given pride of place in the volume: he is the first poet included, his poems are given more space than those of any of the other nineteen poets represented, and Morrison and Motion spend a good part of their introduction discussing him. And to be sure, this anthology both registered and furthered Heaney's reputation in Britain, Ireland, and the United States. However, their positioning of Heaney as the central contemporary *British* poet significantly annoyed him, and he wrote an "Open Letter" in verse protesting his cooptation into a British canon: "be advised / My passport's green. / No glass of ours was ever raised / To toast *The Queen*."[6]

The criticism of the anthology is largely deserved, but its appearance and makeup did help shape British poetry at the end of the century, if primarily by way of resistance or negation. Motion and Morrison were right to suggest that "British poetry is once again undergoing a transition: a body of work has been created which demands, for its appreciation, a reformation of poetic taste."[7] The trouble is that Motion and Morrison ignore a great deal of the work actually indicative of the much broader "transition" that British poetry had been undergoing since the 1960s. And so one significant effect was the appearance of alternative anthologies in its wake. A handful of major anthologies through-out the 1980s and 1990s have Motion and Morrison's book as their implicit or explicit target. Volumes such as Andrew Crozier and Tim Longville's *A Various Art* (1987), Iain Sinclair's *Conductors of Chaos: A Poetry Anthology* (1996), Maggie O'Sullivan's *Out of Everywhere: Linguistically Innovative Poetry by Women in North America and the U.K.* (1996), and Ric Caddel and Peter Quartermain's *Other: British and Irish Poetry Since 1970* (1999) sought to showcase the work of the British Poetry Revival. Others highlighted black British poets or women poets, namely, Jeni Couzyn's *The Bloodaxe Book of Contemporary Women Poets: Eleven British Writers* (1985), Carol Rumens' *Making for the Open: The Chatto Book of Post-Feminist Poetry, 1964–1984* (1985) and *New Women Poets* (1990), James Berry's *News For Babylon: The Chatto Book of West Indian-British Poetry* (1984), and John Muckle's *The New British Poetry, 1968–1988* (1988). Indeed, the central story of British poetry from the late 1970s through the 1990s concerns its increasing openness. As new narratives about Britain are proposed, debated, and lived – about who is and who isn't British; about what Britain is, was, and will be; about Britain as an economic and political unit, and as a cultural and social structure – poetry reflects on them and offers its own set of narratives. These concern the iden-tity of poets and the importance of the concept of identity within poetry, the place of poetry within culture, and the range of practices encompassed by its forms of art. In this chapter, I describe new narratives about poetry that take shape and connect them with narratives circulating in and about Britain itself. The new narratives about British poetry are also narratives *about* narrative in poetry: about how poetry takes up and reimagines storytelling within its for-mal processes. And so this chapter's title has a double valence.[8]

Motion and Morrison catch one aspect of this shift in what we might think of as a fourth claim to go along with the three I describe earlier. British poetry's renewed "interest in narrative" is, for Motion and Morrison, notable because it is characterized by a self-reflexivity or performativity that "exhibit[s] some-thing of the spirit of postmodernism."[9] These narrative poems tend to be oblique, and they are in many instances inversions of Martian "bizzarrerie." A typical Martian poem consists of a strange surface that, once decoded, gives way to a quite conventional account of everyday conventions. In Raine's "A Martian Sends a Postcard Home," the alien of the title describes the accou-terments and behaviors of humans in baroquely estranging terms that stand ready to be deciphered. Once one riddles out the object or action that is being figured ("caxtons are mechanical birds with many wings" = books), the excitement of the poem is largely over.[10] In comparison, the "new narrative" poems that Motion and Morrison describe feature a clarity of surface but lack the contextual depth that would allow for a full understanding. If Martian poems too quickly turn the unknown or strange into the known and familiar, thereby committing themselves to a gimmicky production of newness, then the narrative poems of James Fenton, Muldoon, or Motion himself offer up limpid poetic surfaces that remain partial, inscrutable, or hermetic. Fenton's context-uncertain texts, such as "A Nest of Vampires" or "A Staffordshire Murderer," are exemplary of this trend. And in this sense, one could say that it is Muldoon and not Heaney who becomes the gravitational center of Motion and Morrison's anthology (perhaps only in retrospect) and whose own mode of virtuosic formalism and narrative obliquity provides the model for many poets at the end of the century.

Renewed attention to the narrative resources within poetry coincided with a series of new narratives about the significant changes taking place in England, Scotland, Wales, and Northern Ireland. The Northern Irish Troubles took up a good deal of attention in the 1970s and 1980s, but Britain confronted crises and challenges on a number of other fronts as well. A long economic slump collapsed the postwar political consensus and led to labor confrontations and general debates about the nature of the United Kingdom's economic future, even though the discovery of oil in the North Sea made for brief bursts of revitalization. The great majority of Britain's overseas empire had been dismantled, and growing independence and devolution movements in Scotland and Wales, along with an uneasy entrance into the European Economic Community, helped spur a sense that Britain was, as Tom Nairn has famously put it, "breaking up."[11] Additionally, racial tensions had been increasing throughout the 1970s in many English cities, and they worsened with the rise of the Conservative government at the decade's end.

Kenneth Jackson writes that "more than any change of government since 1945, Margaret Thatcher's election victory was taken as marking a decisive shift in the national mood, politically, intellectually, and culturally."[12] During her time as prime minister (1979–1990), Thatcher oversaw the liberalization of the British economy, the weakening of the welfare state, and the embrace of American-style monetarism and consumer capitalism. Her policies and bearing defined the decade, and she became a locus around which arguments about Britain and British culture revolved, especially after her triumph in the 1982 Falklands War, which led to an overwhelming Conservative victory in the 1983 elections. However fleetingly, she rekindled imperial feeling during the springtime conflict with Argentina, demonstrating the sure, tough-minded leadership that became her signature governing style. She defeated Arthur Scargill and the National Union of Mineworkers after strikes in 1984 and 1985, which subsequently decimated the miners' union and weakened trade unions generally. Her policies toward Northern Ireland appeared intractable. She favored the privatization of public resources and oversaw the denationalization of British Telecom, British Aerospace, Britoil, British Gas, Rolls-Royce, and British Airports. The narrow view of society that she articulated – famously expressing disbelief in its existence apart from individuals and families – marginalized civic and social groupings of all kinds. While southeast England, and especially the greater London metropolitan area, continued to thrive economically, many other parts of Britain were left out. The weakening of local governmental bodies and cultural institutions by the political hegemony in London, the neglect of public services by the Conservative government, continuing deindustrialization throughout the archipelago, and high levels of unemployment in many areas made for widespread unrest and a combustible and polarizing social fabric. As might be expected, Thatcher became a crucial figure within poetry, the symbol of a conservative and retrograde England against whom a number of writers positioned themselves, although Larkin was a great admirer.

Racial and ethnic tensions had been a fairly constant aspect of British life since large-scale immigration from the Caribbean, Africa, and Asia began after the war, as I describe in Chapter 2. By the late 1970s, several changes to British immigration policy had made it increasingly difficult for former colonial subjects to enter Britain, and black and brown Britons faced racism and discrimination in multiple forms. As Paul Gilroy writes, "the 1971 Immigration Act brought an end to primary immigration and instituted a new pattern of internal control and surveillance of black settlers. It was paralleled by a new vocabulary of 'race' and crime which grew in the aftermath of the first panic over 'mugging.'"[13] At the same time, the increasing importance of youth and popular culture, the spread of left-based and radical political organizations from the United States and Europe, and the coming-of-age of the generation born in the decade or so after the war who either came as children to Britain or who were the children of immigrants provided the grounds for concerted resistance to oppression. For Linton Kwesi Johnson, the poet who most forcefully articulated this resistance and a defining figure within black British literature, aesthetic considerations were coupled with political ones. In his early and highly influential books and records, his unique form of dub poetry worked in solidarity with the political goals of the radical black left.

Johnson is a diasporic figure, coming from Jamaica to Brixton in 1963 when he was eleven, but unlike earlier writers like Brathwaite, Salkey, or Walcott, his work is concentrated on life in England, although his primary contribution to British poetry involves his adaptation of a Caribbean cultural form. His dub poetry emerges out of dub music, which features a D.J. speaking, or "toasting," over the instrumental tracks of reggae songs. He joined the British Black Panthers as a teenager, was a member of the Caribbean Artists Movement in the early 1970s, and became a central figure in the Race Today collective later in the decade. His early dub poems focus on two key aspects of black social and political life: the reggae-driven youth scene in Brixton and the tumultuous, often violent relationship between black communities and the police, which for Johnson – as for many others – was the archetypal symbol of the racism and xenophobia of English society and the British state.[14] Drawing from Brathwaite's model of "nation language" as well as from Jamaican dub lyricists, D.J.s, and musicians – such as Bongo Jerry, Burning Spear, I Roy, U Roy, Big Youth, and Mikey Smith – Johnson's dub poetry interweaves Caribbean and black English vernaculars, reggae music, and lyric performance. After two volumes in the mid-1970s, *Voices of the Living and the Dead* (1974) and *Dread Beat and Blood* (1975), Johnson brought out his first album, *Dread Beat and Blood* (1978), which was followed by a third and fourth volume – *Forces of Victory* (1979) and *Inglan Is a Bitch* (1981). These, along with the albums *Forces of Victory* (1979) and *Bass Culture* (1980), established him as a major voice within discussions of race in Britain, as well as a sought-after performer who has toured internationally throughout the past forty years, both as a soloist and with a backing band (primarily with the Dennis Bovell Dub Band).

Johnson's poetry of the 1970s and 1980s alternates among three basic modes: verbal approximations of dub rhythms and reggae music that double as descriptions of the scenes and styles of black urban culture in London, narrative accounts of the oppression of black communities and their confrontations with the Metropolitan police, and polemical refrains about social and political injustice in Britain and the forms of resistance that black Britons must take up. The first mode makes for a sonically charged and highly figural texture:

> Shock-black bubble-doun-beat bouncing
> rock-wise tumble-doun sound music;
> foot-drop find drum, blood story,
> bass history is a moving
>   is a hurting black story.[15]

Here, in the first stanza of "Reggae Sounds," the heavily accented, four-beat lines mime a reggae rhythm while describing the musical scene. Like Langston Hughes's blues poems, Johnson's dub poems toggle between describing dub music and trying to become it. The third and fourth lines locate dub within the larger frame of black history in Britain and throughout the Atlantic world: the drum tells a "blood story," a "bass history" whose rhythms – like Walcott's figuration of the sea – encode the violence and trauma of a diasporic history and its continuing ramifications.[16]

In the second mode, which often works alongside the first, Johnson recounts particular events and social conditions in a forceful public voice, turning his poems into vehicles for community response. Most often, he focuses on confrontations between black citizens and the police, as in "Five Nights of Bleeding," in which the refrain – "madness … madness … war" – refers to the energy of the weekend parties around Brixton, the violence that often follows them, the aggressive tactics of the police, and the response to that aggression. The alteration of the refrain after a passage about the wounding of two policemen – from "madness … madness … war" to "righteous righteous war" – indicates the ideology that underpins Johnson's earlier work.[17] Poems, especially those written in the wake of major confrontations, such as the battles between police and participants during the Notting Hill Carnival in 1976 or during the Brixton riots in 1981, serve as the staging grounds for statements of solidarity and political analysis. Johnson's refrains about English racism – "It Dread Inna Inglan" and "Inglan Is a Bitch" – are expanded into larger polemics that draw on the militant ideologies of the Black Panthers as well as the anticolonial philosophy of Franz Fanon. The subjugation of and discrimination against black people in "Maggi Tatcha's" Britain – both the source and condition of black British "dread" – is Johnson's abiding theme. As Fred D'Aguiar puts it, "a poem by Johnson wasn't simply a record of an event but formed a part of the history surrounding it."[18]

One of the most significant of such poems is "New Craas Massakah," which tells the story of the 1981 New Cross Fire, a racially motivated arson attack on a house in New Cross that caused the death of thirteen black children and the injury of twenty-six during Yvonne Ruddick's sixteenth birthday party. Alternating between short lines that recapitulate the happy jollity of the party followed by the terror of the attack and longer, more decisively paced stanzas that express outrage against the police and the media, "New Craas Massakah" enfolds the characteristic features of Johnson's style into a dense communal elegy. It manages to isolate the various strands of everyday racism within British society while also conveying the uniquely traumatic effect of the New Cross fire on the "whole a black Britn," before setting the rhetorical stage for future action:

> but stap
> yu noh remembah
> how di whole a black Britn did rack wid rage
> how di whole a black Britn tun a fiery red
> nat di callous red af di killah's eyes
> but red wid rage like di flames af di fyah[19]

The ineffective attempts of the police and government to cover up the "cowl facks / bout dat brutal attack," and the willingness of the mainstream media to go along with officially sanctioned stories, leads not to dismay but to a refusal "fi surrendah."[20] Johnson ends the poem with a third iteration of the short-lined lyric that first describes the party and then the fire. The choice to end in narrative rather than rhetoric is significant, especially since so many of Johnson's poems do come to rest in moments of polemical force. Here, "the cowl facks" of the event – both tragedy and crime – are described in simple, rhythmically propulsive tercets, without any additional commentary, as though nothing additional needs to be, or can be, finally said.

While Johnson's work is derived from the improvisational modes of dub and reggae, he has throughout his career emphasized that his poems are composed texts. At the center of dub music is a D.J. who mixes rhythms, phrases, and sound effects over the instrumental background of a reggae song from which lead vocals have been removed. It is both intimate and highly mediated. The D.J. interacts with the audience, and each performance is shaped by its site specificity. However, the intimacy between D.J. and audience is mediated through a highly complex technological apparatus: the sound system that is the D.J.'s instrument. Johnson describes the "dub-lyricist" this way: "The 'dub-lyricist' is the dj turned poet. He intones his lyrics rather than sings them. Dub-lyricism is a new form of (oral) music-poetry, wherein the lyricist overdubs rhythmic phrases on to the rhythm background of a popular song."[21] This splicing together of oral performance and written literature – a version of Édouard Glissant's notion of "oraliture" – is at the heart of Johnson's dub poetry.[22] And one cannot approach a Johnson poem, either experientially or analytically, without attending to the complex interactions between written text and oral performance of that text. But he has differentiated his practice from that of popular musicians by consistently publishing his work in book form, asserting the primacy of his poems as written objects at the same time that those poems reach a much larger audience via Johnson's performances of them – live or recorded – than via the printed book.

His status, as of 2002, as a "Penguin Classic" poet – the first black writer and second living writer to be published in that series – has assured his literary canonicity, but he continues to cultivate an ironic resistance to the notion of canonicity and the field of contemporary poetry, as in the wryly counterfactual poem, "If I Woz a Tap-Natch Poet." In this text, Johnson manages simultaneously to position himself among the great black poets from the Caribbean, Africa, and the United States and to disavow any such move. Johnson's dub poetry was decisive for black British poets in the 1980s and 1990s, and it strongly influenced both those writers who followed up on his use of dialect and dub as well as those who chose to compose primarily in standard English. Some poets, most famously Benjamin Zephaniah, have taken up Johnson's repudiations of the racist ideologies within British society, while others, namely Jean "Binta" Breeze and Patience Agbabi, have triangulated dub with other models of performance or spoken-word poetry. Despite Johnson's ambiguous status within the canon of British poetry in the early 1980s, he was part of a remarkable flourishing of black British literature at the time.

This flourishing occurred just as Thatcher's government fundamentally altered the definition of British citizenship with the 1981 British Nationality Act, which made it dependent on an individual's ability to demonstrate that a forebear was British rather than equating citizenship with the fact of having been born in the country. This shift, from a *jus soli* policy to a de facto *jus sanguinis* definition of British citizenship, cemented the drift of British immigration policy since the early 1960s, essentially racializing the legal concept of Britishness. Ian Baucom writes of the far-reaching 1981 Act: "discarding nine hundred years of legal precedent that recognized a territorial principle as the sole absolute determinant of British identity, the act determined that Britain was, henceforth, a genealogical community ... [T]he 1981 Nationality Act codified a theory of identity that sought to defend the 'native' inhabitants of the island against the claims of their former subjects by defining Britishness as an inheritance of race."[23] Coincident with these legal shifts was a substantial body of work – literary, scholarly, and popular – that examined the longer history of race relations in England, especially in light of the legacy of British imperialism and the centrality of the Transatlantic slave trade within that legacy.

Salman Rushdie's Booker Prize–winning novel, *Midnight's Children* (1981), marked a watershed moment for postcolonial literature, just as Edward Said's *Orientalism* (1978) inaugurated postcolonial studies. Alongside Said and his formative analysis of the racial and imperial ideologies rooted in the canon of English literature, a handful of scholars – many of them associated with the Centre for Contemporary Cultural Studies at the University of Birmingham – sought to investigate the history of race relations in Britain. Key volumes such as Stuart Hall's *Policing the Crisis: Mugging, the State, and Law and Order* (1978) and Paul Gilroy's *"There Ain't No Black in the Union Jack": The Cultural Politics of Race and Nation* (1987) provided theoretical accounts of the changes in the culture and politics of race in Britain, paying particular attention to the events of the 1970s and 1980s. In this way, Gilroy and Hall can be seen as theorizing the historical conditions that Johnson's poems stage. Similarly, Rushdie's novels – *Midnight's Children* and *The Satanic Verses* in particular – both draw upon and influence the work of postcolonial critics such as Said, Gayatri Spivak, and Homi Bhabha. And Rushdie's transformative Booker victory occurred not in isolation but in concert with the successes of other black British writers who were achieving mainstream recognition, such as James Berry, who won the 1981 National Poetry Competition, and Grace Nichols, who won the 1983 Commonwealth Poetry Prize.

Nichols's prizewinning volume, *I Is a Long Memoried Woman*, like Brathwaite's *The Arrivants*, is structured around a transatlantic circuit that retraces the trauma of the African slave trade. The volume comprises a set of linked short poems and features a corporate lyric subject who describes and reflects upon the conditions of slavery and colonialism – the "long memoried woman" who is a lost figure from history (a "child of the middle passage womb"), an avatar for the poet (who was born in Guyana in 1950 and came to the United Kingdom in the late 1970s), and a transhistorical Afro-Caribbean subject ("We the women who toil / unadorn / heads tie with cheap / cotton").[24] The volume's short-lined, free-verse, refrain-filled poems include elegies for those "souls / caught in the Middle Passage / limbo"; songs in praise of African and Caribbean gods, spirits, folk figures, and imagined ancestors; songs of women working on cane plantations; and lyrics in praise of the Caribbean islands, which are "fertile / with brutality."[25] The volume can also be read, loosely, as a lyric *bildungsroman* that tracks the composite figure's life (sometimes in first person and sometimes in third) from childhood through her time as a slave laborer, wife, and mother, all the while working toward the kind of self-possession that appears in the volume's powerful "Epilogue," where the conditions of diaspora and loss make for a regeneration in which a new tongue "has sprung."[26]

Stitched into Nichols's sequence is a set of political poems that use revolutionary figures within Caribbean history – Nanny of the Maroons and Toussaint l'Ouverture primarily – as talismans to spur liberatory thinking in the present. As with earlier poems by Brathwaite and Walcott, part of the challenge for poets writing about the history of slavery and colonization is the absence of that history, its obliteration in the sea and in the hegemonic discourses and institutions of empire. Poetry, then, can become a mode of imaginative reclamation, and Nichols's loosely metaphorical narrative and variable speaker allows her to link a version of her own history to a larger trajectory of African and Caribbean cultural materials. The ocean crossing recounted throughout the volume and concluded in the "Epilogue" is marked by violence and loss, but newness remains possible, even one that remains haunted by what has been lost.

The regeneration promised at the end of *I Is a Long Memoried Woman* is analogous to Walcott's guiding notion of the wound as an enabling figure for postcolonial aesthetics, and Walcott's Adamic stance – the poet as one who can name and create anew out of the depredations of imperial history – has been adopted by a number of poets in his wake.[27] The most sustained such espousal is David Dabydeen's *Turner* (1994), which deconstructs the racial ideologies of empire by reimagining J.M.W. Turner's famous seascape, *Slavers Throwing Overboard the Dead and the Dying* (also known as *Slave Ship* and first displayed in 1840). Dabydeen, who was born in Guyana in 1955 and came to Britain in 1969, has had a varied career as a scholar, poet, novelist, and diplomat and has written extensively about representations of black people within English literature and art. *Turner* is a sequence of twenty-five poems that, as Dabydeen notes, "focuses on the submerged head of the African in the foreground of Turner's painting."[28] Turner's painting was originally praised and purchased by John Ruskin, who described it as the most impressive and sublime of his seascapes yet only mentioned the actual subject of the work in a footnote. Dabydeen takes this footnote, which "reads like an afterthought, something tossed overboard," as his starting point and then organizes the sequence as a set of monologues spoken by the drowned slave in Turner's painting.[29]

Turner is a negative ekphrastic poem: it takes the painting's almost absent subject and imagines a history and life for the nearly unseen figure in its foreground. The central speaker remembers his past before the slavers – who are collectively named Turner throughout – come and take him, details his brief time on the slave ship, narrates his afterlife undersea, and attempts to find some mode of regeneration or recompense. Dabydeen, who moved from writing primarily in dialect in his first volume, *Slave Song* (1984), to mixing dialect poems and standard-English poems in *Coolie Odyssey* (1988) to writing *Turner* in standard English orthography, has differentiated his own project from Brathwaitian "nation language," but, like Brathwaite's, Dabydeen's poetry is immersed in European modernist literature. Once again, Eliot is a key influence. *Turner*, whose twenty-five sections each comprise a single stanza of widely variable lengths, is a richly descriptive poem, although one that rarely calls attention to its own formal textures. The many names of animals, fruits, and birds that dot the poem are invented, which provides the poem with a certain weightlessness – as though the act of nomination that the speaker undertakes is never anything but provisional or counterfactual.

The poem's second central conceit is that the speaker's reawakening under the water is spurred by the appearance of another figure who is tossed overboard, a stillborn child also named Turner. Throughout the poem, the speaker reiterates the moment when the child hits the water, which becomes the catalyst for the poem's extensive act of imagined remembrance. At various points the speaker is positioned as father, mother, and double of the dead child, and the speaker's central dilemma is to conceive of a future that neither he nor the stillborn child ever had. The poem is blankly recursive, repeating its initial event while aiming to find a viable way forward: "stillborn from all the signs"; "It plopped into the water and soon swelled / Like a brumplak seed"; "It plopped into the water from a passing ship"; "It broke the waters and made the years / Stir"; "I gather it in with dead arms"; "I gather it to my body, this grain."[30] The poem continually stages its own failure to move beyond its initial terms, a failure of which the speaker is all too cognizant. Thinking of the stillborn child who repeatedly calls him "nigger" and who drifts "away from / My body of lies," the speaker laments:

> I wanted to teach it
> A redemptive song, fashion new descriptions
> Of things, new colours fountaining out of form.
> I wanted to begin anew in the sea
> But the child would not bear the future
> Nor its inventions.[31]

Both speaker and child have blank histories and impossible futures, "neither ghost / Nor portent of a past or future life," and the poem's concluding litany provides the most thoroughgoing instance of its cultivation of negation:

> No savannah, moon, gods, magicians
> To heal or curse, harvests, ceremonies,
> No men to plough, corn to fatten their herds,
> No stars, no land, no words, no community,
> No mother.[32]

The figure of the mother – at once sea, moon, Africa, the speaker imagining himself to be the mother of the stillborn, the speaker's mother, and the stillborn's birth mother, who lies brutally dying on the ship's deck at the start of the poem – provides a consistent, if unexamined, locus for the poet's creative energies. But here it is the final term in a catalogue of absent plentitude. Dabydeen lists the cultural inheritance that the colonial slave trade has decimated and removes one by one from the text the totems and symbols that have sustained it.

Like Nichols, Dabydeen frames contemporary questions about identity, race, and diaspora through a turn to and attempted reclamation of the past. The maternal figure that threads together Nichols's volume keys its effort towards historical repair, a process that in Dabydeen's *Turner* becomes a ceaseless return to unknowable origins, a circular movement emblematized as a blank or already-foreclosed birth. Both present highly symbolic lyric narratives that imagine a past in order to historicize matters of race, gender, and postcoloniality. A quite different representation of motherhood and the maternal, one that considers these matters within the context of contemporary Britain, appears in Jackie Kay's sequence, *The Adoption Papers* (1991). Kay's autobiographical text, which was broadcast first as a radio play on the BBC's *Drama Now* program in 1990, provides a multivocal account of a young mixed-race girl who has been adopted by a white Scottish couple and whose twin attempts to make a place for herself in a largely white community and to contact her birth mother provide the primary substance of the narrative. Kay differentiates the poem's three speakers – the daughter, the birth mother, and the adoptive mother – by typeface, and the daughter's Palatino font matches that of the rest of the book, which suggests that Kay's own position is nearest that of the adopted daughter. Indeed, Kay was born in Edinburgh in 1961 to a Scottish mother and Nigerian father and adopted by a Scottish couple soon after her birth. Moving chronologically through the daughter's early life and touching down on various key episodes as they are rendered by either the daughter or her two mothers, *The Adoption Papers* charts the competing elements within the process of identity formation in postcolonial Britain. It can be read not only as the story of a single black subject's development but also as a *bildungsroman* for a generation of postcolonial black Britons who either came to Britain at a young age in the decade and a half after the end of the war or who were born in Britain to parents who themselves had recently immigrated. In documenting the coming of age of the protagonist, Kay maps the complexities of being both black and British in the postwar period as those terms were being redefined politically and reconceived socially and culturally.

The Adoption Papers interrogates the legal procedures for adoption in Britain and provides an alternate narrative – a different archive of "papers" – that emphasizes the psychological desires, anxieties, and investments inherent to but also obscured by the formal bureaucracy of adoption. The legal documents that govern the process and so determine the child's "official identity" are remade as lyric texts that examine the fluid intricacies of identity as a lived process. The emotional stakes of the birth and the adoption – the birth mother's sadness and guilt about giving up her child ("I had no other choice / Anyway it's best for her"), the adoptive mother's uneasy position as both mother and not mother ("I am not a mother / until I've signed that piece of paper"), and the child's constant sense of a double inheritance ("My mammy says she's no really my mammy") – are intensified by the racial dynamics at work.[33]

The poem presents these complexities polyphonically: not through the voice of a single "I," but via a ceaseless triangulation of lyric speaking. At times, one of the three speakers controls a long stretch of the text, while at others the speakers alternate stanza by stanza or line by line. As various episodes are recounted – the difficult birth and the child's early health issues; the adoptive parents' search for an agency that will take them; their sudden change of fortune when they mention, "oh you know we don't mind the colour";[34] their attempt to present themselves in the best light to the agent who will judge their fitness to be parents;[35] the adoptive mother's anxious dreams that she will lose her child; conversations between adoptive mother and child about being adopted – the young girl becomes more and more conscious of her own racial and cultural inheritance.

She suffers the persecution of her classmates and teachers as her parents seek to protect her and encourage her, even though they never fully understand the difference that race makes. In "Chapter 7: Black Bottom," the adoptive mother wishes simply to ignore the fact of racial difference, but despite their own wish to avoid thinking about race, their daughter's experiences at school force her parents to take up a proactive and defensive stance, in certain ways mirroring the course of black radical politics of the time (this part of the poem is marked "1967–1971"). The daughter's adoption of Angela Davis as a hero, as well as the birth mother's descriptions of the disapproving stares she faced when dating the Nigerian birth father, each speak to the longer history of postwar race relations in Scotland. The bond between birth mother and daughter is strengthened textually even as it remains unrealized within the narrative, especially within part three of the poem, which covers the 1980s. "Chapter 8: Generations" alternates between the birth mother's pondering of her child's future and the daughter's increasing desire to learn about her own familial past:

> the blood does not bind confusion,
> yet I confess to my contradiction
> I want to know my blood.[36]

Knowledge of one's origins does not assure an unproblematic identity and thereby "bind confusion," but it can help understand, if not solve, the contradictions that underlie one's sense of self. Birth mother and daughter continue to shadow each other as the daughter takes concrete steps to locate her birth mother, calling her maternal grandmother in the Highlands and getting in touch with her mother's sister, who promises that her mother will write. The sequence ends not with a meeting between mother and daughter but with "The Meeting Dream," in which birth mother and daughter spend an awkward and somewhat disappointing day together:

> One dream cuts another open like a gutted fish
> nothing is what it was;
> she is too many imaginings to be flesh and blood.
> There is nothing left to say.
> Neither of us mentions meeting again.[37]

The poem ends by mirroring the form of the opening, in which each speaker is given an opening monologue that establishes her position in the narrative. At the end, however, the order of the monologues shifts: instead of the daughter placed between adoptive mother and birth mother, as in the beginning, the daughter's final passage is also the poem's, making her the narrative's final speaker. This formal assurance is undercut by the tone of each of the final passages: the adoptive mother's confidence in her place as a mother ("Closer than blood. / Thicker than water. Me and my daughter.") is counterpointed with the birth mother's ritual repetition of her original parting from her daughter and then with the daughter's hopeful imagining about what the letter from her birth mother will look like when it arrives in the mail.[38] A final piece of significant paper in a poem filled with vital documents, this yet-to-arrive letter is an emblem of the daughter's multifarious construction of her own identity: based in story, dream, and text and ceaselessly on the move. Kay deconstructs notions of motherhood, race, filiation, and affiliation in order to present a story of one subject's *bildung* that can also serve as a broader investigation of social relations in contemporary Britain.

I have spent the first part of this chapter considering several ways in which poetry has addressed narratives about race and Britishness that have circulated throughout the postwar period and that intensified in the later 1970s and throughout the 1980s. However, narratives about race and ethnic identity have not been the only ones to undergo widespread rethinking. If *The Adoption Papers* uses a family narrative to revise national narratives about gender and race, then Tony Harrison positions his family narrative as an allegory of socioeconomic class in England. The central conflict in Harrison's early books – especially *The Loiners* (1970), the expanding sonnet sequence *The School of Eloquence* (1978 and forward),[39] and *v.* (1985) – is between the linguistic and social fabric of Harrison's white working class background in Leeds and his own calling as a poet in the tradition of both the Latin and Greek classics and the mainline of English poetry.[40] Harrison's poems stage this conflict within heteroglossic forms that mingle the northern dialects of Harrison's Leeds with a heightened literary register that displays his deep learning and linguistic fluency. As we have seen in this and earlier chapters, many poets have worked to thicken the texture and expand the range of English, to make it a network of related but divergent Englishes rather than a standard form of the language – "Received Pronunciation," "BBC English," the English spoken by upper-class communities in the southeast of the country – below which sit a series of non-standard Englishes that are marked racially, ethnically, or socioeconomically. Harrison's contribution to this project has been to render these mixed registers within traditional English forms and meters, with iambic pentameters, hexameters, couplets, and rhyming quatrains serving as the building blocks of his extensive oeuvre. His poems, then, are tensed between their formal virtuosity and their linguistic amalgam as they address the friction between his working-class background and his poetic vocation.

Harrison's style is most clearly visible in what stands for many as his masterpiece, *v.* (1985). Modeled on Thomas Gray's "Elegy Written in a Country Churchyard" and composed during the 1984 miners' strike, the 112 rhyming quatrains of *v.* comprise a graveside elegy for Harrison's parents as he stops in for a quick visit between trains. A sardonic critique of British society in the 1980s, *v.* stages the poet's own conflicted history as an imagined dialogue between himself and a young skinhead who has vandalized the gravestones. The poem became widely known after it was shown on Channel Four in November 1987, and its strong language led to calls that it be banned for obscenity. Its reception history is a major aspect of the poem's context, and the second edition of the poem contains a large section devoted to media responses to its initial broadcast and publication. A poet, playwright, and film writer, Harrison has cultivated a position as a public figure throughout his career, one often complicated by his learned and allusive verse. *v.*'s adamant accessibility has helped it become one of the signal English poems of the late twentieth century.

The poem's narrative arc is limpid, covering the poet's monologue as he stands in the cemetery and considers his and England's past and future:

> Next millennium you'll have to search quite hard
> to find my slab behind the family dead,
> butcher, publican, and baker, now me, bard
> adding poetry to their beef, beer, and bread.[41]

Harrison, as always, remains highly conscious of the difference between the working-class men whose graves surround his parents' (and, one day, his) and his own status as an educated poet. This disparity becomes the central topic of conversation between himself and the skinhead whom he later ventriloquizes, an antagonistic version of his earlier self. The entire graveyard sits above a worked-out mine, and the cemetery – slowly collapsing into the hollow pit below it and covered with graffiti and trash – quite plainly becomes the symbol of a dilapidated nation:

> when going to clear the weeds and rubbish thrown
> on the family plot by football fans, I find
> UNITED graffitied on my parents' stone.
>
> How many British graveyards now this May
> are strewn with rubbish and choked up with weeds

> since families and friends have gone away
> for work or fuller lives, like me from Leeds?[42]

The graffito refers to the local football club whose losses spur drunken vandalism and which for Harrison represents a serendipitous "accident of meaning" that describes his parents in heaven and the unified quality of the nation itself.[43] However, this bit of wishful thinking quickly falls away, and Harrison spends most of his time mulling over the implications of a different piece of graffiti: the "v" whose ubiquity makes it into something like the vandals' collectively anonymous signature. Rather than "UNITED," which might have been a workable motif in an earlier England of postwar consensus, "v" is the central symbol of 1980s Thatcherite Britain. As Harrison writes, "These Vs are all the versuses of life," and the poem cultivates antagonism as its basic stylistic mechanism.[44] Well-wrought quatrains grate against the vulgarities and curses that inhabit them. The poet speaker is set against the imagined skinhead who appears about a third of the way through the text, upbraiding the poet for forgetting his background and for his delusions about art's purpose in a moment of economic calamity and social ruin for England's industrial working class. The skinhead is an avatar of the poet himself – the version of Harrison that he did not become – and as they trade insults, the poet seeks to reoccupy the skinhead's aggressive masculinity and violent pose. Castigated by his other self and forced to face his own complicity in a bourgeois ideology that he seeks to criticize, the poet speaker leaves the cemetery to catch his train.

By this point, the antagonistic engine that drives the poem sputters. The final third of *v.* incorporates nostalgic recollections of his father's and his childhood's Leeds and then details the poet's journey home, where he quickly assumes his middle-class life with his wife (listening to Berg on the stereo, watching news of Northern Ireland and the Persian Gulf on the television). "UNITED" once again is made to stand for marital love as the couple climbs into bed near the poem's end. The final seven quatrains pivot more directly to the reader and recapitulate the poem's beginning. We are returned to the graveyard sometime in "the next millennium," and the poet tells us once again how to find his grave before asking us to "erase the more offensive FUCK and CUNT / but leave, with the worn UNITED, one small v."[45] The "v" – versus, victory, verses – is now graffitied onto Harrison's own imagined gravestone, for which he has – in a mordant reshuffling of the end of Yeats's "Under Ben Bulben" – provided an epitaph as the poem's last stanza:

> *Beneath your feet's a poet, then a pit.*
> *Poetry supporter, if you're hear to find*

how poems can grow from (beat you to it!) SHIT
find the beef, the beer, the bread, then look behind.[46]

The poem's rearguard action is literalized, and Harrison cagily composes an ending that is both a return to the past (the past of the poem's early stanzas, the past of the reader's present, and Harrison's own past) and a leap into the future. Aiming to assure a poem's (and poet's) immortality by lodging it within a future reader is a well-worn literary task, but Harrison's bid is undercut by the nature of the ground itself. The "cavernous hollow" beneath the graveyard, which will "swallow / this place of rest and all the resters down," ensures that such a scene as the poem's conclusion imagines can never happen.[47]

David Kennedy is right to suggest that the force of *v.*'s political and social critique is hampered by the fact that "Harrison seems able to record only the decline of working-class culture and his own anger, bewilderment and impotence at its dissolution and passing."[48] However, the poem in certain ways outflanks its problematic content by so clearly placing itself on such shaky ground. The tension between the poem's multiple manifestations of literariness and its rougher linguistic substance is deliberately unsettled by the projected collapse of its diegetic ground. Dissent not only characterizes the political landscape of Thatcherite Britain and the poem's rhetorical strategy, it also becomes *v.*'s compositional crux. Superficially solving itself by returning to its opening scene and terms, the poem also contains a structural hollow analogous to the pit that underlies the graveyard.

The speaker's complicity in the ideologies that he seeks to critique and the poem's unsatisfactory attempt to resolve this critique within the domestic space of marital love do not vitiate *v.*'s effect, as long as the kind of antagonistic force that drives the poem also shapes a reader's response to it. The final "versus" to mention is the reader's struggle against the attractions of the poem's surfaces. We are, I think, meant to read against the poem as much as we read with it and to keep alive the skepticism that shapes the central dialogue between the poet and skinhead, even if we disagree considerably with both the content and the course of that argument. *v.*, like many of Harrison's poems, is antagonistic and antagonized. It does not, however, seriously question its own formal assumptions. Additionally, the speaker's unreflective capitulation to ideologies of gender and race obscures his class critique. I have already worked through several texts that entwine examinations of race and gender, and I will now consider poetry that works to question and dismantle gender ideologies within a broader analysis of the central premises of English lyric poetry.

If, in the three decades after 1945, there was a scarcity of women poets recognized within the working canons of British poetry, then the next four decades have been much more notable for the prominence and variety of poetry by women. The increasing centrality of women's poetry in Britain is, along with the significant developments in black British poetry, the central story of the 1980s. Fleur Adcock, Liz Lochhead, Anne Stevenson, Penelope Shuttle, Wendy Cope, and Carol Rumens became important figures and found mainstream success, while Denise Riley, Wendy Mulford, Geraldine Monk, and Maggie O'Sullivan drew from the energies of the British Poetry Revival and, alongside American poets such as Lyn Hejinian and Susan Howe, have been at the center of contemporary experimental poetry in English.

The project of "writing back" to a patriarchal English literary tradition, what Adrienne Rich famously called "writing as re-vision," arose out of feminist movements in the 1960s. With Simone de Beauvoir's *The Second Sex* (published in English in 1961) and Betty Friedan's *The Feminine Mystique* (1963) as guiding documents of women's liberation and feminism, and with Stevie Smith and Sylvia Plath serving as key influences, women poets in Britain took a number of distinct paths as they found ways to articulate the particularities of their personal experiences while using their poems to launch critiques of patriarchy. The establishment of feminist presses and journals, such as Virago Press (1973) and *Spare Rib* (1972), respectively, provided outlets for women writers, although there were disagreements about whether constructing a separate canon and discourse of feminist poetry, one that entirely rejected the male literary tradition, was the best course. As Jane Dowson and Alice Entwistle point out, a divide emerged between poets whose careers had been established by the 1970s, such as Elizabeth Jennings and Patricia Beer, who tended to be wary of conflating politics and poetics, and younger writers whose work was more forcefully political and who saw definite links between their poetry and their political aims, such as Gillian Allnutt, Alison Fell, Michèle Roberts, and Jeni Couzyn.[49]

Of course, many women poets in the 1970s and 1980s, including those listed, did not choose between apolitical, personal lyrics and a poetry exclusively committed to feminist politics. For poets like Adcock, Lochhead, and Eavan Boland, lyric accounts of their experiences as women, lovers, wives, mothers, and writers are simultaneously enquiries into larger questions about the gendered nature of social and literary relations. Often, as in Ruth Fainlight's *Sibyls and Others* (1980) and Lochhead's *The Grimm Sisters* (1981) or, later, Gillian Clarke's *The King of Britain's Daughter* (1993) and Carol Ann Duffy's monologues in *The World's Wife* (1999), myths, folktales, and other stories that are sunk deep into European or Western culture are rewritten from a female perspective. Much of this poetry is formally moderate, most often adopting a loosely free-verse norm or adapting traditional meters, but it is thematically and generically adventurous, revising and upending familiar literary scenes and topoi.

The new narratives about gender, sex, economics, and history that are presented in such poems tend not to disrupt or problematize their own formal or discursive unfolding. For writers such as Mulford, Riley, or, as discussed earlier, Veronica Forrest-Thomson, it is just as crucial that poems emerging out of feminist philosophies step outside the representational practices and limits of patriarchal discourses. Influenced by second-wave feminism and by the poststructuralist models of French feminist writers, especially Hélène Cixous and Julia Kristeva, these experimentally minded poets extended the project of deconstructing the gendered ideologies of Western culture into the realm of language.[50] The English poetic tradition is, like the culture from which it emerges, deeply patriarchal, and so the most far-reaching interventions into that tradition lay bare the gendered nature of its basic signifying practices. If lyric poetry in English has relied on a male subject and a female object at its conceptual core, then simply reversing that binary – "writing back" to a patriarchal canon by positioning the lyric subject as female – is a necessary but not sufficient repudiation of the gender ideologies marbling the literary canon. Romantic and post-Romantic lyric poetry is premised upon the delineation of a coherent subject who functions as a poem's speaker and its guiding mind. This subject assumes the power to represent the world and to recreate that world in language. Such a dynamic is part of lyric's deep structure, and it privileges a certain kind of speaker and a certain kind of poetic speech, which is often implicitly male. A female lyric subject falls outside this limiting ideological norm, as Mulford suggests in "Valentine": "she is nowhere constituted and bits / hang off her all the time."[51] The project for a number of feminist poets has been to find a mode of experimental, innovative writing that puts such ideologies under question, to investigate, as Riley puts it, "speech as a sexed thing."[52]

Riley's attempt to locate a viable mode of feminist lyric in *Marxism for Infants* (1977), *Dry Air* (1985), and *Mop Mop Georgette* (1993) coincides with her scholarly work on the discursive construction of gender in *War in the Nursery: Theories of the Child and Mother* (1983) and *"Am I That Name?" Feminism and the Category of "Women" in History* (1988). Altogether, these works comprise a thoroughgoing reclamation of female experience as a crucial subject of intellectual and aesthetic engagement, as well as a ceaselessly self-reflexive critique of systemic patriarchy:

> The work is
> e.g. to write 'she' and for that to be a statement
> of fact only and not a strong image
> of everything which is not-you, which sees you.[53]

This passage, from "A Note on Sex and 'The Reclaiming of Language,'" *Dry Air*'s opening poem, is typical in its combination of a straightforward style with moments of estrangement or purposeful affectation. The quotation marks around the pronoun *she* serve to unmoor the lyric coherence of the poem, which focuses on the experience of a "Savage" returning home from what is called "the New Country." Made into an ethnographic object and then a tourist's souvenir, the primary *she* of the poem is very much not the speculative "*she*" in the quoted passage, which functions as a countertext within the otherwise straightforward description of the "Savage," a *she* who is objectified: "everything which is not-you, which sees you." If "the work" of feminism and of reclaiming language is to "write 'she'" as a "statement / of fact only," then this early poem by Riley productively short-circuits its ability to fulfill that aim. The passage is wary of a too-easy articulation of subjectivity and instead demonstrates the kind of constitutive instability that for Riley is crucial for thinking about terms such as "women." As she writes in *Am I That Name?*, "the suggestion is that 'women' is a simultaneous foundation of and irritant to feminism, and that this is constitutively so ... the dangerous intimacy between subjectification and subjection needs careful calibration."[54]

Such interrogative self-reflexivity is a regular feature of Riley's poetry, and several critics have bristled over what they see as its solipsism. At certain moments, her work runs the risk of excessive self-scrutiny, of what Riley herself recognizes as "attitudinising" ("that's what I do").[55] However, Riley manages to shape this tendency into a mode of lyric in which the subject's position is ceaselessly unsettled and consistently made contingent upon the discursive and historical structures that produce it. As with the recalcitrant "e.g." in the quoted passage or the well-known final line of "Affections Must Not" ("I. neglect. the. house"), Riley's poems often include rough patches, moments that perform resistance to lyric fluency.[56] The value of such a disconcerted lyric texture is that it dispenses with the damaging fiction of a self-sufficient poetic "I." A poem's attempt to produce a coherent subject is shown to be a kind of wrangling rather than an act of mastery:

> Stammering it fights to get
> held and to never get held
> as whatever motors it swells
> to hammer itself out on me.[57]

By presenting instances of lyric speech that are troubled and fissile and by so refusing the reification of the subject, Riley manages to preserve lyric as a potentially progressive mode of aesthetic discourse.

Ideologies of gender and selfhood are among Riley's abiding subjects, and she has taken them up in poems that explore questions of sexuality and objectification (see "Lure, 1963") and the intertwining of gender, domesticity, and economics ("Affections Must Not"). She has addressed English literature's patriarchal foundations ("When It's Time to Go") by rewriting individual poems (such as "Well All Right," a response to Yeats's "Leda and the Swan") and entire genres, as in her wryly demystifying "Pastoral":

> Gents in a landscape hang above their lands.
> Their long keen shadows trace peninsulas on fields.
> Englishness, Welshness, flow blankly out around them.[58]

Even in such satirical moments, her poetry's politics recognize the very uncertain political status of poetry itself. Updating Auden's complex edict that "poetry makes nothing happen" (but is instead "a way of happening") for the quite different situation of 1980s Britain, Riley simultaneously demonstrates the fierce potential of a politically charged poetry and refuses to license the too easy conflation of poetic innovation and political action:

> Not your landscapes stiffened with figurines of an ageing woman
>   politician, it is harder than that
> Not your happy here-we-go-down-together dream of a roseate
>   catastrophe
> Nor your reassuring conviction that whole governments
> Will pale and stagger under the jawbones of your dismembered syntax
> Vain boy![59]

After lampooning Thatcher's England, Riley rebukes the "vain boy[s]" of linguistically-innovative poetry before sardonically abandoning writerly power in the stanza that follows ("What I want please write it for me"). As in this negative litany, Riley's poems move among rhetorical registers, harnessing discursive mobility in lyrics of affective intensity and fierce skepticism.

Like Johnson's dub polemics, Nichols's and Dabydeen's transatlantic reimaginings, Kay's lyric drama, and Harrison's conflicted quatrains, Riley's self-reflexive investigations intervene in a wider set of political and social narratives that took hold throughout Britain in the latter decades of the twentieth century. They are part of a larger effort by poets in the period to reconceive of Britain itself. One way to frame these shifts is to consider how poets reimagined the concept of *home*.[60] As I've pointed out, changes in immigration and citizenship laws fundamentally altered the status of Britain as a homeland. Simultaneously, burgeoning devolution movements in Scotland and, to a lesser degree, Wales, along with the continuation of the Troubles in Northern Ireland, destabilized the notion of homeland from another direction. Even though the 1979 independence referenda in Wales and Scotland did not pass, movements toward greater autonomy gained strength throughout Thatcher's decade in power. Indeed, these movements seem to have been quickened by political reactions against the Thatcher government, especially in Scotland, resulting in successful devolution referenda in Scotland and Wales in 1997, which created the Scottish Assembly and the National Assembly of Wales, respectively. Within England, poets carried on with the local and regional projects of the 1960s and 1970s. Roy Fisher continued his poetic mapping of Birmingham in *A Furnace* (1986).[61] Peter Reading detailed the grim intricacies and sordid materials of "junk Britain," as Tom Paulin described it, in volumes such as *Ukulele Music* (1985) and *Stet* (1986).[62] Hull, in the wake of Larkin's long residence there and Douglas Dunn's attention to the city in *Terry Street* (1969) and *For Love or Nothing* (1974), became a hub of poetic activity and source of material for writers like Peter Didsbury, Sean O'Brien, and Rumens. For poets throughout England, Scotland, Wales, and Northern Ireland, then, the delineation of place and the articulation of locality remained central tasks. And the space and concept of home persisted as a key category of thought, even as the domestic sphere itself was transformed. I conclude, then, with a turn through several poems that attend to the nuanced valences of home.

As we've seen with Larkin, focusing on home often made for disappointed poetry. For Douglas Dunn, who increasingly, although not uncritically, emphasized his Scottish roots in his work after the 1970s, a focus on homeland functioned in tandem with a sense of belatedness, of having to exist in what he calls, in an elegy for Hugh MacDiarmid, "this nocturne of modernity."[63] Dunn's vision tends toward the conservative and nostalgic, imagining a new pastoral nation reborn out of the missteps of industry. In "Galloway Motor Farm," which casts its eye on a field of abandoned automobiles, he writes:

> Scotland, come back
> From the lost ground of your dismantled lands.
> A carelessness has defaced even the bluebell.[64]

Dunn's fellow Scottish poet Edwin Morgan, who by the 1980s was the dominant voice in Scottish poetry and whose 1972 *Glasgow Sonnets* rendered the particulars of urban dilapidation in his hometown ("A shilpit dog fucks grimly by the close. / Late shadows lengthen slowly, slogans fade"), took a much longer view in *Sonnets from Scotland* (1984).[65] In this sequence of fifty-one poems, Morgan tracks Scotland's deep history, beginning in "Slate" in the Paleolithic age and proffering the sonnet as a time-traveling device that can change locations and foci at will. Morgan's transhistorical, extraplanetary, and corporate speaker (most often simply, "we") touches down on various key as well as idiosyncratic landmarks, figures, and episodes throughout the history of civilization in Scotland, moving with a madcap logic towards the present and into a post-cataclysmic future. The scope of Morgan's relentless remapping of Scotland manages to be at once severely local and nearly galactic, circling a particular bit of the planet while moving through time. Reconsidering moments of Scotland's past and imagining instants well beyond the present, the *Sonnets from Scotland* are perfectly titled – they are from Scotland in the way that the *Voyager* spacecraft is "from" Earth: "Scotland was found on Jupiter. That's true."[66]

Aside from Morgan, most poets tended to reconceive notions of home from somewhere nearer to home. Learning "what is meant by home," to mention again a line from Derek Mahon's "Afterlives," was quite a different experience for an exilic Northern Irish poet like Mahon than for postcolonial writers like Fred D'Aguiar or Grace Nichols.[67] D'Aguiar's poem "Home" details a return trip to London in which his experience with "H.M. Customs" at Heathrow reveals the racially constructed nature of British identity and citizenship:

> My passport photo's too open-faced,
> haircut wrong (an afro) for the decade;
> the stamp, British Citizen not bold enough
> for my liking and too much for theirs.[68]

For D'Aguiar's speaker, "home is always elsewhere," even though London serves as a locus of love and affection. The diasporic undertow of D'Aguiar's poem is reversed by Nichols, who turns the anxiety of nonbelonging into a not unambivalent declaration of mobility: "Wherever I hang me knickers – that's my home."[69] The uneasy toggle between *me* and *my*, subtly and knowingly switching from a racially or geographically marked to an unmarked grammatical form of the possessive, reads as an emblem of the vexations of home for British poets late in the twentieth century.

The family dwelling can index nearly the full range of social, political, and cultural issues with which poets wrangled, a usefully malleable figure for a poem's internal questioning of identity, belonging, and subjectivity – the setting, as it were, for British poetry's new narratives in the period. For Mahon, *home* is the word that, off-rhymed with "bomb," signals an experiential and affective disattachment, while for D'Aguiar it indicates a condition of almost existential displacement. Nichols revalues the displacement negatively ensconced in *home* so as to mark a condition of sexual freedom and subjective agency, even if the slip from *me* to *my* signals a bind of another order. At the end of "Coming Home," Rumens evacuates *home* of its sense of intimacy and comfort, presenting it instead as a space of obligation and near deathliness: "how tight the plot that locks us in, / how small our parts, how unchosen."[70] The confining qualities of home, a principal topic for many women poets, is both recognized and complicated by Anne Stevenson: "that four-walled chrysalis / and impediment, home; / that lamp and hearth, that easy fit / of bed to bone."[71] Here, as for Rumens, home is a stand-in for the grave, but it is also a vital and creative space. This dialectical figuration of home is given another twist by Gillian Clarke at the start of "Cofiant," a lyric sequence chronicling her family's history: "Houses we've lived in / inhabit us / and history's restless / in the rooms of the mind."[72] Both subject of and subject to home, *we* inhabit it just as it inhabits, and founds, us. The scalability of *home* as figure and concept makes it particularly useful. It can stand for both family life and national life; it can denote actual houses or connote a sense of origins; it can become a synecdoche for whole societies – or, as in Clarke's quoted passage, it can offer a figural container for subjective and psychological life.

As we've seen, such flexibility also makes the idea of home unstable and uncanny. The intimate estrangement lodged in *home* takes on particular resonance for late-twentieth-century British poets, for whom the material and historical conditions of home were shifting enormously. One of the most intriguing texts of the period, and one that condenses a number of the issues I've taken up in this chapter, is the title poem from Jo Shapcott's *Phrase Book* (1991). Drawing from the Martian manner of Craig Raine, the new narrative obliquities of Fenton and Muldoon, and the euphemizing lexicon of the United States military, "Phrase Book" is an occasionally surreal parable of an Englishwoman who is simultaneously stationed in her house watching television footage of, presumably, the first Gulf War and lost somewhere abroad, using the phrase book of the title to communicate in the local language. The poem exists in several places at once, stacking a sexual encounter, which is seemingly observed by military pilots on their "Side-Looking // Airborne Radar," on top of screen images of war violence.[73] Intertwined within these scenarios is the circuitous story of the speaker's attempt to get home:

> Where is the British Consulate? Please explain.
> What does it mean? What must I do? Where
> can I find? What have I done? I have done
> nothing. Let me pass please. I am an Englishwoman.[74]

Here, in the poem's final lines, the panicked miscommunications display the vertiginous effects of the phrase book's primer-like sentences, just as the military vocabulary estranges the domestic narrative woven through the text. Home, language, personal history, and national identity are each mutually misconstituted, as the crash of technologies warps any attempt at self-definition.

The speaker twice declares her Englishness, but the poem's narrative turmoil belies the assumed sturdiness of this claim. As in Shapcott's wryly alienating text, the new narrative strategies that poets undertook aimed to upset and unsettle received narratives of British culture, whether they had been received from the long tradition or were newly modeled within the Thatcher era's schisms. In doing so, such poems put into question these narratives, finding in the local subtleties of poetic form spaces in which different stories might take shape.

Chapter 7

Platforms and Performances

The 1990s were, in many ways, a heady time for poetry in Britain. An increasing and increasingly diverse number of poets were writing and publishing poems as the century drew to a close, more frequently than ever within the context of newly established creative writing programs and workshops. Concomitantly, more and more poets took up teaching positions at colleges and universities, and poetry as a craft and product became wound more tightly into the institutions of higher education. Poetry prizes proliferated, with major awards like the Forward Prizes (established in 1991) and the T.S. Eliot Prize (inaugurated in 1993) coming with significant cash rewards and even, for a while, televised award ceremonies. A number of programs were launched to increase poetry's public profile, including Poetry on the Underground (1986), National Poetry Day (1994), and Poetry on the Buses (1998). Major individual honors also helped keep poetry in the news: Hughes's assumption of the Laureateship in 1984 (after Larkin declined the post), Walcott's 1992 Nobel Prize, and Heaney's 1995 Nobel. These achievements cemented trends indicative of postwar British poetry more broadly, with the two Nobels saying nearly as much about the advance of Caribbean and Northern Irish poetry and the reorientation of British poetry in the previous several decades as they did about the achievements of each poet individually.

Additionally, there were concerted efforts to sort and canonize the torrent of poetic activity, with a cache of anthologies sizing up the field and promoting its various encampments. This followed a familiar pattern of action and reaction, one that we've seen in previous chapters: Conquest's *New Lines* spawned Alvarez's *The New Poetry*, and Motion and Morrison's *The Penguin Book of Contemporary British Poetry* irked into existence several anthologies eager to combat its limited scope. As the decade drew to a close, anthologies assumed the added burden of summarizing an entire half century's or century's worth of poetry. In *The Penguin Book of Poetry from Britain and Ireland since 1945* (1998), Simon Armitage and Robert Crawford presented a fairly conservative version of a still-evolving and highly debated canon that carried the additional prestige of historical sweep – each phrase in the volume's title asserts a different mode of authority. Keith Tuma's *Anthology of Twentieth-Century British & Irish Poetry*, published by Oxford University Press in 2001, was a major – and controversial – intervention into and renovation of the canon, one that recovered a number of overlooked poets and placed great emphasis on the modernist and experimental strands within the canon at the expense of what we call, as always too simply, the mainstream. Of course, several earlier anthologies had set themselves similar tasks, whether Crozier and Longville's *A Various Art* or Sinclair's *Conductors of Chaos*. However, Tuma's book – with its commanding title, its densely footnoted heft, its formidable publisher, its significant price, and its appearance at the start of a new millennium – made a decisive claim to literary-historical centrality, which caused a good deal of angst for its critics. Anthologies are always polemical, which accounts for nearly all of their flair and much of their interest, but the *fin-de-siècle* moment raised the stakes of such literary-critical skirmishes.

These efforts to promote poetry must be viewed within the context of continued worries about its viability within the publishing world. Although several writers remained big sellers, the overall market for poetry shrank. The fact that Heaney and Hughes accounted for such a huge percentage of contemporary poetry sales is astounding, to be sure, but also a worrying sign, and the huge success of Hughes's *Birthday Letters* (1998), about his relationship with Sylvia Plath, only magnified the imbalance. Poetry had long been a way for publishers to establish cultural prestige rather than to ensure profits. But as more and more multinational corporations have taken over publishing firms, poetry lists have been reduced drastically or cut altogether. Paladin Poetry is an unfortunate example of this trend. An important imprint of Grafton Books (later bought by Collins), Paladin produced John Muckle's *The New British Poetry* anthology in 1988, as well as selections of key British poets like Allen Fisher and Tom Raworth and international figures such as John Ashbery and Octavio Paz. The imprint was discontinued and its print runs pulped after Collins was bought by Rupert Murdoch's News Corporation in 1989 and amalgamated into HarperCollins. The closure of the Oxford Poets series in 1999 was a particular nadir, but it was part of a broader tendency among major trade publishers to thin their lists to established stars and a few select others. One effect of this pattern has been to make space for publishers such as Bloodaxe and Carcanet to become principal forces within the small world of poetry publishing.

Central to a consideration of British poetry in the 1990s and into the present is its complex position within the cultural marketplace, a marketplace responding to the dismantling of much of the postwar welfare state after a decade of Thatcherism, the end of the Cold War, and the hyperextension of

American-style capitalism and consumerism. The "platforms and performances" named in this chapter's title are at times literal – political poetry and performance poetry will be topics – but they also refer to a more fundamental issue. At century's end, ceaselessly burgeoning forms of communication and mass media made for an utterly saturated cultural sphere, a condition that of course endures in the early twenty-first century. Even before the full advent of online culture and social media, poets – just like everybody else – have had to negotiate a dizzying and fully commodified landscape, trapped on the platform of mediatized consumerism that produces hemmed-in choices and presents freedom as being simply one more purchase away. The space between a product's marketing and the product itself has become increasingly negligible, and while it is easier and cheaper to distribute poetry than it ever has been (via print-on-demand services, desktop publishing, and online magazines and journals), the precise implications of imagining poetry as a product have had to be faced anew. As we've seen, many writers in Britain had long been critiquing capitalism and considering the links between poetry and consumerism, but in the 1990s and 2000s this nexus came to the center of the stage. In large part, it remains there.

For a stretch in the early 1990s, the spotlight was occupied by a group of writers yoked together in a promotional campaign dubbed "The New Generation Poets." The idea was hatched at the National Poetry Competition awards event in 1993 and developed by a steering committee of editors and administrators, the driving figures of which were Peter Forbes, then-editor of the Poetry Society's *Poetry Review*, and Bill Swainson, editor at Harvill. A small panel of judges, among whose members were Michael Longley and James Wood, used a loose set of guidelines to choose a group of twenty "New Gen" poets who were announced in January 1994 amidst much media fanfare. The chosen writers gave public readings throughout the country and were promoted on Radio 1, as well as on television and in print journalism.[1] A special issue of the *Poetry Review* featuring the chosen poets paced the spring media rollout. National Poetry Day was established as part of the promotion, and the rolling series of readings, events, interviews, and publications was capped off in October 1994, when an episode of *The South Bank Show* was devoted to New Gen poetry. The aim was to give poetry traction in a crowded media environment and to sell more books, and these young(-ish) poets were commodified within an increasingly celebrity-driven culture as the literary equivalents of pop stars or stand-up comedians. The campaign was overseen by Colman Getty, a large public relations firm, and sponsored by a number of the usual suspects – the major publishers, the Arts Council, and Waterstone's. However, it also relied on much broader support from the establishment, including the

British Council, the Foundation for Sport and the Arts, and Lord Goodman, at the time one of the most significant and well-connected people in Britain, and a lawyer and negotiator for an array of public figures, from Harold Wilson to Edward Heath to Rupert Murdoch.

Much of the New Gen phenomenon seems like a blustery marketing campaign, but it does catch and reflect the more general commodification of British culture occurring at the time, a point that Iain Sinclair makes in his introduction to *Conductors of Chaos*, the most ardent rebuttal to the New Gen narrative. Nearly every corner of the poetry business comes in for criticism by Sinclair, but the harshest barbs are reserved for the New Gen poets, who, he writes, "have arrived in our midst like pod people. They are eternally not-quite-young and they feed on images of blight…They were invented by marketing men, hyped into existence with seemingly fictitious occupations and previous histories dreamt up by Poetry Society copywriters."[2] Unlike many of the groupings we've seen so far, which evolved out of friendships and shared projects, New Gen poets are a prefabricated configuration. Peter Forbes, in his introductory column to the "New Generation Poets" issue of *Poetry Review*, promotes the "distinctiveness and stubborn, even wilful individuality of these poets" rather than conformation to "journalistic clichés of the new pluralism, regionalism, and the rise of the working class voice."[3] Of course, promoting the distinctive individuality of the writers was as much a marketing move as an aesthetic judgment. Nonetheless, from certain angles, the group of twenty writers represented a diverse cross-section of multicultural Britain, and such a presentation of diversity was part of the promotional campaign. There were twelve men and eight women selected. Nine of the poets were born in England and seven in Scotland. Of the remaining four, three were born outside Britain but came to England as children (Moniza Alvi, who was born in Pakistan; David Dabydeen, who was born in Guyana; and Michael Hoffman, who was born in Germany). And there was one fully fledged ex-pat: Michael Donaghy, an Irish American who was born in the Bronx and came to England in his early thirties. Most of the poets have gone on to have significant careers, with several becoming quite famous: Carol Ann Duffy, Simon Armitage, Glyn Maxwell, and Don Paterson, to name the biggest names.[4] The success of the campaign has led to two sequels, with twenty poets chosen as the "Next Generation" in 2004 and another twenty named by the Poetry Society as "Next Generation Poets 2014."

Perhaps predictably, considering that the entire project was conceived from the center of the literary establishment and that it aimed to increase poetry's popularity in a crowded cultural marketplace, much of the New Gen writing fits into a fairly narrow band of formal ambition. Most New Gen poems are short to medium-sized lyrics voiced by clear and consistent speakers that unfold in traditional meters or in loose free verse. There is a preponderance of eclectic character sketches, quirky anecdotes, and ironic self-portraits, many of which are clever, accessible, pleasurably light, and sometimes gently shocking. As with many of the poets discussed in the previous chapter, narrative is prominent and tends at once toward the offhand and the fabular. Many poems veer toward the parabolic or the casually significant, often coming to rest in deflationary moments that are equal parts Auden, Larkin, and Martian, with a Muldoonian twist. Throughout the range of New Gen poems, the manipulation of tone is a chief technique, with the poet's "voice" and stylistic signature becoming central markers of distinction. That is to say, the poets are entirely of their moment, as Stan Smith has pointed out:

> These poets are all Thatcher's Children, products of the entrepreneurial culture of the 1980s. Their generation is that of the Yuppies, the quick City killing, the meteoric rise of talent and fortunes from new and unexpected origins, and their language often has the slick knowingness of such a culture, even when they turn it in irony to bite the hand that feeds them. Though they all variously set themselves in opposition to this ethos, it is everywhere inscribed in their lines.[5]

At its worst, New Gen poetry cultivates a weak postmodernism, a carefully managed and packaged eclecticism whose seeming innovation is simply a consumable newness, a mere play of style. As Smith suggests, an ethos of self-promotion and commodification is often a symptom of this work rather than a problem with which it reckons. But several poets have managed to address this tension from within the maw of their marketing: as when W.N. Herbert provides a raucous deconstruction of the packaging of Scottishness in "Cabaret McGonagall," when Kathleen Jamie examines the odds and ends atop a city dump in order to question the weight of the past on the present in "Mr. and Mrs. Scotland Are Dead," or when Armitage constructs a monumental parody to millennial monumentalism in "Five Eleven Ninety Nine."

Beginning with his first volume, *Zoom!* (1989), Armitage has become a deft artificer of what we might call lyric curios, vignettes of the oddly mundane encounter or eccentric event, best seen in poems like "Goalkeeper with a Cigarette" and "The Tyre." The title poem of *The Dead Sea Poems* (1995) can be read as an ironic parable of the New Gen formation, in which self-absorption becomes mythicized self-regard. In the poem, the speaker enters a cave in order to recover one of the goats he's been driving and finds a dozen caskets that contain "poems written in my own hand."[6] It is never explained how the poems got there or whether the speaker knew that they had been missing, but he takes them and sells them for "twelve times nothing." Later, he sees them "on public display": they have become hugely valuable literary artifacts, and in order to prevent another such loss, he decides to recite his poems again and again

> by singing the whole of the work
> to myself, every page of that innocent,
> everyday, effortless verse, of which this

> is the first.[7]

The poem's self-reflexive, quasi-Borgesian cast – it is the text that it is about – is reminiscent of Hughes's well-known poem "The Thought-Fox." But while that poem concerns the interleaving of perception and composition, Armitage's focuses on its own status as a product. His parable moves through three different ways to envision an aesthetic artifact: first as a near-sacred object, then as a commodity, and finally as something utterly bound to the self, something that isn't discovered or sold but that is realized by being "all / to heart." After two moments at which the speaker is alienated from his poetic labor, the conclusion offers a reconciliation of sorts: the poems are neither totems nor collector's items but rather integral to the self's "everyday" life. The trouble, of course, is that this concluding realization is catalyzed by financial considerations. The speaker goes through the trouble of reciting his poems so completely because he knows "now the price of my early art." By internalizing "the whole of the work," the speaker has become the commodity that he too cheaply sold, just as the poem, with its final words, becomes a self-branding product that announces its own high-end rarity and authenticity ("this // is the first"). The intrigue is primarily a matter of discerning the poem's complex tone, which Armitage keeps productively unsettled. Is its seeming seriousness really a kind of deadpan? Is its puffed-up self-importance in truth a species of self-deprecation? Or is this self-deprecation a backdoor – and knowing – pomposity? How do we position the goat-herder/poet/speaker in relation to Simon Armitage? Most readers are not going to read the poem and imagine that this is something that "happened" to Armitage, as one does with many of the anecdotal texts in his first few volumes. But we also can't easily take the text as a dramatic monologue. The poem's ironies career off each other. It is both a parable and a mock parable, just as "Five Eleven Ninety Nine," the text at the heart of *The Dead Sea Poems*, is at once an extensive and excessive poem about a huge bonfire and a parody that questions such excess.

"Five Eleven Ninety Nine," as its title makes clear, is a Guy Fawkes Night poem that describes in extravagant detail the lengths to which one community goes to build "the fire to end all fires."[8] For 512 lines – divided into five-beat, occasionally rhyming quatrains – the speaker catalogues all the belongings and detritus used to build the fire and then narrates its lighting, the sounds and sights as it crackles and grows, the increasingly self-sabotaging measures to which individuals go to keep it lit, and its inevitable decay. A moment of purgation and catharsis for the town, who "deliver all things combustible," the bonfire is also an all-too-clear millennial symbol.[9] Community ritual becomes rummage sale set aflame, and at one point, a mock-crucifixion is suggested when someone remembers a huge wooden cross sitting in a garage and "the strongest of us bends / and takes its length along his spine."[10] The poem ends after the fire goes out and the people return to their scavenged homes, returning at dawn to view the aftermath:

> We wait, listless, aimless now it's over,
> ready for what follows, what comes after,
> stood beneath an iron sky together,
> awkwardly at first, until whenever.[11]

Any meaning or significance that the event might have had has drained away as they, like good consumers, merely wait for the next thing "until whenever." If only by fact of its length, the poem surely seeks to make an impact, and the monumentalism of its event is mirrored in the vastness of the poem's form. Just as the pyre slowly builds as everyone adds their items to it, so does the poem build itself by enumerating all those items. The "centre pole" of the fire, around and beneath which all of the materials are placed, is replicated metrically by the pentameter norm and stanzaically by the insistent quatrains, and the poem's total of 512 lines seems designed to exceed, just by a little, one possible permutation of the titular date: 511.99.[12] However, this playing of form off content can't help but feel a bit hollow, especially considering the predictability of the narrative arc. The poem certainly seeks to be a kind of satire, either of the specific publicity surrounding the New Gen moment, or of the emptiness of postmodern spectacle more broadly. But its dependence on exactly what it seeks to skewer limits its critical power. It is both a long piece of lyric hype and an attempted mockery of the same.

In contrast to Armitage's quasi- or pseudo-autobiographical anecdotes, in which the force and location of a text's irony are usually equivocal, Carol Ann Duffy's dramatic monologues have such a space clearly built in. Since the appearance of *Standing Female Nude* (1985), Duffy has become most well known for monologues that satirize everything from the educational system ("Head of School") and carnivorism ("A Healthy Meal") to patriarchy more generally. As with a novel in which we distance the narrator-function from the author-function, so in Duffy's ventriloquized lyrics are we able to differentiate between an authorial "I" and the "I" of a poem. This is especially the case because so many of Duffy's personas are so clearly not her, whether the sadistic murderer who speaks in "Psychopath," the French prostitute who models in "Standing Female Nude," or the many historical and mythical women – such as "Mrs. Darwin" or "Queen Kong" – whom Duffy reanimates in *The World's Wife* (1999). Duffy, who has also written popular children's poetry, depends heavily on myths, parables, and folk tales within her large-scale deconstruction of gender ideologies, a project at the center of her first six volumes, from *Standing Female Nude* (1985) through *Feminine Gospels* (2002). As part of her emphasis on the construction of gender and sexuality within Western cultures, Duffy uses the dramatic monologue form to investigate the power of ideology and the ways in which individuals are produced by social and discursive codes well outside their own will or control.

Intriguingly, one of the most poignant such poems features a nonhuman speaker. In "The Dolphins," one of a pair of performing dolphins captive at an aquarium describes the duo's subjugation:

> World is what you swim in, or dance, it is simple.
> We are in our element but we are not free.[13]

Their managed tedium certainly allegorizes the quietly desperate conditions of contemporary life, but it is when the poem is taken on its own terms – as a monologue spoken by a dolphin – that the strange power of Duffy's mimicry is most apparent. The unadorned and deadly earnest language placed in their mouths contrasts utterly with the vapid tricks that they must perform, as in the poem's final lines:

> There is a plastic toy. There is no hope. We sink
> to the limits of this pool until the whistle blows.
> There is a man and our mind knows we will die here.[14]

Joined into one mind, the dolphins report upon their duties and understand their fate, providing a moment of stark fatalism that redirects the charge of anthropomorphization by so fully committing to the pathetic fallacy as a compositional strategy. There is a productive split between the poem's theme – the way in which animals become domesticated and commodified by humans – and the rhetorical unfolding of that theme, wherein the otherness of the dolphins remains strangely other. They are weirdly humanized, given the powers of human language while remaining undifferentiated as human subjects. The single-minded pair – "Our mind" – understands their grim fate, but it is a mind that subtly resists a reader's attempt to sympathize with it, if only because it is eerily plural.

Duffy's critics have sometimes complained that her work is too accessible, that her dependence on a plain style and relatively simple language prevents any larger critique of patriarchy from gaining force. To be sure, Duffy's work does not problematize the ideologies of lyric as does Denise Riley's, nor does it unrig language's basic mechanisms of signification and reference, as we will see when turning to Maggie O'Sullivan's and Geraldine Monk's poetry.[15] Duffy's genius is for remaining within the center of the English literary tradition while working its angles in order to dislodge its presumptions from the inside. "Warming Her Pearls," one of her best known poems, is a cross-class lesbian love poem in which the beloved – "my lady" – is metonymically evoked via the pearls that the speaker, the lady's maid, wears all day in order to keep them warm until her lady needs them for her evening parties. Disrupting the gender roles of the courtly love tradition, Duffy nonetheless retains the basic scaffolding of the blazon in order to depict the maid's desire for her lady, who at the start of the poem appears as a series of isolated limbs and parts:

> Next to my own skin, her pearls. My mistress
> bids me wear them, warm them, until evening
> when I'll brush her hair. At six, I place them
> round her cool, white throat. All day I think of her.[16]

The opening line provides the metonymic logic that governs the poem's unfolding: figuratively and literally (by way of the phrase's placement in the line), "her pearls" mediate the maid's desire for her mistress. Traditionally featuring a male lover/speaker and a female beloved, the blazon genre is here half subverted, with a female subject and a female object. Similarly, the poem presents a very conservative English class structure, even as it undermines this by limning a scene of lesbian desire. The scene, however, features a fairly standard cache of sexualized images and innuendoes – "her milky stones," "my red lips," "her slim hand" – as it yokes together sex and death, sex and money, and pleasure and pain: "All night / I feel their absence and I burn."[17] Duffy's poems are uncannily traditional lyrics, whether her dramatic monologues, the many nonpersona poems in the mid-1990s volumes as well as in *Rapture* (2005) and *The Bees* (2011), or the extended parable-narratives in *Feminine Gospels* (see especially "The Long Queen," "The Map-Woman," and "The Laughter of Stafford Girls' High"). Duffy's wit and humor have helped make her the most popular poet in Britain in the early twenty-first century, a stature both confirmed and furthered when, in 2009, she became the first woman and the first Scot to be named Poet Laureate. Her poems seem utterly accessible and familiar, and for the most part they are, yet there are subtle but vital revisions contained within their forms and generic conventions that require readers to mind the details of her lyric fictions.

Duffy was one of seven Scottish New Gen poets, and whatever its other limitations, the New Gen campaign managed to catch the full force of a late-century Scottish poetry renaissance, just as Motion and Morrison's 1982 anthology, whatever *its* own faults, caught the rise of Northern Irish poetry near its apex. Scottish poetry had been in an upswing since the late 1960s, as earlier chapters have discussed. Tom Leonard, Douglas Dunn, Liz Lochhead, and especially Edwin Morgan became important precursors for younger writers such as Jackie Kay, Frank Kuppner, Robin Robertson, as well as the Scottish New Gen poets: Duffy, Paterson, Jamie, Herbert, John Burnside, Mick Imlah, and Robert Crawford. The publication of Morgan's *Selected Poems* in 1985 was a major event and cemented his status as the key Scottish poet after MacDiarmid. This position was formalized when Morgan was named the first Scots Makar, the Scottish National Poet, a post he held from 2004 until his death in 2010. Donny O'Rourke's anthology, *Dream State: The New Scottish Poets* (1994) and its 2002 expanded version, helped coalesce this distinct body of poetry, which managed to distinguish itself from MacDiarmid's legacy and from that of an earlier generation of male-dominated Scottish poets (which included Morgan and Finlay) that came of age in the 1960s.

These "New Scottish Poets" continued to ask questions about Scottish identity and to work through the complex interrelationships among Scotland's three major languages – English, Scottish Gaelic, and Scots. Just as Morgan and, behind him, MacDiarmid were vital influences for younger Scottish poets in English, so did Scottish Gaelic poets in the twentieth century's latter decades have the towering example of Somhairle MacGill-Eain (Sorley MacLean). In addition, a number of poets wrote in both English and Scots. Herbert's *Dundee Doldrums* (1991) and *Sharawaggi* (1991) – a volume of Scots poetry coauthored with Crawford – blend the dictionary-diving impulse behind MacDiarmid's synthetic Scots with an urban Scots indebted to Leonard's demotic vernacular poetry and simultaneously draw on American Beat and New York School styles. Herbert continues to move back and forth between Scots and English in his work, with his Scots poems often modeling a rowdy reinvention of the ballad tradition and his English poems primarily progressing in streams of data-rich free verse. A heavy information load is typical of Herbert's poems, and, along with Richard Price, he gathered other Scottish poets of similar proclivities into *Contraflow on the Super Highway* (1994), an anthology showcasing a mini-burst of what they dubbed Informationism.

The Scottish Informationists, as their moniker suggests, are interested in the massive amounts of information that technological and scientific advances have produced and put into play, and they use their poems both to display these varieties of information and to consider the effects of such an overload of data. Herbert's wry poems tend to feature large amounts of detail, and his impulse to obsessively enumerate links him not only with his fellow Informationists but also to writers like Armitage, Muldoon, and Peter Reading, as well as to Don Paterson, whose penchant for detail is most clearly apparent in his ongoing series of long poems, "The Alexandrian Library." In "Cabaret McGonagall," Herbert's Informationism appears as a rollicking but gimlet-eyed celebration of contemporary Scottish culture that doubles as a castigation of the marketing of Scottishness and of a society damagingly arrested by popular culture and consumerism:

> Come aa ye dottilt brain-deid lunks,
> ye hibernatin cyber-punks,
> gadget-gadjies, comics-geeks,
> guys wi perfick rat's physiques,
> fowk with fuck-aa social skills,
> fowk that winnae tak thir pills:
> *gin ye cannae even pley fuitball*
> *treh thi Cabaret McGonagall.*[18]

Herbert's anxious depiction of the state of Scottish culture took on special force within continuing debates about Scotland's political future. A narrow majority of voters in the 1979 referendum supported a devolved Scottish government, but Westminster was able to nullify the election because of low voter turnout. This outcome, along with rising disapproval of Thatcher's Conservative government throughout the 1980s, widened the political gap between Scotland and England, and writers and artists in particular became vocal proponents of a more independent Scotland. Such a state of affairs became a reality after a 1997 devolution referendum did gain the necessary support of Scottish voters, and the Scottish Assembly was reestablished in 1999 after a hiatus of 292 years. Scotland's political status continues to be an active question. The September 2014 Scottish independence referendum did not pass, but one outcome of the campaign has been the promise of increased power devolved to Scotland by the government at Westminster. The blossoming of Scottish poetry in the 1980s and 1990s runs in parallel with progress toward a more independent Scotland, and a number of writers took nationalism as a primary theme. However, as Christopher Whyte has argued, one ought to be skeptical of "the transitory but intense love affair which took place between writers and intellectuals and the nationalist movement."[19]

Robert Crawford, a fellow Informationist, has been a central voice in this conversation. In a number of influential scholarly books, he has argued for the centrality of Scottish writers within the history of English literature and culture, and his early volumes of poetry – *A Scottish Assembly* (1990) and *Talkies* (1992) – consider the politics of Scottish nationalism within larger questions about Scotland's role in a global information economy. Like Herbert, Crawford worries about the marketing of Scottishness for the tourist economy, as in his paean to "Inner Glasgow":

> hard nostalgia
> Steam-rivets us to ghosts we love, in murals
>
> Where everybody looks the same and sings
> Of oppression, smokes, drinks lager, shouts out 'fuck'.
> Shops sell us.[20]

Wary of callow attempts to gloss over and profit from a fetishized version of Glasgow's history – what the poem names "Entrepreneurs' industrial / Museum postcard grime" – Crawford wants to capture his sense of an authentic Scottish nation and culture at the same time that he recognizes their implication in global circuits of capitalism.[21] For Crawford, "Scotland," as two consecutive poems with that title have it, is both "glens / Gridded with light" and "semiconductor country."[22] Crawford carries on a particularly Scottish form of Keatsian negative capability known as the "Caledonian antisyzygy." This designates the idea that Scottish literature typically features a "zigzag of contradictions" and a "sudden jostling of contraries," a notion promulgated by MacDiarmid and first named by the Scottish literary critic G. Gregory Smith in *Scottish Literature: Character and Influence* (1919).[23] Without granting the phrase's essentialism, it is useful to reactivate the notion of the antisyzygy to consider how poets have grappled with the torsions of the late twentieth and early twenty-first centuries as Scotland's political and social textures are being reimagined.

One of the most compelling poems of the period and one that brings together contraries so as to jostle notions of Scottish culture is the title poem of Kathleen Jamie's 1994 volume, *The Queen of Sheba*. Along with Duffy, Kay, and Lochhead, Jamie has changed the terms of poetry in Scotland after a century in which males dominated the canon and women writers were marginalized. The massive success of these writers – within a Scottish, British, as well as international context – signals a considerable shift in the representation of women within Scottish literature and a regendering of the concept of Scottish poetry. "The Queen of Sheba" is the opening text of a volume that comprises in part a gallery of girls' and women's lives. The book delves into the perils that young girls face ("Mother-May-I" and "The Shoe"), the economic and sexual oppressions of patriarchy ("Hand Relief"), parabolic sketches of women at various points of life and age ("School Reunion" and "Wee Wifey"), and folk-like narratives of feminist reclamation ("Bairns of Suzie – A Hex," "Den of the Old Men," and "Arraheids"). The title poem licenses the texts that follow, presaging Duffy's gleefully anachronistic fables in *The World's Wife*, but in the form of third-person address rather than dramatic monologue:

> Scotland, you have invoked her name
> just once too often
> in your Presbyterian living rooms.
> She's heard, yea
> even unto heathenish Arabia
> your vixen's bark of poverty, come down
> the family like a lang neb, a thrawn streak,
> a wally dug you never liked
> but can't get shot of.
> She's had enough. She's come.[24]

The parsimonious conservatism of Scottish culture, especially as it is used to marginalize women and maintain patriarchy, is, along with the Queen of Sheba herself, compared to an undesirable or "thrawn" genetic quality ("a lang neb," a long nose) or a family heirloom that just can't be gotten rid of ("a wally dug," a china dog). Rampantly mixing registers as though to combat the uniformity of tradition by way of diction, Jamie crashes together the deliberately antique, the casually conversational, and the blatantly demotic as she reclaims a rhetorical put-down meant to suppress women and girls ("who do you think you are, the Queen of Sheba?") by imagining the arrival of the Queen of Sheba into contemporary Scotland. Displaying the penchant for enumeration and spectacle shared by a number of New Gen poets, Jamie proceeds to narrate the queen's journey from ancient Sheba "to the peat and bracken / of the Pentland hills / across the fit-ba pitch," where her sensual authority overcomes Scotland's latent Calvinism, as she leads "those great soft camels / widdershins round the kirk-yaird."[25] She inspires the women and girls of Scotland to claim independence and power, and the poem rises to a conclusion after a man at the back of the gathered crowd "growls: whae do you think y'ur?" In response,

> a thousand laughing girls and she
> draw our hot breath
> and shout:
> THE QUEEN OF SHEBA!"[26]

A masculinist insult is made into a feminist anthem. The potential ideological oversimplification that the poem offers is mitigated by its position as the
first poem in the volume: its naïvety is tactical, and the poem succeeds as
an apostrophic overture to the increasingly complex investigations of gender
and sexuality that occur after it in *The Queen of Sheba*. Jamie's investigation
continues in her next volume, *Jizzen* (1999), which focuses on motherhood
and pregnancy, drawing its title from an Old Scots term for the *childbed*. As
with a number of New Gen poets, much of the interpretive intricacy has to
do with tone. We are sure that "The Queen of Sheba" courses with irony, especially considering that the poem, which celebrates an ancient female mon-
arch, appeared just as Scotland debated its own place in the United Kingdom,
where another queen had been long installed on the throne. But the poem's
celebration of a progressive politics isn't simply ironic or reactionary. Its mag-
ically real nature allows it to be at once serious and fantastical, and, as with
Duffy's dolphin monologue, the poem never fully flips over into allegory.
Rather, the aim is to allow multiple possibilities to remain in play, a different
sort of antisyzygy.

Jamie's work since *Jizzen* has centralized a topic long present in her work: the
relationship between humans and the environment and the thorough damage
that humans have done to the world. *The Tree House* (2004) and *The Overhaul*
(2012) are filled with short eco-lyrics, miniatures in the style of Michael
Longley, that aim to find "a way to live / on this damp, ambiguous earth."[27]
Jamie most often takes on the stance of a naturalist observing nature in peril,
as at the end of "The Whale-Watcher," for whom the surfacing whales are "like
stitches sewn in a rent / almost beyond repair."[28] As I turn now from New Gen
poetry to late-century work that emanated from well outside the mainstream,
it is worth digressing for a brief moment to linger on an issue that has taken
hold across the spectrum of poetic practice.

A number of poets have adapted the rich traditions of British nature writing to respond to an age of systemic ecological crisis, from Lavinia Greenlaw's
early global-warming poem, "The Recital of Lost Cities," to Duffy's more recent
attention to environmental issues in *The Bees* (see, especially, "Parliament").
Robert Minhinnick is a key figure in British eco-poetry, and he has, along
with Gwyneth Lewis, led a late-century flowering of English poetry in Wales.
Akin to the circumstances in Scotland, the rise of Welsh poetry in English
ran alongside a movement for political devolution, one that resulted in a successful referendum and the establishment of the Welsh Assembly in 1999.[29]
Minhinnick has extended the range of poetry in Wales beyond its usual local
and pastoral remit, writing increasingly expansive poems – mostly in the form
of travelogues or aggregations of brief texts – that range over a variety of international issues, from the wars in Iraq (see "Twenty-Five Laments for Iraq")

to the iniquities of global capitalism (as in "La Otra Orilla"). Minhinnick has long been an environmental activist in Wales, and his work often thematizes or stages ecological matters, as in "The Porthcawl Preludes." In this series, each short poem speaks as a different character in the ecological and human-built network of the Porthcawl shoreline, from the birds above and sea life in the water to the buoys in the bay.

Minhinnick's nautical personifications take their place within one of the richest veins of British nature poetry: texts about, to, or from the perspective of animals. Animal poems are ubiquitous throughout the history of world poetry, and they are prevalent in the full range of British poetry of the past seventy years, from the parabolic or allegorical sketches of Stevie Smith, Hughes, Heaney, Muldoon, or Duffy to the experimental naturalist lyrics of Colin Simms and Helen MacDonald to the Olsonian writing that Harriet Tarlo has dubbed "radical landscape poetry."[30] Animals are at the core of Maggie O'Sullivan's visual and sound poetry, and the densely textured poems in *In the House of the Shaman* (1993) and *Palace of Reptiles* (2002) comprise, among many other things, lyric bestiaries concerned with the many kinds of violence that animals suffer at human hands. Quite a number of ecologically minded poems unfold as mini-dramas in which the speaker functions as an observer of damage or as an avatar of threatened nature. However, O'Sullivan's poems forestall allegory or narrative by unrigging language's ability to communicate meaning and emphasizing the transformative qualities inherent to acts of poetic speech.

To read and hear O'Sullivan's poems is to experience a recital of language coming into being. Instead of grammatically fit sentences and words that have shared lexical meanings, her poems consist of recalcitrant bundles of sonic energy and uncanny semantics, what Peter Middleton calls "her use of non-lexical word-like assemblages of recognisable phonemes."[31] We listen to and watch the sound-prints of words and phrases morph and transmogrify into other words, near-words, echoes, neologisms, nonsense words, stutterings, and linguistic noise. In "Birth Palette," the opening poem in *Palace of Reptiles*, O'Sullivan describes and enacts this process with the conjured phrase, "crushtative bundles."[32] Instead of narrative, discourse, or argument, her poems offer enunciations, acts of language making in which newly forged sonic icons take on talismanic functions within a quasi-ritual context, as in "Hill Figures":

> elved X, chema-
> > tensions
> > chema-
> > > nexions: poisons
>
> > > pins, xins,
> > > > flicted[33]

There is a preponderance of sound effects and sense effects, but there is also an adamant refusal of sense. Not only does the poetry evade paraphrase, it rarely yields even local patches of normative meaning. Her works are at once oral, scriptural, visual, and etymological, and this total activation of the materiality of the signifier is simultaneously a thorough unspooling of the process of signification. In an extended text titled "riverrunning (realizations," first delivered as a talk in 1993, O'Sullivan articulates her poetic practice:

> The works I make Celebrate ORigins/ENtrances – the
> Materiality of Language: its actual contractions &
> expansions, potentialities, prolongments, assemblages –
> the acoustic, visual, oral & sculptural qualities
> within the physical: intervals between; in & beside.[34]

Drawing on the modernist innovations of Stein, Joyce, Kurt Schwitters, and Joseph Beuys, as well as on a genealogy that runs from Hopkins through Bunting to Griffiths and MacSweeney, O'Sullivan seeks to reanimate many of the fundamental energies of lyric poetry by recentering the poet's power of linguistic creation. At the same time, this project has a strong ethical undertow. Its lexical and syntactical experiments aim to reimagine the relationship between humans and the natural world by refashioning the basic mode in which we understand and delineate that world.

O'Sullivan's *In the House of the Shaman* (1993) is concerned primarily with recovering the roots of lyric poetry in chant, spell, and charm, and most texts are focused on the transformative powers of nature and on human attempts to access nature's power. The long poem that opens the volume, "Another Weather System," is a highly oblique consideration of the kinds of violence that humans inflict on animals and the natural world. Its opening phrase depicts both a magical or shamanic space and a violent trap:

> Contorted
> lure
> of
> Circles[35]

The central imagery of the poem has to do with acts of treachery toward nature:

> fur
> at
> beauty.
> Thieves Came

> *WHORLED STINGING*[36]

The often brutal lives of animals are again and again rendered in short phrasal bursts: "*HARES RAN / TOAD SCREAM.*"[37] O'Sullivan continually links moments of violence to acts of writing in order to make terribly clear just how intertwined are the basic mechanisms of human civilization with the systemic violence done to the world: "hooking the bill   tearing the flesh   lining the text."[38] The task, then, is to reconsider our position as a node within a complex system of relations (ecological, cultural, economic, physiological) rather than as the subject or master of that system:

> Wolf
> pattering
> tabor
> this
> appeared
> act
> i
> this
> locate
> space[39]

"i" is here positioned within a "space" in whose energies it participates but does not control; it refuses to act as a grammatical subject but rather remains a particle in a linguistic environment. What is clear throughout, however, is that we have failed at the larger task of reorienting ourselves in relation to the world:

> /in their own death/we have
> lost/we shall never hear/is killed/we
> are cursed/we[40]

While her poems are not exclusively concerned with ecological and environmental matters, they do continually model and ask a reader to undergo a different kind of intersubjective encounter. Reading an O'Sullivan text is never a comfortable or consistent experience. One is always adjusting the terms of engagement in order to remain constantly responsive to shifting conditions. We end up renovating our apparatus for reading every several lines, and our encounter with a text is also a reenactment of it. In this way, the act of reading becomes not consumptive but reciprocal. From one angle, O'Sullivan's compositional practice reasserts the primacy of the author by so thoroughly disabling attempts at comprehension or interpretation. But, from another angle, her texts provide meaningful spaces of readerly engagement. To return to Olson, O'Sullivan's poems are indeed "high-energy constructs," but the energy isn't simply sourced from the author and transferred to the reader. Because

the poems are so deeply inscrutable, they require significant readerly creativity. The possibility for passive consumption of these poems just does not
exist: they offer nearly nothing to one who skims.

O'Sullivan is one of a number of contemporary British poets for whom the
performance of poetry is vital to its realization. She is a remarkable reader
of her own work, and her vibrant performances often help generate critical
approaches to her highly defamiliarizing texts. O'Sullivan occasionally thematizes her work's ritual aspect by construing the poem as a set of instructions
for performance, as in "narcotic properties," which begins "PLACE A SMALL
PALE-CREAM BOWL (TO SIGNIFY / abundance) / on the table-top in front
of you."[41] In "theoretical economies," the poem immediately becomes a multimedia happening:

> Part of 'theoretical economies' is a BANNER.
> It is one six foot length of bamboo pole horizontally
> suspended from the ceiling somewhere in the centre of
> the room.[42]

For O'Sullivan – as well as for Brian Catling, cris cheek, Geraldine Monk, and
others who were associated with Cobbing's projects or who participated in
the Sub Voicive reading series in London that was started by Gilbert Adair
in 1980 – the oral performance of a poem is not merely the delivery of a text
or the live branding of a writer's personality. It is a secondary compositional
process in which the artifactual nature of the poem on the page is recomposed
within the transient and shifting air of the lecture hall or the dank room above
the pub. Whether calling for active audience participation or ambient collaboration, what we might call a performative poem depends upon being read out
loud, usually to other people, with the speaker's entire body taking part in its
realization.

The emphasis on a poem's status as event is vital for such experimentally
minded poets, but it is also at the heart of the widespread emergence of
performance-based and slam poetry in the past several decades. Indeed, this
emergence is one of the shaping features of contemporary poetry in Britain.
In this milieu, organizations like Apples and Snakes have supported performance poets in England, and poets such as Patience Agbabi, Jean "Binta"
Breeze, Lemn Sissay, and Kate Tempest have become major presences on the
scene, drawing on the models of earlier performance writers like Linton Kwesi
Johnson and Louise Bennett. In pioneering research on contemporary British
oral poetics, Nicky Marsh, Peter Middleton, and Victoria Sheppard suggest
that "what we are witnessing in this history of recent poetry performance
are sometimes radical innovations, innovations for which there is either no

precedent or, in cases where there may be some few precursors, little shared consciousness of this history and almost no critical history."[43] Middleton in particular has done significant work constructing theoretical and analytical methods for researching poetry readings and oral performances,[44] although the divide between so-called stage poets and page poets remains significant, and scholarly approaches to performance writing still linger quite a way behind the developments within this body of work.

The concept of performativity in this context isn't limited to the public performance of a completed or in-progress work. Performance is central to the compositional process as well, with the act of writing envisioned as a somatic and physical experience as well as a mental one. A number of poets have articulated this idea, often in texts that theorize their own circumstances of occurrence. Ken Edwards writes, seemingly addressing himself and fellow poets, "launch into writing and you launch into the unnamed future, with language as a cutting edge."[45] cris cheek describes his poems as "documents in conversation with the demotics of attention, not to say at times mundane, but complex occasions of linguistic experience – open to off-the-cuff commentary and exquisite interface, uninvited intervention and reflection."[46] For cheek, who often composes with a recording device to hand, the poem is an intricate combination of intention, attention, inattention, and "uninvited intervention[s]," a process he describes in "Squat" as "Off and On on-going Going / Going on and off."[47] Alan Halsey – who writes an assortment of visual and sound-based poetry and in texts like *Marginalien Marginalia: Irregulars & Gargoyles* practices a mode of bibliographic performativity (fittingly, considering his career as a printer and bookseller) – renders the multiple and overlapping temporalities of composition and performance in "Song-Cycle 1991":

> one must constantly and once
> having noted in a quite
>
> different order this origin or
> that be said to have spoken.[48]

Creation ("this origin or / that") and performance ("be said to have spoken") are combined in a recursive loop, one that is both an ongoing process ("constantly") and an isolable instance ("once"). What it is that "one must" do, say, or make in order to "be said to have spoken" remains inscrutable, but this deconstructed speech act displays the enlacing of composition and realization that catalyzes performance writing.

I'll turn now to one of the most ambitious texts to come out of this configuration of experimental performance writers. Geraldine Monk's *Interregnum* (1994) is one of the key works in recent British poetry, and it brings together many of the topics central to this book. It is a book-length poem about the Pendle witch trials, which took place in Lancashire in 1612, and revivifies the complex trauma of that moment. The Pendle trials are perhaps the most well known witch trials in England, partly because a very large amount of documentary evidence on the incident has survived. They occurred at a moment of deep disquiet, largely due to fears of a Catholic uprising against King James I, who was himself interested in witches and wrote a treatise titled *Demonology* in 1597. The larger fears were confirmed with the discovery of the Gunpowder Plot in 1605, which aimed to strike at the center of the English government, and Guy Fawkes's attempt to blow up the House of Lords was still on many minds. At the center of the Lancashire trials was a nine-year-old girl named Jennet Device who lived near Pendle Hill with her mother (Elizabeth), grandmother (Demdike), and two siblings, Alizon and James. In March 1612, Alizon confessed to bewitching a peddler but also accused a neighboring family, with whom her own family was feuding, of witchcraft and murder. This family then claimed that Demdike herself was a witch, and the magistrate arrested Alizon, Demdike, and two neighbors. Elizabeth Device later held a party on Good Friday and everyone there was arrested, which produced additional accusations and arrests. In August 1612, Jennet Device denounced her mother as a witch, and after a two-day trial, her whole family and a number of others were found guilty. Ten people were hanged at Gallows Hill. In 1613, Thomas Potts, the Lancaster Assizes court reporter, published a popular account of the trials, *The Wonderfull Discoverie of Witches in the Countie of Lancaster*.

Instead of adopting a third-person point of view or coalescing a central character to serve as a protagonist or authorial stand-in, as was Hill's strategy in *Mercian Hymns*, Monk disperses the events surrounding the witch trials by adopting the voices of various of the central actors. At the same time, there is a complex scaffolding that joins the discrete poems into a dramatic architecture. The first of the poem's three major sections, "Nerve Center," sets the scene, but by way of several texts that limn a twentieth-century Pendle filled with tourists, hikers, a biker gang (in "Hallowe'en Bikers"), "shift workers," "drivers," "pagans," and "born agains." The well-provisioned tourists – with their "snap / emergency kits," "Kendal mint cake," and "Fair Isle sweaters" – and New Age pagans who visit Pendle Hill on Halloween are objects of Monk's mild rebuke, but they aren't simply targets of scorn.[49] Their introduction in the first section has a double function: it counterpoints contemporary and early-seventeenth-century Lancashire so as to make *Interregnum* not only an attempt at a lyric history but also a text that models a lyric historiography; in addition, it previews themes and idioms that will be key to the poem's reimagining of the Pendle trials. After the prefatory texts, "Nerve Center" includes a group of five poems under the subheading "Hill Outriders" that presents central thematic loci as *Interregnum* approaches the events of 1612 more directly. "Hill Outriders" includes poems about the economic and social marginality that played a part in the Pendle trials ("Shift Workers"), the spiritual torment felt by the actors (mediated through the figure of Gerard Manley Hopkins in "Jesuit Boy Blues"), the violence of capture and execution (in "Fox Hunt" and "Fox Trot"), and the dream of escape ("Flyer").

The second section, "Palimpsestus," appears as a single unit, with sections of elliptical poetry split by equally elliptical bold-faced phrases. The phrases in bold function as titles to or commentaries on the cryptic free verses that appear with them, and in the first edition of the text, the poems and bolded phrases appeared on facing pages, which made more apparent their discrete simultaneity. But in Monk's *Selected Poems*, the poems and phrases are continuous:[50]

> **...(DISTURBED TRANSFORMATIONS)...**
>
> ...lewd and magical suggestions of
> > form
> > > archways of limbs
> > > > full
> > > fungus breathings...
>
> **...(CORRECTION OF DISFIGUREMENTS)...**[51]

"Palimpsestus" enacts a series of ritual fragments that are spiritual, sexual, hallucinatory, and violent, and the alternation between the two kinds of texts replicates Monk's large-scale attempt to articulate widely distant historical moments, what she calls "pooling centuries."[52] At certain instants, it seems like enchantments or spells are being pronounced, while at others, modern details impinge and the poem becomes a palimpsest of two times. The section features numerous prayers, curses, threats, warnings, transgressive visions, triadic chants, and nonsensical patterns; it performs the "depraved outrage" and "witch weavings" that supposedly featured at the Good Friday gathering held by Elizabeth Device.[53] The physical and psychic extremity described is not attached to a particular subject but rather manifests as a floating set of actions and affects, with the bolded passages guiding a reader through the section, even as they lack a stable deictic space or perspective: "Disturbed Transformations," "Entry Zone of Hallucinations," "Mind Full of Meat and Flowers," "Mouth Dripping Verbal Crucifixions," "Ghosts."[54]

David Kennedy and Christine Kennedy describe *Interregnum* as "a montage of bodily, linguistic, perceptual and temporal transformations which is keyed by one dominant current of transformation: from ecstasy into suffering and back into ecstasy."[55] This montage takes its fullest shape in the final section, by far the longest of the three, where the particulars of the accusations, trials, and executions are restaged.[56] After several prefatory, scene-setting poems, a series of monologues spoken by the main characters is interspersed with descriptions of the trial or songs from the prison cell that describe the prisoners' torments. Monk opens up several lines of investigation, the primary one being about the coercive power of language itself. In all her work, Monk is a weaver of puns and neologisms, which in *Interregnum* often depict visceral textures and erotic spiritualism, as in "Pagans," an early poem in the sequence:

> hula-juggins
> rattling prayseeds
> gimcrack berry-reds
> bead-smear
> bloodclots
> blossom[57]

Here, the playful linguistic performativity serves partly to mock the spiritual pretensions of contemporary New Age spirituality. But as the sequence moves forward, the dangers of language making come to the fore. *Interregnum* is, among many other things, a mesh of speech acts – songs, chants, spells, accusations, counteraccusations, confessions, and judgments. Acts of speech are often made substantive: "More than meat or drink. Better than stars and water. Words birthed. Made flesh. Took wing. Horrids and enormities. Chantcasters."[58] The progression of this passage mimics that of the events in Pendle: ecstatic transformations of language – words as celestial nourishment – become horrid and enormous as they are brought within the realm of the town's religious and legal authorities. As the accused give testimony and undergo questioning, their words become subject to the machinations of discursive power:

> a bleed of double talk
> ever redding torment
> sprouting wound-words[59]

The trial allows those who stand accused of witchcraft to enter the historical record as subjects, but their narratives and speech acts are manipulated by those in power: "we only believe / your truth telling / it like we / want to / hear what we / don't is // lying."[60] The prerogative to create truth via language is, of course, not limited to those in power, and a number of the imagined monologues in the final part of *Interregnum* reflect upon the fictional nature of their stories, most notably in the "Out-Thoughts" of Chattox (the grandmother of the neighboring family):

> But only I was amazed
> by my outbreaks of
> quirky
> metaphors and
> unchallengeable leaps to
> lucidity
> at invention that beggared
> hypocrisy.[61]

Chattox's amazement at her ability to produce imaginative language is simultaneously amazement at the ease with which she is able to invent – to lie about the events in question. Such awareness is not possible for Jennet Device, whose monologue ends the sequence. In "The Eternal Bewilderment of Jennet Device," the nine-year-old girl whose testimony against her mother clinched the guilty verdict does not understand the implications of her words, and the whole series ends with her increasingly regressive linguistic performances:

> I weird sang.   High trilled and skirled.
> I led a merry crab dance.   Bright.
> Kookie-mad.[62]

Still thinking of the entire episode as a kind of game, Jennet's monologue reveals only a fractured and traumatized sense of her family's demise:

> OH MA
> mi maa   mi mother
> mUth   er   ing
> muth   rin
> muR   ther   ing   ringa
> killything-a.   Gran.   Ali.   J.
> killyall thing-s bright XXXXXXXXXX.[63]

A sardonic inversion of the nonsense verses that the tourists sing in *Interregnum*'s very first text, this final poem, with its word shards and warped repetitions, performs a buckling of linguistic ability, one that Jennet shares with those she accused and who have been killed. Central to Monk's performative poetry in *Interregnum* is an investigation into linguistic performativity itself. The events around the Pendle trials were spurred primarily by acts of speech, whether the spells or curses supposedly performed, the accusations that flew between the two families, or the testimonies heard in the court. By incorporating a consideration of performative utterances within an experimental text that is itself deeply performative, Monk provides at once a form of lyric historiography and an immanent critique of language's power to create the reality that it represents.

Part of the charge of poetry such as Monk's or O'Sullivan's is that it refuses to give up the opacity of its materials. Words and phrases hold on to their density, and so instead of asking what a poem means, a reader might ask what a poem does. This isn't simply a matter of bowing to a poem's reflexivity or linguistic autonomy. A poem's resistance to normative, easily exchangeable meaning is neither a sign of its self-determined authority nor a signal that it haughtily refuses all attempts to share in its meaning. Anything that might be construed as its meaning or message is bound up in the form of its performative or enunciative act. A poem's difficulty, then, is not merely a signal of deliberate obscurity. Rather, it may be a necessary and vital effect of its arduous attention to the particularities of its stuff – the knot-filled grain of its thought processes, the dialectical twists of the ideas with which it reckons, the competing valences of the affective structures that it unfolds.

A very different form of energetic ardor appears in the later poetry of Geoffrey Hill, who I have brought to the fore several times throughout this book and whose remarkable resurgence since the late 1990s necessitates that I return to him again. As with Prynne, Hill has produced a body of late poetry that intensifies an already intense oeuvre. His recent proliferation has been more unexpected than Prynne's continual ratcheting of his poetry's internal pressure, because it stands in such stark contrast to the rarity and reticence that defined Hill's earlier career. While Hill's central themes – the history of England; the trauma and brutality of the European twentieth century; the nature of faith and of value; the intertwining of language, power, and civil society; and the obligations of poetry – remain consistent between his pre-1990s works and his post-1996 flowering, his volubility has been surprising. Readers used to the tightly drawn lyrics that characterized his slim output from *For the Unfallen* to *The Mystery of the Charity of Charles Péguy* (1983) – five volumes in total appeared between 1959 and 1996 – have had to significantly shift their pace to keep up with the ten individual volumes that have appeared since 1996. His work has long been characterized as "difficult," and this has functioned as a term of both praise and blame that operates in tandem with the "England's greatest living poet" tag that is regularly applied to him. It isn't necessarily that his later work is more difficult than his earlier work; his poems have always been densely allusive, logically and syntactically compacted, and conceptually complex. But the sheer volume of the late work, as well as its often hermetic verbosity, exponentially increases the demands it places upon readers.

It is one thing to work carefully through the thirteen intricate sonnets that constitute "An Apology for the Revival of Christian Architecture in England," especially as those texts appear in a slim 1978 volume – *Tenebrae* – published seven years after the previous slim volume, *Mercian Hymns*, and five years before the next one, *The Mystery of the Charity of Charles Péguy*. It is quite another thing to work through the 144 poems that comprise *Oraclau/Oracles* (2010), which are modeled on a complex stanza form adapted from Donne and display a new interest in Welsh literature and culture and the Welsh language, offering an entirely new range of allusive possibilities. The task is magnified because *Oraclau/Oracles* is the sixth book Hill has published since the beginning of the new millennium. Indeed, Hill's pace seems to ceaselessly quicken: *Oraclau/Oracles* is one part of a seven-book series titled *The Daybooks*, which is dated "2007–2012" and covers twice as many pages in Hill's collected volume as do the poems published between 1959 and 1996.[64]

Hill's late work ranges widely, from the scathing admonitions of *Canaan* (1996), the prophetic and hectoring cacophony of *Speech! Speech!* (2000), and the somber lyricism of *Without Title* (2006) to the stylized theatrics of *Scenes from Comus* (2005) and large portions of *The Daybooks*. Throughout, and especially in *The Orchards of Syon* (2002), Hill returns to a pastoral mode, albeit a deeply skeptical one that is "forever tangling with England / in her quiet ways of betrayal."[65] In addition to considering abstract matters of theology and philosophy, Hill's "grand and crabby music" is able to accommodate quite specific political rebukes, as in his address "To the High Court of Parliament," which concerns a series of bribery scandals and shady deals that came to light in late 1994.[66] At the start of that poem, the opening text of *Canaan*, Hill asks dismissively, "where's probity in this," and refers to the "slither-frisk" of politicians, whom he goes on to compare to rats invading a birdhouse.[67] The probity that he seeks in civil life extends and is underwritten by his longstanding argument about the necessary probity of literary language and the value and responsibilities of poetry, a line of thinking most fully realized in his well-known essay, "Our Word Is Our Bond." Even as he takes extensive rhetorical and stylistic risks in his later work, his concern is always with the rightness and precision of poetic speech:

> For wordly, read worldly; for in equity, inequity;
> for religious read religiose; for distinction
> detestation. Take accessible to mean
> acceptable, accommodating, openly servile.[68]

In this passage from *The Triumph of Love* (1998), the quest for a just exactitude is linked to a commitment to difficulty, to a nonaccommodation of the demands of a contemporary culture that desires accessibility and immediacy and so receives mediocrity. The demands made by Hill's work upon readers are inextricable from the larger arguments – about language, literature, and civil life – that underlie his work.

His recurrent use of extended sequences and the sheer prodigiousness of his late work produces a form of virtuosically cracked fluency – what he describes as "a knack, a way / with broken speech; a singular welcome / for rough occurrence"[69] – that cuts against the strictures modeled by his earlier poetry.[70] But what binds his late work together and connects it to what came before is its performativity. Whether he is acting the part of wizened scold, eccentric autodidact, or randy old poet in the style of Yeats, Hill's poems rarely lose their texture of public address. They are baroquely staged monologues or verbal cadenzas, with even the most contemplative or prayerful of the poems taking on something of a Prosperian cast, as in this passage from *Al Tempo de' Tremuoti*, the final part of *The Daybooks*:

> There are things here I wish I had not said
> Or thought, even. A mythist and so loath
> To grasp as real the otherness of breath
> I am an old blasphemer and afraid;
>
> Intractability of happenstance
> Reduced to final supplication: Mary
> Mediatrix, absolve my word-memory
> Uprisen in this late self-hallowing trance.[71]

The confession of the first stanza becomes the stylized supplication of the second, but the quatrain's final line rebounds in a moment of self-dramatization: the request to the Virgin Mary for absolution for his art – "my word-memory" – is cancelled by the proclamation of a "self-hallowing trance." The fashioning of one's own holiness or hallowedness becomes, in the circumstances of the poem, a gesture of self-hollowing. In "Our Word Is Our Bond," as he reroutes J.L. Austin's theory of speech acts, Hill provides something of a preemptory gloss: poetry, he writes, "is, in a peculiar way, the most oxymoronic art: its very making is its undoing. In a poet's involvement with language, above all, there is, one would darkly and impetuously claim, an element of helplessness, of being at the mercy of accidents, the prey of one's own presumptuous energy."[72] This incessant double bind marks – in fact, it is – our relationship with language. As Hill writes elsewhere, "our well dug-in / language pitches us as it finds."[73] The irresolvability of this condition, for Hill, does not lead to free play but to a ceaseless strenuousness. However, as the late work makes clear in both its sheer volume and its inventiveness, such dedication to linguistic probity embeds a radical creativity: "Imagination, freakish, dashing every way, / defers annulment."[74]

Hill's late-career torrent, and the unexpected shapes it has taken, is unique, but several of the major British poets born before 1945 have produced significant late-career poetry. While a number of poets complete the great bulk of their writing well before their deaths – Larkin and Bunting would be the major relevant examples – many others continue to compose new poems, and a few find new formal ground in which to toil. Most follow stylistic lines established in their earlier work, as is the case with Hughes, or, in a more intriguing way, Heaney. Like Hill, Heaney was often given the "greatest living poet in English" mantle before his death in 2013, and pairing Heaney with Hill can help me bring this chapter to a close and to preview the conclusion to come. Heaney's final volumes – *Electric Light* (2001), *District and Circle* (2006), and *Human Chain* (2010) – often revisit the ground of his earlier work, whether as part of his late career impulse to "credit marvels" or as full reimaginings of his earlier themes, as in "The Tollund Man in Springtime."[75] By then a global figure and certainly the most well-known poet in the world, Heaney's later poetry inevitably takes on public force. His commitment to the value of poetry as an imaginative counterpressure to the drag of the actual shares something with Hill's declaration at the end of *The Triumph of Love* that a poem ought to be "*a sad / and angry consolation*."[76]

As always in Hill's poetry, each word in this seemingly straightforward phrase is both lure and snare. A poem's sadness and anger are signs of its protest against the state of the world but also measures of its incapacity to do more than register such a protest and perhaps to project a barely glimpsed alternative to the injustice, terror, or destruction that it sees, what Heaney phrases "an elsewhere world."[77] For Hill, a poem is a consolation both because it offers recompense and because it marks its own failure to fully repair that which it can only console. A poem, then, is not simply a comment on conditions but also a form of them. As much as any postwar poet, Heaney and Hill made this enabling difficulty a founding crux of their work. For poets who have begun their careers at the end of the twentieth century or at the start of the twenty-first and for whom poetry as a practice and art occupies an ever-shrinking portion of the cultural landscape, the idea of a poem as a form of consolation might seem untenable or a foolhardy delusion about one's own importance. And yet, poems keep occurring. In the final part of this book, I will survey some of the most captivating poetry to appear in Britain since the millennium's turn, touching down on several texts that continue to push the borders of lyric form so that they might more adequately limn the textures of contemporary experience and more urgently press against the intractable world.

Conclusion: Archipelagic Experiments

A book such as this one edges toward precarity as it approaches the present. It becomes less possible to survey the field as the historical distance closes on the surveyor. One's choices about what to cover become increasingly contingent, and one's speculations occur on ever-shakier ground. New volumes of poetry appear constantly and in seemingly ever-larger numbers, although large commercial publishers bring out fewer and fewer of them.[1] Seeking to comprehensively review and evaluate the past decade or so of British poetry seems an act of hubris or folly, inevitably devolving into a partisan or scatter-shot review-essay or a very long list. Any judgment is premature, and every name mentioned is a name dropped. If as formidable a critic as F.R. Leavis could get things so splendidly wrong in *New Bearings in English Poetry* (1932) by naming Ronald Bottrall as the great hope of English poetry in the 1930s, then perhaps prognostication is not the best path forward. Focusing on the prize-winning volumes from the past ten or fifteen years does not produce a capacious enough picture of twenty-first-century British poetry, but simply railing against the whole machinery of literary awards, the mainstream publishing establishment, and its tight reviewing network is equally limited. Thrilling, perhaps, and necessary, but less useful in this context. So, in this conclusion, I will attempt neither a full summary of recent poetry nor a tendentious essay highlighting the poems that I like best.

Rather, I will focus on two topics in order to shed some light on recent practice. First, I will consider the ways in which poets have extended and compounded linguistic registers in order to accommodate the baggy capacity of contemporary English(es), routing this consideration through a look at the work of Daljit Nagra, Jen Hadfield, and Caroline Bergvall. I will then examine several ways that poets have stretched lyric form, absorbing disparate genres and mediums in order to register the hypermottled modes of contemporary social and cultural life. This final section will feature texts by Alice Oswald and Keston Sutherland. To be sure, there is significant overlap between these two issues, and my separation of them here is merely an analytical gambit. Much of the most intriguing poetry of the new century is profoundly heterogeneous.

Such poems absorb, repel, mutate, and redirect the manifold idioms of advertising, commerce, entertainment, and the culture industry. They fold a huge range of discourses, idiolects, and jargons into their amalgamated forms. In doing so, such poetry problematizes the underpinnings of the writerly act itself, conducting a nearly continuous investigation of the prerogatives and privileges of poetry and of poets. It continues, then, the project of locating and asserting poetry's particular value in contemporary culture.

Before turning to those poets, however, it will help to provide, briefly, some literary-historical context. In many ways, the trends and patterns I've tracked over the previous chapters continue to hold. While its contours have changed, there remains a significant gap between so-called mainstream poetry and work that positions itself as alternative or experimental. Don Paterson's introductory essay for *New British Poetry* (2004), an American anthology he coedited with Charles Simic, definitively marks the battleground: between the kinds of poets included in the anthology, who aim to be understood and enjoyed by readers, and those he dubs "the Postmoderns," poets of tortuously difficult texts who have no interest in actually being read, who rely on a hieratic and cultish elitism, and who – so he worries – are infiltrating themselves deeper and deeper into academia.[2] The vicious pique of Paterson's polemic and the force of the many responses to it suggest the continuing Manichaeism that marks, and somewhat mars, the overall poetry scene. Relatedly, the Poetry Society has kept up its "New Gen" promotional program, with updated lists of "Next Generation Poets" released in 2004 and 2014. The active perpetuation of a chosen mainstream has also been a factor in the continuing impasse, especially since previous New Gen or Next Gen poets have helped select and present later generations. Many of these poets are published by a very small set of publishers, primarily Faber and Faber, Picador, and Jonathan Cape, and the most prized volumes of the past decade – such as Sean O'Brien's *The Drowned Book* (2007), John Burnside's *Black Cat Bone* (2011), Michael Symmons Roberts's *Drysalter* (2013), and David Harsent's *Fire Songs* (2014) – have emerged from this same sector of the market. Each of these volumes is significant on its own terms, but the poetry establishment continues to converge on a fairly limited range of formal choices and aesthetic possibilities. The small to medium-sized first-person meditative or scenic poem remains, for many, the template of choice.

If one aspect of the ecosystem of contemporary British poetry is the enduring importance of a very small number of London-based imprints whose slim volumes dominate the prize circuit and review pages, then another is the increasing centrality of Michael Schmidt's Carcanet Press and Neil Astley's Bloodaxe Books. These two presses produce the great majority of poetry volumes in Britain, publishing a range of American, European, and world poetry, and both maintain strong and varied British and Irish lists. In addition to its single-poet volumes, Bloodaxe has long been known for its popular anthologies, a number of them edited by Astley himself: according to Sarah Broom, Astley's "2002 Bloodaxe anthology *Staying Alive* sold 35,000 copies in its first six months."[3] It has since sold many more and has generated several sequels.

As noted in Chapter 5, Bloodaxe's anthologies of women's poetry have been especially influential, beginning with Jeni Couzyn's *Bloodaxe Book of Contemporary Women Poets* (1985) and continuing with a handful of follow-up volumes by various editorial hands over the past three decades. One of the characteristics of postwar British poetry, and one that is reflected in the makeup of the book in your hands, is that very few women poets rose to prominence in Britain during the three decades after the end of the war. This was largely due to a conservative and patriarchal literary culture, and efforts by feminist writers beginning in the late 1960s and early 1970s started to turn the canonical tide. In a number of ways, the tide has been turned. At the moment of writing, women occupy the three major ceremonial posts for poets in the United Kingdom: Carol Ann Duffy, as mentioned earlier, was named the Poet Laureate in 2009; in 2011, Liz Lochhead assumed the post of Scots Makar, the National Poet of Scotland; and Gillian Clarke has been the National Poet of Wales since 2008. Sinéad Morrissey was named Belfast's first poet laureate in 2013. Additionally, the Contemporary Experimental Women's Poetry Festival, organized by Emily Critchley, was held in Cambridge in 2006 and helped concretize the importance of women poets within experimental circles in Cambridge and beyond. Sexism – both superficial and systemic – remains a considerable and insidious part of the cultures of poetry in Britain, but, at least when looking over the whole of the past seven decades, progress has been made.

For minority poets in Britain, the path has been more complex. Following the generation of poets who came of age during the period of decolonization – most notably Derek Walcott, Kamau Brathwaite, James Berry, and E.A. Markham – a number of black British poets began writing and publishing in the 1970s and early 1980s. As I have discussed in earlier chapters, Linton Kwesi Johnson, Grace Nichols, David Dabydeen, Fred D'Aguiar, and Jackie Kay have had major careers, while Patience Agbabi and Benjamin Zephaniah have become vital presences within performance and spoken-word poetry scenes. Bernardine Evaristo began her career as a poet and has written two important verse novels – *Lara* (1997) and *The Emperor's Babe* (2001) – but she has turned much of her attention to fiction. *Out of Bounds: British Black and Asian*

Poets (2012), edited by Jackie Kay, James Procter, and Gemma Robinson, and published by – who else? – Bloodaxe, has provided a rich map of newer poets, but the major contributors to this volume are well-established figures, such as those just named, and fewer younger black or Asian poets have gained significant prominence in Britain since the turn of the century. One who has is Daljit Nagra.

Along with Kei Miller and Jane Yeh, Nagra is one of three black or Asian writers on the latest list of Next Generation poets, and he has quite quickly become one of the most notable poets in England. Drawing explicitly on Northern Irish poets, as well as on writers such as Kay and Moniza Alvi, Nagra has become widely known for his linguistically exuberant poems about the experiences of Indian immigrants in Britain, especially the Sikh Punjabi community. While the Indian postcolonial novel has long been central to the canon of contemporary British literature, with Salman Rushdie's *Midnight's Children* serving as origin and apex, it has taken longer for a British Indian poetry to develop, with Nagra being one of the first major Indian poets to emerge in postwar Britain. Born outside London and raised both there and in Sheffield, Nagra has been an important part of the performance poetry community at Apples and Snakes and has risen to prominence with two volumes published by Faber and Faber, *Look We Have Coming to Dover!* (2007) and *Tippoo Sultan's Incredible White-Man-Eating Tiger Toy-Machine!!!* (2011). As both titles indicate, Nagra's poetry is driven by an inventive and near-ceaseless enthusiasm. In "Our Town with the Whole of India!," he catalogues the dense richness of Indian culture as it is remade in England, while in poems like "The Furtherance of Mr. Bulram's Education," "A Black History of the English-Speaking Peoples," and "This Man Who Would Be English!," he maps the complexities of a hybrid belonging, when one is caught among identities, languages, cultural practices, and racial categories.

The protagonist and speaker of "This Man Who Would Be English!" begins by aiming to affiliate himself with English culture by watching a football match in a local pub: "Just for kicks I was well in with the English race."[4] But such an affiliation requires a conscious suppression of his own accent and bearing, an act of masking that produces a simultaneous loss of self: "I was one of us, at ease, so long as I passed / my voice into theirs." His repressed cultural, racial, and linguistic differences quickly return to the surface in the form of a phantasm of his mother, who appears on the television as the goalkeeper and reprimands him. The speaker walks home, and the poem ends with a rhyming quatrain spoken, it seems, by his wife, in Punjabi-inflected English. She first disparages the largely white English crowd at the bar ("*D-d-doze err shrubby peeepalll*"), then suggests that the family return to India, and finally refutes his attempted affiliation: "*Lookk lookk ju nott British ju rrr blackkk…!!!*"

Recalling the work of Derek Walcott, Tony Harrison, and others before him, Nagra combines a complex set of cultural and literary anxieties within his distinctive morphology. Like Walcott, he is "divided to the vein" between the racist history of British imperialism and an English literary tradition to which he is drawn. And, like Harrison, his adaptation of Punjabi-English vernacular – which is meant to resist the hegemony of a "Standard English" – also discloses a fear that any such resistance will be appropriated or coopted. In "A Black History of the English-Speaking Peoples," which is set in the new Globe Theatre and considers this precise crux, Nagra asks,

> Am I a noble scruff who hopes a proud
> academy might canonise
> his poems for their faith in canonical allusions?[5]

Moving among registers and vernaculars, Nagra's poetry revisits questions posed in previous contexts by the vexed speaker of Walcott's "A Far Cry from Africa" and the split narrator of Harrison's *v*. He writes from the post-imperial center – looking from, as the conclusion of "A Black History of the English-Speaking Peoples" has it, "the London Eye / at multinationals lying along the sanitized Thames" – and from the center of the literary establishment, as a Faber poet.[6] But he also dislodges those centers by intermeshing the multiple languages of twenty-first-century England, by "babbling our lingoes, flecked by the chalk of Britannia!"[7]

While Nagra extends the linguistic scope of British poetry from the capital of postimperial Britain and hub of global capitalism, Jen Hadfield works from Britain's farthest northern point. A major component of Hadfield's highly praised poetry has been her incorporation and examination of dialect words from Shetland Scots, and *Nigh-No-Place* (2008) especially features a number of poems that turn around a single Shetlandic term that Hadfield has come across during her time there: "Blashey-wadder," "Dead-traa," "Gish," "Glid," "Hüm," "Snuskit," and "Stumba." Hadfield draws at once on Hugh MacDiarmid's synthetic Scots, Tom Leonard's vernacular Glaswegian poems, contemporary Scots poems by W.N. Herbert and Kathleen Jamie, and, a bit more distantly, Seamus Heaney's place-name poems. In *Byssus* (2014), Hadfield's catalogues of flora and fauna, as well as her occasionally surreal parables about the natural world of the Shetlands, most often resemble praise songs and lyric charms that derive – at least partly – from Jerome Rothenberg's work on ethnopoetics.[8]

While Hadfield usually remains within the rough contours of normative English grammar and provides glosses to Shetlandic words, she occasionally moves outside a shared lexis, contriving words that seem like they exist at the joint of English and Shetland Scots but are lexical ghosts. "In Memoriam" both enacts and describes this practice:

> Loving language is wide
> and shallow: sooks, polches
> and wistens it.[9]

Sook appears in several guises in the *OED*, referring to an Australian and New Zealand slang term for a "stupid or timid person," a female blue crab native to the east coast of the United States, and – most relevantly – a Scottish and American dialect term for a cow or for the call used to drive cattle. It is a rare term in Scotland and one that refers usually to a calf, but nowhere in the *OED* does it have the verbal force that Hadfield seems to give it here. It could be, perhaps more straightforwardly, a Scots variant on the verb *sucks*, a reading that would be authorized by the *Dictionary of the Scots Language*.[10] Turning to John J. Graham's *Shetland Dictionary*, to which Hadfield leads her readers in the notes to the volume, enriches this sense.[11] Graham tells us that *sook* is a verb meaning "to dry by exposure to wind" or a noun that describes such a "drying quality."[12] So a bit of digging suggests that, for Hadfield, the act of "loving language" is a "wide and shallow" one and might be likened to the act of *sooking* it, which, given the lexical spread of the word, means something like sucking it dry, as the wind might suck the moisture out of a sheet hanging on the line. A reader might also think about *sook* as a sonic cousin of *soak*, and so imagine *sook* to activate a wonderful dialectic of draught and repletion: *sucking dry* and *soaking wet*. In any case, it is a visceral and sensual sign for the making and loving of language, a mouthy enactment that emerges at the seam of English and Scots, at the hinge between dictionaries.

However, the next two words, which initially seem like verbs in either English or Scots and so would allow the continuation of such a reading, appear in neither the *OED*, the *Dictionary of the Scots Language*, nor Graham's *Shetland Dictionary*. If the first line and a half of this tercet make a claim about the nature of "loving language" (and we might take *loving* as an adjective as well as a verb, allowing us to love language more complexly), then the first word after the colon asks us to perform this love as etymological excavators. As we might when reading Heaney or Hill, we *dig* through the trove of languages. The next two words in the sequence, which seem to complete a trio of verbs that begins with *sooks*, preclude that kind of love. Instead, a reader, having hit upon nothing in her "wide and shallow" pursuit through dictionaries for clues about *polches* and *wistens*, is invited to "lov[e] language" differently: by investing these words with a dynamism that is self-generated, much as Maggie O'Sullivan's word-shards ask a reader to both refurbish meaning and construct it anew. Each word, untethered from a direct denotation, becomes a set of mutable connotations – another form of "wide and shallow" loving. To indicate how the ball might begin to be rolled: *wistens* might take on a sense of *whistles* or *hastens* or *wistful* or *whisper*, each of which can reinflect *sooks*. Of course, these words could simply be local variants that would be quickly understood by someone in the Shetlands, and so my spinning of fanciful etymologies would be misguided, a wrong reading.

But Hadfield, at least based on the evidence of her poetry, is not interested in maintaining a linguistic fence between some cloistered form of Shetlandic Scots and the wider English language context in which her poetry necessarily circulates. In the "Notes" to *Nigh-No-Place*, Hadfield, who was born in Cheshire in Northwest England, avers that she is "not a Shetland dialect speaker" before offering a glossary of Shetland words that "flitted through my vocabulary" and made their way into the book.[13] She has quite quickly become one of the most prominent poets in Britain, with *Nigh-No-Place* winning the T.S. Eliot Prize and *Byssus* published by Picador. Picador, one of the most high-profile English literary presses, is an imprint of Pan Macmillan, which is part of Macmillan Publishers Limited, which, in turn, is a piece of the Georg von Holtzbrinck Publishing Group, a multinational publishing conglomerate based in Stuttgart. This is all simply to map the much larger global circuits that subtend this moment of linguistic play in Hadfield's justly admired poetry. Just as a reader might track the etymological networks that underlie Hadfield's *sooks*, so a different reader might follow the networks of distribution and circulation in which Hadfield's lyric concentrations travel. And both sorts of readings are necessary.

Nagra and Hadfield have extended the project of, as Heaney put it in an early interview, making the English lyric "eat stuff that it has never eaten before."[14] Just as Nagra draws on Northern Irish poets like Heaney and Muldoon, Leonard is an important precursor for Hadfield. In other ways, her poems appear as moderate versions of the more thoroughgoing transformations typical of O'Sullivan and Monk or slightly earlier figures like Griffiths and MacSweeney. Both Hadfield and Nagra intersperse and switch among lexical and sociolinguistic codes, but they maintain the basic generic markers of lyric: brevity, sonic density, and a foundation in an act of speech. For a more disruptive approach to the usual registers of English and of lyric poetry more broadly, we can turn to Caroline Bergvall.

Bergvall works over a broad swath of performance, visual, and literary arts, and many of her texts have other lives as performance and installation pieces. A French-Norwegian writer who has spent a good part of her career in England, Bergvall was the director of a highly innovative program in performance writing at Dartington College of Arts between 1994 and 2000 and is an important theorist of performance writing. Bergvall's conceptual poems often derive from found texts, as in her well-known "Via," which consists of forty-seven different English translations of the opening tercet of Dante's *Commedia*, arranged in alphabetical order. A number of her texts, most notably her extended poem "Goan Atom," move among languages, using one language to distort and metamorphose another. Such macaronic linguistic textures are indebted to avant-garde poetry from early in the twentieth century as well as later sound and concrete poetry. Like Ian Hamilton Finlay and Bob Cobbing, Bergvall has opened the boundaries between literary, visual, and sonic arts. Her work is also connected to the growing body of intermedia and digital poetry, and along with figures like John Cayley and Peter Howard, she is one of the handful of British or Britain-based writers who have produced significant digitally born work.[15]

Bergvall's "Middling English" is an essay that accompanies her "Shorter Chaucer Tales," a series of texts that gathers passages from *The Canterbury Tales*, often interlacing them with contemporary found texts. In it, she writes, "language is its own midden ground," and throughout the essay she argues for a kind of fluctuational language, a "trans-English" that is incessantly remade by the press of other languages.[16] "Poetic art," she suggests, "becomes an occupancy of language made manifest through various platforms, a range of instrumental tools and skills and relativized forms of inscription. From audio performance to complex events, it functions in a logic of relays and of distributive networks, incidentally already inherent in the permutational logic of the alphabetic and indexical systems."[17] For Bergvall, such disruptive and defamiliarizing language has social force. It is "pleasured language, pressured language, language in heated use, harangued language, forms of language revolutionized by action, polemical language structures that propose an intense deliberate reappraisal of the given world and its given forms."[18]

One of the signal examples of Bergvall's pleasured, pressured language use is her long cross-platform poem "About Face." In addition to disrupting one language with another, crossing multiple languages so that they reveal new facets and combinations, "About Face" places performative pressure on the basic mechanisms of language production. First performed in 1999 and first published in *Fig* (2005), the poem, as its title suggests, sets itself around the speaking face, inside its mouth and throat as it struggles towards articulation. As Bergvall writes in a headnote to the poem, she first performed "About Face" after an emergency dental procedure, and "the sutured pain and phantom bone made it difficult to articulate the text to the audience."[19] Unable to perform the smooth "choreography of the physiological mouth into language" during the initial performance, she then made "such processes of marked physical and verbal impediments" a continuing part of the realization of the piece.[20]

The published text of "About Face" incorporates the "micro-frictions" that characterize its verbal performance, as can be seen in the poem's opening passage:

> Begin a f acing
> at a poi nt of motion
> How c lose is near to face a face
> What makes a face how close too near
> Tender nr pace m
> just close enough makes faceless
> too close makes underfaced.[21]

What might sound like a stutter or a misspeaking in an aural performance, or perhaps like a technological glitch in a recorded performance, is rendered literally.[22] The opening presents us with a prototypical lyric stance: a voice beginning to speak. It proceeds to massively undermine this stance by fissuring speech from writing. Listening to Bergvall read the poem and reading the poem on the page are quite different experiences. It is relatively easy for a listener to process the "hesitations, erasures, [and] accidental details" on a recording as a lack of speakerly ability or fluency, a mistake, or a glitch in the medium (such as a file downloading too slowly).[23] Such extraneous materials can be silently categorized as noise. It is, however, much more difficult to treat the stranded letters, cleaved words, and morphological affectations on the page simply as textual "noise." One wants to bring them back into an economy of signification – one wants them to mean something. A face that is too close to one's own loses its facial coherence (becoming, as Bergvall writes, "faceless" or "underfaced"). One sees blurs and disparate surfaces. There is an analogous sort of "too-closeness" in Bergvall's verbal decouplings: a smoothly functioning language system is estranged from itself. Signification becomes blurry or filled with static. Such estrangement is precisely what much poetry does: a blurring or deformation of the literal, a play of sound and figure that overrides denotation and proposition. "About Face" can be seen to provide, then, an intensification of such overriding. If one of the lynchpins of lyric is the fiction of speakerly presence, and if this fiction has at its kernel the phantasm of a voice, then Bergvall's "About Face" seeks to snap the relays that connect these fictional nodes. It is not only that the English language is being disturbed and, so, extended, as in the case of Nagra's and Hadfield's poetry. Bergvall also wants to investigate the ideologies and materials of language itself. This links her more closely with experimental and avant-garde formations in Europe and

North America than it does with much of the English poetic tradition, but among the many conceptual and aesthetic problems that Bergvall's multimedia work confronts are ones central to contemporary lyric poetry. "About Face" expands the possibilities of poetic writing by placing maximal pressure on the integrity of verbal units, offering both a performance in (and with) language and an account of the elided relations between speech and text. It is both a lyric text and a refutation of a narrow version of lyric poetry.

At eleven pages, "About Face" is, relatively speaking, a fairly long poem. If one of the central features of lyric poetry concerns its oblique modes of address – its play of speaker and reader, of an absent though catalytic *I* and a fleshy though variable *you* – then another is its brevity. As opposed to the novelistic, essayistic, or epic, lyric poetry is generally thought of as a compacted act of making – of figural density, affective vim, and enwrapped sound. And, indeed, critical accounts stress the supremacy of the short lyric in postwar British poetry. It is the form that most of the poets have most often employed, primarily in stand-alone lyrics but also as the building blocks of sequences or series. Such extended or accreted lyric forms can be found across the aesthetic spectrum, from Heaney's "Station Island" (1985) to Raworth's *Eternal Sections* (1993). This isn't to say that there aren't important long poems in the post-1945 canon. A handful reach toward epical length – from Lynette Roberts's *Gods With Stainless Ears: A Heroic Poem* (1951) and David Jones's *The Anathemata* (1952) to Walcott's *Omeros* (1990) and Muldoon's "Madoc: A Mystery" (1990) – and, as I discuss in Chapter 3, an important strand of postwar poetry is composed of what C.D. Blanton and Nigel Alderman have dubbed "pocket epics," with Bunting's *Briggflatts* the central exhibit in that generic gallery. There have also been several important multibook projects whose bounds have encompassed large periods of a poet's life and are reminiscent of Pound's *Cantos* and Olson's *The Maximus Poems*, as well as Whitman's lifelong book, *Leaves of Grass*. *War Music*, Christopher Logue's multipart reworking of Homer's *Iliad* published between 1959 and 2005, Allen Fisher's *Place* (1971–1980) and *Gravity as a Consequence of Shape* (1982–2005), and Robert Sheppard's *Twentieth Century Blues* (1989–2000) are all prominent postwar examples. In addition, there have been important cross-genre projects, whether Evaristo's verse novels, Anthony Joseph's lyrical science fiction novel, *The African Origin of UFOs* (2006), Ruth Padel's *Darwin: A Life in Poems* (2009), or Andrea Brady's *Mutability: Scripts for Infancy* (2012), which alternates between discrete lyrics and dated journal-like prose pieces to and about Brady's daughter. There have been, however, fewer intergeneric projects in postwar British poetry, by which I mean texts that incorporate multiple genres into their composition and that also maintain a formal heterogeneity. Roy Fisher's *City* is an early example of a mixed form, although, like Brady's volume, *City* alternates between genres rather than intermeshes them. Several important intergeneric projects appeared within the ferment of the British Poetry Revival, influenced primarily by Olsonian open-field poetics. But there have been relatively few texts from the past several decades that at once expand the remit of poetry by crossing genres or incorporating multiple genres and also remain heterogeneous from page to page and within each page.

One such text is Alice Oswald's *Dart* (2002). As its title suggests, it is set in and around the River Dart in Devon, which flows from high in Dartmoor southeast and becomes a tidal estuary after Totnes before flowing into the sea at Dartmouth. In a prefatory note, Oswald presents the book, which consists of forty-eight pages of unbroken verse and prose, as a kind of lyric field journal that incorporates the conversations that she had "with people who know the river."[24] As Fiona Sampson has suggested, *Dart* is reminiscent of Dylan Thomas's "play for voices," *Under Milk Wood*, and apart from fluid shifts between prose and verse, the only other divisions in the text are marginal notes that indicate a change of speaker.[25] While Oswald links these speakerly characters to the real "life-models" that she met on the Dart, she also notes that these speakers should not be taken to "refer to real people or even fixed fictions."[26] They are, as one passage has it, "swift fragmentary happenings," and while we are presented with a series of character types – "naturalist," "forester," "tin-extractor," "ferryman" – there is no stable diegesis around which a narrative or drama develops.[27] In the prefatory note, Oswald suggests that the distinct voices are linked into what she calls "a sound-map of the river, a songline from the source to the sea," and that all of the voices comprise "the river's mutterings."[28]

The book is thus a collection of voices and a gallery of "found" commentaries, histories, anecdotes, conversations, and monologues, the totality of which aim to take the river's full measure. Via these voices, which are often curtailed or interrupted as Oswald exchanges one for another, we learn about the river's history and ecosystem, its attendant myths and lore, its place in a network of industry and human infrastructure, and the characters that live and work around it. *Dart* takes on many forms, moving from rhyming couplets and long stretches of running verse that mime the river to blocks of conversational prose that appear to be more direct transcriptions of the conversations that Oswald had during the period of composition. At times, the texture of the verse resembles Graham's "The Nightfishing," although without often venturing into the phenomenological territory of the earlier poem. At others, Oswald offers her own variation of "place poetry," with passages resembling the *dinnseanchas* poems of Heaney or John Montague as it names "varieties of water":

Glico of the Running Streams
and Spio of the Boulders-Encaved-In-The-River's-Edges

and all other named varieties of Water
such as Loops and Swirls in their specific dialects
clucking and clapping.[29]

Occasionally it is reminiscent of the washerwomen scene in Joyce's *Finnegans Wake* as the Dart's voices intermingle with each other in the "jostling procession of waters":

why is this flickering water
with its blinks and side-long looks
with its language of oaks
and clicking of its slatey brooks
why is this river not ever
able to leave until it's over?[30]

When it is over, as *Dart* comes to an end, the poem's composite voice gathers itself: "This is me, anonymous, water's soliloquy, // all names, all voices, Slip-Shape, this is Proteus."[31]

Dart is a heterogeneous text, moving between verse and prose and slipping among the many voices that surround the river, some of which Oswald found, some she transfigured, and some she newly fashioned. Indeed, one of the problems that Oswald explores is this: how might a lyric text resist the monologic authority that accrues to the lyric "I"? In *Dart*, Oswald's response is to distribute that "I" among many voices. Much of the book is in the first person, and so there are "I"s everywhere, but these numerous instances of the first-person grammatical subject do not coalesce around a single lyric or narrative subject. But in another way, they do: as Oswald has told us at the outset, the book consists of "the river's mutterings," and so the speaking subject of *Dart* is the River Dart. This is both self-evident and thorny: it provides a homogenous solution to a heterogeneous form. If the "I" of the poem is simply the river itself, then Oswald's method of research and composition, which involved learning from the people who live and work on the river and recording their words, is lost, or at least muted. On an unnumbered page just before and facing the prefatory note to *Dart* from which I have been quoting, there appears a long list of "Acknowledgements." Before including the usual disclaimer about the impossibility of mentioning everyone who "helped with this poem," she goes on to list fifty-seven individuals along with the "Trustees of Dartington Hall." Most of these individuals are listed by first and last name, but Oswald also thanks "Anonymous walker," "3 anonymous poachers," and "Gerry" – just "Gerry." Presumably, Oswald thanks many of the people to whom she spoke about the river and whose words make up much of the text. The "Acknowledgements" are thus something like the credits one would see listed onscreen or named at the end of a broadcast. The interesting question is not about whether these individuals should have been "credited" in Oswald's text, so that instead of an anonymous "I" who speaks about the river, a reader is told that the following words are spoken by, say, "Gerry." It is not a matter of proper citation or about the ethics of found poetry. One imagines that Oswald informed all of her interlocutors about the project and got their permission to draw from their conversations, and one also presumes that she took significant creative license in rescoring her found texts when composing the poem. The cautionary note that appears in the prefatory note – "these [voices] do not refer to real people" – is also, then, something of a disclaimer. We are told that while based on real people's actual words, *Dart* is not a transcription or a documentary. This is relatively straightforward, but the tension between heterogeneity and homogeneity remains, and it is underlined by the intriguing juxtaposition between a long list of "Acknowledgements" to real people and a note that suggests that all of the voices that we are about to read do not "refer to real people." Despite itself, Dart's many-voiced "I" shades into singularity, whether we call that "I," diegetically, the River Dart, or, extradiegetically, Alice Oswald.

John Wilkinson provides a broader perspective on this matter. In *The Lyric Touch*, Wilkinson diagnoses modern lyric's pronominal crisis:

> It can feel as though the lyric poetry of the twentieth-century has been harried past endurance by the problem of the first person singular, the lyric 'I', variously by its pomposity, its frailty, its pretensions and its inadequacy. This cannot be evaded by extirpation of the cursed pronoun, for the depersonalised poem tends to then lay claim to an overweening authority. The first person plural tends to a presumption of common cause or sensibility with the smug or wheedling 'I', and the second person singular or plural to arraign the reader or society from the vantage of the arrogant 'I'.[32]

Displacing the "overweening authority" of the lyric "I" has been a central task of the writers associated with Prynne and Cambridge poetry, a task that is linked to a more thoroughgoing critique of global capitalism. For writers such as Wilkinson, Drew Milne, David Marriott, Andrea Brady, and Keston Sutherland, any cultural or social value that poetry might have relies on a kind of radical negativity, a constant overturning of expected patterns of language and customary literary habits. If, as Wilkinson intimates, the lyric "I" and poetry in general is in constant danger of reification, of being stiffened into an ideologically bankrupt and easily consumable literary product, then the aim must be to ceaselessly resist such capitulation. As we have seen in previous examples – primarily but not exclusively in Prynne's work – this makes for poetry of unremitting difficulty and incessant self-scrutiny, much of which is premised upon a thorough destabilization or whole-scale desertion of the lyric subject. As a final turn in this book, I will consider the stakes of such difficulty as it has appeared in several recent texts of and about the Cambridge formation and as it connects to the notion of formal heterogeneity that I have introduced.

Prynne's centrality to British poetry has become increasingly recognized since the turn of the century, with Randall Stevenson's volume in *The Oxford English Literary History* one of first major indications that the mainstream of English literature had granted Prynne's importance.[33] This wider appreciation has taken place even as Prynne's work of the past two decades has become less and less amenable to explication.[34] It is noteworthy, then, that Fiona Sampson's *Beyond the Lyric: A Map of Contemporary British Poetry,* which for the most part promotes mainstream figures such as Don Paterson and Sean O'Brien, praises the full range of Prynne's body of work, including the more resistant poetry that has appeared since *Her Weasels Wild Returning* (1994).[35] If Sampson's admiration for Prynne is somewhat surprising, then less surprising is her use of Prynne's work to berate younger poets within Prynne's orbit. As discussed in Chapter 4, Prynne himself has remained largely outside the skirmishes that have taken place between mainstream and experimental poets in Britain, publishing little critical prose about contemporary writers. That he largely avoids the machinery of the British poetry business has underscored this sense of Prynne's remoteness, but it has also allowed a narrative of exclusivity and elitism to be forwarded by critics less friendly to Prynne's poetry and that of poets who have travelled in his slipstream.

Since the middle of the 1990s, however, the second and third generations of the Cambridge poetry scene have been more active advocates for their poetics. Drew Milne's *Parataxis* was founded in 1991, and along with *Equofinality*, edited by Rod Mengham and John Wilkinson, and Mengham's *Equipage* press, *Parataxis* became a key outlet for the kind of experimental writing associated with Cambridge poetry, as well as the site of much of its critical prose. Milne's 1993 essay, "Agoraphobia, and the Embarrassment of Manifestos: Notes Towards a Community of Risk," suggests ways that such poetry might form the basis of a more public community. His countermanifesto deliberately relies on the voices of others: he "merely wish[es] to ventriloquize a utopian collective."[36] Excerpts from Prynne's poetry, as well as prose extracts primarily from writers associated with what Milne names "the Cambridge axis," serve as touchstones for Milne's commentary, which aims both to revitalize "the residual and emergent avant-gardes of contemporary poetry" and to provide a relay between what had been (and continues to be) viewed as a hermetic circle of insiders and a more open collective. Part of his goal is to chart a set of possible futures for avant-garde poetry within a British literary culture averse to manifestoes. He writes, "the disparate fragments of contemporary poetics are at a point where a much broader public is within grasp. Thus there is a need to draw together these fragments into a community of risk which can develop a different social basis for a poetry which is both public and private, while transforming the terms of such an opposition." Milne looks backward for a model of such a community, and finds it in the activity around *The English Intelligencer* in the late 1960s. A frustrated contribution from Prynne about the lack of critical exchange in the pages of *The English Intelligencer* is the source of the phrase – "community of risk" – that sutures together Milne's proposals, and his essay ends with a long extract from one of Peter Riley's contributions to the worksheets. That Milne focuses on the founding moment of "the Cambridge axis" is not surprising, but it does warp the texture of his argument. Much earlier in the essay, Milne had written that "above all, and perhaps naively, I am interested in opening up a dialogue between those initiated into the internal markets of contemporary poetry, and those who would like an introduction, or are suspicious of what is apparent." The use of "initiation" here suggests the existence of an enclosure of writers, which somewhat limits, or at least dictates, the terms of the open dialogue that he desires. His decision to quote primarily from fellow members of the "Cambridge axis" threatens to reproduce the "conspiracy of expertise" that he warns against in his essay. Milne makes the case for placing Cambridge poetry within a wider orbit, but also demonstrates the tendency towards a coterie poetics that made Cambridge poetry an appealing target for figures well outside the "axis."

Milne's piece was a product of the early 1990s, but the issues that it raises are still very much alive within debates about experimental British poetry. Some of the same questions about elitism, exclusivity, and politics were raised in a tense exchange between two of Milne's key interlocutors, John Wilkinson and Peter Riley, in the pages of the *Chicago Review* in 2006 and 2007. It began with Wilkinson's review of *The Unconditional: A Lyric*, a long poem by Simon Jarvis, another poet in the "Cambridge axis," whose scholarly work focuses on the intersections between poetry and critical theory and especially on the critical and cognitive possibilities embedded in prosody. He has written extensively on the Frankfurt School and the English Romantic poets and, like Mengham and Milne, teaches at Cambridge. Wilkinson reads the prosody of Jarvis's long poem in the context of Theodor Adorno's negative dialectics and in particular the negative utopianism that striates Adorno's thought. Riley's subsequent letter to the editor is putatively a response to Wilkinson's review, but in actuality it opens a polemical foray over the legacy of Cambridge poetry. It is an occasionally blistering dismissal of ways in which later Cambridge poets like Wilkinson have positioned poetry in relation to politics, as well as of the forms of exclusivity and elitism that Riley sees as inherent to Wilkinson's position. Riley's letter provoked a lengthy and fiery response from Wilkinson, and the exchange is perhaps the most public airing of debates about the consequence of the deeply challenging surfaces that are the most notable feature of Prynne's work and of the poetry produced within his orbit. Picking up on one or two lines of debate between Riley and Wilkinson will allow me to frame my turn to Keston Sutherland, who studied with Prynne, wrote his doctoral dissertation on Prynne and philology, and is at the center of debates about poetic practice and political life in Britain.[37]

Riley's primary concern, for which Wilkinson's review becomes merely a symptomatic pretext, is that the only kind of political agency available to the poetry that would be valued within Wilkinson's circles is one of "total oppositional negation."[38] Riley laments that this requires an abandonment of actual politics and the maintenance of a perpetual position of abstract "crisis," although one that refuses to address actual crises in the world. The problem, he states, is with a "mounting sense of embattled privilege jousting with despair on behalf of humanity."[39] For Riley, "*the poets have decided that there is no hope to be had anywhere and have retreated into language. And there's certainly no hope there, but it gives you the illusion that you're doing something.*"[40] Since language is a "lying instrument," a poem has to occult or conceal anything that might be construed as its "substance or message."[41] Such poems depend on the sort of "conspiracy of expertise" that worried Milne, and what results is an exceedingly small lineage of poets who become near-messianic figures, what Riley calls "a lionization of a handful of extremely selected poets who attain what can only be good old-fashioned 'genius' status."[42] The great bulk of poetry is "silently trash[ed]."[43]

Wilkinson's rejoinder parries Riley by turning his complaints against himself, deflecting his arguments by way of self-deprecating humor (as well as plain-old deprecation), and, at certain points, by knowingly biting on Riley's bait. Two moments in particular are worth centering. The first occurs early on in the letter in which Wilkinson, before he gets down to responding to Riley, offers his essay on Andrea Brady's poetry – which appeared in the same issue of the *Chicago Review* as Riley's letter – as a kind of proleptic answer to some of Riley's concerns. Wilkinson recounts that his essay on Brady "suggested that an exalted and exclusive conception of lyric might be inimical to political effectiveness, and pointed to certain writers whose lyric writing is tied to other modes of writing in a wider political project as more likely to exert a political influence."[44] The second occurs toward the end of the letter, after Wilkinson has fully risen to what he describes as Riley's implicit offer "to be equally oracular." Wilkinson pans back from his local row with Riley to say something about poetry *tout court*:

> Pre-eminently, lyric poetry can act as a specific against dissipation. It can effect a condensation, a new alloy, a new hybrid. This is not the same as a new self, whether for reader or writer, for selfhood always entails a rent in the provisional fabric of poetry. If the alchemy is spiritual, it engenders a new spirit every time, a coming-into-being which never arrives. This happens incidentally to the striving for it. What is produced cannot be vaunted as a totality because it is short-lived and soon to be dispelled.[45]

Wilkinson values lyric poetry's ability to model a form of processual constructivism. That is, a formal unfolding that is neither predetermined nor teleological nor homogenous. And one that doesn't offer "a new self" for either poet or reader. Rather, as he suggests in his comments about his Brady essay, lyric poetry might best be "tied to other modes of writing." A sense of generic instability and structural mutability is inherent to a poem's potential for political efficacy. Formal heterogeneity in this case does not simply indicate a penchant for postmodern play. Rather, the kinds of poems that seem most alive to their historical moment – certainly a moment of large-scale and systemic crisis – provoke continual crises within their local textures so as to produce a ceaseless friction that both resists easy digestibility and reveals new condensations or alloys that couldn't be predicted by the poem's initial terms.

One of the most significant such texts is Keston Sutherland's *Hot White Andy*, which first appeared in an issue of the *Chicago Review* devoted to four contemporary British poets, the same issue in which appears Riley's initial response to Wilkinson's review of Jarvis. The issue remains within "the Cambridge axis," and Sutherland is featured along with Andrea Brady, Chris Goode, and Peter Manson. *Hot White Andy* immediately attracted a good deal of attention, and Sutherland's energetic performance of the poem at several university readings in the spring of 2007 and after has helped ensure its prominence. *Hot White Andy* is a poem that also enfolds a play and a story, and over the course of its 425 lines, it stitches in a vast array of information, citation, allusion, and arcane detail. Sutherland asks his readers to work at a dizzying number of interpretive levels, and his range of reference and rate of linguistic and figural mutation make for a poem of exceeding difficulty. Needless to say, a full reading of the poem is well out of my scope here. But even a brief glance at *Hot White Andy* will help display Sutherland's radical extension of lyric possibilities.

The poem is many minded and multivalent, "thinking in a roundabout manner and by means of bricolage," as one of Sutherland's dramatic personae puts it.[46] But it is also, at its core, an extended love poem, albeit a deeply idiosyncratic one bound up in Sutherland's more systemic Marxian critique of capitalism and consumerism. Introducing the poem at a reading in Helsinki in 2010, Sutherland explains that he tried to write "a love poem to a random person in the world" (although, as Jennifer Cooke and others have pointed out, Sutherland has also described the poem in more personal terms).[47] His Google search returned "Andrew Cheng," who is (or was at the time when the poem was written) an exports manager at a tungsten production company in Wuhan, China.[48] The properties, applications, and industrial and military uses of tungsten provide a good deal of the poem's imagery, especially its use in welding, and this motif offers something like an *ars poetica*. The construction of a poem, and of a love poem in particular, is likened to a heavy industrial process, both the chemical production of tungsten alloys and the applications of those products. In this way, the text saturates itself in the processes and materials of multinational industry, another form of its examination of global capitalism. Because love itself has been thoroughly commodified, Sutherland needs to construct a romantic relationship that is almost unfathomable in order to locate love's revolutionary potential. And so he writes a passionate, seriously felt love poem to someone he doesn't know. *Hot White Andy* contains all sorts of local ironies and moments of mordant humor, but the poem as a whole is deeply serious, although its urgency is, as Wilkinson and Sam Ladkin have suggested, of a preposterous kind.[49]

The poem is in many ways operatic, moving between extended long-line passages of "hot manic recitative" and strangely fashioned lyric arias that appear as stair-step quatrains of affective and sexual energy condensed into halting syntax.[50] This is to drastically oversimplify the poem's complex structure, and such a dichotomy between recitative and aria does not account for the narrative sections of the poem – especially in part "B" – nor the mini-drama that appears in part "A: Turbo," the third and final section. But as a heuristic device, the operatic analogy does at least provide a point of interpretive access. *Hot White Andy*'s opening passage would, in this scheme, constitute a "hot manic recitative":

> Lavrov and the Stock Wizard levitate over to
> the blackened dogmatic catwalk and you eat them. Now swap
> *buy* for *eat*, then *fuck* for *buy*, then *ruminate* for *fuck*,
> phlegmophrenic, want to go to the windfarm,

> *Your* • kids menu lips swinging in the Cathex-Wizz monoplex;
> *Your* • face lifting triple its age in Wuhan die-cut peel lids;
> ng pick *Your* out the reregulated loner PAT to to screw white
> chocolate to the bone. The tension in an unsprung
> *r* trap co
>   →   The tension in an unsprung trap.[51]

Even merely glossing all of the obscure terms in this passage would take a while, and Sutherland's poetry seems destined for the kind of close commentaries that predominate in the criticism on Prynne's work. Some of the oddities in this opening passage have clear referents, but many are hermetic or newfangled. According to Wilkinson, "Peter Lavrovich Lavrov was a nineteenth-century Russian socialist revolutionary who anticipated Mao Zedong in recognising that in countries where capitalist development was rudimentary, the peasantry could be an engine of socialist transformation. But Lavrov has morphed into Sergey Lavrov, a career bureaucrat and now Russia's Foreign Minister."[52] Wilkinson goes on to suggest that "the Stock Wizard" is a Warren Buffett–like figure, and so the opening pairing of "Lavrov and the Stock Wizard" concretizes the poem's interest in the dangers of global capitalism by triangulating the United States, Russia, and China. The next constellation links eating, sex, shopping, and thinking, and it sets the basic coordinates that will occupy Sutherland throughout. Against the abstraction of the commodity form, *Hot White Andy* asserts continually the body's fleshiness, even as it has preestranged itself by cathecting on a love object that is not one at all.

The (•) that fissures the pronoun *your* from its possessions – its children and its face – and that on the page seems like an extraneous remainder is, in Sutherland's performance, a cue for a vocal gesture in which he blows straight into the microphone with his hands over his mouth, producing a brief popping sound. In an opening that offers all manner of too-easy exchange, the bullet point (•) resists the ideologies of consumption and disposal that surround it. Like Bergvall's morphological noise, it is intractable on the page but enlivening in the air and on the voice. Similarly, the marooned and excessive letters and phonemes in the following lines can be conceptualized as the equivalent to industrial dross – "ng," "to to," "r trap co" – that fall out of an economy of linguistic exchange. The poem's opening passage sets itself among disposable products, alienated bodies, and unfathomable systems of global finance, and in important ways *Hot White Andy* never leaves this space.

As it frantically and seriously pursues its random love object, other characters momentarily come into the foreground, both near namesakes of the Andy Cheng caught in Google's trawl and other random figures who appear more substantively within the poem's dreamlike diegesis. The love poem unfurls amidst a revolving inventory of popular culture references, Internet detritus, and fractured news crawl that attends the poem's composition. Shards of found texts interrupt throughout, and there are a number of passages of straightforward mimetic force, but more often than not, a reader is in a vertiginous, perilous position, unable to make clear linkages and exchanges from line to line and passage to passage, caught in the poem's metrical energy but unable to categorize that energy or to form relays between textual moments. Along the way, Sutherland addresses – in brief and extravagant ways – the wars in Iraq and Afghanistan, police brutality and economic inequality in the United States, the Geneva Conventions, and the economic rise of China within his larger consideration of capitalism's global spread and its damaging logic of exchange and endless growth, asking

> what is
> it for this rapture of transitivity, this equivalence hypodermic,
> the infinity of desire?[53]

As in Sutherland's later book, *The Odes to TL61P*, which takes as its putative praise object the product number for a replacement part of a Hotpoint washer-dryer unit, *Hot White Andy* locates a seemingly random point in the unthinkable totality of global capitalism and consumerism around which to construct his adamant critique.

Like Prynne's "Chromatin," the litany of the poem's final seven lines provides a species of rhetorical closure but forestalls a full resolution by continuing to withhold grammatical and semantic linkages:

> I accumulate you: sky crated in Binzel and *'Change*, crated in
>   illumination,
> I accumulate you: hot sky deserted by Abner and tax phosphor.
> The superpower to come is love itself. Articles 2
> up and the Antepasséist 0. But since this is my only life
> I accumulate you Andrew Lumocolor, not fit for waiting
> away uptight in fire shopped to spit, but a real man
> accumulating men, desire and intensity until I die.[54]

The end of the poem positions love as "the superpower to come," but it remains caught within a process of exchange and accumulation, replaying earlier textual moments that are now even further untethered. Andy Cheng, the poem's object of desire, becomes in his final iteration also a sign for writing itself, as "Lumocolor" can refer to a particular brand of pens and markers produced by the German company Staedtler. The poem's final lines are both rousing and wary, bringing the lengthy parade of exchanges to a close by focusing on the singularity of a life and its inevitable death, but they are also skeptical of the ramifications of doing so, especially given the damaging masculinism that is involved with such accumulative powers.

Hot White Andy is, to be sure, tremendously difficult, and many of its difficulties remain inscrutable. While the objects of Sutherland's attention and critique are clearly evident – Andy Cheng, China, consumerism, capitalism, love – the approaches that he takes to these objects are never fully prescripted, and the innumerable materials that do not assimilate themselves into the poem's course give this text a messy openness that helps dampen its more tendentious bent. The poem's staged narcissism and bathos are diffused within its drastic heterogeneity, and even the knottiest moments can become sites for an important kind of textual intimacy:

> cuff slung hot across the abraded
> jar shows particul | me screams
> me despite
> me I love you, rope 1
> You are so running out of time. Run impressed rope / trap out of it.
> *Run.*[55]

In this moment of, perhaps, escape from danger, the sheer strangeness of the juxtaposed materials makes for precisely what Wilkinson called for: short-lived condensations, new and soon-to-be-dispelled alloys that both model crisis and combat it with something like care. The multiple levels of violence in the earlier lines give way, momentarily, to love, but perhaps more poignantly to a warning: "*Run.*"

Against the multiple crises of global wars, globalized finance, and globe-killing industry, *Hot White Andy* aims to position love as a potentially revolutionary feeling. Like much of the poetry that has emerged out of the Cambridge formation in the past several decades, it is embroiled in perpetual crises of representation, figuration, and form. Crisis often serves as a topic or an underlying theme, but it is more significantly a systemic textual operation. To be sure, there are hazards to such unremitting forms of fragmentation and negation, some of which Peter Riley describes in his riposte to Wilkinson. The syllable-by-syllable strain that characterizes Prynne's later work, as well as other poems within the "Cambridge axis," can potentially locate generative spaces of poetic thought and agency. However, a risk is certainly run: such poetry sets up so many obstacles for even the most flexible and game reader that it may inevitably remain within a small circle of the already converted. Milne and Wilkinson have considered such recalcitrant poetry as part of a broader political conversation, but basing a poetic practice on a continual estrangement of language's basic communicative functions comes with perils.

For the most part, however, such risks are necessary, and, as I hope to have shown over the course of this conclusion and of the volume as a whole, they are not in the exclusive domain of poets associated with Prynne and Cambridge or even of the experimental end of the spectrum of British poetry. Such risks are inextricable from the large-scale and multivalent crises that have characterized both Britain and the globe in the early twenty-first century. Since the terrorist attacks in the United States on September 11, 2001, and especially after the bombings in the London Underground on July 7, 2005, the specter of terrorism and the encroachment of the security state have deeply marked life in Britain, and renewed debates about immigration and the nature of Britishness have introduced new forms of racism and xenophobia. The British economy weakened during the early years of the new century, and the global financial collapse in 2008 had a massive impact, with austerity measures leading to large cuts in a broad range of social services, significant protests against the dominance of corporate interests in matters of politics and civil society, and outrage at the vast economic imbalances that structure contemporary life. When one also takes into account the perilous state of the world's ecological system, it isn't difficult to conclude that it might just be crisis all the way down, leading to either great urgency or plaintive despair.

Whether or not individual poems directly register such crises or incorporate a practice of crisis into their forms, the historical circumstances that surround them can't help but appear. As I have aimed to show throughout this book, poems are entangled in their context, but they aren't necessarily determined by it. Many poems make transhistorical linkages and aim to project themselves into a far future. Such bids are, of course, central to art. At the same time, poems are linguistic and cultural artifacts that comprise unique perspectives on the granularities of their moment. British poetry since 1945 has provided a rich artifactual array, and the major texts of the period might be said to compose a counterhistory, an alternate story of the last seventy years. The substance of this counterhistory would not only be found in poems' themes and topics or merely in the ideologies and attitudes that can be drawn from them. It would also appear in the tilting of a rhyme, the twist of a metaphor, or the buckling of a line. It might surface within the play of an etymology or in the deictic pantomime between *you* and *I*. The politics of poems reside in their concrete poetics, but this isn't to say that poets can't make explicit political statements in poems without reducing themselves to oratory. Nor is this to suggest that any particular form or genre comes with its ideology preloaded. Forms are not neutral, but neither are they determined by their prior use. As Wilkinson suggests, and as many of the poets in this book have demonstrated, poems can provide new condensations of affect, experience, and thought, even and perhaps especially when they use well-worn materials.

The canon of post-1945 British poetry is still in emergence. Some parts of the picture are well established, if in need of reassessment or additional scrutiny, while others remain obscure. While the impact of Larkin and the Movement poets or of Heaney and Northern Irish poetry is clear, our understanding of concurrent developments – such as the British Poetry Revival or the rise of black British poetry in the 1950s and 1960s – is still progressing. If there is a small handful of poets who are solidly established as major figures and who are likely to remain so in upcoming decades, then there are also many handfuls whose work is only now coming into view. And if there are poets who are major on the scene at present, then there are many others who are under the radar and whose later emergence will retroactively shift the story of our contemporary moment. As I indicated at the start of this chapter, mapping the present of British poetry is chancy, and there are certainly whole swathes of intriguing territory that I haven't had space to cover or that I haven't fully charted yet. But in sketching the contours of this canon and lingering in a more sustained manner on a cache of poets and poems, I have aimed to present a usable guide to its key features and most pressing issues. In doing so, I have burrowed again and again into the local textures of individual poems, for it is often in a poem's crevices that its complex substance is best found. A poem might be outwardly, actively political, reflecting on or railing against the iniquities and horrors of the world. It might curl inward, remaining within the orbit of the individual subject or thinking through the relation between a subject and its surround. A poem might praise, celebrate, document, push on, or revolt against its world. It might do all of these at once. Or it might be impossible to say precisely how a poem imagines itself in relation to whatever world it draws. A poem's task or strategy is inextricable from its intricate course of attention and composition. For many of the poems that I've examined throughout this book, the courses taken have been multiple or recursive, circular or curtailed. Many have taken several routes at once, while others have eschewed movement almost entirely. In each case, though, they have sought to locate some path of imaginative thought and feeling whose traces remain in the compounds of their formal acts. In so doing, they tell us something vital both about their intrinsic densities and the complex moment out of which they transpired.

Notes

Introduction

1 Al Alvarez (ed.), *The New Poetry* (Harmondsworth, Middlesex: Penguin, 1966 [1962]), 21.

2 In *The Failure of Conservatism in Modern British Poetry*, Duncan provides his primary proposal: "a minority of British poets have fabulous skills with the unfamiliar, the spontaneous, the improvised, the intimate, and the experimental, and so get attacked or ignored" (Cambridge: Salt Publishing, 2003), 3.

3 See Keith Tuma, *Fishing by Obstinate Isles: Modern and Postmodern British Poetry and American Readers* (Evanston, IL: Northwestern University Press, 1998).

4 There are, of course, many excellent studies of postwar British poetry. For general works, see the "Further Reading" suggestions at the end of this volume. I have included more particular bibliographical information on specific poets and poems, as well as all references, within the notes.

5 There are several additional concessions I should make at the outset. For numerous reasons, this book cannot consider poetry in the other languages of the British Isles apart from English. Nor can it take into account matters of translation more generally, whether of European or world poetry into English, of British poetry into other languages, or of important translations made by poets such as Christopher Middleton, Michael Hoffman, Derek Mahon, or Seamus Heaney.

6 For studies of Anglophone postcolonial poetry, see Jahan Ramazani, *The Hybrid Muse: Postcolonial Poetry in English* (Chicago and London: University of Chicago Press, 2001) and *A Transnational Poetics* (Chicago and London: University of Chicago Press, 2009); and Rajeev S. Patke, *Postcolonial Poetry in English* (Oxford and New York: Oxford University Press, 2006).

7 Alan Sinfield, *Literature, Politics and Culture in Postwar Britain* (London: Continuum, 2004 [1997]), 7.

8 Wendy Webster, *Englishness and Empire, 1939–1965* (Oxford: Oxford University Press, 2005), 61.

9 Anthony Sampson, *Anatomy of Britain* (London: Hodder and Stoughton, 1962), 620.

10 Sinfield, *Literature, Politics and Culture in Postwar Britain*, 304.

11 T.S. Eliot, *Christianity and Culture: The Idea of a Christian Society and Notes Toward the Definition of Culture* (New York and London: Harcourt Brace, 1976), 50–51.

12 Stephen Spender, *Poetry Since 1939* (London: Longmans Green & Company, 1946), 12.

13 Ibid., 10.

14 Philip Larkin, *Required Writing: Miscellaneous Pieces, 1955–1982* (London: Faber and Faber, 1983), 123.

15 James Keery has provided a detailed account of the Apocalyptics and English poetry in the 1940s, which appears as a series of lengthy essays published in the *PN Review* under the general title "The Burning Baby and the Bath Water." See *PN Review* 29.4 (March–April 2003), 29.5 (May–June 2003), 29.6 (July–August 2003), 30.2 (November–December 2003), 30.4 (March–April 2004), 30.5 (May–June 2004), 31.1 (September–October 2004), 31.6 (July–August 2005), 32.6 (July–August 2006), and 33.1 (September–October 2006). Also see Arthur Edward Salmon, *Poets of the Apocalypse* (Boston: Twayne Publishers, 1983).

16 Henry Treece, *How I See Apocalypse* (London: Lindsay Drummond, 1946), 76.

17 Spender, *Poetry Since 1939*, 57–58.

18 Ibid., 45.

19 Kenneth Rexroth (ed.), *The New British Poets: An Anthology* (New York: New Directions, 1949), xvii.

20 See John Goodby, *The Poetry of Dylan Thomas: Under the Spelling Wall* (Liverpool: Liverpool University Press, 2013), 425n1.

21 See ibid., 371–432.

22 Dylan Thomas, *Collected Poems, 1934–1952* (New York: New Directions, 1971 [1952]), 178.

23 Ibid., 179.

24 Ibid., xv.

1 The Movement and Its Discontents

1 Anthony Hartley, "Poets of the Fifties," *The Spectator*, August 27, 1954, 260–261, at 261.

2 Ibid., 260.

3 [J.D. Scott], "In the Movement," *The Spectator*, October 1, 1954, 399–400, at 399.

4 Ibid., 400.

5 Robert Conquest (ed.), *New Lines: An Anthology* (London: Macmillan, 1956), xv.

6 Ibid., xi.

7 Ibid., xiv.

8 Ibid., xv.

9 Ibid., xv.

10 Ibid., xv.

11 Ibid., xv.

12 Ibid., xiv, xvi.

13 Ibid., 1.

14 Ibid., 1.

15 Ibid., 25, 45.

16 Ibid., 72.

17 Ibid., 72.

18 Philip Larkin, *Collected Poems,* ed. Anthony Thwaite (New York: Farrar, Straus and Giroux, 2004), 52.

19 Edna Longley, "Larkin, Decadence and the Lyric Poem," in James Booth (ed.), *New Larkins for Old: Critical Essays* (Basingstoke: Macmillan, 2000), 29–50, at 29.

20 See Nigel Alderman, " 'The Life With a Hole in It': Philip Larkin and the Condition of England," *Textual Practice*, 8.2 (1994), 279–301.

21 Larkin, *Collected Poems*, 58–59. All quotations from this poem come from these two pages.

22 Ibid., 117, 100.

23 Ibid., 80.

24 All quotations from this poem are taken from Larkin, *Collected Poems*, 92–94.

25 Donald Davie, *Thomas Hardy and British Poetry* (New York: Oxford University Press, 1972), 71, 73.

26 Tom Paulin, *Minotaur: Poetry and the Nation State* (Cambridge, MA: Harvard University Press, 1992), 285–286.

27 Andrew Motion, *Philip Larkin: A Writer's Life* (New York: Farrar, Straus and Giroux, 1993), 288.

28 Philip Larkin, *Required Writing: Miscellaneous Pieces, 1955–1982* (London: Faber and Faber, 1983), 55.

29 Blake Morrison, *The Movement: English Poetry of the 1950s* (Oxford: Oxford University Press, 1980), 53.

30 Ibid., 238.

31 Al Alvarez (ed.), *The New Poetry* (Harmondsworth, Middlesex: Penguin, 1966 [1962]), 21.

32 Ibid., 22, 23.

33 Ibid., 23, 24.

34 Ibid., 24–25.

35 Ibid., 32.

36 For a valuable analysis of the similarities between Conquest's and Alvarez's polemics, see Andrew Crozier, "Thrills and Frills: Poetry as Figures of Empirical Lyricism," in Alan Sinfield (ed.), *Society and Literature, 1945–1970* (London: Methuen, 1983), 199–233.

37 Dick Hebidge, *Subculture: The Meaning of Style* (London and New York: Routledge, 1988 [1979]), 46.

38 Nigel Alderman and Michael Thurston, *Reading Postwar British and Irish Poetry* (Chichester, West Sussex: Wiley-Blackwell, 2014), 55.

39 Randall Stevenson, *The Oxford English Literary History, Volume 12. 1960–2000: The Last of England?* (Oxford: Oxford University Press, 2004), 152–153.

40 Thom Gunn, *Collected Poems* (New York: Farrar, Straus and Giroux, 1994), 39.

41 Ibid., 39.

42 Martin Pumphrey, "Play, Fantasy and Strange Laughter," *Critical Quarterly*, 28.3 (1986), 85–96, at 85–86.

43 Stevie Smith, *Collected Poems* (New York: New Directions Press, 1983), 204.

44 Ibid., 571, 265.

45 Christopher Ricks, "Stevie Smith: 'Truth Is Great and Will Prevail in a Bit,'" *Grand Street*, 1.1 (1981), 147–157, at 148.

46 Smith, *Collected Poems*, 407.

47 Ibid., 133.

48 Ibid., 303.

49 Ibid., 303.

50 Quoted in Romana Huk, *Stevie Smith: Between the Lines* (Basingstoke: Palgrave Macmillan, 2005), 283.

51 Robert Conquest (ed.), *New Lines – II* (London: Macmillan, 1963), xxviii.

52 Quoted in Ian Sansom, "'Listen': W. S. Graham," in Ralph Pite and Hester Jones (eds.), *W. S. Graham: Speaking Towards You* (Liverpool: Liverpool University Press, 2004), 11–23, at 16.

53 On Graham, see Matthew Francis, *Where the People Are: Language and Community in the Poetry of W. S. Graham* (Cambridge: Salt Publishing, 2004); and Tony Lopez, *The Poetry of W. S. Graham* (Edinburgh: Edinburgh University Press, 1989). Also see Michael and Margaret Snow (eds.), *The Nightfisherman: Selected Letters of W. S. Graham* (Manchester: Carcanet, 1999).

54 W. S. Graham, *New Collected Poems*, ed. Matthew Francis (London: Faber and Faber, 2004), 4.

55 Edwin Morgan, "The Sea, the Desert, the City: Environment and Language in W. S. Graham, Hamish Henderson, and Tom Leonard," *The Yearbook of English Studies*, 17 (1987), 31–45, at 31.

56 Graham, *New Collected Poems*, 188.

57 Ibid., 19.

58 Ibid., 162.

59 Ibid., 117.

60 Ibid., 105.

61 Ibid., 110.

62 Ibid., 106.

63 Ibid., 116.

64 Ibid., 107, 109, 110, 113.

65 Jon Silkin (ed.), *Poetry of the Committed Individual: A* Stand *Anthology of Poetry* (Harmondsworth, Middlesex: Penguin Books, 1973), 26.

66 G. S. Fraser, "Formal and Relaxed," *The New Statesman*, October 31, 1959, 590.

67 Donald Davie, *Articulate Energy: An Inquiry into the Syntax of English Poetry* (London: Routledge & Kegan Paul, 1955), 129.

68 Vincent Sherry, *The Uncommon Tongue: The Poetry and Criticism of Geoffrey Hill* (Ann Arbor: The University of Michigan Press, 1987), 29.

69 Geoffrey Hill, *Broken Hierarchies: Poems 1952–2012*, ed. Kenneth Haynes (Oxford: Oxford University Press, 2013), 16.

70 T. S. Eliot, *Selected Prose* (Harmondsworth, Middlesex: Penguin Books, 1953), 25.

71 Hill, *Broken Hierarchies*, 3.

72 Ibid., 4.

73 Ibid., 5.

74 Ibid., 18, 16.

75 Ibid., 30.

76 Ibid., 14.

77 Ibid., 17.

78 Ibid., 16.

2 Decolonizing Poetry

1 Anne Spry Rush, *Bonds of Empire: West Indians and Britishness from Victoria to Decolonization* (Oxford: Oxford University Press, 2011), 22.

2 See Wendy Webster, *Englishness and Empire, 1939–1965* (Oxford: Oxford University Press, 2005).

3 Louise Bennett, "Colonization in Reverse," in Jahan Ramazani (ed.), *The Norton Anthology of Modern and Contemporary Poetry* (New York: Norton, 2003), II, 173.

4 Rush, *Bonds of Empire*, 170.

5 Ashley Dawson, *Mongrel Nation: Diasporic Culture and the Making of Postcolonial Britain* (Ann Arbor: The University of Michigan Press, 2007), 6.

6 Derek Walcott, *Collected Poems, 1948–1984* (New York: Farrar, Straus and Giroux, 1986), 18.

7 Ibid., 18.

8 Martin Carter, *University of Hunger: Collected Poems and Selected Prose*, ed. Gemma Robinson (Northumberland: Bloodaxe Books, 2006), 100.

9 Ibid., 84.

10 Ibid., 85.

11 Ibid., 124.

12 See Gail Low, *Publishing the Postcolonial: Anglophone West African and Caribbean Writing in the UK, 1948–1968* (London: Routledge, 2010).

13 Bruce King, *The Oxford English Literary History, Volume 13. 1948–2000: The Internationalization of English Literature* (Oxford: Oxford University Press, 2004), 69.

14 See Low, *Publishing the Postcolonial*, 93–120. On the role of the BBC in the West Indies in the period, see Rush, *Bonds of Empire*, 148–207. For a more general study, see Simon Potter, *Broadcasting Empire: The BBC and the British World, 1922–1970* (Oxford: Oxford University Press, 2012).

15 Paul Breslin, *Nobody's Nation: Reading Derek Walcott* (Chicago and London: University of Chicago Press, 2001), 17–18.

16 On Walcott's poetry, see Breslin, *Nobody's Nation: Reading Derek Walcott*; Jahan Ramazani, *The Hybrid Muse: Postcolonial Poetry in English* (Chicago and London: University of Chicago Press, 2001), 49–72; Bruce King, *Derek Walcott: A Caribbean Life* (Oxford: Oxford University Press, 2001); and Rei Terada, *Derek Walcott's Poetry: American Mimicry* (Boston: Northeastern University Press, 1992).

17 Low, *Publishing the Postcolonial*, 112.

18 Walcott, *Collected Poems, 1948–1984*, 97.

19 Quoted in Breslin, *Nobody's Nation: Reading Derek Walcott*, 3.

20 Derek Walcott, *What the Twilight Says* (New York: Farrar, Straus and Giroux, 1998), 39.

21 Walcott, *Collected Poems, 1948–1984*, 46, 44.

22 Ibid., 114, 86.

23 Ibid., 88.

24 Ibid., 364.

25 Ibid., 367.

26 Ibid., 346.

27 William Shakespeare, *Henry V*, III.ii; James Joyce, *Ulysses*, ed. Jeri Johnson (Oxford: Oxford University Press, 2008 [1993]), 317.

28 See Gail Low, "At Home? Discoursing on the Commonwealth at the 1965 Commonwealth Arts Festival," *The Journal of Commonwealth Literature*, 48.1 (2013), 97–111.

29 My account of CAM is heavily indebted to Anne Walmsley's valuable history, *The Caribbean Artists Movement, 1966–1972* (London and Port of Spain: New Beacon Books, 1992).

30 Walmsley, *The Caribbean Artists Movement*, 61.

31 Edward Kamau Brathwaite, *History of the Voice: The Development of Nation Language in Anglophone Caribbean Poetry* (London and Port of Spain: New Beacon Books, 1984), 5–6.

32 Ibid., 7.

33 Ibid., 7.

34 Ibid., 13.

35 Ibid., 13.

36 Ibid., 42n55.

37 Quoted in Walmsley, *The Caribbean Artists Movement*, 260. The talk was titled "The Function of the Writer in the Caribbean."

38 On Brathwaite's work, see Timothy Reiss (ed.), *For the Geography of a Soul: Emerging Perspectives on Kamau Brathwaite* (Trenton, NJ: African World Press, 2001); Gordon Rohlehr, *Pathfinder: Black Awakening in* The Arrivants *of Edward Kamau Brathwaite* (Port of Spain: Gordon Rohlehr, 1981); and Stewart Brown (ed.), *The Art of Kamau Brathwaite* (Bridgend, Wales: Seren Press, 1991).

39 Edward Brathwaite, *The Arrivants: A New World Trilogy* (Oxford: Oxford University Press, 1973), 42, 43.

40 Ibid., 44–45.

41 Brathwaite, *History of the Voice*, 46n59.

42 Brathwaite, *The Arrivants*, 48.

43 Ibid., 49.

44 Ibid., 49.

45 Ibid., 15, 24, 34, 42, 50.

46 Lawrence Breiner, *An Introduction to West Indian Poetry* (Cambridge: Cambridge University Press, 1998), 178.

47 Brathwaite, *The Arrivants*, 150.

48 Simon Gikandi, "E.K. Brathwaite and the Poetics of the Voice: The Allegory of History in 'Rights of Passage,'" *Callaloo*, 14.3 (1991), 727–736, at 728.

49 Brathwaite, *The Arrivants*, 269–270.

50 Jahan Ramazani, *A Transnational Poetics* (Chicago and London: University of Chicago Press, 2009), 101.

51 For a thorough survey of West Indian poetry, see Breiner, *An Introduction to West Indian Poetry*. Also see Charles W. Pollard, *New World Modernisms: T.S. Eliot, Derek Walcott, and Kamau Brathwaite* (Charlottesville: University of Virginia Press, 2004); Silvio Torres-Saillant, *Caribbean Poetics: Toward an Aesthetic of West Indian Literature* (Cambridge: Cambridge University Press, 1997); and Lee Jenkins, *The Language of Caribbean Poetry: Boundaries of Expression* (Gainesville: University Press of Florida, 2004).

52 Gareth Griffiths, *African Literatures in English: East and West* (Harlow: Longman, 2000), 79.

53 On Okigbo's life and work, see Sunday O. Anozie, *Christopher Okigbo: Creative Rhetoric* (London: Evans, 1972); Uzoma Esonwanne (ed.), *Critical Essays on Christopher Okigbo* (New York: G.K. Hall, 2000); Donatus I. Nwoga (ed.), *Critical Perspectives on Christopher Okigbo* (Washington, DC: Three Continents Press, 1984); and Obi Nwakanma, *Christopher Okigbo 1930–1967: Thirsting for Sunlight* (Woodbridge: James Currey, 2010).

54 Christopher Okigbo, *Collected Poems* (London: Heinemann, 1986), xxvi.

55 "Interview with Marjory Whitelaw, 1965," *Journal of Commonwealth Literature*, 9 (July 1970), 28–37. Reprinted in Esonwanne (ed.), *Critical Essays on Christopher Okigbo*, 59.

56 Okigbo, *Collected Poems*, 19, 24, 25, 23.

57 Ibid., 19, 29, 20.

58 Ibid., 62.

59 Ibid., 62.

60 Ibid., 62.

61 Ibid., 89, 92, 93, 98, 94.

62 Ted Hughes, *Collected Poems*, ed. Paul Keegan (New York: Farrar, Straus and Giroux, 2003), 21.

63 Ibid., 22.
64 Ibid., 22.
65 Ibid., 240.
66 Ibid., 244.
67 Ibid., 84, 85.
68 Ibid., 85.
69 Ibid., 85.

3 Local Modernism

1 Jed Esty, *A Shrinking Island: Modernism and National Culture in England* (Princeton, NJ: Princeton University Press, 2004), 5, 2.
2 Ibid., 2.
3 See Robert Hewison, *The Heritage Industry: Britain in Decline* (London: Methuen, 1987).
4 Philip Larkin, *Collected Poems*, ed. Anthony Thwaite (New York: Farrar, Straus and Giroux, 2004), 151, 134.
5 Nigel Alderman, "Introduction: Pocket Epics: British Poetry After Modernism," *Yale Journal of Criticism*, 13.1 (2000), 1–2, at 1.
6 John Kerrigan, "Divided Kingdoms and the Local Epic: *Mercian Hymns* to *The King of Britain's Daughter*," *The Yale Journal of Criticism*, 13.1 (2000), 3–21, at 4.
7 Roy Fisher, *The Long and the Short of It: Poems 1955–2005* (Northumberland: Bloodaxe Books, 2005), 285.
8 John Kerrigan, "Roy Fisher on Location," in John Kerrigan and Peter Robinson (eds.), *The Thing about Roy Fisher: Critical Studies* (Liverpool: Liverpool University Press, 2000), 16–46, at 39.
9 Peter Barry, "'Birmingham's what I think with': Roy Fisher's Composite-Epic," *The Yale Journal of Criticism*, 13.1 (2000), 87–105, at 87.
10 Kerrigan, "Roy Fisher on Location," 20.
11 For the second and final version of *City*, Fisher leaves out Shayer's "Preface," the original subtitles ("Introduction," "The Place – The Day," and "Coda"), three poems ("Toyland," "The Judgment," and the quasi-ballad "Do Not Remain Too Much Alone"), and several mainly biographical or narrative paragraphs. He adds a handful of descriptive prose paragraphs as well as two poems ("The Sun Hacks" and "The Park"). Many of the prose paragraphs added to the final text of *City* first appear in "The Hallucinations: City II," a nine-page typescript supplement to *City* published by Migrant Press in Autumn 1962. The overall effect of the changes is to downplay the realist, biographical aspects of *City* in favor of a mode of place writing organized around a perceiving "I" who "sees with" Birmingham.
12 Fisher, *The Long and the Short of It*, 39–40.
13 Ibid., 39.
14 Ibid., 37–38.

15 Ibid., 36, 38, 39.

16 Ibid., 35.

17 On Bunting's biography, see Richard Burton, *A Strong Song Tows Us: The Life of Basil Bunting* (Oxford: Prospecta Press, 2013). Also see Tom Pickard, "Sketches from 'My Voice Locked In: The Lives of Basil Bunting,'" *Chicago Review*, 44.3-4 (1998), 75–96; Keith Aldritt, *The Poet as Spy: The Life and Wild Times of Basil Bunting* (London: Aurum Press, 1998); and Richard Caddel, *Basil Bunting: A Northern Life* (Newcastle: Newcastle Libraries and Information Service and the Basil Bunting Poetry Centre, 1997).

18 The major studies of Bunting's work are Victoria Forde, *The Poetry of Basil Bunting* (Newcastle upon Tyne: Bloodaxe Books, 1991); and Peter Makin, *Bunting: The Shaping of His Verse* (Oxford: Clarendon Press, 1992). Also see Carroll R. Terrell (ed.), *Basil Bunting: Man and Poet* (Orono, ME: National Poetry Foundation, 1981); and James McGonigal and Richard Price (eds.), *The Star You Steer By: Basil Bunting and British Modernism* (Amsterdam: Editions Rodopi, 2000).

19 T.S. Eliot (ed.), *Literary Essays of Ezra Pound* (New York: New Directions, 1968), 3.

20 See Keith Tuma, "Pound, Eliot, Yeats, Auden, and Basil Bunting in the Thirties," *Sagetrieb: A Journal Devoted to Poets in the Imagist/Objectivist Tradition*, 10.1–2 (Spring-Fall 1991), 99–121; and John Seed, "An English Objectivist? Basil Bunting's Other England," *Chicago Review*, 44.3–4 (1998), 114–126.

21 Eric Mottram, "'An Acknowledged Land': Love and Poetry in Bunting's Sonatas," in Terrell (ed.), *Basil Bunting: Man and Poet*, 77–105, at 96.

22 Bunting's diagram of the structure of *Briggflatts* has been reproduced in many essays and articles. It resembles a profile of a mountain range or a cardiogram and is meant to show the multiple climaxes in each section. For Bunting's own discussion of the diagram, see his 1970 interview with Peter Quartermain and Warren Tallman: "Basil Bunting Talks About *Briggflatts*," *Agenda*, 16.1 (Spring 1978), 8–19.

23 Basil Bunting, *Complete Poems* (New York: New Directions, 2000), 59.

24 Ibid., 59.

25 Ibid., 59.

26 Ibid., 59.

27 Ibid., 62.

28 Ibid., 63.

29 Ibid., 64, 65.

30 Ibid., 66.

31 Ibid., 68.

32 Basil Bunting, "A Note on Briggflatts," *Briggflatts* (Northumberland: Bloodaxe Books, 2009), 40. This note, first published in 1989, was left deliberately unpublished by Bunting during his life and is his sole prose statement on the poem.

33 Bunting, *Complete Poems*, 69, 70.

34 Ibid., 71.

35 Ibid., 71.

36 Ibid., 72.

37 Ibid., 73.
38 Ibid., 73.
39 Ibid., 73.
40 Ibid., 73.
41 Ibid., 74.
42 Ibid., 74.
43 Ibid., 74.
44 Ibid., 75.
45 Ibid., 75.
46 Ibid., 76, 77.
47 Ibid., 77.
48 Ibid., 77.
49 Ibid., 78.
50 Ibid., 78.
51 Ibid., 78.
52 Ibid., 79.
53 Geoffrey Hill, *Broken Hierarchies: Poems 1952–2012*, ed. Kenneth Haynes (Oxford: Oxford University Press, 2013), 83.
54 Ibid., 83.
55 Ibid., 99.
56 Ibid., 83.
57 On *Mercian Hymns*'s entanglements with British politics in its contemporary moment, see William Wootten, "Rhetoric and Violence in Geoffrey Hill's *Mercian Hymns* and the Speeches of Enoch Powell," *Cambridge Quarterly*, 29.1 (2000), 1–15.
58 Hill, *Broken Hierarchies*, 89.
59 Ibid., 89.
60 Ibid., 95.
61 Ibid., 111.
62 Ibid., 96.
63 Ibid., 102.
64 Ibid., 97, 110.
65 Ibid., 111, 112.
66 C.D. Blanton, "Nominal Devolutions: Poetic Substance and the Critique of Political Economy," *Yale Journal of Criticism*, 13.1 (Summer 2000), 129–151, at 133.
67 Bunting, *Complete Poems*, 61.
68 Peter Riley, *The Derbyshire Poems* (Exeter: Shearsman Books, 2010), 9.
69 Ibid., 177, 175.
70 Ibid., 177.
71 Ibid., 177.
72 Ibid., 179.
73 Ibid., 27.

74 Ibid., 63.
75 Ibid., 183.
76 Ibid., 183.
77 Ibid., 15.
78 Ibid., 15.

4 Late Modernism

1 For a brief but crucial account, see Eric Mottram, "The British Poetry Revival, 1960–1975," in Robert Hampson and Peter Barry (eds.), *New British Poetries: The Scope of the Possible* (Manchester: Manchester University Press, 1993), 15–50.

2 Robert Sheppard, *The Poetry of Saying: British Poetry and Its Discontents 1950–2000* (Liverpool: Liverpool University Press, 2005), 35–36.

3 Richard Price, "CAT-Scanning the Little Magazine," in Peter Robinson (ed.), *The Oxford Handbook of Contemporary British and Irish Poetry* (Oxford: Oxford University Press, 2013), 173–190, at 188.

4 On little magazines and small press poetry in postwar Britain, see Wolfgang Görtschacher, *Little Magazine Profiles: The Little Magazines in Great Britain, 1939–1993* (Salzburg: University of Salzburg Press, 1993); David Miller and Richard Price, *British Poetry Magazines, 1914–2000* (London: British Library, 2006); and R.J. Ellis, "Mapping the United Kingdom Little Magazine Field," in Hampson and Barry (eds.), *New British Poetries: The Scope of the Possible*, 72–103.

5 For an account of poetry publishing in the postwar period, see Matthew Sperling, "Books and the Market: Trade Publishers, State Subsidies, and Small Presses," in Robinson (ed.), *The Oxford Handbook of Contemporary British and Irish Poetry*, 191–212.

6 Mottram, "The British Poetry Revival, 1960–1975," 15.

7 For an extended account of events at the Poetry Society, see Peter Barry, *Poetry Wars: British Poetry of the 1970s and the Battle of Earls Court* (Cambridge: Salt Publishing, 2006). Also see Robert Sheppard, *When Bad Times Made for Good Poetry: Episodes in the History of the Poetics of Innovation* (Exeter: Shearsman Books, 2011), 14–30.

8 J.H. Prynne, *Poems* (Fremantle, Western Australia: Fremantle Arts Centre Press and Northumberland: Bloodaxe Books, 2005), n.p.

9 See Keith Tuma, *Fishing by Obstinate Isles: Modern and Postmodern British Poetry and American Readers* (Evanston, IL: Northwestern University Press, 1998).

10 Many of the best essays on Raworth appear in a special issue of *The Gig*, which also includes a detailed bibliography by Nate Dorward. See *Removed for Further Study: The Poetry of Tom Raworth*, *The Gig*, 13–14 (May 2003).

11 Tom Raworth, *Collected Poems* (Manchester: Carcanet, 2003), 212–213.

12 Brian Reed, "Carry on, England: Tom Raworth's 'West Wind,' Intuition, and Neo-Avant-Garde Poetics," *Contemporary Literature*, 47.2 (Summer 2006), 170–206, at 177.

13 Raworth, *Collected Poems*, 254.

14 For two versions of this argument, see John Barrell, "Subject and Sentence: The Poetry of Tom Raworth," *Critical Inquiry*, 17.2 (1991), 386–410; and Sheppard, *The Poetry of Saying*, 171–193.

15 Charles Olson, "Projective Verse," in Donald M. Allen (ed.), *The New American Poetry* (New York: Grove Press, 1960), 386–400, at 387.

16 Ibid., 387.

17 Raworth, *Collected Poems*, 201–202.

18 T.S. Eliot, *Collected Poems 1909–1962* (New York: Harcourt Brace, 1991 [1963]), 53.

19 For an argument about the importance of recognizing such variety, see Drew Milne, "Neo-Modernism and Avant-Garde Orientations," in Nigel Alderman and C.D. Blanton (eds.), *A Concise Companion to Postwar British and Irish Poetry* (Chichester, West Sussex: Wiley-Blackwell, 2009), 155–175.

20 John Wilkinson, *The Lyric Touch: Essays on the Poetry of Excess* (Cambridge: Salt Publishing, 2007), 115.

21 And there are of course a number of poets in the Cambridge orbit on whom I do not have space to dwell, notably Douglas Oliver and John Riley.

22 Wilkinson, *The Lyric Touch*, 120–121.

23 Ibid., 121.

24 See Crozier's note on the project's history that is included in *The English Intelligencer* archive held at New York University (Fales Library. NYU. The English Intelligencer Archive. MSS 012. Series A. Folder 1. Box 1.).

25 One high point in the journal occurred with the transition from Crozier's editorship to Riley's, when Riley's "Working Notes on British Prehistory: or, Archaeological Guesswork One," formed a bridge between the last bundle of pages assembled by Crozier and the beginning of Series 2, which appeared in March 1967 and featured several responses to Riley's "Working Notes," including several from Prynne, culminating in his "A Note on Metal."

26 Crozier published fourteen small-press volumes and chapbooks during his lifetime, as well as a collected volume, *All Where Each Is* (East Sussex: Allardyce, Barnett, 1985).

27 Edward Larrissy, "Poets of *A Various Art*: J.H. Prynne, Veronica Forrest-Thomson, Andrew Crozier," in James Acheson and Romana Huk (eds.), *Contemporary British Poetry: Essays in Theory and Criticism* (Albany: SUNY Press, 1996), 63–79, at 75.

28 Ian Brinton (ed.), *An Andrew Crozier Reader* (Manchester: Carcanet, 2012), 154.

29 See ibid., 96.

30 Ibid., 97.

31 Ibid., 98.

32 Ibid., 98.

33 Ibid., 99, 102.

34 Ibid., 99.

35 Veronica Forrest-Thomson, *Poetic Artifice: A Theory of Twentieth-Century Poetry* (Manchester: Manchester University Press, 1978), 2.

36 Ibid., xi.

37 Ibid., 6.

38 Ibid., 89, 74.

39 Ibid., xiv.

40 Veronica Forrest-Thomson, *Collected Poems*, ed. Anthony Barnett (Exeter: Shearsman Books and East Sussex: Allardyce Book, 2008), 123. All subsequent quotations are taken from this page.

41 Ibid., 180.

42 Forrest-Thomson, *Poetic Artifice*, 50.

43 For a detailed bibliography of all of Prynne's work and secondary criticism on it, see *The Bibliography of J.H. Prynne* (prynnebibliography.wordpress.com). See especially Simon Jarvis, "Quality and the Non-identical in J.H. Prynne's 'Aristeas, in Seven Years,'" *Parataxis*, 1 (1991), 69–86; N.H. Reeve and Richard Kerridge, *Nearly Too Much: The Poetry of J.H. Prynne* (Liverpool: Liverpool University Press, 1995); D.S. Marriott, "Contemporary British Poetry and Resistance: Reading J.H. Prynne," *Parataxis*, 8-9 (1996), 159–74; Drew Milne, "Speculative Assertions: Reading J.H. Prynne's *Poems*," *Parataxis*, 10 (2001), 67–86; Charles Altieri, "An Aspect of Prynne's Poetics: Autonomy as a Lyric Ideal," *The Gig*, 10 (2001), 38–51; Kevin Nolan, "Capital Calves: Undertaking an Overview," *Jacket*, 24 (November 2003), http://jacketmagazine.com/24/nolan.html; Anthony Mellors, *Late Modernist Poetics: From Pound to Prynne* (Manchester: Manchester University Press, 2005); Peter Middleton, *Performance, Readership, and Consumption in Contemporary Poetry* (Tuscaloosa: University of Alabama Press, 2005); John Wilkinson, *The Lyric Touch*; Keston Sutherland, "XL Prynne," in Ian Brinton (ed.), *A Manner of Utterance: The Poetry of J.H. Prynne* (Exeter: Shearsman Books, 2009), 104–132; and Christopher Nealon, "The Prynne Reflex," *The Claudius App IV*, http://theclaudiusapp.com/4-nealon.html.

44 J.H. Prynne, *Poems* (Northumberland: Bloodaxe Books, 2015), 13.

45 Ibid., 128.

46 Ibid., 15.

47 Ibid., 15.

48 See Wilkinson, *The Lyric Touch*, 121–122.

49 Ibid., 122.

50 Prynne, *Poems*, 51.

51 Ibid., 65.

52 Ibid., 66.

53 Ibid., 66.

54 Reeve and Kerridge, *Nearly Too Much: The Poetry of J.H. Prynne*, 133.

55 Prynne, *Poems*, 172.

56 See Ryan Dobran (ed.), *Glossator: Practice and Theory of the Commentary*, 2: On the Poems of J.H. Prynne (2010). For Prynne's own commentaries, see *They That*

Haue Powre to Hurt; A Specimen of a Commentary on Shake-speares Sonnets, 94 (Cambridge: privately printed, 2001); *Field Notes: "The Solitary Reaper" and Others* (Cambridge: Barque Press, 2007); and *George Herbert, "Love [III]": A Discursive Commentary* (Cambridge: Barque Press, 2011).

57 J.H. Prynne, "Mental Ears and Poetic Work," *Chicago Review*, 55.1 (Winter 2010), 126–157, at 141.

58 See J.H. Prynne, "Poetic Thought," *Textual Practice*, 24.4 (2010), 595–606.

59 Prynne, *Poems*, 225.

60 Prynne, "Mental Ears and Poetic Work," 132.

61 John James, *Berlin Return* (London and Liverpool: Grosseteste Press, 1983), 27.

62 Ibid., 55.

63 John James, *A Theory of Poetry* (Cambridge: Street Editions, 1977), n.p.

64 James, *Berlin Return*, 23.

65 Barry MacSweeney, *Wolf Tongue: Selected Poems 1965–2000* (Northumberland: Bloodaxe Books, 2003), 111.

66 For an extended reading of MacSweeney's work, see Clive Bush, *Out of Dissent: A Study of Five Contemporary British Poets* (London: Talus Editions, 1997), 304–416.

67 MacSweeney, *Wolf Tongue*, 75.

68 Ibid., 118.

69 Barry MacSweeney, *Odes: 1971–1978* (London: Trigram Press, 1978), 49.

70 Barry MacSweeney, *Hellhound Memos* (London: The Many Press, 1993), 11.

71 MacSweeney, *Wolf Tongue*, 103.

72 Bill Griffiths, *Cycles* (London: Pirates Press and Writers Forum, 1976), n.p. Also see *Future Exiles, 3 London Poets: Allen Fisher, Bill Griffiths, Brian Catling* (London: HarperCollins, 1992), 215.

73 For a description of Griffiths's dazzling books and pamphlets, see Alan Halsey, "Pirate Press: A Bibliographical Excursion," in William Rowe (ed.), *The Salt Companion to Bill Griffiths* (Cambridge: Salt Publishing, 2007), 55–71.

74 For an account of Cobbing's work in its multiple aesthetic contexts, see Sheppard, *When Bad Times Made for Good Poetry*, 214–232.

75 Quoted in Tuma, *Fishing by Obstinate Isles*, 212.

76 Bob Cobbing, *Ballet of the Speech Organs: Bob Cobbing on Bob Cobbing*, as interviewed by Steven Ross Smith (Saskatoon and Toronto: Underwhich Editions, 1998), 2.

77 Ibid., 14.

78 Bob Cobbing, *Sensations of the Retina* ([London]: grOnk IS 15, 1978), n.p. Available online at http://ubumexico.centro.org.mx/text/vp/cobbing_sensation_of_the_retina_1978.pdf.

79 Edwin Morgan, *Selected Poems* (Manchester: Carcanet Press, 2000), 66.

80 Ibid., 23–24.

81 Tom Leonard, *Outside the Narrative: Poems 1965–2009* (West Devonshire: Etruscan Books and Edinburgh: Word Power Books, 2009), 19.

82 Edwin Morgan, "Early Finlay," in Alec Finlay (ed.), *Wood Notes Wild: Essays on the Poetry and Art of Ian Hamilton Finlay* (Edinburgh: Polygon, 1995), 16–24, at 20.

83 On Finlay's work, see Yves Abrioux and Stephen Bann, *Ian Hamilton Finlay: A Visual Primer* (Cambridge: The MIT Press, 1992); Finlay (ed.), *Wood Notes Wild*; Stephen Scobie, *Earthquakes and Explorations: Language and Painting from Cubism to Concrete Poetry* (Toronto: University of Toronto Press, 1997), 169–194; and Nicholas Zurbrugg, "Ian Hamilton Finlay and Concrete Poetry," in Acheson and Huk (eds.), *Contemporary British Poetry*, 113–141.

84 Ian Hamilton Finlay, *A Model of Order: Selected Letters on Poetry and Making*, ed. Thomas A. Clark (Glasgow: WAX366, 2009), 21–23.

85 See Stephen Bann's pioneering 1977 essay, "Ian Hamilton Finlay: An Imaginary Portrait," reprinted in Finlay (ed.), *Wood Notes Wild*, 54–81.

86 Ian Hamilton Finlay, *Poems to Hear and See* (New York: Macmillan and London: Collier-Macmillan, 1971), n.p.

87 Robert Hampson, "Producing the Unknown: Language and Ideology in Contemporary Poetry," in Hampson and Barry (eds.), *New British Poetries*, 134–155, at 138.

88 Allen Fisher, "The Poetics of the Complexity Manifold," *boundary 2*, 26.1 (Spring 1999), 115–118, at 115.

89 Allen Fisher, *Place* (East Sussex: Reality Street Editions, 2005), 9.

90 Ibid., 14.

91 Ibid., 33.

92 Ibid., 173, 159.

93 Ibid., 129.

94 Ibid., 157.

95 Ibid., 93–94.

96 Ibid., 300.

97 Ibid., 385.

98 Ibid., 83.

99 Ibid., 404.

100 Wilkinson, *The Lyric Touch*, 177.

5 The North

1 The crucial books on postwar Northern Irish poetry are Clair Wills, *Improprieties: Politics and Sexuality in Northern Irish Poetry* (Oxford: Clarendon Press, 1993); Edna Longley, *Poetry in the Wars* (Newcastle upon Tyne: Bloodaxe Books, 1986) and *The Living Stream: Literature and Revisionism in Ireland* (Newcastle upon Tyne: Bloodaxe Books, 1994); Peter McDonald, *Mistaken Identities: Poetry and Northern Ireland* (Oxford: Clarendon Press, 1997); Heather Clark, *The Ulster Renaissance: Poetry in Belfast, 1962–1972* (Oxford: Oxford University Press, 2006); and Shane Alcobia-Murphy, *Sympathetic Ink: Intertextual Relations in Northern Irish Poetry* (Liverpool: Liverpool University Press, 2006). Also see Neil Corcoran (ed.), *The Chosen Ground: Essays on the Contemporary Poetry of Northern Ireland* (Bridgend, Wales: Seren, 1992).

2 See Ann Bridgwood and John Hampson (eds.), *Rhyme and Reason: Developing Contemporary Poetry* (London: Arts Council of England, 2000), 23.

3 This is only the barest sketch of the context of the Troubles. For more detailed accounts, see David McKittrick and David McVea, *Making Sense of the Troubles: A History of the Northern Ireland Conflict* (London: Viking, 2012); Sabine Wichert, *Northern Ireland Since 1945* (London: Longman, 1991); Thomas Hennessey, *A History of Northern Ireland, 1920–1996* (New York: St. Martin's Press, 1997); and Jonathan Tonge, *Northern Ireland* (Cambridge: Polity, 2006).

4 Terence Brown, "A Northern Renaissance: Poets from the North of Ireland, 1965–1980," in *Ireland's Literature: Selected Essays* (Mullingar, Ireland: Lilliput Press, 1988), 203–221, at 215.

5 Derek Mahon, *Collected Poems* (Loughcrew, Ireland: Gallery Press, 2001), 59.

6 Fran Brearton has produced the most substantial readings of Longley's work. See *The Great War in Modern Poetry: W.B. Yeats to Michael Longley* (Oxford: Oxford University Press, 2000) and *Reading Michael Longley* (Northumberland: Bloodaxe Books, 2006).

7 Michael Longley, *Collected Poems* (London: Jonathan Cape, 2006), 62. All references to this poem come from this page.

8 Ibid., 54.

9 Christopher Ricks, *The Force of Poetry* (Oxford: Oxford University Press, 1984), esp. 34–59. For a mobilization of Ricks's formulation within an argument about Heaney's Romanticism, see Guinn Batten, "Heaney's Wordsworth and the Poetics of Displacement," in Bernard O'Donoghue (ed.), *The Cambridge Companion to Seamus Heaney* (Cambridge: Cambridge University Press, 2009), 178–191.

10 Seamus Heaney, *Poems, 1965–1975* (New York: Farrar, Straus and Giroux [Noonday Press], 1988), 40.

11 Ibid., 103.

12 Ibid., 103, 183.

13 Ibid., 220.

14 Ibid., 3, 51.

15 Seamus Heaney, *Preoccupations: Selected Prose, 1968–1978* (New York: Farrar, Straus and Giroux [Noonday Press], 1988), 41.

16 Ibid., 56.

17 The secondary bibliography on Heaney is voluminous, with a first wave of introductory studies and critical guides beginning to appear in the early 1980s and a second wave of more specialized monographs in the 2000s. Of the first sort, see Bernard O'Donoghue, *Seamus Heaney and the Language of Poetry* (New York: Harvester Wheatsheaf, 1994); Neil Corcoran, *The Poetry of Seamus Heaney: A Critical Study* (London: Faber and Faber, 1998); and Helen Vendler, *Seamus Heaney* (Cambridge, MA: Harvard University Press, 1998). Of the second sort, see Meg Tyler, *A Singing Contest: Conventions of Sound in the Poetry of Seamus Heaney* (London: Routledge, 2005); and Richard Rankin Russell, *Poetry and Peace: Michael Longley, Seamus*

Heaney, and Northern Ireland (Notre Dame, IN: University of Notre Dame Press, 2010), as well as his *Seamus Heaney's Regions* (Notre Dame, IN: University of Notre Dame Press, 2014). Many of the key reviews and essays are included in Tony Curtis (ed.), *The Art of Seamus Heaney* (Bridgend, Wales: Seren, 2001); and Michael Allen (ed.), *Seamus Heaney* (New York: St. Martin's Press, 1997).

18 Richard Finneran (ed.), *The Collected Poems of W.B. Yeats*, rev. 2nd ed. (New York: Scribner, 1996), 202.

19 Some of the most famous critical pieces on Heaney are about *North*. For a range of responses, from the most enthusiastic to the most skeptical, see essays by Cruise O'Brien, Longley, Deane, Lloyd, and Coughlan in Allen (ed.), *Seamus Heaney*.

20 One can extend this suite by considering "Come to the Bower," which precedes "Bog Queen," as a prefatory poem, and "Kinship" as a kind of epilogue.

21 Heaney, *Poems, 1965–1975*, 189.

22 Ibid., 191.

23 Ibid., 191.

24 Ibid., 191.

25 Ibid., 193. All subsequent references to this poem are taken from this page.

26 Seamus Heaney, *Opened Ground: Selected Poems 1966–1996* (New York: Farrar, Straus and Giroux, 1999), 114. All subsequent references to this poem are taken from this page.

27 Heaney, *Poems, 1965–1975*, 126.

28 Mahon, *Collected Poems*, 64–65.

29 Ibid., 65.

30 Ibid., 59.

31 Ibid., 89–90. All subsequent references to this poem come from these pages.

32 For an extended account, see my *Continuity and Change in Irish Poetry, 1966–2010* (Cambridge: Cambridge University Press, 2012).

33 Tom Paulin, *Selected Poems, 1972–1990* (London: Faber and Faber), 43.

34 Ibid., 43.

35 Ibid., 43.

36 Ibid., 53.

37 Ibid., 11.

38 Ciaran Carson, *The Irish for No* (Winston-Salem, NC: Wake Forest University Press, 1987), 31.

39 Ibid., 31.

40 Ciaran Carson, *Belfast Confetti* (Winston-Salem, NC: Wake Forest University Press, 1992), 105.

41 Ibid., 108.

42 Ibid., 106.

43 Ibid., 108.

44 Ibid., 108.

45 On McGuckian's poetry, in addition to sources listed earlier, see Shane Alcobia-Murphy and Richard Kirkland (eds.), *Medbh McGuckian: The Interior of*

Words (Cork: Cork University Press, 2010); and Leontia Flynn, *Reading Medbh McGuckian* (Dublin: Irish Academic Press, 2014).

46 Medbh McGuckian, *Venus and the Rain* (Loughcrew, Ireland: Gallery Press, 1994 [1984]), 32.

47 Ibid., 32.

48 Medbh McGuckian, *On Ballycastle Beach* (Winston-Salem, NC: Wake Forest University Press, 1988), 59.

49 See Wills, *Improprieties: Politics and Sexuality in Northern Irish Poetry*, 158–193.

50 In addition to sources listed earlier, see Clair Wills, *Reading Paul Muldoon* (Newcastle upon Tyne: Bloodaxe Books, 1998); Tim Kendall, *Paul Muldoon* (Chester Springs, PA: Dufour Editions, 1996); Tim Kendall (ed.), *Paul Muldoon: Critical Essays* (Liverpool: Liverpool University Press, 2004); and Elmer Kennedy-Andrews (ed.), *Paul Muldoon: Poetry, Prose, Drama* (Gerrards Cross: Colin Smythe, 2006).

51 Paul Muldoon, *Poems 1968–1998* (New York: Farrar, Straus and Giroux, 2001), 84.

52 Ibid., 161.

53 Ibid., 81.

54 Ibid., 127.

55 Ibid., 146–147.

6 New Narratives

1 Blake Morrison and Andrew Motion (eds.), *The Penguin Book of Contemporary British Poetry* (Harmondsworth, Middlesex: Penguin, 1982), 11.

2 Ibid., 11.

3 Ibid., 12.

4 Ibid., 17, 16–17.

5 Ibid., 17.

6 Seamus Heaney, "An Open Letter," *Ireland's Field Day* (Notre Dame, IN: Notre Dame University Press, 1986 [1983]), 25.

7 Morrison and Motion (eds.), *The Penguin Book of Contemporary British Poetry*, 11.

8 For an early articulation of this notion, see John Kerrigan, "The New Narrative," *London Review of Books*, 6.3 (February 16, 1984), 22–23.

9 Morrison and Motion (eds.), *The Penguin Book of Contemporary British Poetry*, 19, 20.

10 Craig Raine, *A Martian Sends a Postcard Home* (Oxford: Oxford University Press, 1979), 1.

11 See Tom Nairn, *The Break-Up of Britain: Crisis and Neo-Nationalism* (London: New Left Books, 1977).

12 Kenneth Jackson, *Britain since 1945: The People's Peace* (Oxford: Oxford University Press, 2001), 437.

13 Paul Gilroy, *"There Ain't No Black in the Union Jack": The Cultural Politics of Race and Nation* (London: Hutchinson, 1987), 117.

14 For a reading of LKJ within the context of British politics in the 1970s and 1980s, see Ashley Dawson, *Mongrel Nation: Diasporic Culture and the Making of Modern Britain* (Ann Arbor: The University of Michigan Press, 2007), 73–94.

15 Linton Kwesi Johnson, *Mi Revalueshanary Fren: Selected Poems* (Keene, NY: Ausable Press, 2006), 15.

16 As in a number of Johnson's poems, the final stanza repeats the first, although in several recordings of the poem, Johnson changes "hurting" to "haunting," a significant alteration that makes black history into an ambiguously active presence.

17 Johnson, *Mi Revalueshanary Fren*, 5.

18 Fred D'Aguiar, "Have You Been Here Long? Black Poetry in Britain," in Robert Hampson and Peter Barry (eds.), *New British Poetries: The Scope of the Possible* (Manchester: Manchester University Press, 1993), 51–71, at 57.

19 Johnson, *Mi Revalueshanary Fren*, 54.

20 Ibid., 53, 56.

21 Linton Kwesi Johnson, "Jamaican Rebel Music," *Race and Class*, 17.4 (1976), 397–412, at 398.

22 See Édouard Glissant, *Caribbean Discourse: Selected Essays* (Charlottesville: University of Virginia Press, 1992).

23 Ian Baucom, *Out of Place: Englishness, Empire, and the Locations of Identity* (Princeton, NJ: Princeton University Press, 1999), 8.

24 Grace Nichols, *I Is a Long Memoried Woman* (London: Karnac House, 1983), 5, 12.

25 Ibid., 16, 31.

26 Ibid., 87.

27 See Jahan Ramazani, *The Hybrid Muse: Postcolonial Poetry in English* (Chicago and London: University of Chicago Press, 2001), 49–71.

28 David Dabydeen, *Turner: New and Selected Poems* (Leeds: Peepal Tree, 1995), 7.

29 Ibid., 7.

30 Ibid., 9, 10, 13, 21, 26, 27.

31 Ibid., 41

32 Ibid., 24, 42.

33 Jackie Kay, *The Adoption Papers* (Newcastle upon Tyne: Bloodaxe Books, 1991), 17, 16, 21.

34 Ibid., 14

35 This episode, which is told in "Chapter 3: The Waiting Lists," includes a subtle critique of British politics in the 1960s. Ahead of the social worker's visit, the adoptive mother hides all signs of the couple's communist sympathies – books by Marx and Engels, a poster of Paul Robeson, copies of *The Daily Worker* – but leaves "a bust of Burns / my detective stories / and the Complete Works of Shelley" in view (15). This suggests that while symbols of left politics need to be hidden in order to conform to what counts as "ordinary" (15) and therefore acceptable in 1960s

Britain, earlier avatars of radicalism – Burns and Shelley – can remain because their Britishness will signify much more intensely than their politics.

36 Ibid., 29.

37 Ibid., 33.

38 Ibid., 34.

39 Harrison generally works in a 16-line sonnet form, adapted from George Meredith's *Modern Love* sequence.

40 On Harrison's work, see Neil Astley and Rosemary Burton (eds.), *Tony Harrison* (Newcastle upon Tyne: Bloodaxe Books, 1991); and Sandie Byrne (ed.), *Tony Harrison: Loiner* (Oxford: Clarendon Press, 1997).

41 Tony Harrison, *Selected Poems* (London: Penguin, 2006), 236.

42 Ibid., 238.

43 Ibid., 240.

44 Ibid., 238.

45 Ibid., 249.

46 Ibid., 249.

47 Ibid., 245.

48 David Kennedy, " 'Past Never Found': Class, Dissent and the Contexts of Tony Harrison's *v.*," *English*, 58.221 (2009), 162–181, at 169.

49 Jane Dowson and Alice Entwistle, *A History of Twentieth-Century Women's Poetry* (Cambridge: Cambridge University Press, 2005), 101.

50 On British women's experimental poetry, see Linda Kinnahan, *Lyric Interventions: Feminism, Experimental Poetry, and Contemporary Discourse* (Iowa City: University of Iowa Press, 2004); and David Kennedy and Christine Kennedy, *Women's Experimental Poetry in Britain 1970–2010: Body, Time and Locale* (Liverpool: Liverpool University Press, 2013).

51 Wendy Mulford, "Valentine," in Gillian Allnutt, Fred D'Aguiar, Ken Edwards, and Eric Mottram (eds.), *The New British Poetry: 1968–1988* (London: Paladin, 1988), 207.

52 Denise Riley, *Dry Air* (London: Virago Press, 1985), 10.

53 Ibid., 7. All further references to this poem come from this page.

54 Denise Riley, *"Am I That Name?": Feminism and the Category of "Women" in History* (Minneapolis: University of Minnesota Press, 1988), 17.

55 Denise Riley, *Mop Mop Georgette* (Cambridge: Reality Street, 1993), 23.

56 Riley, *Dry Air*, 27.

57 Riley, *Mop Mop Georgette*, 36.

58 Ibid., 44.

59 Ibid., 60.

60 For an extended treatment of this theme, see Robert Crawford, *Identifying Poets: Self and Territory in Twentieth-Century Poetry* (Edinburgh: Edinburgh University Press, 1993).

61 *A Furnace* is one of the most significant British poems of the last thirty years. Only the constraints of space and my aim to discuss as many poets substantively as possible prevent a consideration of it here.

62 Tom Paulin, *Minotaur: Poetry and the Nation State* (London: Faber and Faber, 1992), 287.

63 Douglas Dunn, *St. Kilda's Parliament* (London: Faber and Faber, 1981), 20.

64 Ibid., 27.

65 Edwin Morgan, *Selected Poems* (Manchester: Carcanet, 2000), 82.

66 Ibid., 150.

67 Derek Mahon, *Collected Poems* (Loughcrew, Ireland: Gallery Press, 2001), 59.

68 Fred D'Aguiar, *British Subjects* (Newcastle upon Tyne: Bloodaxe Books, 1993), 14.

69 Grace Nichols, *Lazy Thoughts of a Lazy Woman* (London: Virago, 1989), 10.

70 Carol Rumens, "Coming Home," in Morrison and Motion (eds.), *The Penguin Book of Contemporary British Poetry*, 160.

71 Anne Stevenson, *Collected Poems 1955–1995* (Newcastle upon Tyne: Bloodaxe Books, 2000), 72.

72 Gillian Clarke, *Collected Poems* (Manchester: Carcanet, 1997), 121.

73 Jo Shapcott, *Phrase Book* (Oxford: Oxford University Press, 1992), 26.

74 Ibid., 27.

7 Platforms and Performances

1 For an account of how plans evolved, see *Poetry Review*, 84.1 (Spring 1994), 52–53.

2 Iain Sinclair, "Infamous and Invisible: A Manifesto for Those Who Do Not Believe in Such Things," in Iain Sinclair (ed.), *Conductors of Chaos: A Poetry Anthology* (London: Picador, 1996), xiii–xx, at xvi.

3 Peter Forbes, "Talking about the New Generation," *Poetry Review*, 84.1 (Spring 1994), 4–6, at 4.

4 Here are the poets as announced by David Lister in *The Independent*: "Moniza Alvi; Simon Armitage; John Burnside, 39, knowledge engineer, who was born in Dunfermline; Robert Crawford, 34, a lecturer from St Andrews; David Dabydeen, 37, a lecturer at Warwick University; Michael Donaghy, 38, a folk musician and teacher; Carol Ann Duffy, 38, a writer and poet; Ian Duhig, 39, from Leeds works in a drug rehabilitation centre; Elizabeth Garrett, 35, works in the Bodleian Library at Oxford; Lavinia Greenlaw, 31, works for the London Arts Board; W N Herbert, 32, from Dundee, a writer-in-residence; Michael Hoffmann, 36, a writer and translator; Mick Imlah, 37, who has been a model for a clothing firm; Kathleen Jamie, 31, a writer-in-residence in the Orkneys; Sarah Maguire, 36, a writer-in-residence at a men's prison; Glyn Maxwell, 31, a publisher's editor; Jamie McKendrick, 38, a part-time teacher; Don Paterson; Pauline Stainer, 52, who has worked in a mental hospital, pub and library; Susan Wicks, 46, a teacher" (*The Independent*, January 13, 1994, 19).

5 Stan Smith, "The Things that Words Give a Name To: The 'New Generation' Poets and the Politics of the Hyperreal," *Critical Survey*, 8.3 (1996), 306–322, at 312.

6 Simon Armitage, *The Dead Sea Poems* (London: Faber and Faber, 1995), 1.

7 Ibid., 2. All further references to this poem come from this page.

8 Ibid., 36.

9 Ibid., 37.

10 Ibid., 50.

11 Ibid., 57.

12 Ibid., 36.

13 Carol Ann Duffy, *Selected Poems* (London: Penguin Books, 1994), 25.

14 Ibid., 26.

15 However, for an argument about the linguistically innovative aspects of Duffy's poetry, see Stan Smith, "'What Like Is It?': Duffy's *différance*," in Angelica Michelis and Antony Rowland (eds.), *The Poetry of Carol Ann Duffy: "Choosing Tough Words"* (Manchester: Manchester University Press, 2003), 143–168.

16 Duffy, *Selected Poems*, 60.

17 Ibid., 60, 61.

18 W.N. Herbert, *Cabaret McGonagall* (Newcastle upon Tyne: Bloodaxe Books, 1996), 87.

19 Christopher Whyte, *Modern Scottish Poetry* (Edinburgh: Edinburgh University Press, 2004), 210.

20 Robert Crawford, *Selected Poems* (London: Jonathan Cape, 2005), 9.

21 Ibid., 9.

22 Ibid., 16, 17.

23 See Duncan Glen (ed.), *Selected Essays of Hugh MacDiarmid* (London: Jonathan Cape, 1969), 58.

24 Kathleen Jamie, *The Queen of Sheba* (Newcastle upon Tyne: Bloodaxe Books, 1994), 9.

25 Ibid., 9, 10.

26 Ibid., 11.

27 Kathleen Jamie, *The Tree House* (London: Picador, 2004), 7.

28 Ibid., 25.

29 On contemporary Welsh poetry in English, see Daniel G. Williams (ed.), *Slanderous Tongues: Essays on Welsh Poetry in English 1970–2005* (Bridgend, Wales: Seren, 2010); Ian Gregson, *The New Poetry in Wales* (Cardiff: University of Wales Press, 2007); and Alice Entwistle, *Poetry, Geography, Gender: Women Rewriting Contemporary Wales* (Cardiff: University of Wales Press, 2013).

30 See Harriet Tarlo (ed.), *The Ground Aslant: An Anthology of Radical Landscape Poetry* (Exeter: Shearsman Books, 2011).

31 Peter Middleton, "'Ear Loads': Neologisms and Sound Poetry in Maggie O'Sullivan's *Palace of Reptiles*," *Journal of British and Irish Innovative Poetry*, 2.1 (2010), 1–20, at 2.

32 Maggie O'Sullivan, *Palace of Reptiles* (Willowdale, Ontario: The Gig, 2003), 11.

33 Maggie O'Sullivan, *In the House of the Shaman* (London and Cambridge: Reality Street, 1993), 56.

34 O'Sullivan, *Palace of Reptiles*, 64.

35 O'Sullivan, *In the House of the Shaman*, 9.

36 Ibid., 9.

37 Ibid., 10.

38 Ibid., 14.

39 Ibid., 21.

40 Ibid., 23.

41 O'Sullivan, *Palace of Reptiles*, 16.

42 Ibid., 19.

43 Nicky Marsh, Peter Middleton, and Victoria Sheppard, "'Blasts of Language': Changes in Oral Poetics in Britain since 1965," *Oral Tradition*, 21.1 (2006), 44–67, at 65.

44 See Peter Middleton, *Distant Reading: Performance, Readership, and Consumption in Contemporary Poetry* (Tuscaloosa: University of Alabama Press, 2005).

45 Ken Edwards, "Provisionally," in Richard Caddel and Peter Quartermain (eds.), *Other: British and Irish Poetry Since 1970* (Hanover, NH and London: Wesleyan University Press, 1999), 57.

46 cris cheek, *Part: Short Life Housing* (Toronto: The Gig, 2009), ix.

47 Ibid., 145.

48 Alan Halsey, *Not Everything Remotely: Selected Poems 1978–2005* (Cambridge: Salt Publishing, 2006), 156.

49 Geraldine Monk, *Selected Poems* (Cambridge: Salt Publishing, 2003), 101.

50 For a detailed description of the differences between the two editions, see Christine Kennedy and David Kennedy, *Women's Experimental Poetry in Britain 1970–2010: Body, Time and Locale* (Liverpool: Liverpool University Press, 2013), 74–75.

51 Monk, *Selected Poems*, 112.

52 Ibid., 111.

53 Ibid., 114, 116.

54 Ibid., 112, 113, 114, 117, 121.

55 Christine Kennedy and David Kennedy, "Poetry, Difficulty, and Geraldine Monk's *Interregnum*," in Scott Thurston (ed.), *The Salt Companion to Geraldine Monk* (Cambridge: Salt Publishing, 2007), 11–25, at 23.

56 This section is untitled in the 2003 Salt *Selected Poems* edition but was titled "Interregnum" in the original edition, which was published in 1994 by Creation Books.

57 Monk, *Selected Poems*, 104.

58 Ibid., 124.

59 Ibid., 137.

60 Ibid., 134.

61 Ibid., 140.

62 Ibid., 163.

63 Ibid., 163.

64 In my count here, I include *Ludo*, a section of poems that appears just before *The Daybooks* in *Broken Hierarchies: Poems 1952–2012*. It is described as the "Epigraphs and Colophons to *The Daybooks*" and constitutes a full sequence in its own right.

65 Geoffrey Hill, *Broken Hierarchies: Poems 1952–2012*, ed. Kenneth Haynes (Oxford: Oxford University Press, 2013), 417.

66 Ibid., 430.

67 Ibid., 171.

68 Ibid., 250.

69 Ibid., 369.

70 Apart from the discrete lyrics that make up *Canaan* (1996), *Without Title* (2006), and *A Treatise of Civil Power* (2007), all of the post-1980s poetry in Hill's 2013 collected volume appears in numbered series. Of the thirteen sequences, eleven are composed of uniform shapes: *Hymns to Our Lady of Chartres* (1982–2012), of twenty-one poems, each of five quatrains; *Speech! Speech!* (2000), of 120 twelve-line stanzas; *The Orchards of Syon* (2002), of 68 twenty-four-line stanzas; the three parts of *Scenes from Comus* (2005), of 20 ten-line stanzas, 80 stanzas of either seven or nine lines, and 20 twelve-line stanzas, respectively; and *Pindarics* (2005–2012), of thirty-four poems of twenty-three lines each. Each of the first five of the six parts of *The Daybooks* (2007–2012) features a single form: *Expostulations on the Volcano* contains fifty-four poems, each of five rhyming quatrains; *Liber Illustrium Virorium* has 54 rhyming stanzas, each of twenty-one lines; *Oraclau/Oracles* consists of 144 nine-line stanzas that each rhyme abbacccddd; *Clavics* of 42 thirty-line poems that adapt George Herbert's pattern poetry; and *Odi Barbare* of fifty-two poems, each of six quatrains, that adopt a stanza form from Sidney's *Old Arcadia*. The final section, *Al Tempo de' Tremuoti*, is made up of ninety-five poems that range from two to ten quatrains. The remaining sequences are nonisomorphic: *The Triumph of Love* (1998) consists of 150 variable-length stanzas, and *Ludo* (2011) of sixty-four poems in a variety of complex verse patterns.

71 Hill, *Broken Hierarchies*, 895.

72 Geoffrey Hill, *Collected Critical Writings*, ed. Kenneth Haynes (Oxford: Oxford University Press, 2008), 155.

73 Hill, *Broken Hierarchies*, 500.

74 Ibid., 501.

75 Seamus Heaney, *Seeing Things* (New York: Farrar, Straus and Giroux, 1991), 52.

76 Hill, *Broken Hierarchies*, 286 [italics original].

77 Seamus Heaney, *Human Chain* (New York: Farrar, Straus and Giroux, 2010), 44.

Conclusion: Archipelagic Experiments

1 For a trenchant analysis of the extraordinary rate of production of poetry volumes in the contemporary Northern American context, see Craig Dworkin, "Seja Marginal," in *The Consequences of Innovation: 21st Century Poetics*, ed. Craig Dworkin (New York: Roof Books, 2008), 7–24.

2 See Don Paterson, "Introduction," in Don Paterson and Charles Simic (eds.), *New British Poetry* (Saint Paul, MN: Graywolf Press, 2004), xxiii–xxxv.

3 Sarah Broom, *Contemporary British and Irish Poetry: An Introduction* (Basingstoke: Palgrave Macmillan, 2006), 5.

4 Daljit Nagra, *Look We Have Coming to Dover!* (London: Faber and Faber, 2007), 15. Further references to this poem are taken from this page.

5 Daljit Nagra, *Tippoo Sultan's Incredible White-Man-Eating Tiger Toy-Machine!!!* (London: Faber and Faber, 2011), 51.

6 Ibid., 53.

7 Nagra, *Look We Have Coming to Dover!*, 32.

8 See, in particular, Jerome Rothenberg, *Technicians of the Sacred: A Range of Poetries from Africa, America, Asia & Oceania* (Berkeley: University of California Press, 1985 [1968]).

9 Jen Hadfield, *Byssus* (London: Picador, 2014), 42.

10 See *DSL: Dictionary of the Scots Language*, http://www.dsl.ac.uk/entry/snd/souk.

11 Hadfield, *Byssus*, 69.

12 John J. Graham, *Shetland Dictionary*, http://www.shetlanddialect.org.uk/john-j-grahams-shetland-dictionary.php?word=2325.

13 Jen Hadfield, *Nigh-No-Place* (Northumberland: Bloodaxe Books, 2008), 64.

14 Harriet Cooke, interview with Seamus Heaney [untitled], *Irish Times*, December 6, 1973, 8.

15 For John Cayley's work, see http://programmatology.shadoof.net. For *xylo* and other examples of Peter Howard's digital poetry, see http://www.peterhoward.org. On digital poetry more generally, see Chris Funkhauser, *Prehistoric Digital Poetry: An Archaeology of Forms, 1959–1995* (Tuscaloosa: University of Alabama Press, 2007) and *New Directions in Digital Poetry* (New York and London: Continuum, 2007); and Adalaide Morris and Thomas Swiss (eds.), *New Media Poetics: Contexts, Technotexts, and Theories* (Cambridge: MIT Press, 2006).

16 Caroline Bergvall, *Meddle English* (Callicoon, NY: Nightboat Books, 2011), 6, 14.

17 Ibid., 15–16.

18 Ibid., 17.

19 Caroline Bergvall, *Fig* (Cambridge: Salt Publishing, 2005), 33.

20 Ibid., 33.

21 Ibid., 33, 35.

22 An audio version of Bergvall performing the poem is available on the *PennSound* website: http://writing.upenn.edu/pennsound/x/Bergvall.php.

23 Caroline Bergvall, "In the Place of Writing," in Romana Huk (ed.), *Assembling Alternatives: Reading Postmodern Poetries Transnationally* (Middletown, CT: Wesleyan University Press, 2003), 327–337, at 329.

24 Alice Oswald, *Dart* (London: Faber and Faber, 2002), n.p.

25 Fiona Sampson, *Beyond the Lyric: A Map of Contemporary British Poetry* (London: Chatto & Windus, 2012), 159.

26 Oswald, *Dart*, n.p.

27 Ibid., 44.

28 Ibid., n.p.

29 Ibid., 17.

30 Ibid., 43.

31 Ibid., 48.

32 John Wilkinson, *The Lyric Touch: Essays on the Poetry of Excess* (Cambridge: Salt Publishing, 2007), 187.

33 See Randall Stevenson, *The Oxford English Literary History, Volume 12. 1960–2000: The Last of England?* (Oxford: Oxford University Press, 2004), esp. 230–237.

34 On Prynne's late poetry, see Joe Luna and Jow Lindsay Walton (eds.), *On the Late Poetry of J.H. Prynne* (Brighton: Hi Zero & Sad Press, 2014).

35 See Sampson, *Beyond the Lyric*, 271–276.

36 Drew Milne, "Agoraphobia, and the Embarrassment of Manifestos: Notes Towards a Community of Risk," *Parataxis*, 3 (1993), 25–39. Reprinted in *Jacket* 20 (December 2002), http://jacketmagazine.com/20/pt-dm-agora.html. All subsequent quotations are taken from this web page.

37 Wilkinson's review appears in *Chicago Review*, 52.2–4 (Autumn 2006), 369–375; Riley's letter to the editor ["Dear *Chicago Review*"] in 53.1 (Spring 2007), 221–227; and Wilkinson's response to Riley ["Dear *Chicago Review*"] in 53.2–3 (Autumn 2007), 231–238.

38 Peter Riley, "Dear *Chicago Review*," 222.

39 Ibid., 223.

40 Ibid., 224 [italics original].

41 Ibid., 223, 225.

42 Ibid., 226.

43 Ibid., 227.

44 John Wilkinson, "Dear *Chicago Review*," 231.

45 Ibid., 237.

46 Keston Sutherland, "Hot White Andy," *Chicago Review*, 53.1 (2007), 73–87, at 83.

47 Jennifer Cooke, "The Laughter of Narcissism: Loving *Hot White Andy* and the Troubling Chain of Equivalence," in *Complicities: British Poetry 1945–2007*, edited by Robin Purves and Sam Ladkin (Czech Republic: Litteraria Pragensia, 2007), 323–340, at 329.

48 Sutherland's reading at the 2010 "Helsinki Poetry Mash!" is available at http://www.youtube.com/watch?v=tB96rk8VKLg.

49 Sam Ladkin, "Problems for Lyric Poetry," in Purves and Ladkin (eds.), *Complicities: British Poetry 1945–2007*, 271–322, at 314.

50 Sutherland, "Hot White Andy," 75.

51 Ibid., 75.

52 John Wilkinson, "Mandarin Ducks and Chee-chee Chokes" [a review of *Hot White Andy*], *Jacket*, 35 (Early 2008), http://jacketmagazine.com/35/r-sutherland-rb-wilkinson.shtml.

53 Sutherland, "Hot White Andy," 80.

54 Ibid., 87.

55 Ibid., 81.

Further Reading

This list contains general studies of postwar British poetry. Articles and books on specific poets and topics are included in the relevant notes.

Alderman, Nigel, and C.D. Blanton, editors. "Pocket Epics: British Poetry After Modernism." *Yale Journal of Criticism*, 13.1 (2000), 1–151.
    editors. *A Concise Companion to Postwar British and Irish Poetry*. Chichester, West Sussex: Wiley-Blackwell, 2009.
Alderman, Nigel, and Michael Thurston. *Reading Postwar British and Irish Poetry*. Chichester, West Sussex: Wiley-Blackwell, 2014.
Barry, Peter. *Contemporary British Poetry and the City*. Manchester: Manchester University Press, 2000.
    Poetry Wars: British Poetry of the 1970s and the Battle of Earls Court. Cambridge: Salt Publishing, 2006.
Booth, Martin. *British Poetry 1964–1984: Driving through the Barricades*. London: Routledge & Kegan Paul, 1985.
Broom, Sarah. *Contemporary British and Irish Poetry: An Introduction*. Basingstoke: Palgrave Macmillan, 2006.
Bush, Clive. *Out of Dissent: A Study of Five Contemporary British Poets*. London: Talus, 1997.
Conran, Anthony. *Frontiers in Anglo-Welsh Poetry*. Cardiff: University of Wales Press, 1997.
Corcoran, Neil. *English Poetry since 1940*. London: Longman, 1993.
Corcoran, Neil, editor. *The Cambridge Companion to Twentieth-Century English Poetry*. Cambridge: Cambridge University Press, 2007.
Davie, Donald. *Thomas Hardy and British Poetry*. Oxford: Oxford University Press, 1972.
    Under Briggflatts: A History of Poetry in Great Britain, 1960–1988. Manchester: Carcanet, 1989.
Day, Gary, and Brian Docherty, editors. *British Poetry from the 1950s to the 1990s: Politics and Art*. Basingstoke: Macmillan, 1997.
Dowson, Jane, editor. *The Cambridge Companion to Twentieth-Century British and Irish Women's Poetry*. Cambridge: Cambridge University Press, 2011.
Dowson, Jane, and Alice Entwistle. *A History of Twentieth-Century British Women's Poetry*. Cambridge: Cambridge University Press, 2005.

Duncan, Andrew. *Centre and Periphery in Modern British Poetry.*
    Liverpool: Liverpool University Press, 2005.
    The Council of Heresy: A Primer of Poetry in a Balkanised Terrain.
    Exeter: Shearsman Books, 2009.
    The Failure of Conservatism in Modern British Poetry. Cambridge: Salt
    Publishing, 2003.
    *Origins of the Underground: British Poetry Between Apocryphon and Incident
    Light, 1933–1979.* Cambridge: Salt Publishing, 2008.
Entwistle, Alice. *Poetry, Geography, Gender: Women Rewriting Contemporary
    Wales.* Cardiff: University of Wales Press, 2013.
Gregson, Ian. *Contemporary Poetry and Postmodernism: Dialogue and
    Estrangement.* Basingstoke: Macmillan, 1996.
    The New Poetry in Wales. Cardiff: University of Wales Press, 2007.
Hampson, Robert, and Peter Barry, editors. *New British Poetries: The Scope of the
    Possible.* Manchester: Manchester University Press, 1993.
Hart, Matthew. *Nations of Nothing but Poetry: Modernism, Transnationalism, and
    Synthetic Vernacular Poetry.* New York: Oxford University Press, 2010.
Homberger, Eric. *The Art of the Real: Poetry in England and America Since 1939.*
    London: Dent and Totowa, NJ: Rowman and Littlefield, 1977.
Hooker, Jeremy. *Imagining Wales: A View of Modern Welsh Writing in English.*
    Cardiff: University of Wales Press, 2001.
Huk, Romana, and James Acheson, editors. *Contemporary British Poetry: Essays
    in Theory and Criticism.* Albany: State University of New York
    Press, 1996.
Ingelbien, Raphaël. *Misreading England: Poetry and Nationhood since the Second
    World War.* Amsterdam: Editions Rodopi, 2002.
Johnston, Dillon. *The Poetic Economies of England and Ireland, 1912–2000.*
    Basingstoke: Palgrave Macmillan, 2001.
Kennedy, David. *New Relations: The Refashioning of British Poetry, 1980–1994.*
    Bridgend, Wales: Seren Books, 1996.
Kennedy, David, and Christine Kennedy. *Women's Experimental Poetry in Britain
    1970–2010: Body, Time and Locale.* Liverpool: Liverpool University
    Press, 2013.
Kinnahan, Linda. *Lyric Interventions: Feminism, Experimental Poetry, and
    Contemporary Discourse.* Iowa City: University of Iowa Press, 2004.
Leader, Zachary, editor. *The Movement Reconsidered: Essays on Larkin, Amis,
    Gunn, Davie, and Their Contemporaries.* Oxford: Oxford University
    Press, 2009.
Longley, Edna. *The Living Stream: Literature and Revisionism in Ireland.*
    Newcastle upon Tyne: Bloodaxe Books, 1994.
    Poetry in the Wars. Newcastle upon Tyne: Bloodaxe Books, 1986.
Ludwig, Hans-Werner, and Lothar Fietz, editors. *Poetry in the British
    Isles: Non-Metropolitan Perspectives.* Cardiff: University of Wales
    Press, 1995.

Mackay, Peter, Edna Longley, and Fran Brearton, editors. *Modern Irish and Scottish Poetry*. Cambridge: Cambridge University Press, 2011.

McDonald, Peter. *Serious Poetry: Form and Authority from Yeats to Hill*. Oxford: Clarendon Press and New York: Oxford University Press, 2002.

McGuire, Matt, and Colin Nicholson, editors. *The Edinburgh Companion to Contemporary Scottish Poetry*. Edinburgh: Edinburgh University Press, 2009.

Merriman, Emily Taylor, and Adrian Grafe, editors. *Intimate Exposure: Essays on the Public–Private Divide in British Poetry since 1950*. Jefferson, NC: McFarland, 2010.

Middleton, Peter. *Distant Reading: Performance, Readership, and Consumption in Contemporary Poetry*. Tuscaloosa: University of Alabama Press, 2005.

Miller, David, and Richard Price. *British Poetry Magazines, 1914–2000: A History and Bibliography of "Little Magazines."* London and Newcastle: The British Library and the Oak Knoll Press, 2006.

Morrison, Blake. *The Movement: English Poetry and Fiction of the 1950s*. Oxford: Oxford University Press, 1980.

O'Brien, Sean. *The Deregulated Muse: Essays on Contemporary British and Irish Poetry*. Newcastle upon Tyne: Bloodaxe Books, 1998.

Patke, Rajeev S. *Postcolonial Poetry in English*. Oxford: Oxford University Press, 2006.

Picot, Edward. *Outcasts from Eden: Ideas of Landscape in British Poetry since 1945*. Liverpool: Liverpool University Press, 1997.

Pollard, Charles W. *New World Modernisms: T.S. Eliot, Derek Walcott, and Kamau Brathwaite*. Charlottesville: University of Virginia Press, 2004.

Pollard, Natalie. *Speaking to You: Contemporary Poetry and Public Address*. Oxford: Oxford University Press, 2012.

Purves, Robin, and Sam Ladkin, editors. *Complicities: British Poetry 1945–2007*. Prague: Litteraria Pragensia, 2007.

Ramazani, Jahan. *The Hybrid Muse: Postcolonial Poetry in English*. Chicago and London: University of Chicago Press, 2001.

A Transnational Poetics. Chicago and London: University of Chicago Press, 2009.

Redmond, John. *Poetry and Privacy: Questioning Public Interpretations of Contemporary British and Irish Poetry*. Bridgend, Wales: Seren Books, 2013.

Robinson, Peter. *Twentieth Century Poetry: Selves and Situations*. Oxford: Oxford University Press, 2005.

Robinson, Peter, editor. *The Oxford Handbook of Contemporary British and Irish Poetry*. Oxford: Oxford University Press, 2013.

Sampson, Fiona. *Beyond the Lyric: A Map of Contemporary British Poetry*. London: Chatto & Windus, 2012.

Sheppard, Robert. *The Poetry of Saying: British Poetry and Its Discontents 1950–2000*. Liverpool: Liverpool University Press, 2005.

When Bad Times Made for Good Poetry: Episodes in the History of the Poetics of Innovation. Exeter: Shearsman Books, 2011.

Sinfield, Alan. *Literature, Politics, and Culture in Postwar Britain.* Berkeley: University of California Press, 1989.

Smith, Stan. *Poetry and Displacement.* Liverpool: Liverpool University Press, 2007.

Stevenson, Randall. *The Oxford English Literary History, Volume 12. 1960–2000: The Last of England?* Oxford: Oxford University Press, 2004.

Trotter, David. *The Making of the Reader: Language and Subjectivity in Modern American, English and Irish Poetry.* London: Macmillan, 1984.

Tuma, Keith. *Fishing by Obstinate Isles: Modern and Postmodern British Poetry and American Readers.* Evanston, IL: Northwestern University Press, 1998.

Wheatley, David. *Contemporary British Poetry: Readers' Guide to Essential Criticism.* London: Palgrave Macmillan, 2014.

Whyte, Christopher. *Modern Scottish Poetry.* Edinburgh: Edinburgh University Press, 2004.

Wilkinson, John. *The Lyric Touch: Essays on the Poetry of Excess.* Cambridge: Salt Publishing, 2007.

Williams, Daniel G., editor. *Slanderous Tongues: Essays on Welsh Poetry in English 1970–2005.* Bridgend, Wales: Seren Books, 2010.

Wootten, William. *The Alvarez Generation: Thom Gunn, Geoffrey Hill, Ted Hughes, Sylvia Plath, and Peter Porter.* Liverpool: Liverpool University Press, 2015.

Index

Cambridge Introductions to Literature

Authors

Margaret Atwood   Heidi Macpherson

Jane Austen   Janet Todd

Samuel Beckett   Ronan McDonald

Walter Benjamin   David Ferris

Lord Byron   Richard Lansdown

Chekhov   James N. Loehlin

J. M. Coetzee   Dominic Head

Samuel Taylor Coleridge   John Worthen

Joseph Conrad   John Peters

Jacques Derrida   Leslie Hill

Charles Dickens   Jon Mee

Emily Dickinson   Wendy Martin

George Eliot   Nancy Henry

T. S. Eliot   John Xiros Cooper

William Faulkner   Theresa M. Towner

F. Scott Fitzgerald   Kirk Curnutt

Michel Foucault   Lisa Downing

Robert Frost   Robert Faggen

Gabriel Garcia Marquez   Gerald Martin

Nathaniel Hawthorne   Leland S. Person

Zora Neale Hurston   Lovalerie King

James Joyce   Eric Bulson

Thomas Mann   Todd Kontje

Christopher Marlowe   Tom Rutter

Herman Melville   Kevin J. Hayes

Milton   Stephen B. Dobranski

Toni Morrison   Tessa Roynon

George Orwell   John Rodden and John Rossi

Sylvia Plath   Jo Gill

Edgar Allan Poe   Benjamin F. Fisher

Ezra Pound   Ira Nadel

Marcel Proust   Adam Watt

Jean Rhys   Elaine Savory

Edward Said   Conor McCarthy

Shakespeare   Emma Smith

Shakespeare's Comedies   Penny Gay

Shakespeare's History Plays   Warren Chernaik

Shakespeare's Poetry   Michael Schoenfeldt

Shakespeare's Tragedies   Janette Dillon

Harriet Beecher Stowe   Sarah Robbins

Mark Twain   Peter Messent

Edith Wharton   Pamela Knights

Walt Whitman   M. Jimmie Killingsworth

Virginia Woolf   Jane Goldman

William Wordsworth   Emma Mason

W. B. Yeats   David Holdeman

Topics

American Literary Realism   Phillip Barrish

The American Short Story   Martin Scofield

Anglo-Saxon Literature   Hugh Magennis

Comedy   Eric Weitz

Creative Writing   David Morley